Expert SQL Server
2008 Development

Alastair Aitchison
Adam Machanic

Apress®

Expert SQL Server 2008 Development

ISBN-13 (pbk): 978-1-4302-7213-7

ISBN-13 (electronic): 978-1-4302-7212-0

9 8 7 6 5 4 3 2 1

Trademarked names may appear in this book. Rather than use a trademark symbol with every occurrence of a trademarked name, we use the names only in an editorial fashion and to the benefit of the trademark owner, with no intention of infringement of the trademark.

President and Publisher: Paul Manning
Lead Editor: Jonathan Gennick
Technical Reviewer: Evan Terry
Editorial Board: Clay Andres, Steve Anglin, Mark Beckner, Ewan Buckingham, Gary Cornell, Jonathan Gennick, Jonathan Hassell, Michelle Lowman, Matthew Moodie, Duncan Parkes, Jeffrey Pepper, Frank Pohlmann, Douglas Pundick, Ben Renow-Clarke, Dominic Shakeshaft, Matt Wade, Tom Welsh
Coordinating Editor: Mary Tobin
Copy Editor: Damon Larson
Compositor: Bytheway Publishing Services
Indexer: Barbara Palumbo
Artist: April Milne
Cover Designer: Anna Ishchenko

Distributed to the book trade worldwide by Springer-Verlag New York, Inc., 233 Spring Street, 6th Floor, New York, NY 10013. Phone 1-800-SPRINGER, fax 201-348-4505, e-mail orders-ny@springer-sbm.com, or visit http://www.springeronline.com.

For information on translations, please e-mail info@apress.com, or visit http://www.apress.com.

Apress and friends of ED books may be purchased in bulk for academic, corporate, or promotional use. eBook versions and licenses are also available for most titles. For more information, reference our Special Bulk Sales–eBook Licensing web page at http://www.apress.com/info/bulksales.

The information in this book is distributed on an "as is" basis, without warranty. Although every precaution has been taken in the preparation of this work, neither the author(s) nor Apress shall have any liability to any person or entity with respect to any loss or damage caused or alleged to be caused directly or indirectly by the information contained in this work.

The source code for this book is available to readers at http://www.apress.com. You will need to answer questions pertaining to this book in order to successfully download the code.

For Clare and Douglas

Contents at a Glance

Contents

About the Author

Alastair Aitchison is a freelance technology consultant based in Norwich, England. He has experience across a wide variety of software and service platforms, and has worked with SQL Server 2008 since the earliest technical previews were made publicly available. He has implemented various SQL Server solutions requiring highly concurrent processes and large data warehouses in the financial services sector, combined with reporting and analytical capability based on the Microsoft business intelligence stack. Alastair has a particular interest in analysis of spatial data, and is the author of *Beginning Spatial with SQL Server 2008* (Apress, 2009). He speaks at user groups and conferences, and is a highly active contributor to several online support communities, including the Microsoft SQL Server Developer Center forums.

About the Technical Reviewer

 **Evan Terry** is the Chief Technical Consultant at The Clegg Company, specializing in data management, information and data architecture, database systems, and business intelligence. His past and current clients include the State of Idaho, Albertsons, American Honda Motors, and Toyota Motor Sales, USA. He is the coauthor of *Beginning Relational Data Modeling*, has published several articles in DM Review, and has presented at industry conferences and conducted private workshops on the subjects of data and information quality, and information management. He has also been the technical reviewer of several Apress books relating to SQL Server databases. For questions or consulting needs, Evan can be reached at evan_terry@cleggcompany.com.

Acknowledgments

When I was asked to write this book, I jumped at the chance to work with the great bunch of folks at Apress again. I am particularly lucky to have the assistance once more of two hugely talented individuals, in the form of Jonathan Gennick and Evan Terry. As my editor, Jonathan has encouraged, taught, and mentored me through the authoring process, and has never wavered in his support even when the going got a bit tough (which, as in any publication schedule, at times it did!). Evan not only provided the benefit of his wealth of technical knowledge, but also his authoring expertise, and at times he simply provided a sensible voice of reason, all of which helped to improve the book significantly. I would also like to thank Mary Tobin, who managed to keep track of all the deadlines and project management issues, Damon Larson, for correcting my wayward use of the English language, and all the other individuals who helped get this book into the form that you are now holding in your hands. Thank you all.

My family have once again had to endure me spending long hours typing away at the keyboard, and I thank them for their tolerance, patience, and support. I couldn't do anything without them.

And thankyou to you, the reader, for purchasing this book. I hope that you find the content interesting, useful, and above all, enjoyable to read.

Preface

I've worked with Microsoft SQL Server for nearly ten years now, and I've used SQL Server 2008 since the very first preview version was made available to the public. One thing I have noticed is that, with every new release, SQL Server grows ever more powerful, and ever more complex. There is now a huge array of features that go way beyond the core functionality expected from a database system and, with so many different facets to cover, it is becoming ever harder to be a SQL Server "expert". SQL Server developers are no longer simply expected to be proficent in writing T-SQL code, but also in XML and SQLCLR (and knowing when to use each). You no longer execute a query to get a single result set from an isolated database, but handle multiple active result sets derived from queries across distributed servers. The types of information stored in modern databases represent not just character, numeric, and binary data, but complex data such as spatial, hierarchical, and filestream data.

Attempting to comprehensively cover any one of these topics alone would easily generate enough material to fill an entire book, so I'm not even going to try doing so. Instead, I'm going to concentrate on what I believe you need to know to create high-quality database applications, based on my own practical experience. I'm not going to waste pages discussing the ins and outs of some obscure or little-used feature, unless I can show you a genuine use case for it. Nor will I insult your intelligence by laboriously explaining the basics – I'll assume that you're already familiar with the straightforward examples covered in Books Online, and now want to take your knowledge further.

All of the examples used in this book are based on real-life scenarios that I've encountered, and they show you how to deal with problems that you're likely to face in most typical SQL Server environments. I promise not to show you seemingly perfect solutions, which you then discover only work in the artificially-cleansed "AdventureWorks" world; as developers we work with imperfect data, and I'll try to show you examples that deal with the warts and all. The code examples were tested using the SQL Server 2008 Developer Edition with Service Pack 1 installed, but should work on all editions of SQL Server 2008 unless explicitly stated otherwise.

Finally, I hope that you enjoy reading this book and thinking about the issues discussed. The reason why I enjoy database development is that it presents a never-ending set of puzzles to solve – and even when you think you have found the optimum answer to a problem, there is always the possibility of finding an even better solution in the future. While you shouldn't let this search for perfection detract you from the job at hand (sometimes, "good enough" is all you need), there are always new techniques to learn, and alternative methods to explore. I hope that you might learn some of them in the pages that follow.

CHAPTER 1

Software Development Methodologies for the Database World

Databases are software. Therefore, database application development should be treated in the same manner as any other form of software development. Yet, all too often, the database is thought of as a secondary entity when development teams discuss architecture and test plans, and many database developers are still not aware of, or do not apply, standard software development best practices to database applications.

Almost every software application requires some form of data store. Many developers go beyond simply persisting application data, instead creating applications that are **data driven**. A data-driven application is one that is designed to dynamically change its behavior based on data—a better term might, in fact, be **data dependent**.

Given this dependency upon data and databases, the developers who specialize in this field have no choice but to become not only competent software developers, but also absolute experts at accessing and managing data. Data is the central, controlling factor that dictates the value that any application can bring to its users. Without the data, there is no need for the application.

The primary purpose of this book is to encourage Microsoft SQL Server developers to become more integrated with mainstream software development. These pages stress rigorous testing, well-thought-out architectures, and careful attention to interdependencies. Proper consideration of these areas is the hallmark of an expert software developer—and database professionals, as core members of any software development team, simply cannot afford to lack this expertise.

In this chapter, I will present an overview of software development and architectural matters as they apply to the world of database applications. Some of the topics covered are hotly debated in the development community, and I will try to cover both sides, even when presenting what I believe to be the most compelling argument. Still, I encourage you to think carefully about these issues rather than taking my—or anyone else's—word as the absolute truth. Software architecture is a constantly changing field. Only through careful reflection on a case-by-case basis can you hope to identify and understand the "best" possible solution for any given situation.

Architecture Revisited

Software architecture is a large, complex topic, partly due to the fact that software architects often like to make things as complex as possible. The truth is that writing first-class software doesn't involve nearly as much complexity as many architects would lead you to believe. Extremely high-quality designs are possible merely by understanding and applying a few basic principles. The three most important concepts that every software developer must know in order to succeed are **coupling**, **cohesion**, and **encapsulation**:

- **Coupling** refers to the amount of dependency of one module within a system upon another module in the same system. It can also refer to the amount of dependency that exists between different systems. Modules, or systems, are said to be **tightly coupled** when they depend on each other to such an extent that a change in one necessitates a change to the other. This is clearly undesirable, as it can create a complex (and, sometimes, obscure) network of dependencies between different modules of the system, so that an apparently simple change in one module may require identification of and associated changes made to a wide variety of disparate modules throughout the application. Software developers should strive instead to produce the opposite: **loosely coupled** modules and systems, which can be easily isolated and amended without affecting the rest of the system.

- **Cohesion** refers to the degree that a particular module or component provides a single, well-defined aspect of functionality to the application as a whole. **Strongly cohesive** modules, which have only one function, are said to be more desirable than **weakly cohesive** modules, which perform many operations and therefore may be less maintainable and reusable.

- **Encapsulation** refers to how well the underlying implementation of a module is hidden from the rest of the system. As you will see, this concept is essentially the combination of loose coupling and strong cohesion. Logic is said to be **encapsulated** within a module if the module's methods or properties do not expose design decisions about its internal behaviors.

Unfortunately, these qualitative definitions are somewhat difficult to apply, and in real systems, there is a significant amount of subjectivity involved in determining whether a given module is or is not tightly coupled to some other module, whether a routine is cohesive, or whether logic is properly encapsulated. There is no objective method of measuring these concepts within an application. Generally, developers will discuss these ideas using comparative terms—for instance, a module may be said to be *less* tightly coupled to another module than it was before its interfaces were **refactored**. But it might be difficult to say whether or not a given module *is* tightly coupled to another, in absolute terms, without some means of comparing the nature of its coupling. Let's take a look at a couple of examples to clarify things.

What is Refactoring?

Refactoring is the practice of reviewing and revising existing code, while not adding any new features or changing functionality—essentially, cleaning up what's there to make it work better. This is one of those areas that management teams tend to despise, because it adds no tangible value to the application from a sales point of view, and entails revisiting sections of code that had previously been considered "finished."

Coupling

First, let's look at an example that illustrates basic coupling. The following class might be defined to model a car dealership's stock (to keep the examples simple, I'll give code listings in this section based on a simplified and scaled-down C#-like syntax):

```
class Dealership
{
    // Name of the dealership
    string Name;

    // Address of the dealership
    string Address;

    // Cars that the dealership has
    Car[] Cars;

    // Define the Car subclass
    class Car
    {
        // Make of the car
        string Make;

        // Model of the car
        string Model;
    }
}
```

This class has three fields: the name of the dealership and address are both strings, but the collection of the dealership's cars is typed based on a subclass, **Car**. In a world without people who are buying cars, this class works fine—but, unfortunately, the way in which it is modeled forces us to tightly couple any class that has a car instance to the dealer. Take the owner of a car, for example:

```
class CarOwner
{
    // Name of the car owner
    string name;

    // The car owner's cars
    Dealership.Car[] Cars
}
```

Notice that the **CarOwner**'s cars are actually instances of **Dealership.Car**; in order to own a car, it seems to be presupposed that there must have been a dealership involved. This doesn't leave any room for cars sold directly by their owner—or stolen cars, for that matter! There are a variety of ways of fixing this kind of coupling, the simplest of which would be to not define **Car** as a subclass, but rather as its own stand-alone class. Doing so would mean that a **CarOwner** would be coupled to a **Car**, as would a **Dealership**—but a **CarOwner** and a **Dealership** would not be coupled at all. This makes sense and more accurately models the real world.

Cohesion

To demonstrate the principle of cohesion, consider the following method that might be defined in a banking application:

```
bool TransferFunds(
    Account AccountFrom,
    Account AccountTo,
    decimal Amount)
{
    if (AccountFrom.Balance >= Amount)
        AccountFrom.Balance -= Amount;
    else
        return(false);

    AccountTo.Balance += Amount;
    return(true);
}
```

Keeping in mind that this code is highly simplified and lacks basic error handling and other traits that would be necessary in a real banking application, ponder the fact that what this method basically does is withdraw funds from the **AccountFrom** account and deposit them into the **AccountTo** account. That's not much of a problem in itself, but now think of how much infrastructure (e.g., error-handling code) is missing from this method. It can probably be assumed that somewhere in this same banking application there are also methods called **Withdraw** and **Deposit**, which do the exact same things, and which would also require the same infrastructure code. The **TransferFunds** method has been made weakly cohesive because, in performing a transfer, it requires the same functionality as provided by the individual **Withdraw** and **Deposit** methods, only using completely different code.

A more strongly cohesive version of the same method might be something along the lines of the following:

```
bool TransferFunds(
    Account AccountFrom,
    Account AccountTo,
    decimal Amount)
{
    bool success = false;
    success = Withdraw(AccountFrom, Amount);

    if (!success)
        return(false);

    success = Deposit(AccountTo, Amount);

    if (!success)
        return(false);
    else
        return(true);
}
```

Although I've already noted the lack of basic exception handling and other constructs that would exist in a production version of this kind of code, it's important to stress that the main missing piece is some form of a transaction. Should the withdrawal succeed, followed by an unsuccessful deposit, this code as-is would result in the funds effectively vanishing into thin air. Always make sure to carefully test whether your mission-critical code is atomic; either everything should succeed or nothing should. There is no room for in-between—especially when you're dealing with people's funds!

Encapsulation

Of the three topics discussed in this section, encapsulation is probably the most important for a database developer to understand. Look back at the more cohesive version of the **TransferFunds** method, and think about what the associated **Withdraw** method might look like—something like this, perhaps:

```
bool Withdraw(Account AccountFrom, decimal Amount)
{
    if (AccountFrom.Balance >= Amount)
    {
        AccountFrom.Balance -= Amount;
        return(true);
    }
    else
        return(false);
}
```

In this case, the **Account** class exposes a property called **Balance**, which the **Withdraw** method can manipulate. But what if an error existed in **Withdraw**, and some code path allowed **Balance** to be manipulated without first checking to make sure the funds existed? To avoid this situation, it should not have been made possible to set the value for **Balance** from the **Withdraw** method directly. Instead, the **Account** class should define its *own* **Withdraw** method. By doing so, the class would control its own data and rules internally—and not have to rely on any consumer to properly do so. The key objective here is to implement the logic exactly once and reuse it as many times as necessary, instead of unnecessarily recoding the logic wherever it needs to be used.

Interfaces

The only purpose of a module in an application is to do something at the request of a consumer (i.e., another module or system). For instance, a database system would be worthless if there were no way to store or retrieve data. Therefore, a system must expose **interfaces**, well-known methods and properties that other modules can use to make requests. A module's interfaces are the gateway to its functionality, and these are the arbiters of what goes into or comes out of the module.

Interface design is where the concepts of coupling and encapsulation really take on meaning. If an interface fails to encapsulate enough of the module's internal design, consumers may have to rely upon some knowledge of the module, thereby tightly coupling the consumer to the module. In such a situation, any change to the module's internal implementation may require a modification to the implementation of the consumer.

Interfaces As Contracts

An interface can be said to be a **contract** expressed between the module and its consumers. The contract states that if the consumer specifies a certain set of parameters to the interface, a certain set of values will be returned. Simplicity is usually the key here; avoid defining interfaces that change the number or type of values returned depending on the input. For instance, a stored procedure that returns additional columns if a user passes in a certain argument may be an example of a poorly designed interface.

Many programming languages allow routines to define **explicit contracts**. This means that the input parameters are well defined, and the outputs are known at compile time. Unfortunately, T-SQL stored procedures in SQL Server only define inputs, and the procedure itself can dynamically change its defined outputs. In these cases, it is up to the developer to ensure that the expected outputs are well documented and that unit tests exist to validate them (see Chapter 3 for information on unit testing).Throughout this book, I refer to a contract enforced via documentation and testing as an **implied contract**.

Interface Design

Knowing how to measure successful interface design is a difficult question. Generally speaking, you should try to look at it from a maintenance point of view. If, in six months' time, you were to completely rewrite the module for performance or other reasons, can you ensure that all inputs and outputs will remain the same?

For example, consider the following stored procedure signature:

```
CREATE PROCEDURE GetAllEmployeeData
    --Columns to order by, comma-delimited
    @OrderBy varchar(400) = NULL
```

Assume that this stored procedure does exactly what its name implies—it returns all data from the **Employees** table, for every employee in the database. This stored procedure takes the **@OrderBy** parameter, which is defined (according to the comment) as "columns to order by," with the additional prescription that the columns should be comma-delimited.

The interface issues here are fairly significant. First of all, an interface should not only hide internal behavior, but also leave no question as to how a valid set of input arguments will alter the routine's output. In this case, a consumer of this stored procedure might expect that, internally, the comma-delimited list will simply be appended to a dynamic SQL statement. Does that mean that changing the order of the column names within the list will change the outputs? And, are the **ASC** or **DESC** keywords acceptable? The contract defined by the interface is not specific enough to make that clear.

Secondly, the consumer of this stored procedure must have a list of columns in the **Employees** table in order to know the valid values that may be passed in the comma-delimited list. Should the list of columns be hard-coded in the application, or retrieved in some other way? And, it is not clear if all of the columns of the table are valid inputs. What about a **Photo** column, defined as **varbinary(max)**, which contains a JPEG image of the employee's photo? Does it make sense to allow a consumer to specify that column for sorting?

These kinds of interface issues can cause real problems from a maintenance point of view. Consider the amount of effort that would be required to simply change the name of a column in the **Employees** table, if three different applications were all using this stored procedure and had their own hard-coded lists of sortable column names. And what should happen if the query is initially implemented as dynamic SQL, but needs to be changed later to use static SQL in order to avoid recompilation costs? Will it be possible to detect which applications assumed that the **ASC** and **DESC** keywords could be used, before they throw exceptions at runtime?

The central message I hope to have conveyed here is that extreme flexibility and solid, maintainable interfaces may not go hand in hand in many situations. If your goal is to develop truly robust software, you will often find that flexibility must be cut back. But remember that in most cases there are perfectly sound workarounds that do not sacrifice any of the real flexibility intended by the original interface. For instance, in this example, the interface could be rewritten in a number of ways to maintain all of the possible functionality. One such version follows:

```
CREATE PROCEDURE GetAllEmployeeData
    @OrderByName int = 0,
    @OrderByNameASC bit = 1,
    @OrderBySalary int = 0,
    @OrderBySalaryASC bit = 1,
    -- Other columns ...
```

In this modified version of the interface, each column that a consumer can select for ordering has two associated parameters: one parameter specifying the order in which to sort the columns, and a second parameter that specifies whether to order ascending or descending. So if a consumer passes a value of **2** for the **@OrderByName** parameter and a value of **1** for the **@OrderBySalary** parameter, the result will be sorted first by salary, and then by name. A consumer can further modify the sort by manipulating the **@OrderByNameASC** and **@OrderBySalaryASC** parameters to specify the sort direction for each column.

This version of the interface exposes nothing about the internal implementation of the stored procedure. The developer is free to use any technique he or she chooses in order to return the correct results in the most effective manner. In addition, the consumer has no need for knowledge of the actual column names of the **Employees** table. The column containing an employee's name may be called **Name** or may be called **EmpName**. Or, there may be two columns, one containing a first name and one a last name. Since the consumer requires no knowledge of these names, they can be modified as necessary as the data changes, and since the consumer is not coupled to the routine-based knowledge of the column name, no change to the consumer will be necessary. Note that this same reasoning can also be applied to suggest that end users and applications should only access data exposed as a view rather than directly accessing base tables in the database. Views can provide a layer of abstraction that enable changes to be made to the underlying tables, while the properties of the view are maintained.

Note that this example only discussed inputs to the interface. Keep in mind that outputs (e.g., result sets) are just as important, and these should also be documented in the contract. I recommend always using the **AS** keyword to create column aliases as necessary, so that interfaces can continue to return the same outputs even if there are changes to the underlying tables. As mentioned before, I also recommend that developers avoid returning extra data, such as additional columns or result sets, based on input arguments. Doing so can create stored procedures that are difficult to test and maintain.

Exceptions are a Vital Part of Any Interface

One important type of output, which developers often fail to consider when thinking about implied contracts, are the **exceptions** that a given method can throw should things go awry. Many methods throw well-defined exceptions in certain situations, but if these exceptions are not adequately documented, their well-intended purpose becomes rather wasted. By making sure to properly document exceptions, you enable clients to catch and handle the exceptions you've foreseen, in addition to helping developers understand what can go wrong and code defensively against possible issues. It is almost always better to follow a code path around a potential problem than to have to deal with an exception.

Integrating Databases and Object-Oriented Systems

A major issue that seems to make database development a lot more difficult than it should be isn't development-related at all, but rather a question of architecture. Object-oriented frameworks and database systems generally do not play well together, primarily because they have a different set of core goals. Object-oriented systems are designed to model business entities from an action standpoint—what can the business entity do, and what can other entities do to or with it? Databases, on the other hand, are more concerned with relationships between entities, and much less concerned with the activities in which they are involved.

It's clear that we have two incompatible paradigms for modeling business entities. Yet both are necessary components of almost every application and must be leveraged together toward the common goal: serving the user. To that end, it's important that database developers know what belongs where, and when to pass the buck back up to their application developer brethren. Unfortunately, the question of how to appropriately model the parts of any given business process can quickly drive one into a gray area. How should you decide between implementation in the database vs. implementation in the application?

The central argument on many a database forum since time immemorial (or at least since the dawn of the Internet) has been what to do with that ever-present required "logic." Sadly, try as we might, developers have still not figured out how to develop an application without the need to implement business requirements. And so the debate rages on. Does "business logic" belong in the database? In the application tier? What about the user interface? And what impact do newer application architectures have on this age-old question?

A Brief History of Logic Placement

Once upon a time, computers were simply called "computers." They spent their days and nights serving up little bits of data to "dumb" terminals. Back then there wasn't much of a difference between an application and its data, so there were few questions to ask, and fewer answers to give, about the architectural issues we debate today.

But, over time, the winds of change blew through the air-conditioned data centers of the world, and the systems previously called "computers" became known as "mainframes"—the new computer on the rack in the mid-1960s was the "minicomputer." Smaller and cheaper than the mainframes, the "minis" quickly grew in popularity. Their relative low cost compared to the mainframes meant that it was now fiscally possible to scale out applications by running them on multiple machines. Plus, these machines were inexpensive enough that they could even be used directly by end users as an alternative to the previously ubiquitous dumb terminals. During this same period we also saw the first commercially available database systems, such as the Adabas database management system (DBMS).

The advent of the minis signaled multiple changes in the application architecture landscape. In addition to the multiserver scale-out alternatives, the fact that end users were beginning to run machines more powerful than terminals meant that some of an application's work could be offloaded to the user-interface (UI) tier in certain cases. Instead of harnessing only the power of one server, workloads could now be distributed in order to create more scalable applications.

As time went on, the "microcomputers" (ancestors of today's Intel- and AMD-based systems) started getting more and more powerful, and eventually the minis disappeared. However, the client/server-based architecture that had its genesis during the minicomputer era did not die; application developers found that it could be much cheaper to offload work to clients than to purchase bigger servers.

The late 1990s saw yet another paradigm shift in architectural trends—strangely, back toward the world of mainframes and dumb terminals. Web servers replaced the mainframe systems as centralized data and UI systems, and browsers took on the role previously filled by the terminals. Essentially, this brought application architecture full circle, but with one key difference: the modern web-based data center is characterized by "farms" of *commodity servers*—cheap, standardized, and easily replaced hardware, rather than a single monolithic mainframe.

The latest trend toward cloud-based computing looks set to pose another serious challenge to the traditional view of architectural design decisions. In a cloud-based model, applications make use of shared, virtualized server resources, normally provided by a third-party as a service over the internet. Vendors such as Amazon, Google, and Microsoft already offer cloud-based database services, but at the time of writing, these are all still at a very embryonic stage. The current implementation of SQL Server Data Services, for example, has severe restrictions on bandwidth and storage which mean that, in most cases, it is not a viable replacement to a dedicated data center. However, there is growing momentum behind the move to the cloud, and it will be interesting to see what effect this has on data architecture decisions over the next few years.

When considering these questions, an important point to remember is that a single database may be shared by multiple applications, which in turn expose multiple user interfaces, as illustrated in Figure 1-1.

Database developers must strive to ensure that data is sufficiently encapsulated to allow it to be shared among multiple applications, while ensuring that the logic of disparate applications does not collide and put the entire database into an inconsistent state. Encapsulating to this level requires careful partitioning of logic, especially data validation rules.

Rules and logic can be segmented into three basic groups:

- Data logic
- Business logic
- Application logic

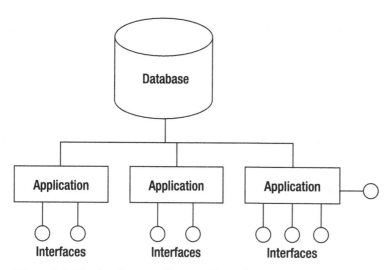

Figure 1-1. The database application hierarchy

When designing an application, it's important to understand these divisions and consider where in the application hierarchy any given piece of logic should be placed in order to ensure reusability.

Data Logic

Data logic defines the conditions that must be true for the data in the database to be in a consistent, noncorrupt state. Database developers are no doubt familiar with implementing these rules in the form of primary and foreign key constraints, check constraints, triggers, and the like. Data rules do not dictate *how* the data can be manipulated or *when* it should be manipulated; rather, data rules dictate the state that the data must end up in once any process is finished.

It's important to remember that data is not "just data" in most applications—rather, the data in the database models the actual business. Therefore, data rules must mirror all rules that drive the business itself. For example, if you were designing a database to support a banking application, you might be presented with a business rule that states that certain types of accounts are not allowed to be overdrawn. In order to properly enforce this rule for both the current application and all possible future applications, it must be implemented centrally, at the level of the data itself. If the data is guaranteed to be consistent, applications must only worry about what to *do* with the data.

As a general guideline, you should try to implement as many data rules as necessary in order to avoid the possibility of data quality problems. The database is the holder of the data, and as such should act as the final arbiter of the question of what data does or does not qualify to be persisted. Any validation rule that is central to the business is central to the data, and vice versa. In the course of my work with numerous database-backed applications, I've never seen one with too many data rules; but I've very often seen databases in which the lack of enough rules caused data integrity issues.

Where Do the Data Rules Really Belong?

Many object-oriented zealots would argue that the correct solution is not a database at all, but rather an interface bus, which acts as a façade over the database and takes control of all communications to and from the database. While this approach would work in theory, there are a few issues. First of all, this approach completely ignores the idea of database-enforced data integrity and turns the database layer into a mere storage container, failing to take advantage of any of the in-built features offered by almost all modern databases designed specifically for that purpose. Furthermore, such an interface layer will still have to communicate with the database, and therefore database code will have to be written at some level anyway. Writing such an interface layer may eliminate some database code, but it only defers the necessity of working with the database. Finally, in my admittedly subjective view, application layers are not as stable or long-lasting as databases in many cases. While applications and application architectures come and go, databases seem to have an extremely long life in the enterprise. The same rules would apply to a do-it-all interface bus. All of these issues are probably one big reason that although I've heard architects argue this issue for years, I've never seen such a system implemented.

Business Logic

The term **business logic** is generally used in software development circles as a vague catch-all for anything an application does that isn't UI related and that involves at least one conditional branch. In other words, this term is overused and has no real meaning.

Luckily, software development is an ever-changing field, and we don't have to stick with the accepted lack of definition. Business logic, for the purpose of this text, is defined as any rule or process that dictates how or when to manipulate data in order to change the state of the data, but that does not dictate how to persist or validate the data. An example of this would be the logic required to render raw data into a report suitable for end users. The raw data, which we might assume has already been subjected to data logic rules, can be passed through business logic in order to determine the aggregations and analyses appropriate for answering the questions that the end user might pose. Should this data need to be persisted in its new form within a database, it must once again be subjected to data rules; remember that the database should always make the final decision on whether any given piece of data is allowed.

So does business logic belong in the database? The answer is a definite "maybe." As a database developer, your main concerns tend to revolve around data integrity and performance. Other factors (such as overall application architecture) notwithstanding, this means that in general practice you should try to put the business logic in the tier in which it can deliver the best performance, or in which it can be reused with the most ease. For instance, if many applications share the same data and each have similar reporting needs, it might make more sense to design stored procedures that render the data into the correct format for the reports, rather than implementing similar reports in each application.

Performance vs. Design vs. Reality

Architecture purists might argue that performance should have no bearing on application design; it's an implementation detail, and can be solved at the code level. Those of us who've been in the trenches and have had to deal with the reality of poorly designed architectures know that this is not the case. Performance is, in fact, inexorably tied to design in virtually every application. Consider chatty interfaces that send too much data or require too many client requests to fill the user's screen with the requested information, or applications that must go back to a central server for key functionality with every user request. In many cases, these performance flaws can be identified—and fixed—during the design phase, before they are allowed to materialize. However, it's important not to go over the top in this respect: designs should not become overly contorted in order to avoid anticipated "performance problems" that may never occur.

Application Logic

If data logic *definitely* belongs in the database, and business logic *may* have a place in the database, application logic is the set of rules that should be kept as far away from the central data as possible. The rules that make up application logic include such things as user interface behaviors, string and number formatting rules, localization, and other related issues that are generally tied to user interfaces. Given the application hierarchy discussed previously (one database that might be shared by many applications, which in turn might be shared by many user interfaces), it's clear that mingling user interface data with application or central business data can raise severe coupling issues and ultimately reduce the possibility for sharing of data.

Note that I'm not implying that you should always avoid persisting UI-related entities in a database. Doing so certainly makes sense for many applications. What I am warning against is the risk of failing to draw a sufficiently distinct line between user interface elements and the rest of the application's data. Whenever possible, make sure to create different tables, preferably in different schemas or even entirely different databases, in order to store purely application-related data. This will enable you to keep the application decoupled from the data as much as possible.

The "Object-Relational Impedance Mismatch"

The primary stumbling block that makes it difficult to move information between object-oriented systems and relational databases is that the two types of systems are incompatible from a basic design point of view. Relational databases are designed using the rules of normalization, which help to ensure data integrity by splitting information into tables interrelated by keys. Object-oriented systems, on the other hand, tend to be much more lax in this area. It is quite common for objects to contain data that, while related, might not be modeled in a database in a single table.

For example, consider the following class, for a product in a retail system:

```
class Product
{
    string UPC;
    string Name;
    string Description;
    decimal Price;
```

```
    datetime UpdatedDate;
}
```

At first glance, the fields defined in this class seem to relate to one another quite readily, and one might expect that they would always belong in a single table in a database. However, it's possible that this product class represents only a point-in-time view of any given product, as of its last-updated date. In the database, the data could be modeled as follows:

```
CREATE TABLE Products
(
    UPC varchar(20) PRIMARY KEY,
    Name varchar(50)
);
```

```
CREATE TABLE ProductHistory
(
    UPC varchar(20) FOREIGN KEY REFERENCES Products (UPC),
    Description varchar(100),
    Price decimal,
    UpdatedDate datetime,
    PRIMARY KEY (UPC, UpdatedDate)
);
```

The important thing to note here is that the object representation of data may not have any bearing on how the data happens to be modeled in the database, and vice versa. The object-oriented and relational worlds each have their own goals and means to attain those goals, and developers should not attempt to wedge them together, lest functionality is reduced.

Are Tables Really Classes in Disguise?

It is sometimes stated in introductory database textbooks that tables can be compared to classes, and rows to instances of a class (i.e., objects). This makes a lot of sense at first; tables, like classes, define a set of attributes (known as columns) for an entity. They can also define (loosely) a set of methods for an entity, in the form of triggers.

However, that is where the similarities end. The key foundations of an object-oriented system are inheritance and polymorphism, both of which are difficult if not impossible to represent in SQL databases. Furthermore, the access path to related information in databases and object-oriented systems is quite different. An entity in an object-oriented system can "have" a child entity, which is generally accessed using a "dot" notation. For instance, a bookstore object might have a collection of books:

```
Books = BookStore.Books;
```

In this object-oriented example, the bookstore "has" the books. But in SQL databases this kind of relationship between entities is maintained via keys, where the child entity points to its parent. Rather than the bookstore having the books, the relationship between the entities is expressed the other way around, where the books maintain a foreign key that points back to the bookstore:

```
CREATE TABLE BookStores
(
    BookStoreId int PRIMARY KEY
```

13

```
);

CREATE TABLE Books
(
    BookStoreId int REFERENCES BookStores (BookStoreId),
    BookName varchar(50),
    Quantity int,
    PRIMARY KEY (BookStoreId, BookName)
);
```

While the object-oriented and SQL representations can store the same information, they do so differently enough that it does not make sense to say that a table represents a class, at least in current SQL databases.

Modeling Inheritance

In object-oriented design, there are two basic relationships that can exist between objects: "has-a" relationships, where an object "has" an instance of another object (e.g., a bookstore has books), and "is-a" relationships, where an object's type is a subtype (or *subclass*) of another object (e.g., a bookstore is a type of store). In an SQL database, "has-a" relationships are quite common, whereas "is-a" relationships can be difficult to achieve.

Consider a table called "Products," which might represent the entity class of all products available for sale by a company. This table may have columns (attributes) that typically belong to a product, such as "price," "weight," and "UPC." These common attributes are applicable to all products that the company sells. However, the company may sell many subclasses of products, each with their own specific sets of additional attributes. For instance, if the company sells both books and DVDs, the books might have a "page count," whereas the DVDs would probably have "length" and "format" attributes.

Subclassing in the object-oriented world is done via inheritance models that are implemented in languages such as C#. In these models, a given entity can be a member of a subclass, and still generally treated as a member of the *superclass* in code that works at that level. This makes it possible to seamlessly deal with both books and DVDs in the checkout part of a point-of-sale application, while keeping separate attributes about each subclass for use in other parts of the application where they are needed.

In SQL databases, modeling inheritance can be tricky. The following code listing shows one way that it can be approached:

```
CREATE TABLE Products
(
    UPC int NOT NULL PRIMARY KEY,
    Weight decimal NOT NULL,
    Price decimal NOT NULL
);

CREATE TABLE Books
(
    UPC int NOT NULL PRIMARY KEY
        REFERENCES Products (UPC),
    PageCount int NOT NULL
);
```

```
CREATE TABLE DVDs
(
    UPC int NOT NULL PRIMARY KEY
        REFERENCES Products (UPC),
    LengthInMinutes decimal NOT NULL,
    Format varchar(4) NOT NULL
        CHECK (Format IN ('NTSC', 'PAL'))
);
```

The database structure created using this code listing is illustrated in Figure 1-2.

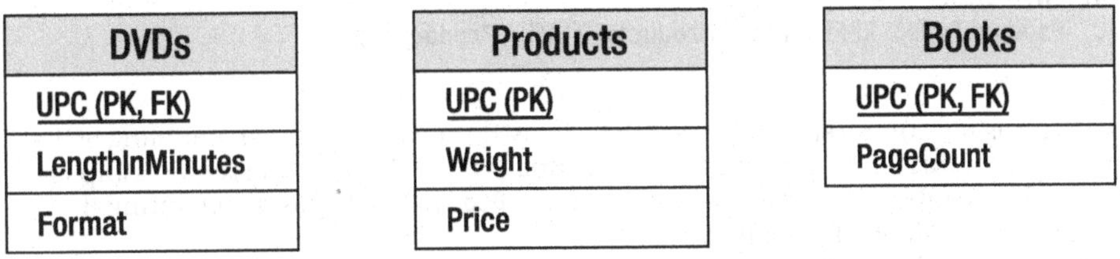

DVDs		Products		Books
UPC (PK, FK)		UPC (PK)		UPC (PK, FK)
LengthInMinutes		Weight		PageCount
Format		Price		

Figure 1-2. Modeling CREATE TABLE DVDs inheritance in a SQL database

Although this model successfully establishes books and DVDs as subtypes for products, it has a couple of serious problems. First of all, there is no way of enforcing uniqueness of subtypes in this model as it stands. A single UPC can belong to both the **Books** and **DVDs** subtypes simultaneously. That makes little sense in the real world in most cases (although it might be possible that a certain book ships with a DVD, in which case this model could make sense).

Another issue is access to attributes. In an object-oriented system, a subclass automatically inherits all of the attributes of its superclass; a book entity would contain all of the attributes of both books and general products. However, that is not the case in the model presented here. Getting general product attributes when looking at data for books or DVDs requires a join back to the **Products** table. This really breaks down the overall sense of working with a subtype.

Solving these problems is not impossible, but it takes some work. One method of guaranteeing uniqueness among subtypes involves populating the supertype with an additional attribute identifying the subtype of each instance. The following tables show how this solution could be implemented:

```
CREATE TABLE Products
(
    UPC int NOT NULL PRIMARY KEY,
    Weight decimal NOT NULL,
    Price decimal NOT NULL,
    ProductType char(1) NOT NULL
        CHECK (ProductType IN ('B', 'D')),
    UNIQUE (UPC, ProductType)
);

CREATE TABLE Books
(
    UPC int NOT NULL PRIMARY KEY,
    ProductType char(1) NOT NULL
        CHECK (ProductType = 'B'),
```

```
    PageCount int NOT NULL,
    FOREIGN KEY (UPC, ProductType) REFERENCES Products (UPC, ProductType)
);

CREATE TABLE DVDs
(
    UPC int NOT NULL PRIMARY KEY,
    ProductType char(1) NOT NULL
        CHECK (ProductType = 'D'),
    LengthInMinutes decimal NOT NULL,
    Format varchar(4) NOT NULL
        CHECK (Format IN ('NTSC', 'PAL')),
    FOREIGN KEY (UPC, ProductType) REFERENCES Products (UPC, ProductType)
);
```

By defining the subtype as part of the supertype, a **UNIQUE** constraint can be created, enabling SQL Server to enforce that only one subtype for each instance of a supertype is allowed. The relationship is further enforced in each subtype table by a **CHECK** constraint on the **ProductType** column, ensuring that only the correct product types are allowed to be inserted.

It is possible to extend this method even further using indexed views and **INSTEAD OF** triggers. A view can be created for each subtype, which encapsulates the join necessary to retrieve the supertype's attributes. By creating views to hide the joins, a consumer does not have to be aware of the subtype/supertype relationship, thereby fixing the attribute access problem. The indexing helps with performance, and the triggers allow the views to be updateable.

It is possible in SQL databases to represent almost any relationship that can be embodied in an object-oriented system, but it's important that database developers understand the intricacies of doing so. Mapping object-oriented data into a database (properly) is often not at all straightforward, and for complex object graphs can be quite a challenge.

The "Lots of Null Columns" Inheritance Model

An all-too-common design for modeling inheritance in the database is to create a single table with all of the columns for the supertype in addition to all of the columns for each subtype, the latter nullable. This design is fraught with issues and should be avoided. The basic problem is that the attributes that constitute a subtype become mixed, and therefore confused. For example, it is impossible to look at the table and find out what attributes belong to a book instead of a DVD. The only way to make the determination is to look it up in the documentation (if it exists) or evaluate the code. Furthermore, data integrity is all but lost. It becomes difficult to enforce that only certain attributes should be non-**NULL** for certain subtypes, and even more difficult to figure out what to do in the event that an attribute that should be **NULL** isn't—what does NTSC format mean for a book? Was it populated due to a bug in the code, or does this book really have a playback format? In a properly modeled system, this question would be impossible to ask.

ORM: A Solution That Creates Many Problems

One solution to overcoming the problems that exist between relationship and object-oriented systems is to turn to tools known as *object-relational mappers (ORMs)*, which attempt to automatically map objects to databases.

Many of these tools exist, including the open source nHibernate project, and Microsoft's own Entity Framework. Each of these tools comes with its own features and functions, but the basic idea is the same in most cases: the developer "plugs" the ORM tool into an existing object-oriented system and tells the tool which columns in the database map to each field of each class. The ORM tool interrogates the object system as well as the database to figure out how to write SQL to retrieve the data into object form and persist it back to the database if it changes. This is all done automatically and somewhat seamlessly.

Some tools go one step further, creating a database for the preexisting objects, if one does not already exist. These tools work based on the assumption that classes and tables can be mapped in one-to-one correspondence in most cases, which, as previously mentioned, is generally *not* true. Therefore these tools often end up producing incredibly flawed database designs.

One company I did some work for had used a popular Java-based ORM tool for its e-commerce application. The tool mapped "has-a" relationships from an object-centric rather than table-centric point of view, and as a result the database had a **Products** table with a foreign key to an **Orders** table. The Java developers working for the company were forced to insert fake orders into the system in order to allow the firm to sell new products.

While ORM does have some benefits, and the abstraction from any specific database can aid in creating portable code, I believe that the current set of available tools do not work well enough to make them viable for enterprise software development. Aside from the issues with the tools that create database tables based on classes, the two primary issues that concern me are both performance related:

> First of all, ORM tools tend to think in terms of objects rather than collections of related data (i.e., tables). Each class has its own data access methods produced by the ORM tool, and each time data is needed, these methods query the database on a granular level for just the rows necessary. This means that (depending on how connection pooling is handled) a lot of database connections are opened and closed on a regular basis, and the overall interface to retrieve the data is quite "chatty." SQL DBMSs tend to be much more efficient at returning data in bulk than a row at a time; it's generally better to query for a product and all of its related data at once than to ask for the product, and then request related data in a separate query.

> Second, query tuning may be difficult if ORM tools are relied upon too heavily. In SQL databases, there are often many logically equivalent ways of writing any given query, each of which may have distinct performance characteristics. The current crop of ORM tools does not intelligently monitor for and automatically fix possible issues with poorly written queries, and developers using these tools are often taken by surprise when the system fails to scale because of improperly written queries.

ORM tools have improved dramatically over the last couple of years, and will undoubtedly continue to do so as time goes on. However, even in the most recent version of the Microsoft Entity Framework (.NET 4.0 Beta 1), there are substantial deficiencies in the SQL code generated that lead to database queries that are ugly at best, and frequently suboptimal. I feel that any such automatically generated ORM code will never be able to compete performance-wise with manually crafted queries, and a better return on investment can be made by carefully designing object-database interfaces by hand.

Introducing the Database-As-API Mindset

By far the most important issue to be wary of when writing data interchange interfaces between object systems and database systems is coupling. Object systems and the databases they use as back ends should be carefully partitioned in order to ensure that, in most cases, changes to one layer do not necessitate changes to the other layer. This is important in both worlds; if a change to the database requires an application change, it can often be expensive to recompile and redeploy the application. Likewise, if application logic changes necessitate database changes, it can be difficult to know how changing the data structures or constraints will affect other applications that may need the same data.

To combat these issues, database developers must resolve to adhere rigidly to a solid set of encapsulated interfaces between the database system and the objects. I call this the **database-as-API** mindset.

An **application programming interface** (API) is a set of interfaces that allows a system to interact with another system. An API is intended to be a complete access methodology for the system it exposes. In database terms, this means that an API would expose public interfaces for retrieving data from, inserting data into, and updating data in the database.

A set of database interfaces should comply with the same basic design rule as other interfaces: well-known, standardized sets of inputs that result in well-known, standardized sets of outputs. This set of interfaces should completely encapsulate all implementation details, including table and column names, keys, indexes, and queries. An application that uses the data from a database should not require knowledge of internal information—the application should only need to know that data can be retrieved and persisted using certain methods.

In order to define such an interface, the first step is to define stored procedures for all external database access. Table-direct access to data is clearly a violation of proper encapsulation and interface design, and views may or may not suffice. Stored procedures are the only construct available in SQL Server that can provide the type of interfaces necessary for a comprehensive data API.

Web Services as a Standard API Layer

It's worth noting that the database-as-API mindset that I'm proposing requires the use of stored procedures as an interface to the data, but does not get into the detail of what protocol you use to access those stored procedures. Many software shops have discovered that web services are a good way to provide a standard, cross-platform interface layer, such as using ADO.NET data services to produce a RESTful web service based on an entity data model. Whether using web services is superior to using other protocols is something that must be decided on a per-case basis; like any other technology, they can certainly be used in the wrong way or in the wrong scenario. Keep in mind that web services require a lot more network bandwidth and follow different authentication rules than other protocols that SQL Server supports—their use may end up causing more problems than they solve.

By using stored procedures with correctly defined interfaces and full encapsulation of information, coupling between the application and the database will be greatly reduced, resulting in a database system that is much easier to maintain and evolve over time.

It is difficult to stress the importance that stored procedures play in a well-designed SQL Server database system in only a few paragraphs. In order to reinforce the idea that the database must be thought of as an API rather than a persistence layer, this topic will be revisited throughout the book with examples that deal with interfaces to outside systems.

The Great Balancing Act

When it comes down to it, the real goal of software development is to produce working software that customers will want to use, in addition to software that can be easily fixed or extended as time and needs progress. But, when developing a piece of software, there are hard limits that constrain what can actually be achieved. No project has a limitless quantity of time or money, so sacrifices must often be made in one area in order to allow for a higher-priority requirement in another.

The database is, in most cases, the center of the applications it drives. The data controls the applications, to a great extent, and without the data the applications would not be worth much. Likewise, the database is often where applications face real challenges in terms of performance, maintainability, and other critical success factors. It is quite common for application developers to push these issues as far down into the data tier as possible, and in the absence of a data architect, this leaves the database developer as the person responsible for balancing the needs of the entire application.

Attempting to strike the right balance generally involves a trade-off between the following areas:

- Performance

- Testability

- Maintainability

- Security

- Allowing for future requirements

Balancing the demands of these competing facets is not an easy task. What follows are some initial thoughts on these issues; examples throughout the remainder of the book will serve to illustrate them in more detail.

Performance

We live in an increasingly impatient society. Customers and management place demands that must be met *now* (or sometimes yesterday). We want fast food, fast cars, and fast service, and are constantly in search of instant gratification of all types. That need for speed certainly applies to the world of database development. Users continuously seem to feel that applications just aren't performing as fast as they should, even when those applications are doing a tremendous amount of work. It sometimes feels as though users would prefer to have *any* data as fast as possible, rather than the *correct* data if it means waiting a bit longer.

The problem, of course, is that performance isn't easy, and can throw the entire balance off. Building a truly high-performance application often involves sacrifice. Functionality might have to be trimmed (less work for the application to do means it will be faster), security might have to be reduced (less authorization cycles means less work), or inefficient code might have to be rewritten in arcane, unmaintainable ways in order to squeeze every last CPU cycle out of the server.

So how do we reconcile this need for extreme performance—which many seem to care about to the exclusion of all else—with the need for development best practices? Unfortunately, the answer is that sometimes we can only do as well as we can do. Most of the time, if we find ourselves in a position in which a user is complaining about performance and we're going to lose money or a job if it's not remedied, the user doesn't want to hear about why fixing the performance problem will increase coupling and decrease maintainability. The user just wants the software to work fast—and we have no choice but to deliver.

A fortunate fact about sticking with best practices is that they're often considered to be the best way to do things for several reasons. Keeping a close watch on issues of coupling, cohesion, and proper encapsulation throughout the development cycle can not only reduce the incidence of performance problems, but will also make fixing most of them a whole lot easier. And on those few occasions where you need to break some "perfect" code to get it working as fast as necessary, know that it's not your fault—society put you in this position!

Testability

It is inadvisable, to say the least, to ship any product without thoroughly testing it. However, it is common to see developers exploit anti-patterns that make proper testing difficult or impossible. Many of these problems result from attempts to produce "flexible" modules or interfaces—instead of properly partitioning functionality and paying close attention to cohesion, it is sometimes tempting to create "all-singing, all-dancing," monolithic routines that try to do it all.

Development of these kinds of routines produces software that can never be fully tested. The combinatorial explosion of possible use cases for a single routine can be immense—even though, in most cases, the number of actual combinations that users of the application will exploit is far more limited.

Think very carefully before implementing a flexible solution merely for the sake of flexibility. Does it really need to be that flexible? Will the functionality really be exploited in full right away, or can it be slowly extended later as required?

Maintainability

Throughout the lifespan of an application, various modules and routines will require maintenance and revision in the form of enhancements and bug fixes. The issues that make routines more or less maintainable are similar to those that influence testability, with a few twists.

When determining how testable a given routine is, we are generally only concerned with whether the interface is stable enough to allow the authoring of test cases. For determining the level of maintainability, we are also concerned with exposed interfaces, but for slightly different reasons. From a maintainability point of view, the most important interface issue is coupling. Tightly coupled routines tend to carry a higher maintenance cost, as any changes have to be propagated to multiple routines instead of being made in a single place.

The issue of maintainability also goes beyond the interface into the actual implementation. A routine may have a stable, simple interface, yet have a convoluted, undocumented implementation that is difficult to work with. Generally speaking, the more lines of code in a routine, the more difficult maintenance becomes; but since large routines may also be a sign of a cohesion problem, such an issue should be caught early in the design process if developers are paying attention.

As with testability, maintainability is somewhat influenced by attempts to create "flexible" interfaces. On one hand, flexibility of an interface can increase coupling between routines by requiring the caller to have too much knowledge of parameter combinations, overrideable options, and the like. On the other hand, routines with flexible interfaces can sometimes be more easily maintained, at least at the beginning of a project. In some cases, making routines as generic as possible can result in fewer total routines needed by a system, and therefore less code to maintain. However, as features are added, the ease with which these generic routines can be modified tends to break down due to the increased complexity that each new option or parameter brings. Oftentimes, therefore, it may be advantageous early in a project to aim for some flexibility, and then refactor later when maintainability begins to suffer.

Maintainability is also tied in with testability in one other key way: the better a routine can be tested, the easier it will be to modify. Breaking changes are not as much of an issue when tests exist that can quickly validate new approaches to implementation.

Security

In an age in which identity theft makes the news almost every night, and a computer left open on the Internet will be compromised within 30 seconds, it is little wonder that security is considered one of the most important areas when developing software applications. Security is, however, also one of the most complex areas, and complexity can hide flaws that a trained attacker can easily exploit.

Complex security schemes can also have a huge impact on whether a given piece of software is testable and maintainable. From a testing standpoint, a developer needs to consider whether a given security scheme will create too many variables to make testing feasible. For instance, if users are divided into groups and each group has distinct security privileges, should each set of tests be run for each group of users? How many test combinations are necessary to exercise before the application can be considered "fully" tested?

From a maintenance point of view, complexity from a security standpoint is equally dangerous as complexity of any other type of implementation. The more complex a given routine is, the more difficult (and therefore more expensive) it will be to maintain.

In a data-dependent application, much of the security responsibility will generally get pushed into the data tier. The security responsibilities of the data tier or database will generally include areas such as authentication to the application, authorization to view data, and availability of data. Encapsulating these security responsibilities in database routines can be a win from an overall application maintainability perspective, but care must be taken to ensure that the database routines do not become so bogged down that their maintainability, testability, or performance suffer.

Allowing for Future Requirements

In a dynamic environment, where you face ever-changing customer requirements and additional feature requests, it is easy to give too much attention to tomorrow's enhancements, instead of concentrating on today's bugs. Looking through many technical specifications and data dictionaries, it's common to see the phrase "reserved for future use." Developers want to believe that adding complexity up front will work to their advantage by allowing less work to be done later in the development process. However, this approach of second-guessing future requirements frequently backfires, producing software full of maintenance baggage. These pieces of code must be carried around by the development team and kept up to date in order to compile the application, but often go totally unused for years at a time.

Even SQL Server itself even suffers from these problems. For example, according to Books Online, the `NUM_INPUT_PARAMS`, `NUM_OUTPUT_PARAMS`, and `NUM_RESULT_SETS` returned by the `sp_stored_procedures` stored procedure in SQL Server 2008 are reserved for future use (`http://msdn.microsoft.com/en-us/library/ms190504.aspx`), just as they were in SQL Server 2005 (`http://msdn.microsoft.com/en-us/library/ms190504(SQL.90).aspx`).

In one 15-year-old application I worked on, the initial development team had been especially active in prepopulating the code base with features reserved for the future. Alas, several years, a few rounds of layoffs, and lots of staff turnovers later, and no members of the original team were left. The remaining developers who had to deal with the 2 million–line application were afraid of removing anything lest it would break some long-forgotten feature that some user still relied upon. It was a dismal scene, to say the least, and it's difficult to imagine just how much time was wasted over the years keeping all of that redundant code up to date.

Although that example is extreme (certainly by far the worst I've come across), it teaches us to adhere to the golden rule of software development: the **KISS** principle (keep it simple, stupid). Keep your software projects as straightforward as they can possibly be. Adding new features tomorrow should always be a secondary concern to delivering a robust, working product today.

Summary

Applications depend upon databases for much more than mere data persistence, and database developers must have an understanding of the entire application development process in order to create truly effective database systems.

By understanding architectural concepts such as coupling, cohesion, and encapsulation, database developers can define modular data interfaces that allow for great gains in ongoing maintenance and testing. Database developers must also understand how best to map data from object-oriented systems into database structures, in order to effectively persist and manipulate the data.

This chapter has provided an introduction to these ideas. The concepts presented here will be revisited in various examples throughout the remainder of the book.

CHAPTER 2

■ ■ ■

Best Practices for Database Programming

Software development is not just a practical discipline performed by coders, but also an area of academic research and theory. There is now a great body of knowledge concerning software development, and lengthy academic papers have been written to propose, dissect, and discuss different approaches to development. Various methodologies have emerged, including test-driven development (TDD), agile and extreme programming (XP), and defensive programming, and there have been countless arguments concerning the benefits afforded by each of these schools of thought.

The practices described in this chapter, and the approach taken throughout the rest of this book, are most closely aligned with the philosophy of defensive programming. However, the topics discussed here can be applied just as readily in any environment. While software theorists may argue the finer differences between different methodologies (and undoubtedly, they do differ in some respects), when it comes down to it, the underlying features of good programming remain the same whatever methodology you apply.

I do not intend to provide an exhaustive, objective guide as to what constitutes best practice, but rather to highlight some of the standards that I believe demonstrate the level of professionalism that database developers require in order to do a good job. I will present the justification of each argument from a defensive point of view, but remember that they are generally equally valid in other environments.

Defensive Programming

Defensive programming is a methodology used in software development that suggests that developers should proactively anticipate and make allowances for (or "defend against") unforeseen future events. The objective of defensive programming is to create applications that can remain robust and effective, even when faced with unexpected situations.

Defensive programming essentially involves taking a pessimistic view of the world—if something can go wrong, it will: network resources will become unavailable halfway through a transaction; required files will be absent or corrupt; users will input data in any number of ways different from that expected, and so on. Rather than leave anything to chance, a defensive programmer will have predicted the possibility of these eventualities, and will have written appropriate handling code to check for and deal with these situations. This means that potential error conditions can be detected and handled before an actual error occurs.

Note that defensive programming does not necessarily enable an application to continue when exceptional circumstances occur, but it does make it possible for the system to behave in a predictable, controlled way—degrading gracefully, rather than risking a crash with unknown consequences. In many cases, it may be possible to identify and isolate a particular component responsible for a failure, allowing the rest of the application to continue functioning.

There is no definitive list of defensive programming practices, but adopting a defensive stance to development is generally agreed to include the following principles:

- Keep things simple (or KISS—keep it simple, stupid). Applications are not made powerful and effective by their complexity, but by their elegant simplicity. Complexity allows bugs to be concealed, and should be avoided in both application design and in coding practice itself.

- "If it ain't broke, fix it anyway." Rather than waiting for things to break, defensive programming encourages continuous, proactive testing and future-proofing of an application against possible breaking changes in the future.

- Be challenging, thorough, and cautious at all stages and development. "What if?" analyses should be conducted in order to identify possible exceptional scenarios that might occur during normal (and abnormal) application usage.

- Extensive code reviews and testing should be conducted with different peer groups, including other developers or technical teams, consultants, end users, and management. Each of these different groups may have different implicit assumptions that might not be considered by a closed development team.

- Assumptions should be avoided wherever possible. If an application requires a certain condition to be true in order to function correctly, there should be an explicit assertion to this effect, and relevant code paths should be inserted to check and act accordingly based on the result.

- Applications should be built from short, highly cohesive, loosely coupled modules. Modules that are well encapsulated in this way can be thoroughly tested in isolation, and then confidently reused throughout the application. Reusing specific code modules, rather than duplicating functionality, reduces the chances of introducing new bugs.

Throughout the remainder of this chapter, I'll be providing simple examples of what I believe to be best practices demonstrating each of these principles, and these concepts will be continually reexamined in later chapters of this book.

Attitudes to Defensive Programming

The key advantages of taking a defensive approach to programming are essentially twofold:

- Defensive applications are typically robust and stable, require fewer essential bug fixes, and are more resilient to situations that may otherwise lead to expensive failures or crashes. As a result, they have a long expected lifespan, and relatively cheap ongoing maintenance costs.

- In many cases, defensive programming can lead to an improved user experience. By actively foreseeing and allowing for exceptional circumstances, errors can be caught *before* they occur, rather than having to be handled afterward. Exceptions can be isolated and handled with a minimum negative effect on user experience, rather than propagating an entire system failure. Even in the case of extreme unexpected conditions being encountered, the system can still degrade gracefully and act according to documented behavior.

However, as with any school of thought, defensive programming is not without its opponents. Some of the criticisms commonly made of defensive coding are listed following. In each case, I've tried to give a reasoned response to each criticism.

Defensive code takes longer to develop.

It is certainly true that following a defensive methodology can result in a longer up-front development time when compared to applications developed following other software practices. Defensive programming places a strong emphasis on the initial requirements-gathering and architecture design phases, which may be longer and more involved than in some methodologies. Coding itself takes longer because additional code paths may need to be added to handle checks and assertions of assumptions. Code must be subjected to an extensive review that is both challenging and thorough, and then must undergo rigorous testing. All these factors contribute to the fact that the overall development and release cycle for defensive software is longer than in other approaches.

There is a particularly stark contrast between defensive programming and so-called "agile" development practices, which focus on releasing frequent iterative changes on a very accelerated development and release cycle. However, this does not necessarily mean that defensive code takes longer to develop when considered over the full life cycle of an application. The additional care and caution invested in code at the initial stages of development are typically paid back over the life of the project, because there is less need for code fixes to be deployed once the project has gone live.

Writing code that anticipates and handles every possible scenario makes defensive applications bloated.

Code bloat suggests that an application contains unnecessary, inefficient, or wasteful code. Defensive code protects against events that may be *unlikely* to happen, but that certainly doesn't mean that they can't happen. Taking actions to explicitly test for and handle exceptional circumstances up front can save lots of hours spent possibly tracing and debugging in the future. Defensive applications may contain more total lines of code than other applications, but all of that code should be well designed, with a clear purpose. Note that the label of "defensive programming" is sometimes misused: the addition of unnecessary checks at every opportunity without consideration or justification is *not* defensive programming. Such actions lead to code that is both complex and rigid. Remember that true defensive programming promotes simplicity, modularization, and code reuse, which actually reduces code bloat.

Defensive programming hides bugs that then go unfixed, rather than making them visible.

This is perhaps the most common misconception applied to defensive practices, which manifests from a failure to understand the fundamental attitude toward errors in defensive applications. By explicitly identifying and checking exceptional scenarios, defensive programming actually takes a very proactive approach to the identification of errors. However, having encountered a condition that could lead to an exceptional circumstance, defensive applications are designed to fail gracefully—that is, at the point of development, potential scenarios that may lead to exceptions are identified and code paths are created to handle them. To demonstrate this in practical terms, consider the following code listing, which describes a simple stored procedure to divide one number by another:

```
CREATE PROCEDURE Divide (
  @x decimal(18,2),
  @y decimal(18,2)
  )
  AS BEGIN
    SELECT @x / @y
  END;
GO
```

Based on the code as written previously, it would be very easy to cause an exception using this procedure if, for example, the supplied value of @y was 0. If you were simply trying to prevent the error message from occurring, it would be possible to consume (or "swallow") the exception in a catch block, as follows:

```
ALTER PROCEDURE Divide (
  @x decimal(18,2),
  @y decimal(18,2)
  )
  AS BEGIN
    BEGIN TRY
      SELECT @x / @y
    END TRY
    BEGIN CATCH
      /* Do Nothing */
    END CATCH
  END;
GO
```

However, it is important to realize that the preceding code listing is *not* defensive—it does nothing to prevent the exceptional circumstance from occurring, and its only effect is to allow the system to continue operating, pretending that nothing bad has happened. **Exception hiding** such as this can be very dangerous, and makes it almost impossible to ensure the correct functioning of an application. The defensive approach would be, before attempting to perform the division, to explicitly check that all the requirements for that operation to be successful are met. This means asserting such things as making sure that values for @x and @y are supplied (i.e., they are not **NULL**), that @y is not equal to zero, that the supplied values lie within the range that can be stored within the **decimal(18,2)** datatype, and so on.

The following code listing provides a simplified defensive approach to this same procedure:

```
ALTER PROCEDURE Divide (
  @x decimal(18,2),
  @y decimal(18,2)
  )
  AS BEGIN
    IF @x IS NULL OR @y IS NULL
      BEGIN
        PRINT 'Please supply values for @x and @y';
        RETURN;
      END
```

```
  IF @y = 0
    BEGIN
      PRINT '@y cannot be equal to 0';
      RETURN;
    END

  BEGIN TRY
    SELECT @x / @y
  END TRY
  BEGIN CATCH
    PRINT 'An unhandled exception occurred';
  END CATCH
END;
GO
```

For the purposes of the preceding example, each assertion was accompanied by a simple **PRINT** statement to advise which of the conditions necessary for the procedure to execute failed. In real life, these code paths may handle such assertions in a number of ways—typically logging the error, reporting a message to the user, and attempting to continue system operation if it is possible to do so. In doing so, they prevent the kind of unpredictable behavior associated with an exception that has not been expected.

Defensive programming can be contrasted to the **fail fast** methodology, which focuses on immediate recognition of any errors encountered by causing the application to halt whenever an exception occurs. Just because the defensive approach doesn't espouse ringing alarm bells and flashing lights doesn't mean that it hides errors—it just reports them more elegantly to the end user and, if possible, continues operation of the core part of the system.

Why Use a Defensive Approach to Database Development?

As stated previously, defensive programming is not the only software development methodology that can be applied to database development. Other common approaches include TDD, XP, and fail-fast development. So why have I chosen to focus on just defensive programming in this chapter, and throughout this book in general? I believe that defensive programming is the most appropriate approach for database development for the following reasons:

> **Database applications tend to have a longer expected lifespan than other software applications**. Although it may be an overused stereotype to suggest that database professionals are the sensible, fastidious people of the software development world, the fact is that database development tends to be more slow-moving and cautious than other technologies. Web applications, for example, may be revised and relaunched on a nearly annual basis, in order to take advantage of whatever technology is current at the time. In contrast, database development tends to be slow and steady, and a database application may remain current for many years without any need for updating from a technological point of view. As a result, it is easier to justify the greater up-front development cost associated with defensive programming. The benefits of reliability and bug resistance will typically be enjoyed for a longer period.

> **Users (and management) are less tolerant of bugs in database applications**. Most end users have come to tolerate and even expect bugs in desktop and web software. While undoubtedly a cause of frustration, many people are routinely in

the habit of hitting Ctrl+Alt+Delete to reset their machine when a web browser hangs, or because some application fails to shut down correctly. However, the same tolerance that is shown to personal desktop software is not typically extended to corporate database applications. Recent highly publicized scandals in which bugs have been exploited in the systems of several governments and large organizations have further heightened the general public's ultrasensitivity toward anything that might present a risk to database integrity.

Any bugs that do exist in database applications can have more severe consequences than in other software. It can be argued that people are absolutely right to be more worried about database bugs than bugs in other software. An unexpected error in a desktop application may lead to a document or file becoming corrupt, which is a nuisance and might lead to unnecessary rework. But an unexpected error in a database may lead to important personal, confidential, or sensitive data being placed at risk, which can have rather more serious consequences. The nature of data typically stored in a database warrants a cautious, thorough approach to development, such as defensive programming provides.

Designing for Longevity

Consumer software applications have an increasingly short expected shelf life, with compressed release cycles pushing out one release barely before the predecessor has hit the shelves. However, this does not have to be the case. Well-designed, defensively programmed applications can continue to operate for many years. In one organization I worked for, a short-term tactical management information data store was created so that essential business reporting functions could continue while the organization's systems went through an integration following a merger. Despite only being required for an immediate post-merger period, the (rather unfortunately named) Short Term Management Information database continued to be used for up to ten years later, as it remained more reliable and robust than subsequent attempted replacements.

And let that be a lesson in choosing descriptive names for your databases that won't age with time!

Best Practice SQL Programming Techniques

Having looked at some of the theory behind different software methodologies, and in particular the defensive approach to programming, you're now probably wondering about how to put this into practice. As in any methodology, defensive programming is more concerned with the mindset with which you should approach development than prescribing a definitive set of rules to follow. As a result, this section will only provide examples that illustrate the overall concepts involved, and should not be treated as an exhaustive list. I'll try to keep the actual examples as simple as possible in every case, so that you can concentrate on the reasons I consider these to be best practices, rather than the code itself.

Identify Hidden Assumptions in Your Code

One of the core tenets of defensive programming is to identify all of the assumptions that lie behind the proper functioning of your code. Once these assumptions have been identified, the function can either be adjusted to remove the dependency on them, or explicitly test each condition and make provisions should it not hold true. In some cases, "hidden" assumptions exist as a result of code failing to be sufficiently explicit.

To demonstrate this concept, consider the following code listing, which creates and populates a **Customers** and an **Orders** table:

```
CREATE TABLE Customers(
  CustID int,
  Name varchar(32),
  Address varchar(255));

INSERT INTO Customers(CustID, Name, Address) VALUES
  (1, 'Bob Smith', 'Flat 1, 27 Heigham Street'),
  (2, 'Tony James', '87 Long Road');
GO

CREATE TABLE Orders(
  OrderID INT,
  CustID INT,
  OrderDate DATE);

INSERT INTO Orders(OrderID, CustID, OrderDate) VALUES
  (1, 1, '2008-01-01'),
  (2, 1, '2008-03-04'),
  (3, 2, '2008-03-07');
GO
```

Now consider the following query to select a list of every customer order, which uses columns from both tables:

```
SELECT
  Name,
  Address,
  OrderID
FROM
  Customers c
  JOIN Orders o ON c.CustID = o.CustID;
GO
```

The query executes successfully and we get the results expected:

Bob Smith	Flat 1, 27 Heigham Street	1
Bob Smith	Flat 1, 27 Heigham Street	2
Tony James	87 Long Road	3

But what is the hidden assumption? The column names listed in the **SELECT** query were not qualified with table names, so what would happen if the table structure were to change in the future? Suppose that an **Address** column were added to the **Orders** table to enable a separate delivery address to be attached to each order, rather than relying on the address in the **Customers** table:

```
ALTER TABLE Orders ADD Address varchar(255);
GO
```

The unqualified column name, **Address**, specified in the **SELECT** query, is now ambiguous, and if we attempt to run the original query again we receive an error:

```
Msg 209, Level 16, State 1, Line 1

Ambiguous column name 'Address'.
```

By not recognizing and correcting the hidden assumption contained in the original code, the query subsequently broke as a result of the additional column being added to the **Orders** table. The simple practice that could have prevented this error would have been to ensure that all column names were prefixed with the appropriate table name or alias:

```
SELECT
  c.Name,
  c.Address,
  o.OrderID
FROM
  Customers c
  JOIN Orders o ON c.CustID = o.CustID;
GO
```

In the previous case, it was pretty easy to spot the hidden assumption, because SQL Server gave a descriptive error message that would enable any developer to locate and fix the broken code fairly quickly. However, sometimes you may not be so fortunate, as shown in the following example.

Suppose that you had a table, **MainData**, containing some simple values, as shown in the following code listing:

```
CREATE TABLE MainData(
  ID int,
  Value char(3));
GO
```

```
INSERT INTO MainData(ID, Value) VALUES
  (1, 'abc'), (2, 'def'), (3, 'ghi'), (4, 'jkl');
GO
```

Now suppose that every change made to the **MainData** table was to be recorded in an associated **ChangeLog** table. The following code demonstrates this structure, together with a mechanism to automatically populate the **ChangeLog** table by means of an **UPDATE** trigger attached to the **MainData** table:

```
CREATE TABLE ChangeLog(
  ChangeID int IDENTITY(1,1),
  RowID int,
  OldValue char(3),
  NewValue char(3),
  ChangeDate datetime);
GO

CREATE TRIGGER DataUpdate ON MainData
FOR UPDATE
AS
  DECLARE @ID int;
  SELECT @ID = ID FROM INSERTED;

  DECLARE @OldValue varchar(32);
  SELECT @OldValue = Value FROM DELETED;

  DECLARE @NewValue varchar(32);
  SELECT @NewValue = Value FROM INSERTED;

  INSERT INTO ChangeLog(RowID, OldValue, NewValue, ChangeDate)
  VALUES(@ID, @OldValue, @NewValue, GetDate());
GO
```

We can test the trigger by running a simple **UPDATE** query against the **MainData** table:

```
UPDATE MainData SET Value = 'aaa' WHERE ID = 1;
GO
```

The query appears to be functioning correctly—SQL Server Management Studio reports the following:

```
(1 row(s) affected)
```

```
(1 row(s) affected)
```

And, as expected, we find that one row has been updated in the `MainData` table:

ID	Value
1	aaa
2	def
3	ghi
4	jkl

and an associated row has been created in the `ChangeLog` table:

ChangeID	RowID	OldValue	NewValue	ChangeDate
1	1	abc	aaa	2009-06-15 14:11:09.770

However, once again, there is a hidden assumption in the code. Within the trigger logic, the variables `@ID`, `@OldValue`, and `@NewValue` are assigned values that will be inserted into the `ChangeLog` table. Clearly, each of these scalar variables can only be assigned a single value, so what would happen if you were to attempt to update two or more rows in a single statement?

```
UPDATE MainData SET Value = 'zzz' WHERE ID IN (2,3,4);
GO
```

If you haven't worked it out yet, perhaps the messages reported by SQL Server Management Studio will give you a clue as to the result:

```
(1 row(s) affected)
```

```
(3 row(s) affected)
```

The result in this case is that all three rows affected by the **UPDATE** statement have been changed in the **MainData** table:

ID	Value
1	aaa
2	zzz
3	zzz
4	zzz

but only the first update has been logged:

ChangeID	RowID	OldValue	NewValue	ChangeDate
1	1	abc	aaa	2009-06-15 14:11:09.770
2	2	def	zzz	2009-06-15 15:18:11.007

The failure to foresee the possibility of multiple rows being updated in a single statement led to a silent failure on this occasion, which is much more dangerous than the overt error given in the previous example. Had this scenario been actively considered, it would have been easy to recode the procedure to deal with such an event by making a subtle alteration to the trigger syntax, as shown here:

```
ALTER TRIGGER DataUpdate ON MainData
FOR UPDATE
AS
  INSERT INTO ChangeLog(RowID, OldValue, NewValue, ChangeDate)
  SELECT i.ID, d.Value, i.Value, GetDate()
  FROM INSERTED i JOIN DELETED d ON i.ID = d.ID;
GO
```

Don't Take Shortcuts

It is human nature to want to take shortcuts if we believe that they will allow us to avoid work that we feel is unnecessary. In programming terms, there are often shortcuts that provide a convenient, concise way of achieving a given task in fewer lines of code than other, more standard methods. However, these shortcut methods can come with associated risks. Most commonly, shortcut methods require less code because they rely on some assumed default values rather than those explicitly stated within the procedure. As such, they can only be applied in situations where the conditions imposed by those default values hold true.

By relying on a default value, shortcut methods may increase the rigidity of your code and also introduce an external dependency—the default value may vary depending on server configuration, or change between different versions of SQL Server. Taking shortcuts therefore reduces the portability of code, and introduces assumptions that can break in the future.

To demonstrate, consider what happens when you **CAST** a value to a **varchar** datatype without explicitly declaring the appropriate data length:

```
SELECT CAST ('This example seems to work ok' AS varchar);
GO
```

The query appears to work correctly, and results in the following output:

```
This example seems to work ok
```

It seems to be a common misunderstanding among some developers that omitting the length for the **varchar** type as the target of a **CAST** operation results in SQL Server dynamically assigning a length sufficient to accommodate all of the characters of the input. However, this is not the case, as demonstrated in the following code listing:

```
SELECT CAST ('This demonstrates the problem of relying on default datatype length'
AS varchar);
GO
```

```
This demonstrates the problem
```

If not explicitly specified, when **CAST**ing to a character datatype, SQL Server defaults to a length of 30 characters. In the second example, the input string is silently truncated to 30 characters, even though there is no obvious indication in the code to this effect. If this was the intention, it would have been much clearer to explicitly state **varchar(30)** to draw attention to the fact that this was a planned truncation, rather than simply omitting the data length.

Another example of a shortcut sometimes made is to rely on implicit **CAST**s between datatypes. Consider the following code listing:

```
DECLARE
  @x int = 5,
  @y int = 9,
  @Rate decimal(18,2);

SET @Rate  = 1.9 * @x / @y;

SELECT 1000 * @Rate;
GO
```

In this example, **@Rate** is a multiplicative factor whose value is determined by the ratio of two parameters, **@x** and **@y**, multiplied by a hard-coded scale factor of 1.9. When applied to the value **1000**, as in this example, the result is as follows:

```
1060
```

Now let's suppose that management makes a decision to change the calculation used to determine @Rate, and increases the scale factor from 1.9 to 2. The obvious (but incorrect) solution would be to amend the code as follows:

```
DECLARE
  @x int = 5,
  @y int = 9,
  @Rate decimal(18,2);

SET @Rate = 2 * @x / @y;

SELECT 1000 * @Rate;
GO
```

```
1000
```

Rather than increasing the rate as intended, the change has actually negated the effect of applying any rate to the supplied value of **1000**. The problem now is that the sum used to determine **@Rate** is a purely integer calculation, 2 * 5 / 9. In integer mathematics, this equates to 1. In the previous example, the hard-coded value of 1.9 caused an implicit cast of both **@x** and **@y** parameters to the **decimal** type, so the sum was calculated with decimal precision.

This example may seem trivial when considered in isolation, but can be a source of unexpected behavior and unnecessary bug-chasing when nested deep in the belly of some complex code. To avoid these complications, it is always best to explicitly state the type and precision of any parameters used in a calculation, and avoid implicit **CAST**s between them.

Another problem with using shortcuts is that they can obscure what the developer intended the purpose of the code to be. If we cannot tell what a line of code is *meant* to do, it is incredibly hard to test whether it is achieving its purpose or not. Consider the following code listing:

```
DECLARE @Date datetime = '03/05/1979';
SELECT @Date + 365;
```

At first sight, this seems fairly innocuous: take a specific date and add 365. But there are actually several shortcuts used here that add ambiguity as to what the intended purpose of this code is:

> The first shortcut is in the implicit **CAST** from the string value **'03/05/1979'** to a **datetime**. As I'm sure you know, there are numerous ways of presenting date formats around the world, and 03/05/1979 is ambiguous. In the United Kingdom it means the 3rd of May, but to American readers it means the 5th of March. The result of the implicit cast will depend upon the locale of the server on which the function is performed.

> Even if the dd/mm/yyyy or mm/dd/yyyy ordering is resolved, there is still ambiguity regarding the input value. The datatype chosen is **datetime**, which stores both a date and time component, but the value assigned to **@Date** does not specify a time, so this code relies on SQL Server's default value of midnight: 00:00:00. However, perhaps it was not the developer's intention to specify an instance in time, but rather the whole of a calendar day. If so, should the original **@Date** parameter be specified using the **date** datatype instead? And what about the result of the **SELECT** query—should that also be a **date**?

Finally, the code specifies the addition of the integer 365 with a **datetime** value. When applied to a date value, the + operator adds the given number of days, so this appears to be a shortcut in place of using the **DATEADD** method to add 365 days. But, is *this* a shortcut to adding 1 year? If so, this is another example of a shortcut that relies on an assumption—in this case, that the year in question has 365 days.

The combination of these factors has meant that it is unclear whether the true intention of this simple line of code is

```
SELECT DATEADD(DAY, 365, '1979-03-05');
```

which leads to the following result:

```
1980-03-04 00:00:00.000
```

or whether the code is a shortcut for the following:

```
SELECT CAST(DATEADD(YEAR, 1, '1979-05-03') AS date);
```

which would lead to a rather different output:

```
1980-05-03
```

■ **Note** For further discussion of issues related to temporal data, please refer to Chapter 11.

Perhaps the most well-known example of a shortcut method is the use of **SELECT** * in order to retrieve every column of data from a table, rather than listing the individual columns by name. As in the first example of this chapter, the risk here is that any change to the table structure in the future will lead to the structure of the result set returned by this query *silently* changing. At best, this may result in columns of data being retrieved that are then never used, leading to inefficiency. At worst, this may lead to very serious errors (consider what would happen if the columns of data in the results are sent to another function that references them by index position rather than column name, or the possibility of the results of any **UNION** queries failing because the number and type of columns in two sets fail to match). There are many other reasons why **SELECT** * should be avoided, such as the addition of unnecessary rows to the query precluding the use of covering indexes, which may lead to a substantial degradation in query performance.

Testing

Defensive practice places a very strong emphasis on the importance of testing and code review throughout the development process. In order to defend against situations that might occur in a live production environment, an application should be tested under the same conditions that it will experience in the real world. In fact, defensive programming suggests that you should test under extreme conditions (**stress testing**)—if you can make a robust, performant application that can cope with severe pressure, then you can be more certain it will cope with the normal demands that will be expected of it. In addition to performance testing, there are functional tests and unit tests to consider, which ensure that every part of the application is behaving as expected according to its contract, and performing the correct function. These tests will be discussed in more detail in the next chapter.

When testing an application, it is important to consider the sample data on which tests will be based. You should not artificially cleanse the data on which you will be testing your code, or rely on artificially generated data. If the application is expected to perform against production data, then it should be tested against a fair representation of that data, warts and all. Doing so will ensure that the application can cope with the sorts of imperfect data typically found in all applications—missing or incomplete values, incorrectly formatted strings, **NULL**s, and so on. Random sampling methods can be used to ensure that the test data represents a fair sample of the overall data set, but it is also important for defensive testing to ensure that applications are tested against extreme edge cases, as it is these unusual conditions that may otherwise lead to exceptions.

Even if test data is created to ensure a statistically fair representation of real-world data, and is carefully chosen to include edge cases, there are still inherent issues about how defensively guaranteed an application can be when only tested on a relatively small volume of test data. Some exceptional circumstances only arise in a full-scale environment. Performance implications are an obvious example: if you only conduct performance tests on the basis of a couple of thousand rows of data, then don't be surprised when the application fails to perform against millions of rows in the live environment (you'll be amazed at the number of times I've seen applications signed off on the basis of a performance test against a drastically reduced size of data). Nor should you simply assume that the performance of your application will scale predictably with the number of rows of data involved. With careful query design and well-tuned indexes, some applications may scale very well against large data sets. The performance of other applications, however, may degrade exponentially (such as when working with Cartesian products created from **CROSS JOIN**s between tables). Defensive testing should be conducted with consideration not only of the volumes of data against which the application is expected to use now, but also by factoring in an allowance for expected future growth.

Another consideration when testing is the effect of multiple users on a system. There are many functions that, when tested in isolation, are proven to pass in a consistent, repeatable manner. However, these same tests can fail in the presence of concurrency—that is, multiple requests for the same resource on the database. To demonstrate this, the following code listing creates a simple table containing two integer columns, **x** and **y**, and a **rowversion** column, **v**.

```
CREATE TABLE XandY (
  x int,
  y int,
  v rowversion);

INSERT INTO XandY (x, y) VALUES (0, 0);
GO
```

The following code executes a loop that reads the current values from the **XandY** table, increments the value of **x** by 1, and then writes the new values back to the table. The loop is set to run for 100,000 iterations, and the loop counter only increments if the **rowversion** column, **v**, has not changed since the values were last read.

```
SET NOCOUNT ON;
DECLARE
  @x int,
  @y int,
  @v rowversion,
```

```
  @success int = 0;
WHILE @success < 100000
BEGIN
  -- Retrieve existing values
  SELECT
    @x = x,
    @y = y,
    @v = v
  FROM XandY

  -- Increase x by 1
  SET @x = @x + 1;

  SET TRANSACTION ISOLATION LEVEL READ COMMITTED;
  BEGIN TRANSACTION
    IF EXISTS(SELECT 1 FROM XandY WHERE v = @v)
      BEGIN
        UPDATE XandY
          SET
            x = @x,
            y = @y
          WHERE v = @v;
        SET @success = @success + 1;
      END
  COMMIT;
END
GO
```

Executing this code leads, as you'd expect, to the value of the **x** column being increased to 100,000:

x	y	v
100000	0	0x00000000001EA0B9

Now let's try running the same query in a concurrent situation. First, let's reset the table to its initial values, as follows:

```
UPDATE XandY SET x = 0;
GO
```

Now open up a new query in SQL Server Management Studio and enter the following code:

```
SET NOCOUNT ON;

DECLARE
  @x int,
  @y int,
  @v rowversion,
  @success int = 0;
```

```
WHILE @success < 100000
BEGIN
  -- Retrieve existing values
  SELECT
    @x = x,
    @y = y,
    @v = v
  FROM XandY

  -- Increase y by 1
  SET @y = @y + 1;

  SET TRANSACTION ISOLATION LEVEL READ COMMITTED;
  BEGIN TRANSACTION
    IF EXISTS(SELECT 1 FROM XandY WHERE v = @v)
      BEGIN
        UPDATE XandY
          SET
            x = @x,
            y = @y
          WHERE v = @v;
        SET @success = @success + 1;
      END
  COMMIT;
END
GO
```

This second query is identical to the first in every respect except that, instead of incrementing the value of **@x** by 1, it increments the value of **@y** by 1. It then writes both values back to the table, as before. So, if we were to run both queries, we would expect the values of both **x** and **y** to be 100,000, right? To find out, execute the first query, which updates the value of **x**. While it is still executing, execute the second script, which updates the value of **y**. After a few minutes, once both queries have finished, checking the contents of the **XandY** table on my laptop gives the following results:

x	y	v
99899	99019	0x000000000021ACCC

Despite apparently containing some degree of allowance for concurrency (by testing that the value of **@rowversion** has remained unchanged before committing the update), when tested in an environment with other concurrent queries, these queries have failed to behave as designed. An explanation of why this has occurred, and methods to deal with such situations, will be explained in Chapter 9.

Code Review

Whereas testing is generally an automated process, code review is a human-led activity that involves peer groups manually reviewing the code behind an application. The two activities of automated testing and human code review are complementary and can detect different areas for code improvement. While automated test suites can very easily check whether routines are producing the correct output in a given number of test scenarios, it is very difficult for them to conclusively state that a routine is coded in the most robust or efficient way, that correct logic is being applied, or the coding standards followed best practice. In these cases, code review is a more effective approach.

Consider the following code listing, which demonstrates a T-SQL function used to test whether a given e-mail address is valid:

```
DECLARE @email_address varchar(255);
IF (
     CHARINDEX(' ',LTRIM(RTRIM(@email_address))) = 0
  AND   LEFT(LTRIM(@email_address),1) <> '@'
  AND   RIGHT(RTRIM(@email_address),1) <> '.'
  AND   CHARINDEX('.',@email_address ,CHARINDEX('@',@email_address)) -
CHARINDEX('@',@email_address ) > 1
  AND   LEN(LTRIM(RTRIM(@email_address ))) -
LEN(REPLACE(LTRIM(RTRIM(@email_address)),'@','')) = 1
  AND   CHARINDEX('.',REVERSE(LTRIM(RTRIM(@email_address)))) >= 3
  AND   (CHARINDEX('.@',@email_address ) = 0 AND CHARINDEX('..',@email_address ) = 0)
)
    PRINT  'The supplied email address is valid';
ELSE
    PRINT 'The supplied email address is not valid';
```

This code might well pass functional tests to suggest that, based on a set of test email addresses provided, the function correctly identifies whether the format of a supplied e-mail address is valid. However, during a code review, an experienced developer could look at this code and point out that it could be much better implemented as a user-defined function using the regular expression methods provided by the .NET Base Class Library, such as shown here:

```
SELECT dbo.RegExMatch('\b[A-Z0-9._%+-]+@[A-Z0-9.-]+\.[A-Z]{2,4}\b', @email_address);
```

Note that this example assumes that you have registered a function called **RegExMatch** that implements the **Match** method of the .NET **System.Text.RegularExpressions.Regex** class. While both methods achieve the same end result, rewriting the code in this way creates a routine that is more efficient and maintainable, and also promotes reusability, since the suggested **RegExMatch** function could be used to match regular expression patterns in other situations, such as checking whether a phone number is valid.

Challenging and open code review has a significant effect on improving the quality of software code, but it can be a costly exercise, and the effort required to conduct a thorough code review across an entire application is not warranted in all situations. One of the advantages of well-encapsulated code is that those modules that are most likely to benefit from the exercise can be isolated and reviewed separately from the rest of the application.

Validate All Input

Defensive programming suggests that you should never trust any external input—don't make assumptions about its type (e.g. alphabetic or numeric), its length, its content, or even its existence! These rules apply not just to user input sent from an application UI or web page, but also to any external file or web resource on which the application relies.

A good defensive stance is to assume that all input is invalid and may lead to exceptional circumstances unless proved otherwise. There are a number of techniques that can be used to ensure that input is valid and safe to use:

- Data can be "massaged." For example, bad characters can be replaced or escaped. However, there are some difficulties associated in identifying exactly what data needs to be treated, and knowing the best way in which to handle it. Silently modifying input affects data integrity and is generally not recommended unless it cannot be avoided.

- Data can be checked against a "blacklist" of potentially dangerous input and rejected if it is found to contain known bad items. For example, input should not be allowed to contain SQL keywords such as **DELETE** or **DROP**, or contain nonalphanumeric characters.

- Input can be accepted only if it consists solely of content specified by a "whitelist" of allowed content. From a UI point of view, you can consider this as equivalent to allowing users to only select values from a predefined drop-down list, rather than a free-text box. This is arguably the most secure method, but is also the most rigid, and is too restrictive to be used in many practical applications.

All of these approaches are susceptible to flaws. For example, consider that you were using the **ISNUMERIC()** function to test whether user input only contained numeric values. You might expect the result of the following to reject the input:

```
DECLARE @Input varchar(32) = '10E2';
SELECT ISNUMERIC(@Input);
```

Most exceptions occur as the result of unforeseen but essentially benign circumstances. However, when dealing with user input, you should always be aware of the possibility of deliberate, malicious attacks that are targeted to exploit any weaknesses exposed in a system that has not been thoroughly defended. Perhaps the most widely known defensive programming techniques concern the prevention of **SQL injection** attacks. That is, when a user deliberately tries to insert and execute malicious code as part of user input supplied to an application.

SQL injection attacks typically take advantage of poorly implemented functions that construct and execute dynamic SQL-based on unvalidated user input. Consider the following example:

```
CREATE PROCEDURE Hackable
    @Input varchar(32)
AS BEGIN
  DECLARE @sql varchar(256) = 'SELECT status FROM sys.sysusers WHERE name = ''' + @Input +
'''';
  EXECUTE(@sql);
END
```

The intended purpose of this code is fairly straightforward—it returns the status of the user supplied in the parameter **@Input**. So, it could be used in the following way to find out the status of the user John:

```
EXEC Hackable 'John';
GO
```

But what if, instead of entering the value **John**, the user entered the input **'public'' or 1=1 --'**, as follows?

```
EXEC Hackable @Input='public'' or 1=1 --';
GO
```

This would lead to the SQL statement generated as follows:

```
SELECT status FROM sys.sysusers WHERE name = 'public' OR 1 = 1;
```

The condition **OR 1 = 1** appended to the end of the query will always evaluate to true, so the effect will be to make the query list every row in the **sys.sysusers** table.

Despite this being a simple and well-known weakness, it is still alarmingly common. Defending against such glaring security holes can easily be achieved, and various techniques for doing so are discussed in Chapter 6.

Future-proof Your Code

In order to prevent the risk of bugs appearing, it makes sense to ensure that any defensive code adheres to the latest standards. There are no ways to guarantee that code will remain resilient, but one habit that you should definitely adopt is to ensure that you rewrite any old code that relies on deprecated features, and do not use any deprecated features in new development in order to reduce the chances of exceptions occurring in the future.

Deprecated features refer to features that, while still currently in use, have been superseded by alternative replacements. While they may still be available for use (to ensure backward compatibility), you should not develop applications using features that are known to be deprecated. Consider the following code listing:

```
CREATE TABLE ExpertSqlServerDevelopment.dbo.Deprecated (
  EmployeeID int DEFAULT 0,
  Forename varchar(32) DEFAULT '',
  Surname varchar(32) DEFAULT '',
  Photo image NULL
);

CREATE INDEX ixDeprecated ON Deprecated(EmployeeID);
DROP INDEX Deprecated.ixDeprecated;

INSERT INTO ExpertSqlServerDevelopment.dbo.Deprecated (
  EmployeeID, Forename, Surname, Photo) VALUES
(1, 'Bob', 'Smith', DEFAULT),
(2, 'Benny', 'Jackson', DEFAULT)

SET ROWCOUNT 1;
SELECT 'Name' = ForeName + ' ' + Surname
FROM ExpertSqlServerDevelopment.dbo.Deprecated
ORDER BY ExpertSqlServerDevelopment.dbo.Deprecated.EmployeeID
SET ROWCOUNT 0;
```

This query works as expected in SQL Server 2008, but makes use of a number of deprecated features, which should be avoided. Fortunately, spotting usage of deprecated features is easy—the `sys.dm_os_performance_counters` dynamic management view (DMV) maintains a count of every time a deprecated feature is used, and can be interrogated as follows:

```
SELECT
    object_name,
    instance_name,
    cntr_value
FROM sys.dm_os_performance_counters
WHERE
    object_name = 'SQLServer:Deprecated Features'
    AND cntr_value > 0;
```

A related, although perhaps more serious, threat to defensive applications is code that relies on *undocumented* features. Many such features exist in SQL Server—the following code listing demonstrates the undocumented **sp_MSForEachTable** stored procedure, for example, which can be used to execute a supplied query against every table in a database.

```
EXEC sp_MSforeachtable "EXEC sp_spaceused '?'";
```

While it is certain that deprecated features will be removed at some point in the future, that time scale is generally known, and there is usually a documented upgrade path to ensure that any functionality previously provided by features that are deprecated will be replaced by an alternative method. Undocumented features, in contrast, may break at any time without warning, and there may be no clear upgrade path. I strongly recommend that you avoid such risky (and almost always unnecessary) practices.

Limit Your Exposure

If defensive programming is designed to ensure that an application can cope with the occurrence of exceptional events, one basic defensive technique is to limit the number of such events that can occur. It follows logically that exceptions can only occur in features that are running, so don't install more features than necessary—by reducing the application surface area, you limit your exposure to potential attacks. Don't grant **EXTERNAL_ACCESS** to an assembly when **SAFE** will do. Don't enable features such as database mail unless they add value or are strictly required by your application.

All users should be authenticated, and only authorized to access those resources that are required, for the period of time for which they are required. Unused accounts should be removed immediately, and unnecessary permissions revoked. Doing so reduces the chance of the system being compromised by an attack, and is discussed in more detail in Chapter 5.

If the security of a system is compromised, employing encryption may help to limit any damage caused. Different encryption methods are discussed in Chapter 6.

Exercise Good Coding Etiquette

Good coding etiquette, by which I refer to practices such as clearly commented code, consistent layout, and well-named variables, should be considered a vital part of *any* software development methodology, and not specifically related to defensive programming. I have chosen to include it here, partly because I consider it so vital that it can never be restated too often, but also because the nature of defensive programming emphasizes these areas more than other approaches, for the following reasons:

As stated previously, the aim of defensive programming is to minimize the risk of errors occurring as a result of future unforeseen events. Those future events may be construed to include future maintenance and enhancements made to the code. By creating clear, well-documented code now, you enhance its future understandability, reducing the chances that bugs will be accidentally introduced when it is next addressed.

Furthermore, since defensive programming aims to create robust, resilient applications, these applications may continue running for a very long duration without any need for manual intervention. When they are next reviewed some years later, the development team responsible may be very different, or the original developers may no longer remember why a certain approach was taken. It is vitally important that this information be documented and clearly visible in the code itself, so that errors or new assumptions are not introduced that could damage the stability of the application.

Code that is well *laid* out often goes hand in hand with code that is well *thought* out. By undertaking such simple steps as indenting code blocks, for example, you can easily identify steps that lie within a loop, and those that are outside the loop, preventing careless mistakes. Most IDEs and code editors provide layout features that will automatically apply a consistent format for tabs, whitespace, capitalization and so on, and these settings can normally be customized to match whatever coding standards are in place in a given organization.

Well-laid-out, meaningfully commented code will make it easier for thorough code review. If the code needs to be revised, it will be much easier to quickly establish the best method to do so.

Finally, if a bug is discovered in a section of code, it is much easier to track down within a well-coded function, and hence resolved with the minimum amount of disruption.

For these reasons, I believe exercising good code etiquette to be a key part of defensive programming. In the following sections, I'll make a few observations on some specific aspects of coding etiquette.

Comments

Everybody knows that comments are an important part of any code, and yet few of us comment our code as well as we should (one reason commonly put forward is that developers prefer to *write* code rather than *writing about* code). Almost every school of thought on best coding practice states that you should make liberal use of comments in code, and defensive programming is no different. Well-written comments make it easier to tell what a function is aiming to achieve and why it has been written a certain way, which by implication means that it is easier to spot any bugs or assumptions made that could break that code.

Good comments should give additional information to whoever is reading the code—not simply point out the obvious or restate information that could easily be found in Books Online. The following comment, for example, is not helpful:

```
-- Set x to 5
SET @x = 5;
```

In general, comments should explain why a certain approach has been taken and what the developer is aiming to achieve. Using comments to describe *expected* behavior makes it much easier to identify cases of *unexpected* behavior. In general it is not necessary to simply comment what a built-in function does, but there may be exceptions to this rule. For example, at a single glance, can you say what you expect the result of the following to be?

```
DECLARE @y int = 2010, @c int, @n int, @k int, @i int, @j int, @l int, @m int,
@d int;
SET @c = (@y / 100);
SET @n = @y - 19 * (@y / 19);
SET @k = (@c - 17) / 25;
SET @i = @c - @c / 4 - ( @c - @k) / 3 + 19 * @n + 15;
SET @i = @i - 30 * (@i / 30);
SET @i = @i - (@i / 28) * (1 - (@i / 28) * (29 / (@i + 1)) * ((21 - @n) / 11));
SET @j = @y + @y / 4 + @i + 2 - @c + @c / 4;
SET @j = @j - 7 * (@j / 7);
SET @l = @i - @j;
SET @m = 3 + (@l + 40) / 44;
SET @d = @l + 28 - 31 * ( @m / 4 );
SELECT CAST(CONVERT(char(4),@y) + '-' + RIGHT('0' + CONVERT(varchar(2),@m),2) + '-'
+ RIGHT('0' + CONVERT(varchar(2),@d),2) AS DateTime);
```

I actually encountered the previous function in a production application, where it was being used to determine whether employees were entitled to a bonus because they had worked on a public holiday. In case you haven't figured it out, the result gives you the date of Easter Sunday in any given year (specified using the variable @y). The code actually fulfils its purpose, but without any comments it took me a long time to find out what that purpose was!

In many cases, you can obviate the need for writing explicit comments by using **self-documenting** code—choosing well-named variables, column aliases, and table aliases. Consider the following code:

```
SELECT DATEPART(Y, '20090617');
```

In most programming languages, the character **Y** used in a date format function denotes the year associated with a date. It may therefore seem reasonable to expect the preceding code to return the full year of the supplied date, **2009**, or perhaps just the final digit of the year, **9**. To explain the actual result of **168**, the code could have easily been made self-documenting by replacing the **Y** with **DAYOFYEAR** (for which it is an abbreviation):

```
SELECT DATEPART(DAYOFYEAR, '20090617');
```

Indentations and Statement Blocks

Code indentations and liberal use of whitespace can help to identify logical blocks of code, loops, and batches, creating code that is understandable, easily maintained, and less likely to have bugs introduced in the future. However, these practices clearly have no direct effect on the execution of the code itself. It is therefore vitally important that the visual layout of code reinforces its logical behavior, as poorly presented code may actually be misleading. Consider the following example:

```
IF 1 = 1
  PRINT 'True';
ELSE
```

```
  PRINT 'False';
  PRINT 'Then Print this';
```

In this case, the indentation on the final line of code makes it appear to be part of the **ELSE** clause, but this is not the case, and the result **Then Print this** will be printed irrespective of the result of the test.

To avoid such misleading situations, I always recommend the liberal use of statement blocks marked by **BEGIN** and **END**, even if a block contains only one statement, as follows:

```
IF 1 = 1
  BEGIN
    PRINT 'True';
  END
ELSE
  BEGIN
    PRINT 'False';
  END
PRINT 'Then Print This';
```

Another misleading practice that can easily be avoided is the failure to use parentheses to explicitly demonstrate the order in which the components of a query are resolved. Consider the following code listing:

```
DECLARE @Table TABLE (x int, y int);
INSERT INTO @Table VALUES (1,1), (1,2), (2,1), (2,2), (3,1), (3,2);

SELECT *
FROM @Table
WHERE
  x = 1 AND
  y = 1 OR y = 2;
GO
```

In this case, as before, the code indentation actually detracts from the true logic of the code, which is to select all rows where **x=1 AND y=1**, or where **y=2**.

If All Else Fails. . .

A fundamental feature of defensive programming is to make assertions to ensure that exceptional circumstances do not occur. It can be argued that, if the ideal of defensive programming were ever truly realized, it would not be necessary to implement exception-handling code, since any potential scenarios that could lead to exceptions would have been identified and handled before they were allowed to occur. Unfortunately, it is not practically possible to explicitly test all exceptional scenarios and, in the real-world, exception and error handling remain very important parts of any software application. For a detailed discussion of exception and error handling in SQL Server, please refer to Chapter 4.

Creating a Healthy Development Environment

The best applications are not created by the individual brilliance of one or two coders, but by the coordinated, effective collaboration of a development team. Successful defensive development is most likely to occur when coding is a shared, open activity.

The benefits of collaborative coding are that you can draw on a shared pool of technical knowledge and resources to ensure that coding is thorough and accurate. Different people will be able to critically examine code from a number of different points of view, which helps to identify any assumptions that might have gone unnoticed by a single developer.

If developers work in isolation, they may introduce dependencies that present a risk to the future maintainability of the code. If only one developer knows the intricacies of a particularly complex section of code and then that developer leaves or is unavailable, you may encounter difficulties maintaining that code in the future. In fact, individual competiveness between developers can lead to developers *deliberately* adding complexity to an application. Coders may seek to ensure that only they understand how a particular section of complex code works, either as a way of flaunting their technical knowledge, for reasons of personal pride, or as a way of creating a dependence on them—making themselves indispensable and ensuring their future job security. All of these create an unhealthy development environment and are likely to negatively affect the quality of any code produced.

Managers responsible for development teams should try to foster an environment of continued professional development, in which shared learning and best practice are key. Software development is a constantly changing area—what is considered best practice now may well be obsolete within a few years. In order to make sure that applications remain cutting edge, individual training of developers and knowledge-sharing between peers should be promoted and encouraged.

The success (or otherwise) of attempts to implement defensive development may also be influenced by wider corporate decisions, including reward systems. For example, a company may implement a reward scheme that pays individual bonuses for any developer that discovers and solves bugs in live applications. Although presumably designed to improve software quality, the effect may actually be completely the opposite—after all, what is the incentive to code defensively (preventing errors before they occur) when it removes the opportunity for a developer to allow bugs through and personally receive the reward for fixing them later? Such policies are likely to encourage competitive, individualistic behavior where developers only look after themselves, instead of taking actions based on the best interests of the project.

Another factor affecting the success of defensive development concerns the way in which budget and project deadlines are managed. Penalties are normally incurred for delivering software projects after deadline. It is an unfortunate fact that, when deadlines are brought forward or budgets slashed, it is defensive practices (such as rigorous testing) that management regard as nonessential, and are among the first to be dropped from the scope of the project.

Managers that demand quick-fix solutions based on unrealistic short-term time scales are likely to encourage piecemeal coding practices that create holes. These are unlikely to use defensive programming and will not stand up to rigorous testing. Software development must be crafted with patience and care, yet management demands often necessitate that shortcuts must be taken, and rarely can truly defensive programming projects be seen to completion. For these reasons, true defensive programming might be seen as an ideal, rather than an achievable objective.

Summary

Defensive programming practices aim to improve the resilience and reliability of software applications when faced with unforeseen circumstances. Given the typical expected lifespan of database applications and the potential severity of the consequences should a bug occur, it makes sense to adopt a defensive approach to ensure that the applications remain robust over a long period of time, and that the need for ongoing maintenance is kept to a minimum.

In this chapter, I have demonstrated a few simplistic examples of what I consider to be best practice in SQL programming, and illustrated how they relate to the defensive programming methodology. Throughout the rest of the book, I will continue to show in more detail how to adopt a defensive stance across a range of development scenarios.

CHAPTER 3

■ ■ ■

Testing Database Routines

What defines a great developer? Is it the ability to code complex routines quickly and accurately? The ability to implement business requirements correctly, within budget, and on schedule? Or perhaps it can be defined by how quickly the developer can track down and fix bugs in the application—or the inverse, the lack of bugs in the developer's code?

All of these are certainly attributes of a great developer, but in most cases they don't manifest themselves merely due to raw skill. The hallmark of a truly great developer, and what allows these qualities to shine through, is a thorough understanding of the importance of testing.

By creating unit tests early on in the development process, developers can continuously validate interfaces and test for exceptions and regressions. Carefully designed functional tests ensure compliance with business requirements. And performance testing—the kind of testing that always seems to get the most attention—can be used to find out whether the application can actually handle the anticipated amount of traffic.

Unfortunately, like various other practices that are better established in the application development community, testing hasn't yet caught on much with database professionals. Although some development shops performance test stored procedures and other database code, it is rare to see database developers writing data-specific unit tests.

There is no good reason that database developers should not write just as many—or more—tests than their application developer counterparts. It makes little sense to test a data-dependent application without validating the data pieces that drive the application components!

This chapter provides a brief introduction to the world of software testing and how testing techniques can be applied in database development scenarios. Software testing is a huge field, complete with much of its own lingo, so my intention is to concentrate only on those areas that I believe to be most important for database developers.

Approaches to Testing

There are a number of testing methodologies within the world of quality assurance, but in general, all types of software tests can be split into two groups:

- **Black box** testing refers to tests that make assumptions only about inputs and outputs of the module being tested, and as such do not validate intermediate conditions. The internal workings of the module are not exposed to (or required by) the tester—hence they are contained within a "black box."

- **White box** testing, on the other hand, includes any test in which the internal implementation of the routine or function being tested is known and validated by the tester. White box testing is also called "open-box" testing, as the tester is allowed to look inside the module to see how it operates, rather than just examining its inputs and outputs.

Within each of these broad divisions are a number of specific tests designed to target different particular areas of the application in question. Examples of black box tests include unit tests, security tests, and basic performance tests such as stress tests and endurance tests. As the testing phase progresses, target areas are identified that require further testing, and the types of tests performed tend to shift from black box to white box to focus on specific internal elements.

From a database development perspective, examples of white box tests include functional tests that validate the internal working of a module, tests that perform data validation, and cases when performance tuning requires thorough knowledge of data access methods. For instance, retrieving and analyzing query plans during a performance test is an example of white box testing against a stored procedure.

Unit and Functional Testing

Developing software with a specific concentration on the data tier can have a benefit when it comes to testing: there aren't too many types of tests that you need to be familiar with. Arguably, the two most important types of test are those that verify that the application behaves as it is meant to, and returns the correct results. This is the purpose of unit tests and functional tests.

Unit tests are black box tests that verify the contracts exposed by interfaces. For instance, a unit test of a stored procedure should validate that, given a certain set of inputs, the stored procedure returns the correct set of output results, as defined by the interface of the stored procedure being tested. The term *correct* as used here is important to define carefully. It means "correct" only insofar as what is defined as the contract for the stored procedure; the actual data returned is not important. So, as long as the results represent valid values in the correct format and of the correct datatypes given the interface's contract, a unit test should pass. Phrased another way, unit tests test the ability of interfaces to communicate with the outside world exactly as their contracts say they will.

Functional tests, as their name implies, verify the functionality of whatever is being tested. In testing nomenclature, the term *functional test* has a much vaguer meaning than *unit test*. It can mean any kind of test, at any level of an application, that tests whether that piece of the application works properly—in other words, that it performs the appropriate sequence of operations to deliver the correct final result as expected. For a simple stored procedure that selects data from the database, this asks the question of whether the stored procedure returning the *correct data*? Again, I will carefully define the term *correct*. This time, *correct* means both the kind of validation done for a unit test (data must be in the correct format), as well as a deeper validation of the accuracy of the actual values returned. The logic required for this kind of validation means that a functional test is a white box test in the database world, compared to the black box of unit testing.

Let's take a look at an example to make these ideas a bit clearer. Consider the following stored procedure, which might be used for a banking application:

```
CREATE PROCEDURE GetAggregateTransactionHistory
    @CustomerId int
AS
BEGIN
    SET NOCOUNT ON;
```

```
SELECT
    SUM
    (
        CASE TransactionType
            WHEN 'Deposit' THEN Amount
            ELSE 0
        END
    ) AS TotalDeposits,
    SUM
    (
        CASE TransactionType
            WHEN 'Withdrawal' THEN Amount
            ELSE 0
        END
    ) AS TotalWithdrawals
    FROM TransactionHistory
    WHERE
        CustomerId = @CustomerId;
END;
```

This stored procedure's implied contract states that, given the input of a customer ID into the @CustomerId parameter, a result set of two columns and zero or one rows will be output (the contract does not imply anything about invalid customer IDs or customers who have not made any transactions). The column names in the output result set will be TotalDeposits and TotalWithdrawals, and the datatypes of the columns will be the same as the datatype of the Amount column in the TransactionHistory table (we'll assume it's decimal).

What if the Customer Doesn't Exist?

The output of the GetAggregateTransactionHistory stored procedure will be the same whether you pass in a valid customer ID for a customer that happens to have had no transactions, or an invalid customer ID. Either way, the procedure will return no rows. Depending on the requirements of a particular situation, it might make sense to make the interface richer by changing the rules a bit, only returning no rows if an invalid customer ID is passed in. That way, the caller will be able to identify invalid data and give the user an appropriate error message rather than implying that the nonexistent customer made no transactions.

A unit test against this stored procedure should do nothing more than validate the interface. A customer ID should be passed in, and the unit test should interrogate the output result set (or lack thereof) to ensure that there are two columns of the correct name and datatype and zero or one rows. No verification of data is necessary; it would be out of scope, for instance, to find out whether the aggregate information was accurate or not—that would be the job of a functional test.

The reason that we draw such a distinction between unit tests and functional tests is that when testing pure interface compliance, we want to put ourselves in the position of someone programming against the interface from a higher layer. Is the interface working as documented, providing the appropriate level of encapsulation and returning data in the correct format?

Each interface in the system will need one or more of these tests (see the "How Many Tests Are Needed?" section later in the chapter), so they need to be kept focused and lightweight. Programming full white box tests against every interface may not be feasible, and it might be simpler to test the validity of data at a higher layer, such as via the user interface itself. In the case of the `GetAggregateTransactionHistory` stored procedure, writing a functional test would essentially entail rewriting the entire stored procedure again—hardly a good use of developer time.

Unit Testing Frameworks

Unit testing is made easier through the use of unit testing frameworks, which provide structured programming interfaces designed to assist with quickly testing software. These frameworks generally make use of **debug assertions**, which allow the developer to specify those conditions that make a test true or false.

A debug assertion is a special kind of macro that is turned on only when a piece of software is compiled in debug mode. It accepts an expression as input and throws an exception if the expression is false; otherwise, it returns **true** (or **void**, in some languages). For instance, the following assertion would always throw an exception:

```
Assert(1 == 0);
```

Assertions allow a developer to self-document assumptions made by the code of a routine. If a routine expects that a variable is in a certain state at a certain time, an assertion can be used in order to help make sure that assumption is enforced as the code matures. If, at any time in the future, a change in the code invalidates that assumption, an exception will be thrown should the developer making the change hit the assertion during testing or debugging.

In unit testing, assertions serve much the same purpose. They allow the tester to control what conditions make the unit test return **true** or **false**. If any assertion throws an exception in a unit test, the entire test is considered to have failed.

Unit testing frameworks exist for virtually every language and platform, including T-SQL (for example, the TSQLUnit project available from **http://sourceforge.net/projects/tsqlunit**). Personally, I find unit testing in T-SQL to be cumbersome compared to other languages, and prefer to write my tests in a .NET language using the .NET unit testing framework, NUnit (**http://www.nunit.org**).

Providing an in-depth guide to coding against unit testing frameworks is outside the scope of this book, but given that unit testing stored procedures is still somewhat of a mystery to many developers, I will provide a basic set of rules to follow. When writing stored procedure unit tests, the following basic steps can be followed:

1. First, determine what assumptions should be made about the stored procedure's interface. What are the result sets that will be returned? What are the datatypes of the columns, and how many columns will there be? Does the contract make any guarantees about a certain number of rows?

2. Next, write code necessary to execute the stored procedure to be tested. If you're using NUnit, I find that the easiest way of exposing the relevant output is to use ADO.NET to fill a DataSet with the result of the stored procedure, where it can subsequently be interrogated. Be careful at this stage; you want to test the stored procedure, not your data access framework. You might be tempted to call the stored procedure using the same method as in the application itself. However, this would be a mistake, as you would end up testing both the stored procedure and that method. Given that you only

need to fill a DataSet, recoding the data access in the unit test should not be a major burden, and will keep you from testing parts of the code that you don't intend to.

3. Finally, use one assertion for each assumption you're making about the stored procedure; that means one assertion per column name, one per column datatype, one for the row count if necessary, and so on. Err on the side of using too many assertions—it's better to have to remove an assumption later because it turns out to be incorrect than to not have had an assumption there to begin with and have your unit test pass when the interface is actually not working correctly.

The following code listing gives an example of what an NUnit test of the GetAggregateTransactionHistory stored procedure might look like:

```
[TestMethod]
public void TestAggregateTransactionHistory()
{
    // Set up a command object
    SqlCommand comm = new SqlCommand();

    // Set up the connection
    comm.Connection = new SqlConnection(
        @"server=serverName; trusted_connection=true;");

    // Define the procedure call
    comm.CommandText = "GetAggregateTransactionHistory";
    comm.CommandType = CommandType.StoredProcedure;

    comm.Parameters.AddWithValue("@CustomerId", 123);

    // Create a DataSet for the results
    DataSet ds = new DataSet();

    // Define a DataAdapter to fill a DataSet
    SqlDataAdapter adapter = new SqlDataAdapter();
    adapter.SelectCommand = comm;

    try
    {
        // Fill the dataset
        adapter.Fill(ds);
    }
    catch
    {
        Assert.Fail("Exception occurred!");
    }

    // Now we have the results -- validate them...

    // There must be exactly one returned result set
    Assert.IsTrue(
```

```
        ds.Tables.Count == 1,
        "Result set count != 1");

    DataTable dt = ds.Tables[0];

    // There must be exactly two columns returned
    Assert.IsTrue(
        dt.Columns.Count == 2,
        "Column count != 2");

    // There must be columns called TotalDeposits and TotalWithdrawals
    Assert.IsTrue(
        dt.Columns.IndexOf("TotalDeposits") > -1,
        "Column TotalDeposits does not exist");

    Assert.IsTrue(
        dt.Columns.IndexOf("TotalWithdrawals") > -1,
        "Column TotalWithdrawals does not exist");

    // Both columns must be decimal
    Assert.IsTrue(
        dt.Columns["TotalDeposits"].DataType == typeof(decimal),
        "TotalDeposits data type is incorrect");

    Assert.IsTrue(
        dt.Columns["TotalWithdrawals"].DataType == typeof(decimal),
        "TotalWithdrawals data type is incorrect");

    // There must be zero or one rows returned
    Assert.IsTrue(
        dt.Rows.Count <= 1,
        "Too many rows returned");
}
```

Although it might be disturbing to note that the unit test is over twice as long as the stored procedure it is testing, keep in mind that most of this code can be easily turned into a template for quick reuse. As noted before, you might be tempted to refactor common unit test code into a data access library, but be careful lest you end up testing your test framework instead of the actual routine you're attempting to test. Many hours can be wasted debugging working code trying to figure out why the unit test is failing, when it's actually the fault of some code the unit test is relying on to do its job.

Unit tests allow for quick, automated verification of interfaces. In essence, they help you as a developer to guarantee that in making changes to a system you didn't break anything obvious. In that way, they are invaluable. Developing against a system with a well-established set of unit tests is a joy, as each developer no longer needs to worry about breaking some other component due to an interface change. The unit tests will complain if anything needs to be fixed.

Regression Testing

As you build up a set of unit tests for a particular application, the tests will eventually come to serve as a **regression suite**, which will help to guard against **regression bugs**—bugs that occur when a developer breaks functionality that used to work. Any change to an interface—intentional or not—will cause unit tests to fail (assuming that the tests have been written correctly). For the intentional changes, the solution is to rewrite the unit test accordingly. But it is these unintentional changes for which we create unit tests, and which regression testing targets.

Experience has shown that fixing bugs in an application often introduces other bugs. It can be difficult to substantiate how often this happens in real development scenarios, but it has been suggested that figures as high as 50 percent can occur in some cases. By building a regression suite, the cost of fixing these "side effect" bugs is greatly reduced. They can be discovered and mended during the development phase, instead of being reported by end users once the application has already been deployed.

Regression testing is also the key to some newer software development methodologies, such as agile development and extreme programming (XP). As these methodologies increase in popularity, and their adoption filters through to the database world, it can be expected that database developers will begin to adopt some of these techniques more readily.

Guidelines for Implementing Database Testing Processes and Procedures

Of all the possible elements that make up a testing strategy, there is really only one key to success: consistency. Tests must be repeatable, and must be run the same way every time, with only well-known (i.e., understood and documented) variables changed. Inconsistency, or a lack of knowledge concerning those variables that might have changed between tests, can mean that any problems identified during testing will be difficult to trace.

Development teams should strive to build a suite of tests that are run at least once for every release of the application, if not more often. These tests should be automated and easy to run. Preferably, the suite of tests should be modular, so that if a developer is working on one part of the application, the subset of tests that apply to only that section can be easily exercised in order to validate any changes.

Continuous Testing

Once you've built a set of automated tests, you're one step away from a fully automatic testing environment. Such an environment should retrieve the latest code from the source control repository, run appropriate build scripts to compile a working version of the application, and run through the entire test suite. Many software development shops use this technique to run their tests several times a day, throwing alerts almost instantly if problem code is checked in. This kind of rigorous automated testing is called continuous integration, and it's a great way to take some of the testing burden out of the hands of developers while still making sure that all of the tests get run as often as (or even more often than) necessary. A great free tool to help set up continuous integration in .NET environments is CruiseControl.NET, available at `http://sourceforge.net/projects/ccnet`.

Testers must also pay particular attention to any data used to conduct the tests. It can often be beneficial to generate test data sets that include every possible case the application is likely to see. Such a set of data can guarantee consistency between test runs, as it can be restored to its original state. It can also guarantee that rare edge cases are tested that might otherwise not be seen.

It's also recommended that a copy of actual production data (if available) be used for testing near the end of any given test period, rather than relying on artificially generated test data. Oftentimes, generated sets can lack the realism needed to bring to light obscure issues that only real users can manage to bring out of an application.

Why Is Testing Important?

It can be argued that the only purpose of software is to be used by end users, and therefore the only purpose of testing is to make sure that those end users don't encounter issues. Thus, there are two important goals that testing hopes to achieve:

- Testing finds problems that need to be fixed.

- Testing ensures that no problems need to be fixed.

Eventually, all software must be tested. If not fully tested by developers or a quality assurance team, an application will be tested by the end users trying to use the software. Unfortunately, this is a great way to lose credibility; users are generally not pleased with buggy software.

Testing by development and quality assurance teams validates the software. Each kind of testing that is performed validates a specific piece of the puzzle, and if a complete test suite is used (and the tests are passed), the team can be fairly certain that the software has a minimal number of bugs, performance defects, and other issues. Since the database is an increasingly important component in most applications, testing the database makes sense; if the database has problems, they will propagate to the rest of the application.

What Kind of Testing Is Important?

From the perspective of a database developer, only a few types of tests are really necessary in the majority of cases. Databases should be tested for the following issues:

- **Interface consistency** should be validated in order to guarantee that applications have a stable structure for data access.

- **Data availability** and **authorization tests** are similar to interface consistency tests, but more focused on *who* can get data from the database than *how* the data should be retrieved.

- **Authentication tests** verify whether valid users can log in, and whether invalid users are refused access. These kinds of tests are only important if the database is being used for authenticating users.

- **Performance tests** are important for verifying that the user experience will be positive, and that users will not have to wait longer than necessary for data. Performance testing may involve **load tests**, which monitor the performance of the database under a given load; **saturation tests**, which attempt to overwhelm the system by constantly adding load and/or removing resources from it until it breaks; and, **endurance tests**, which place a continuous demand on the database over a sustained period of time.

- **Regression testing** covers every other type of test, but generally focuses on uncovering issues that were previously fixed. A regression test is a test that validates that a fix still works.

How Many Tests Are Needed?

Although most development teams lack a sufficient number of tests to test the application thoroughly, in some cases the opposite is true. Too many tests can be just as much of a problem as not enough tests; writing tests can be time-consuming, and tests must be maintained along with the rest of the software whenever functionality changes. It's important to balance the need for thorough testing with the realities of time and monetary constraints.

A good starting point for database testing is to create one unit test per interface parameter "class," or group of inputs. For example, consider the following stored procedure interface:

```
CREATE PROCEDURE SearchProducts
    SearchText varchar(100) = NULL,
    PriceLessThan decimal = NULL,
    ProductCategory int = NULL
```

This stored procedure returns data about products based on three parameters, each of which is optional, based on the following (documented) rules:

- A user can search for text in the product's description.

- A user can search for products where the price is less than a given input price.

- A user can combine a text search or price search with an additional filter on a certain product category, so that only results from that category are returned.

- A user cannot search on both text and price simultaneously. This condition should return an error.

- Any other combination of inputs should result in an error.

In order to validate the stored procedure's interface, one unit test is necessary for each of these conditions. The unit tests that pass in valid input arguments should verify that the stored procedure returns a valid output result set per its implied contract. The unit tests for the invalid combinations of arguments should verify that an error occurs when these combinations are used. Known errors are part of an interface's implied contract (see Chapter 4 for more information on this topic).

In addition to these unit tests, an additional regression test should be produced for each known issue that has been fixed within the stored procedure, in order to ensure that the procedure's functionality does not degenerate over time.

Although this seems like a massive number of tests, keep in mind that these tests can—and should—share the same base code. The individual tests will have to do nothing more than pass the correct parameters to a parameterized base test.

Will Management Buy In?

It's an unfortunate fact that many management teams believe that testing is either an unnecessary waste of time or not something that should be a well-integrated part of the software development process at all. Many software shops, especially smaller ones, have no dedicated quality assurance staff, and such compressed development schedules that little testing gets done, making full functionality testing nearly impossible.

Several companies I've done work for have been in this situation, and it never results in the time or money savings that management thinks it will. On the contrary, time and money is actually *wasted* by lack of testing.

A test process that is well integrated into development finds most bugs up front, when they are created, rather than later on. A developer who is currently working on enhancing a given module has an in-depth understanding of the code at that moment. As soon as he or she moves on to another module, that knowledge will start to wane as focus moves on to other parts of the application. If defects are discovered and reported while the developer is still in the trenches, the developer will not need to relearn the code in order to fix the problem, thereby saving a lot of time. These time savings translate directly into increased productivity, as developers end up spending more time working on new features, and less on fixing defects.

If management teams refuse to listen to reason and allocate additional development time for proper testing, try doing it anyway. Methodologies such as test-driven development (TDD), in which you write the tests first, and then create routines that pass the tests, can greatly enhance overall developer productivity. Adopting a testing strategy—with or without management approval—can mean better, faster output, which in the end will help to ensure success.

Performance Monitoring Tools

Verification using unit, functional, and regression tests is extremely important for thoroughly testing that an application behaves correctly, but it is performance testing that really gets the attention of most developers. Performance testing is imperative for ensuring a positive user experience. Users don't want to wait any longer than absolutely necessary for data.

Performance testing relies on collecting, reviewing, and analyzing performance data for different aspects of the system. Before going into details about how to analyze the performance of a system, it is therefore necessary to look at some of the tools that can be used to capture such data. SQL Server 2008 provides a number of in-built tools that allow DBAs and developers to store or view real-time information about activity taking place on the server, including the following:

- SQL Server Profiler

- Server-side traces

- System Monitor console

- Dynamic Management Views (DMVs)

- Extended Events

- Data Collector

There are also a number of third-party monitoring tools available that can measure, aggregate, and present performance data in different ways. In this section, I'll discuss some of the different methods of monitoring performance, and the type of situations in which they can be used.

■ **Note** Access to performance monitoring tools in many organizations is restricted to database or system administrators. However, most of the tools described in this section allow for performance logs to be saved, so if you have insufficient permissions to be able to monitor performance, another sufficiently privileged user may be able to profile the performance of a server and export the results for you.

Real-Time Client-Side Monitoring

The Profiler tool that ships with SQL Server 2008 is extremely useful and very easy to use. Simply load the Profiler application and point it to the instance of SQL Server that you want to monitor, and it will report real-time information based on around 200 different events. However, for most performance monitoring work, there are only a few key events that you'll need to worry about.

When initially baselining an application, I generally start by looking at only the `SQL:BatchCompleted` and `RPC:Completed` events. Each of these events fires on completion of queries; the only difference between them is that `RPC:Completed` fires on completion of a remote procedure call (RPC), whereas `SQL:BatchCompleted` fires on completion of a SQL batch—different access methods, same end result.

The most valuable columns available for both of these events are `CPU`, `Reads`, `Writes`, and `Duration`:

- The `CPU` column reports the amount of CPU time, in milliseconds, spent parsing, compiling, and executing the query. Due to the fact that this column includes compilation time, it is common to see the reported amount of time drop on consecutive queries, thanks to plan caching.

- The `Reads` column reports the number of **logical** reads performed by the query. A logical I/O occurs any time SQL Server's query engine requests data, whether from the physical disk or from the buffer cache. If you see high numbers in this column, it may not necessarily indicate a performance problem, because the majority of data may be read from cache. However, even reading data from memory does cost the server in terms of CPU time, so it is a good idea to try to keep any kind of reads to a minimum.

- The `Writes` column reports the number of **physical** writes performed by the query. This means that only writes that were actually persisted to disk during the course of the query will be reported.

- The `Duration` column reports the total time elapsed for the call, in milliseconds. The duration of a query is a direct reflection on the user experience, so this is generally the one to start with. If the application is performing slowly, you can find the worst offending queries using this column.

By reviewing the high-level information contained in these columns, you can identify potential candidates for further investigation. First, think about limits that need to be set for any given query in the system. What is the maximum amount of time that a query can be allowed to run? What should the average amount of run time be? By aggregating the `Duration` column, you can determine whether these times have been exceeded.

Once you've isolated possible problem areas (see the "Granular Analysis" section later in the chapter), you can delve deeper in with more in-depth sets of events. For instance, the `Scan:Started` event can be used to identify possible queries that are making inefficient use of indexes and therefore may be causing I/O problems. The `SP:Recompile` event, on the other hand, indicates queries that are getting recompiled by the query optimizer, and may therefore be consuming larger-than-necessary amounts of CPU time.

Server-Side Traces

While SQL Server Profiler is a convenient and useful tool, it does have some limitations. The main problem is that, in order to facilitate real-time data collection and display, SQL Server needs to continually stream the data back to the tool—and there is an overhead associated with doing so. As such, the very act of attempting to monitor performance may have a negative effect on the performance of the system being measured, leading to biased results (the "observer effect").

In an extremely high-transaction performance test, you should strive to minimize the impact of monitoring on results of the test by using **server-side traces** instead of the Profiler tool. A server-side trace runs in the background on the SQL server, saving its results to a local file on the server instead of streaming them to the client.

It is possible to define the parameters for a server-side trace manually in T-SQL, but to do so is a laborious and unnecessary process. A better approach is to create a server-side trace based on a trace definition exported from the SQL Server Profiler tool, as explained in the following steps:

1. First, use SQL Server Profiler to define the events, columns, and filters required for the trace.

2. Select File > Export > Script Trace Definition > For SQL Server 2005 – 2008, and select a file name to save the script.

3. Once the script has been saved, open it in SQL Server Management Studio. This file contains the T-SQL code required to start a trace based on the parameters supplied.

4. Edit the following line of the script, by specifying a valid output path and file name for the trace results where indicated:

```
exec @rc = sp_trace_create @TraceID output, 0, N'InsertFileNameHere',
@maxfilesize, NULL
```

■ **Note** The specified file name should not include an extension of any kind. One will automatically be added by the trace.

---

5. You might also wish to modify the value of the @maxfilesize parameter, which by default is set to 5MB. Increasing the maximum file size will help to minimize the number of rollover files created during the trace. I generally set this to 200MB as a starting point.

6. Once you have finished editing, execute the script. The trace will begin collecting data in the background, and the generated script will return a trace identifier, TraceID, which you should make note of as it will be required to control the trace later.

After following these steps, the trace will be running, and the output of all specified events will be written to the log file, so now is the time to execute your test suite. When you are done tracing, you must stop and close the trace by using the **sp_trace_setstatus** stored procedure, supplying the **TraceID** trace identifier returned when the trace was started. This is demonstrated in the following code listing (in this case the trace identifier is listed as **99**):

```
EXEC sp_trace_setstatus @traceid=99, @status=0;
EXEC sp_trace_setstatus @traceid=99, @status=2;
GO
```

Once the trace is stopped and closed, the **sys.fn_trace_gettable** function can be used to read the data from the trace file. This function takes two arguments: a full path to the trace file name—including the **.trc** extension automatically added by SQL Server—and the maximum number of rollover files to read. The following T-SQL would be used to read the trace file from the path **C:\Traces\myTrace.trc**. The number of rollover files is set high enough that all of the data will be read back, even if the trace rolled over to new files several times:

```
SELECT *
FROM sys.fn_trace_gettable('C:\Traces\myTrace.trc', 999);
GO
```

Once selected in this way, the trace data can be used just like any other data in SQL Server. It can be inserted into a table, queried, or aggregated in any number of ways in order to evaluate which queries are potentially causing problems.

System Monitoring

For a bigger-picture view of the overall performance of a server, system performance counters are an invaluable resource. These counters can be read using the System Monitor console (aka Performance Monitor, or **perfmon.exe**, depending on the operating system under which your SQL Server instance is running), although many load-testing tools have integrated system counter collection and reporting mechanisms. Similar to SQL Server trace events, there are hundreds of counters from which to choose—but only a handful generally need to be monitored when doing an initial performance evaluation of a SQL Server installation.

The following counters are a good starting point for determining what kinds of performance issues to look for:

- **Processor:% Processor Time** reports the total processor time with respect to the available capacity of the server. If this counter is above 70 percent during peak load periods, it may be worthwhile to begin investigating which routines are making heavy use of CPU time.

- **PhysicalDisk:Avg. Disk Queue Length** indicates whether processes have to wait to use disk resources. As a disk is fulfilling requests (i.e., reading and writing data), requests that cannot be immediately filled are queued. Too many simultaneous requests results in wait times, which can mean query performance problems. It's a good idea to make sure that queue lengths stay below 1 (meaning, effectively, that there is no queue) whenever possible.

- **PhysicalDisk:Disk Read Bytes/sec** and **PhysicalDisk:Disk Write Bytes/sec** report the number of bytes read from and written to the disk, respectively. These figures are not especially interesting on their own, but coupled with Avg. Disk Queue Length can help to explain problems. Slow **SELECT** queries coupled with high physical reads and low queue lengths can indicate that the buffer cache is not being effectively utilized. Slow DML queries coupled with high physical writes and high queue lengths are a typical indication of disk contention, and a good sign that you might want to evaluate how to reduce index fragmentation in order to decrease insert and update times.

- **SQLServer:Locks:Average Wait Time (ms)** reports the average amount of time that queries are waiting on locks. Decreasing lock contention can be quite a challenge, but it can be solved in some cases by using either dirty reads (the **READ UNCOMMITTED** isolation level) or row versioning (the **SNAPSHOT** isolation level). See Chapter 9 for a discussion of these and other options.

- **SQLServer:Buffer Manager:Page life expectancy** is the average amount of time, in seconds, that pages remain in buffer cache memory after they are read off of the disk. This counter, coupled with Disk Read Bytes/sec, can help to indicate where disk bottlenecks are occurring—or, it might simply indicate that your server needs more RAM. Either way, values below 300 (i.e., 5 minutes) may indicate that you have a problem in this area.

- **SQLServer:Plan Cache:Cache Hit Ratio** and **SQLServer:Plan Cache:Cached Pages** are counters that deal with the query plan cache. The Cache Hit Ratio counter is the ratio of cache hits to lookups—in other words, what percentage of issued queries are already in the cache. During a performance run, this number should generally start out low (assuming you've rebooted the SQL server before starting in order to put it into a consistent state) and go up during the course of the run. Toward the end, you should see this number fairly near to 100, indicating that almost all queries are cached. The Cached Pages counter indicates how many 8KB pages of memory are being used for the procedure cache. A low Cache Hit Ratio combined with a high Cached Pages value means that you need to consider fixing the dynamic SQL being used by the system. See Chapter 8 for information on techniques for solving dynamic SQL problems.

■ **Tip** SQL Server Profiler has the ability to import saved performance counter logs in order to correlate them with traces. This can be useful for helping to pinpoint the cause of especially large spikes in areas such as CPU time and disk utilization.

Dynamic Management Views (DMVs)

The dynamic management views exposed by SQL Server 2008 contain a variety of server- and database-level information that can be used to assist in performance measurement. The `sys.dm_os_performance_counters` DMV contains over 1,000 rows of high-level performance counters maintained by the server, including common measures concerning I/O, locks, buffers, and log usage. Querying this DMV presents an alternative method of collecting much of the same data that is exposed via the performance monitoring console.

In addition to `sys.dm_os_performance_counters`, there are many other DMVs that contain information useful for performance monitoring purposes. The following list shows a few of the DMVs that I find to be most helpful for performance measurement and tuning:

- **sys.dm_exec_query_stats**: Provides performance statistics for queries whose plans are currently in the cache. When joined to **sys.dm_exec_sql_text** and **sys.dm_exec_query_plan**, it is possible to analyze the performance of individual troublesome batches in relation to their SQL and query plan.

- **sys.dm_db_index_usage_stats**, **sys.dm_db_index_physical_stats**, and **sys.dm_db_index_operational_stats**: These three views display information that is useful for index tuning, including reporting the number of seeks and scans performed against each index, the degree of index fragmentation, and possible index contention and blocking issues.

- **sys.dm_os_wait_stats**: This records information regarding requests that were forced to wait—in other words, any request that could not immediately be satisfied by the server because of unavailability of I/O or CPU resource.

- **sys.dm_os_waiting_tasks** and **sys.dm_tran_locks**: Information on waiting tasks and locks, contained in these two tables respectively, can be combined to help identify blocking situations.

■ **Caution** DMVs generally report any timings measured in microseconds (1/1,000,000 of a second), whereas most other performance measuring tools report timings in milliseconds (1/1,000 of a second).

Analyzing the detailed information contained in these DMVs allows you to understand the root cause of many performance issues, and identify the appropriate course of action to rectify them. For example, suppose that **sys.dm_os_wait_stats** on a poorly performing server showed a significant number of I/O waits (e.g., high values for **PAGEIOLATCH**, **LOGMGR**, or **IO_COMPLETION**), but hardly any waits for CPU resource. Clearly, the performance issues in this case will not be resolved by upgrading the server CPU—there is an I/O bottleneck and the appropriate solution involves finding a way to shorten I/O response times, or reducing the I/O requirements of the query.

■ **Note** DMVs store preaggregated, cumulative statistics since the server was last restarted. In order to reset wait statistics before running a performance test, you can use **DBCC SQLPERF** with the **CLEAR** option—for example, **DBCC SQLPERF ('sys.dm_os_wait_stats', CLEAR);**.

Extended Events

Extended events make up a flexible, multipurpose eventing system introduced in SQL Server 2008 that can be used in a wide variety of scenarios, including performance testing. There are over 250 predefined events, some of which mirror traditional trace event triggers, including **RPC:Completed**, **sp_completed**, and **lock_timeout**, although there are also many others. The payload (i.e., the columns of data) collected when an event fires can then be delivered to a variety of synchronous and asynchronous targets. This flexible framework for handling extended events allows you to build a customized performance monitoring system, which collects very specific measurements and delivers them in a variety of formats to meet your monitoring requirements.

One of the shortcomings of the monitoring tools introduced previously is that they tend to collect performance indicators that are aggregated at predefined levels. The wait statistics exposed in **sys.dm_os_wait_stats**, for example, might indicate that an I/O bottleneck is occurring at a server-wide level. However, based on this information alone, we cannot tell which queries or sessions were affected, or for how long they were made to wait. By leveraging extended events such as **sqlos.wait_info** and **sqlos.wait_info_external**, it is possible to gather specific wait statistics at the session or statement levels. Performance statistics gathered using extended events can be further refined by the addition of predicates, which specify, for example, to only gather information on specific types of wait, those that occur a certain number of times, or those that exceed a minimum wait time.

The following code listing illustrates how to create a new extended event session that records all statements that encounter waits (triggered by the **sqlos.wait_info** event), and saves them to a log file on the server:

```
CREATE EVENT SESSION WaitMonitor ON SERVER
ADD EVENT sqlos.wait_info(
  ACTION(
    sqlserver.sql_text,
    sqlserver.plan_handle)
    WHERE total_duration > 0
)
ADD TARGET package0.asynchronous_file_target(
  SET filename = N'c:\wait.xel',
      metadatafile = N'c:\wait.xem');
GO
```

When you are ready to start the log, run the following:

```
ALTER EVENT SESSION WaitMonitor ON SERVER
STATE = start;
GO
```

Once the session is started, the **sql_text** and **plan_handle** actions will be collected every time the **sqlos_wait_info** event fires and delivered to the specified target. Notice that in this example I specify an asynchronous file target, which means that SQL Server execution will continue while event data is sent to and saved in the target file. If events are fired more quickly than they can be handled, they will be stored in a buffer while waiting to be saved to the target. The size of this buffer is determined by the **MAX_MEMORY** event session variable, which by default is set to 4MB. If events continue to be sent after the buffer is full, then there may be the risk of events being lost from the session and not saved to the target. Synchronous targets do not have this risk, but they may exhibit worse performance because any tasks that fire events are made to wait for the last event to be fully consumed by the target before being allowed to continue.

To stop the **WaitMonitor** session, execute the following code listing:

```
ALTER EVENT SESSION WaitMonitor ON SERVER
STATE = stop;
GO
```

The payload captured by the extended event session is saved to the file target in XML format. To analyze the data contained within this file, it can be loaded back into SQL Server using the `sys.fn_xe_file_target_read_file` method, and then queried using XQuery syntax, as shown in the following query:

```
SELECT
  xe_data.value('(/event/action[@name=''sql_text'']/value)[1]','varchar(max)')
    AS sql_text,
  xe_data.value('(/event/@timestamp)[1]','datetime')
    AS timestamp,
  xe_data.value('(/event/data[@name=''wait_type'']/text)[1]','varchar(50)')
    AS wait_type,
  xe_data.value('(/event/data[@name=''total_duration'']/value)[1]','int')
    AS total_duration,
  xe_data.value('(/event/data[@name=''signal_duration'']/value)[1]','int')
    AS signal_duration
FROM (
  SELECT
  CAST(event_data AS xml) AS xe_data
  FROM
  sys.fn_xe_file_target_read_file('c:\wait_*.xel', 'c:\wait_*.xem', null, null)
  ) x;
GO
```

■ **Note** Extended Events can be used in many more situations than the simple example shown here. For more information, and examples of other possible uses, see Books Online: `http://msdn.microsoft.com/en-us/library/bb630354.aspx`.

Data Collector

The Data Collector allows you to automatically collect performance data from DMVs and certain system performance counters and upload them to a central management data warehouse (MDW) at regular intervals according to a specified schedule. There are three predefined system collection sets that come with SQL Server and, of these, the most useful from a performance tuning point of view is the *server activity collection set*. The server activity collection set combines information from DMVs including `sys.dm_os_wait_stats`, `sys.dm_exec_sessions`, `sys.dm_exec_requests`, and `sys.dm_os_waiting_tasks`, with various SQL Server and OS performance counters to provide an overview of CPU, disk I/O, memory, and network resource usage on the server. By default, each measure is sampled every 60 seconds, and the collected data is uploaded to the MDW every 15 minutes, where it is kept for 14 days before being purged. If required, you can adjust the definition, frequency, and duration of counters collected by creating your own custom data collection set based on the performance counter's collector type.

Whereas the other profiling tools previously discussed are primarily useful for short-term diagnosis and testing focused on a particular target area, the data collector is a useful tool for monitoring long-term trends in performance. Historical performance data can be collected and persisted over a long period of time, and comparisons can be drawn of the relative performance of a server over several months, or even years. The data collector also provides preformatted, drill-down tabular reports and graphs that make it relatively easy to identify major problem areas at a glance. Figure 3-1 illustrates a default report generated from the server activity collection set.

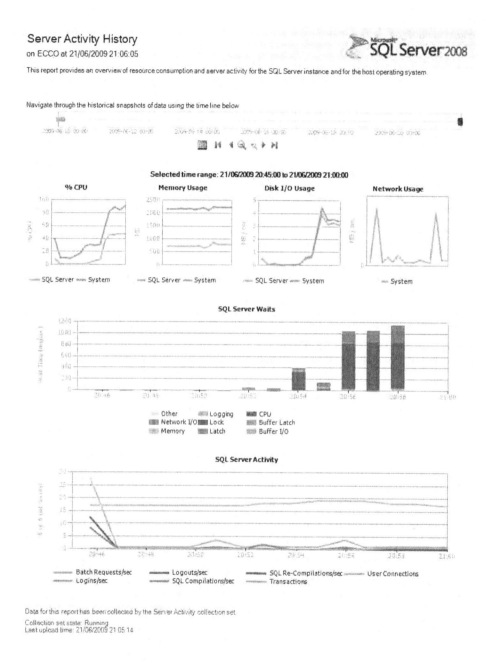

Figure 3-1. The server activity collection report

Analyzing Performance Data

In the previous section, I discussed how to capture SQL Server performance data using a number of different tools and techniques. In this section, let's now consider what data you should monitor, and how to analyze it in order to build up a profile of how a database is performing.

Note that while the techniques discussed here may help you identify bottlenecks and other performance issues, they do not deal with how to fix those problems. Throughout the remainder of the book, various examples will discuss how to look at code from a performance-minded point of view and how to solve some problems, but keep in mind that this book is not intended as a thorough guide to query performance tuning. I highly recommend that readers searching for a more detailed guide invest in a book dedicated to the subject, such as *SQL Server 2008 Query Performance Tuning Distilled*, by Grant Fritchey and Sajal Dam (Apress, 2009).

Capturing Baseline Metrics

Just as with unit and functional testing, having an overall process in place is extremely important when it comes to performance evaluation. Performance tests should be repeatable and should be done in an environment that can be rolled back to duplicate the same conditions for multiple test runs.

Keep in mind that any component in the application may be contributing in some way to performance, so starting from the same point each time is imperative. I recommend using a test database that can be restored to its original state each time, as well as rebooting all servers involved in the test just before beginning a run, in order to make sure that the test starts with the same initial conditions each time. Another option that might be easier than backing up and restoring a test database is using SQL Server 2008's database snapshot feature, or, if you use a virtualized environment, restoring a saved state from a virtual machine image. Try each technique in your own environment to determine which fits best into your testing system.

In addition to making sure the servers are in the same state, you should also collect exactly the same performance counters, query trace data and other metrics in precisely the same way for each test run. Consistency is the key to validating not only that changes are effective, but also measuring *how* effective they are.

During a testing process, the first test that is run should be used as a **baseline**. The metrics captured during the baseline test will be used to compare results for later runs. As problems are solved, or if test conditions change (e.g., if you need to collect more performance counters in a certain area), you should establish a new baseline from which to go forward. Keep in mind that fixing issues in one area of an application might have an impact on performance of another area. For instance, a given query may be I/O-bound, whereas another may be CPU-bound. By fixing the I/O problems for the first query, you may introduce greater CPU utilization, which in turn will cause the other query to degrade in performance if they are run simultaneously.

Baselining metrics in a database environment is generally a fairly straightforward process. Server-side traces should be used to capture performance data, including query duration and resources used. This data can then be aggregated to determine minimum, maximum, and average statistics for queries. In order to determine which resources are starved, performance counters can be used to track server utilization. As changes are made to fix performance issues, the baseline data can be analyzed against other test data in order to establish performance trends.

Big-Picture Analysis

Once you have set up performance counters and traces, you are ready to begin actual performance testing. But this raises the question, "Where to begin?" Especially in a large legacy application, running an end-to-end performance test can be a daunting task.

A first step is to determine what kinds of unit and functional tests exist, and evaluate whether they can be used as starting points for performance tests. Some load testing tools, such as Microsoft's Visual Studio Team System 2008, have the ability to directly load-test prebuilt unit tests. However, most commercial load tools are designed to exercise applications or web code directly. Try to collect as many tests as possible to cover the most-used parts of the application. Absolute coverage is nice, but is unrealistic in many cases.

The next step is to implement a load testing suite using the prebuilt unit and functional tests. Depending on which load tool you are using, this can take some time. The key is to make sure that the load tool passes random or semirandom inputs into any function that goes back to the database, in order to simulate real traffic and make sure that caching does not play too big a part in skewing numbers. Nonrandom inputs can mask disk I/O issues caused by buffer cache recycling.

Set goals for the test to determine what level of load you need to test at. If you are testing on a system that mirrors the application's production environment, try to test at a load equal to that which the application encounters during peak periods. If the test servers are less powerful than the production systems, scale back appropriately. Note that it can be difficult to test against servers that aren't scaled the same as production systems. For instance, if the production database system has eight processors and is attached to a dedicated storage area network (SAN), and the test database system has four processors and internal drives, there may be an I/O mismatch. In this situation it might be advisable to modify SQL Server's processor affinity on the test system such that less processor power is available, which will make the available processor to available disk I/O ratio fall into line with the actual environment in which code needs to run.

In addition to making sure that the test and production systems are scaled similarly, make sure that the SQL Server configurations in both systems are similar. For example, ensure that the maximum degree of parallelism is set similarly so that processors will be used the same way in queries on both the test and production systems. Likewise, you should monitor the RAM options to ensure that they are configured to equivalent percentages on both systems—so if your production system has 16GB of RAM but SQL Server's maximum server memory setting is 12GB, you'll want to set your test system to use 75 percent of the available RAM as well.

Once user goals are set, load tests should generally be configured to step up load slowly, rather than immediately hit the server with the peak number of users. Gradually increasing load during the test creates a more accurate simulation of a typical production environment, in which a server may get rebooted during a maintenance period, then slowly accept user requests and warm up its caches before encountering a larger number of requests during more active times of the day. Note that step testing may not be an accurate figure if you're testing a situation such as a cluster failover, in which a server may be subjected to a full load immediately upon starting up.

The goal of a big-picture test is to see how the system scales overall. Try to look at general trends in the performance counters to determine whether the system can handle load spikes, or generally sustained load over long periods of time (again, depending on actual application usage patterns, if possible). Data captured during this period can be used later for more granular analysis of specific components.

Granular Analysis

If the results of a big-picture test show that certain areas need work, a more granular investigation into specific routines will generally be necessary. Using aggregated trace data collected from a full system test, it's important to evaluate both individual queries and *groups* of queries that are long-running or resource intensive.

While it is often tempting to look only at the worst offending queries—for instance, those with the maximum duration—this may not tell the complete story. For instance, you may notice that certain stored procedures are taking longer than others to run during peak load. These procedures may be responsible for longer user interface wait times, but the individual stored procedure with the longest duration may not necessarily indicate the single longest user interface wait time. This is due to the fact that many applications call more than one stored procedure every time the interface needs to be updated with additional data. In these cases it is important to group procedures that are called together and aggregate their total resource utilization.

When aggregating the combined performance impact of a group of queries, it is important to consider the way in which those procedures are called:

- If stored procedures are called sequentially, their individual durations should be added together in order to determine the total user wait time for that group, and the maximum resource utilization of any procedure in the group should be recorded.

- If, on the other hand, all of the procedures are called simultaneously in parallel (for instance, on different connections), resource utilization should be totaled in order to determine the group's overall impact on the system, and the duration of the longest-running individual query should be noted.

For example, assume that in a given system, whenever a user logs in, three different stored procedures are called to get data for the first screen. Table 3-1 shows the average data collected for these stored procedures.

Table 3-1. Stored Procedures Called After Login, with Averaged Data

Stored Procedure	Duration (ms)	CPU	Reads	Writes
LogSessionStart	422	10	140	1
GetSessionData	224	210	3384	0
GetUserInfo	305	166	6408	0

If the system calls these stored procedures sequentially, the total duration that should be recorded for this group is 951 ms (422 + 224 + 305). Since each is called individually, total system impact at any given time will only be as much as the maximum values for each of the given columns. So we record 210 for CPU, 6408 for Reads, and 1 for Writes.

On the other hand, if these stored procedures are called simultaneously, the impact will be much different. Total duration will only be as much as the longest running of the three—422ms (assuming, of course, that the system has enough resources available to handle all three requests at the same time). However, CPU time during the run should be recorded as 386, Reads as 9932, and Writes as 1.

By grouping stored procedures in this way, the total impact for a given feature can be assessed. It may be the case that individually long-running stored procedures are not the primary performance culprits, and are actually being overshadowed by groups of seemingly less resource-intensive stored procedures. This can also be an issue with cursors that are doing a large number of very small fetch operations. Each individual fetch may fall under the radar, but taken as a whole, it may become clear that the cursor is using a lot of resources.

Another benefit of this kind of grouping is that further aggregation is possible. For instance, given these figures, it is possible to determine how much impact a certain number of users logging in simultaneously would have on the system. That information can be useful when trying to reach specific scalability goals.

Fixing Problems: Is It Sufficient to Focus on the Obvious?

When evaluating the performance of a system and trying to determine where to look to fix problems, it can be tempting to focus on the obvious worst offenders first. However, some care should be taken to make effective use of your time; in many cases what appear to be the obvious problems are actually side effects of other, more subtle issues.

Looking at duration alone is often the easiest mistake to make when analyzing performance issues. Duration tells a major part of the story, but it does not necessarily indicate a performance problem with that stored procedure. It may indicate that the query had to wait for some other query—or queries—to complete, or that the query was competing with other queries for resources. When performance tuning, it is best to be suspicious of long-running queries with very low reported resource utilization. These are often not the real culprits at all.

By using the granular analysis technique and aggregating, it is often possible to find the real offenders more easily. For instance, in one fairly high-transaction system, a procedure was getting called from time to time that was writing 10MB of data to the disk. This procedure reported a high duration, which was interpreted as a possible performance problem. Unfortunately there wasn't much to tune in that stored procedure, but further aggregate analysis revealed another stored procedure in the system that was getting called over 1,000 times a minute and writing as much as 50KB to the disk each time it was called. Each call to the second stored procedure reported a small enough duration that it did not appear to be causing performance problems, yet as it turned out it was causing issues in other areas. By tuning it and reducing the amount of data it was writing on each call, the average duration of the first stored procedure was reduced dramatically.

Summary

Software testing is a complex field, but it is necessary that developers understand enough of it to make the development process more effective. By implementing testing processes during development, more robust software can be delivered with less expense.

Database developers, like application developers, must learn to exploit unit tests in order to increase software project success rates. Database routines will definitely benefit from unit testing, although performance testing is extremely important as well—and much more popular with management teams.

During performance testing, make sure to carefully analyze the data. By recombining the numbers in various ways based on application usage patterns, it is often possible to discover performance issues that are not obvious from the raw numbers. SQL Server 2008 ships with a variety of methods for collecting and presenting performance counters, and I'll be using these to analyze the relative performance of different approaches taken in later chapters throughout the book.

Testing is one of the important factors that helps differentiate good developers from truly great ones. If you're not already testing your software during the development process, the methodologies presented here can help you to implement a set of procedures that will get you closer to the next level.

■ ■ ■

CHAPTER 4

Errors and Exceptions

As software developers, we often daydream of a Utopian world of bug-free software—developed under the shade of a palm tree on a remote island while sipping a long, fruity cocktail. But, alas, back in the real world, hordes of developers sit in cubicle farms gulping acrid coffee, fighting bugs that are not always their fault or under their control in any way.

Exceptions can occur in even the most stringently tested software, simply because it is not possible to check every error condition in advance. For instance, do you know what will happen if a janitor, while cleaning the data-center floor, accidentally slops some mop water into the fan enclosure of the database server? It might crash, or it might not; it might just cause some component to fail somewhere deep in the app, sending up a strange error message.

Although most exceptions won't be so far out of the realm of testability, it is certainly important to understand how to deal with them when and if they occur. It is also imperative that SQL Server developers understand how to work with errors—both those thrown by the server itself and custom errors built specifically for when problems occur during the runtime of an application.

Exceptions vs. Errors

The terms **exception** and **error**, while often used interchangeably by developers, actually refer to slightly different conditions:

> An **error** can occur if something goes wrong during the course of a program, even though it can be purely informational in nature. For instance, the message displayed by a program informing a user that a question mark is an invalid character for a file name is considered to be an error message. However, this may or may not mean that the program itself is in an invalid state.

> An **exception**, on the other hand, is an error that is the result of an **exceptional circumstance**. For example, if a network library is being used to send packets, and the network connection is suddenly dropped due to someone unplugging a cable, the library might throw an exception. An exception tells the calling code that something went wrong and the routine aborted unexpectedly. If the caller does not **handle** the exception (i.e., capture it), its execution will also abort. This process will keep repeating until the exception is handled, or until it reaches the highest level of the call stack, at which point the entire program will fail.

Another way to think about exceptions and errors is to think of errors as occurrences that are *expected* by the program. The error message that is displayed when a file name contains an invalid character is informational in nature because the developer of the program predicted that such an event would occur and created a code path specifically to deal with it. A dropped network connection, on the other hand, could be caused by any number of circumstances and therefore is much more difficult to handle specifically. Instead, the solution is to raise an exception and fail. The exception can then be handled by a routine higher in the call stack, which can decide what course of action to take in order to solve the problem.

What Defines an "Exceptional" Circumstance?

There is some debate in the software community as to whether exceptions should really be used only for exceptional circumstances, or whether it is acceptable to use them as part of the regular operation of a program. For example, some programmers choose to define a large number of different custom exceptions, and then deliberately raise these exceptions as a method of controlling the flow of an application. There are some possible benefits to this approach: raising an exception is a useful way to break out of a routine immediately, however deeply nested in the call stack that routine might be; and, an exception can be used to describe conditions that would be difficult to express in the normal return value of a method. However convenient it may seem to use exceptions in such scenarios, they clearly represent an abuse of the intended purpose of exception-handling code (which, remember, is to deal with *exceptional* circumstances). Furthermore, making lots of exception calls can make your code hard to read, and debugging can be made more difficult, since debuggers generally implement special behavior whenever exceptions are encountered. As a result, exception-laden code is more difficult to maintain when compared to code that relies on more standard control flow structures.

In my opinion, you should raise exceptions only to describe truly exceptional circumstances. Furthermore, due to the fact that exceptions can cause abort conditions, they should be used sparingly. However, there is certainly an upside to using exceptions over errors, which is that it's more difficult for the caller to ignore an exception, since it will cause code to abort if not properly handled. If you're designing an interface that needs to ensure that the caller definitely sees a certain condition when and if it occurs, it might make sense to use an exception rather than an error.

As in almost all cases, the decision is very dependent on the context of your application, so do not feel obliged to stick to my opinion!

How Exceptions Work in SQL Server

The first step in understanding how to handle errors and exceptions in SQL Server is to take a look at how the server itself deals with error conditions. Unlike many other programming languages, SQL Server has an exception model that involves different behaviors for different types of exceptions. This can cause unexpected behavior when error conditions do occur, so careful programming is essential when dealing with T-SQL exceptions.

To begin with, think about connecting to a SQL Server and issuing some T-SQL. First, you must establish a **connection** to the server by issuing login credentials. The connection also determines what database will be used as the default for scope resolution (i.e., finding objects—more on this in a bit). Once connected, you can issue a **batch** of T-SQL. A batch consists of one or more T-SQL **statements**, which will be compiled together to form an execution plan.

The behavior of the exceptions thrown by SQL Server mostly follows this same pattern: depending on the type of exception, a statement, a batch, or an entire connection may be aborted. Let's take a look at some practical examples to see this in action.

Statement-Level Exceptions

A statement-level exception aborts only the current statement that is running within a batch of T-SQL, allowing any subsequent statements within the batch to run. To see this behavior, you can use SQL Server Management Studio to execute a batch that includes an exception, followed by a **PRINT** statement. For instance:

```
SELECT POWER(2, 32);
PRINT 'This will print!';
GO
```

Running this batch results in the following output:

```
Msg 232, Level 16, State 3, Line 1

Arithmetic overflow error for type int, value = 4294967296.000000.

This will print!
```

When this batch was run, the attempt to calculate **POWER(2, 32)** caused an integer overflow, which threw the exception. However, only the **SELECT** statement was aborted. The rest of the batch continued to run, which, in this case, meant that the **PRINT** statement still printed its message.

Batch-Level Exceptions

Unlike a statement-level exception, a batch-level exception does not allow the rest of the batch to continue running. The statement that throws the exception will be aborted, and any remaining statements in the batch will not be run. An example of a batch-aborting exception is an invalid conversion, such as the following:

```
SELECT CONVERT(int, 'abc');
PRINT 'This will NOT print!';
GO
```

The output of this batch is as follows:

```
Msg 245, Level 16, State 1, Line 1
Conversion failed when converting the varchar value 'abc' to data type int.
```

In this case, the conversion exception occurred in the **SELECT** statement, which aborted the batch at that point. The **PRINT** statement was not allowed to run, although if the batch had contained any valid statements *before* the exception, these would have been executed successfully.

Batch-level exceptions might be easily confused with connection-level exceptions (which drop the connection to the server), but after a batch-level exception, the connection is still free to send other batches. For instance:

```
SELECT CONVERT(int, 'abc');
GO
PRINT 'This will print!';
GO
```

In this case there are two batches sent to SQL Server, separated by the batch separator, **GO**. The first batch throws a conversion exception, but the second batch is still run. This results in the following output:

```
Msg 245, Level 16, State 1, Line 2

Conversion failed when converting the varchar value 'abc' to data type int.

This will print!
```

Batch-level exceptions do not affect only the scope in which the exception occurs. The exception will **bubble up** to the next level of execution, aborting every call in the stack. This can be illustrated by creating the following stored procedure:

```
CREATE PROCEDURE ConversionException
AS
BEGIN
    SELECT CONVERT(int, 'abc');
END;
GO
```

Running this stored procedure followed by a **PRINT** shows that, even when an exception occurs in an inner scope (within the stored procedure), the outer batch is still aborted:

```
EXEC ConversionException;
PRINT 'This will NOT print!';
GO
```

The result of this batch is the same as if no stored procedure was used:

```
Msg 245, Level 16, State 1, Line 4
Conversion failed when converting the varchar value 'abc' to data type int.
```

Parsing and Scope-Resolution Exceptions

Exceptions that occur during parsing or during the scope-resolution phase of compilation appear at first to behave just like batch-level exceptions. However, they actually have a slightly different behavior. If the exception occurs in the same scope as the rest of the batch, these exceptions will behave just like a batch-level exception. If, on the other hand, an exception occurs in a lower level of scope, these exceptions will behave just like statement-level exceptions—at least, as far as the outer batch is concerned.

As an example, consider the following batch, which includes a malformed **SELECT** statement (this is a parse exception):

```
SELECTxzy FROM SomeTable;
PRINT 'This will NOT print!';
GO
```

In this case, the **PRINT** statement is not run, because the whole batch is discarded during the parse phase. The output is the following exception message:

```
Msg 156, Level 15, State 1, Line 1
Incorrect syntax near the keyword 'FROM'.
```

To see the difference in behavior, the **SELECT** statement can be executed as dynamic SQL using the **EXEC** function. This causes the **SELECT** statement to execute in a different scope, changing the exception behavior from batch-like to statement-like. Try running the following T-SQL to observe the change:

```
EXEC('SELECTxzy FROM SomeTable');
PRINT 'This will print!';
GO
```

The **PRINT** statement is now executed, even though the exception occurred:

```
Msg 156, Level 15, State 1, Line 1

Incorrect syntax near the keyword 'FROM'.

This will print!
```

This type of exception behavior also occurs during **scope resolution**. Essentially, SQL Server processes queries in two phases. The first phase parses and validates the query and ensures that the T-SQL is well formed. The second phase is the compilation phase, during which an execution plan is built and objects referenced in the query are resolved. If a query is submitted to SQL Server via ad hoc SQL from an application or dynamic SQL within a stored procedure, these two phases happen together. However, within the context of stored procedures, SQL Server exploits **late binding**. This means that the parse phase happens when the stored procedure is created, and the compile phase (and therefore scope resolution) occurs only when the stored procedure is executed.

To see what this means, create the following stored procedure (assuming that a table called SomeTable does not exist in the current database):

```
CREATE PROCEDURE NonExistentTable
AS
BEGIN
    SELECT xyz
    FROM SomeTable;
END;
GO
```

Although SomeTable does not exist, the stored procedure is created—the T-SQL parses without any errors. However, upon running the stored procedure, an exception is thrown:

```
EXEC NonExistentTable;
GO
```

This leads to

```
Msg 208, Level 16, State 1, Procedure NonExistentTable, Line 4
Invalid object name 'SomeTable'.
```

Like the parse exception, scope-resolution exceptions behave similarly to batch-level exceptions within the same scope, and similarly to statement-level exceptions in the outer scope. Since the stored procedure creates a new scope, hitting this exception within the procedure aborts the rest of the procedure, but any T-SQL encountered in the calling batch after execution of the procedure will still run. For instance:

```
EXEC NonExistentTable;
PRINT 'This will print!';
GO
```

leads to the following result:

```
Msg 208, Level 16, State 1, Procedure NonExistentTable, Line 4

Invalid object name 'SomeTable'.

This will print!
```

Connection and Server-Level Exceptions

Some exceptions thrown by SQL Server can be so severe that they abort the entire connection, or cause the server itself to crash. These types of connection- and server-level exceptions are generally caused by internal SQL Server bugs, and are thankfully quite rare. At the time of writing, I cannot provide any examples of these types of exceptions, as I am not aware of any reproducible conditions in SQL Server 2008 that cause them.

The XACT_ABORT Setting

Although users do not have much control over the behavior of exceptions thrown by SQL Server, there is one setting that can be modified on a per-connection basis. Turning on the **XACT_ABORT** setting makes all statement-level exceptions behave like batch-level exceptions. This means that control will always be immediately returned to the client any time an exception is thrown by SQL Server during execution of a query (assuming the exception is not handled).

To enable **XACT_ABORT** for a connection, the following T-SQL is used:

```
SET XACT_ABORT ON;
```

This setting will remain enabled for the entire connection—even if it was set in a lower level of scope, such as in a stored procedure or dynamic SQL—until it is disabled using the following T-SQL:

```
SET XACT_ABORT OFF;
```

To illustrate the effect of this setting on the behavior of exceptions, let's review a couple of the exceptions already covered. Recall that the following integer overflow exception operates at the statement level:

```
SELECT POWER(2, 32);
PRINT 'This will print!';
GO
```

Enabling the **XACT_ABORT** setting before running this T-SQL changes the output, resulting in the **PRINT** statement not getting executed:

```
SET XACT_ABORT ON;
SELECT POWER(2, 32);
PRINT 'This will NOT print!';
GO
```

The output from running this batch is as follows:

```
Msg 232, Level 16, State 3, Line 2
Arithmetic overflow error for type int, value = 4294967296.000000.
```

Note that **XACT_ABORT** only affects the behavior of runtime errors, not those generated during compilation. Recall the previous example that demonstrated a parsing exception occurring in a lower scope using the **EXEC** function:

```
EXEC('SELECTxzy FROM SomeTable');
PRINT 'This will print!';
GO
```

The result of this code listing will remain the same, regardless of the **XACT_ABORT** setting, resulting in the **PRINT** statement being evaluated even after the exception occurs.

In addition to controlling exception behavior, **XACT_ABORT** also modifies how transactions behave when exceptions occur. See the section "Transactions and Exceptions" later in this chapter for more information.

Dissecting an Error Message

A SQL Server exception has a few different component parts, each of which are represented within the text of the error message. Each exception has an associated error number, error level, and state. Error messages can also contain additional diagnostic information including line numbers and the name of the procedure in which the exception occurred.

Error Number

The error number of an exception is listed following the text **Msg** within the error text. For example, the error number of the following exception is 156:

```
Msg 156, Level 15, State 1, Line 1
Incorrect syntax near the keyword 'FROM'.
```

SQL Server generally returns the error message with the exception, so having the error number usually doesn't assist from a problem-solving point of view. However, there are times when knowing the error number can be of use. Examples include use of the **@@ERROR** function, or when doing specialized error handling using the **TRY**/**CATCH** syntax (see the sections "Exception 'Handling' Using @@ERROR" and "SQL Server's TRY/CATCH Syntax" later in the chapter for details on these topics).

The error number can also be used to look up the localized translation of the error message from the **sys.messages** catalog view. The **message_id** column contains the error number, and the **language_id** column can be used to get the message in the correct language. For example, the following T-SQL returns the English text for error 208:

```
SELECT text
FROM sys.messages
WHERE
    message_id = 208
    AND language_id = 1033;
GO
```

The output of this query is an error message template, shown here:

```
Invalid object name '%.*ls'.
```

See the section "SQL Server's RAISERROR Function" for more information about error message templates.

Error Level

The **Level** tag within an error message indicates a number between 1 and 25. This number can sometimes be used to either classify an exception or determine its severity. Unfortunately, the key word is "sometimes": the error levels assigned by SQL Server are highly inconsistent and should generally not be used in order to make decisions about how to handle exceptions.

The following exception, based on its error message, is of error level 15:

```
Msg 156, Level 15, State 1, Line 1
Incorrect syntax near the keyword 'FROM'.
```

The error levels for each exception can be queried from the **sys.messages** view, using the **severity** column. A severity of less than 11 indicates that a message is a **warning**. If severity is 11 or greater, the message is considered to be an **error** and can be broken down into the following documented categories:

- **Error levels 11 through 16** are documented as "errors that can be corrected by the user." The majority of exceptions thrown by SQL Server are in this range, including constraint violations, parsing and compilation errors, and most other runtime exceptions.

- **Error levels 17 through 19** are more serious exceptions. These include out-of-memory exceptions, disk space exceptions, internal SQL Server errors, and other similar violations. Many of these are automatically logged to the SQL Server error log when they are thrown. You can identify those exceptions that are logged by examining the **is_event_logged** column of the **sys.messages** table.

- **Error levels 20 through 25** are fatal connection and server-level exceptions. These include various types of data corruption, network, logging, and other critical errors. Virtually all of the exceptions at this level are automatically logged.

Although the error levels that make up each range are individually documented in Books Online (**http://msdn2.microsoft.com/en-us/library/ms164086.aspx**), this information is inconsistent or incorrect in many cases. For instance, according to documentation, severity level 11 indicates errors where "the given object or entity does not exist." However, error 208, "Invalid object name," is a level-16 exception. Many other errors have equally unpredictable levels, and it is recommended that you do not program client software to rely on the error levels for handling logic.

In addition to inconsistency regarding the relative severity of different errors, there is, for the most part, no discernable pattern regarding the severity level of an error and whether that error will behave on the statement or batch level. For instance, both errors 245 ("Conversion failed") and 515 ("Cannot insert the value NULL . . . column does not allow nulls") are level-16 exceptions. However, 245 is a batch-level exception, whereas 515 acts at the statement level.

Error State

Each exception has a **State** tag, which contains information about the exception that is used internally by SQL Server. The values that SQL Server uses for this tag are not documented, so this tag is generally not helpful. The following exception has a state of 1:

```
Msg 156, Level 15, State 1, Line 1
Incorrect syntax near the keyword 'FROM'.
```

Additional Information

In addition to the error number, level, and state, many errors also carry additional information about the line number on which the exception occurred and the procedure in which it occurred, if relevant. The following error message indicates that an invalid object name was referenced on line 4 of the procedure NonExistentTable:

```
Msg 208, Level 16, State 1, Procedure NonExistentTable, Line 4
Invalid object name 'SomeTable'.
```

If an exception does not occur within a procedure, the line number refers to the line in the batch in which the statement that caused the exception was sent.

Be careful not to confuse batches separated with **GO** with a single batch. Consider the following T-SQL:

```
SELECT 1;
GO
SELECT 2;
GO
SELECT 1/0;
GO
```

In this case, although a divide-by-zero exception occurs on line 5 of the code listing itself, the exception message will report that the exception was encountered on line 1:

```
(1 row(s) affected)



 (1 row(s) affected)

Msg 8134, Level 16, State 1, Line 1

Divide by zero error encountered.
```

The reason for the reset of the line number is that **GO** is not actually a T-SQL command. **GO** is an identifier recognized by SQL Server client tools (e.g., SQL Server Management Studio and SQLCMD) that tells the client to separate the query into batches, sending each to SQL Server one after another. This seemingly erroneous line number reported in the previous example occurs because each batch is sent separately to the query engine. SQL Server does not know that on the client (e.g., in SQL Server Management Studio) these batches are all displayed together on the screen. As far as SQL Server is concerned, these are three completely separate units of T-SQL that happen to be sent on the same connection.

SQL Server's RAISERROR Function

In addition to the exceptions that SQL Server itself throws, users can raise exceptions within T-SQL by using a function called **RAISERROR**. The general form for this function is as follows:

```
RAISERROR ( { msg_id | msg_str | @local_variable }
    { ,severity ,state }
    [ ,argument [ ,...n ] ] )
    [ WITH option [ ,...n ] ]
```

The first argument can be an ad hoc message in the form of a string or variable, or a valid error number from the **message_id** column of **sys.messages**. If a string is specified, it can include format designators that can then be filled using the optional arguments specified at the end of the function call.

The second argument, **severity**, can be used to enforce some level of control over the behavior of the exception, similar to the way in which SQL Server uses error levels. For the most part, the same exception ranges apply: exception levels between 1 and 10 result in a warning, levels between 11 and 18 are considered normal user errors, and those above 18 are considered serious and can only be raised by members of the **sysadmin** fixed-server role. User exceptions raised over level 20, just like those raised by SQL Server, cause the connection to break. Beyond these ranges, there is no real control afforded to user-raised exceptions, and all are considered to be statement level—this is even true with **XACT_ABORT** set.

■ **Note** **XACT_ABORT** does not impact the behavior of the **RAISERROR** statement.

The **state** argument can be any value between 1 and 127, and has no effect on the behavior of the exception. It can be used to add additional coded information to be carried by the exception—but it's probably just as easy to add that data to the error message itself in most cases.

The simplest way to use **RAISERROR** is to pass in a string containing an error message, and set the appropriate error level and state. For general exceptions, I usually use severity 16 and a value of 1 for **state**:

```
RAISERROR('General exception', 16, 1);
```

This results in the following output:

```
Msg 50000, Level 16, State 1, Line 1
General exception
```

Note that the error number generated in this case is 50000, which is the generic user-defined error number that will be used whenever passing in a string for the first argument to **RAISERROR**.

> ■ **Caution** Previous versions of SQL Server allowed RAISERROR syntax specifying the error number and message number as follows: `RAISERROR 50000 'General exception'`. This syntax is deprecated in SQL Server 2008 and should not be used.

Formatting Error Messages

When defining error messages, it is generally useful to format the text in some way. For example, think about how you might write code to work with a number of product IDs, dynamically retrieved, in a loop. You might have a local variable called **@ProductId**, which contains the ID of the product that the code is currently working with. If so, you might wish to define a custom exception that should be thrown when a problem occurs—and it would probably be a good idea to return the current value of **@ProductId** along with the error message.

In this case, there are a couple of ways of sending back the data with the exception. The first is to dynamically build an error message string:

```
DECLARE @ProductId int;
SET @ProductId = 100;

/* ... problem occurs ... */

DECLARE @ErrorMessage varchar(200);
SET @ErrorMessage =
    'Problem with ProductId ' + CONVERT(varchar, @ProductId);

RAISERROR(@ErrorMessage, 16, 1);
```

Executing this batch results in the following output:

```
Msg 50000, Level 16, State 1, Line 10
Problem with ProductId 100
```

While this works for this case, dynamically building up error messages is not the most elegant development practice. A better approach is to make use of a format designator and to pass **@ProductId** as an optional parameter, as shown in the following code listing:

```
DECLARE @ProductId int;
SET @ProductId = 100;

/* ... problem occurs ... */

RAISERROR('Problem with ProductId %i', 16, 1, @ProductId);
```

Executing this batch results in the same output as before, but requires quite a bit less code, and you don't have to worry about defining extra variables or building up messy conversion code. The **%i** embedded in the error message is a format designator that means "integer." The other most commonly used format designator is **%s**, for "string."

You can embed as many designators as necessary in an error message, and they will be substituted in the order in which optional arguments are appended. For example:

```
DECLARE @ProductId1 int;
SET @ProductId1 = 100;

DECLARE @ProductId2 int;
SET @ProductId2 = 200;

DECLARE @ProductId3 int;
SET @ProductId3 = 300;

/* ... problem occurs ... */

RAISERROR('Problem with ProductIds %i, %i, %i',
    16, 1, @ProductId1, @ProductId2, @ProductId3);
```

This results in the following output:

```
Msg 50000, Level 16, State 1, Line 12
Problem with ProductIds 100, 200, 300
```

■ **Note** Readers familiar with C programming will notice that the format designators used by **RAISERROR** are the same as those used by the C language's **printf** function. For a complete list of the supported designators, see the "RAISERROR (Transact-SQL)" topic in SQL Server 2008 Books Online.

Creating Persistent Custom Error Messages

Formatting messages using format designators instead of building up strings dynamically is a step in the right direction, but it does not solve one final problem: what if you need to use the same error message in multiple places? You could simply use the same exact arguments to **RAISERROR** in each routine in which the exception is needed, but that might cause a maintenance headache if you ever needed to change the error message. In addition, each of the exceptions would only be able to use the default user-defined error number, 50000, making programming against these custom exceptions much more difficult.

Luckily, SQL Server takes care of these problems quite nicely, by providing a mechanism by which custom error messages can be added to **sys.messages**. Exceptions using these error messages can then be raised by using **RAISERROR** and passing in the custom error number as the first parameter.

To create a persistent custom error message, use the **sp_addmessage** stored procedure. This stored procedure allows the user to specify custom messages for message numbers over 50000. In addition to an error message, users can specify a default severity. Messages added using **sp_addmessage** are scoped at the server level, so if you have multiple applications hosted on the same server, be aware of whether they define custom messages and whether there is any overlap—you may need to set up a new instance of SQL Server for one or more of the applications in order to allow them to create their exceptions. When developing new applications that use custom messages, try to choose a well-defined range in which to create your messages, in order to avoid overlaps with other applications in shared environments. Remember that you can use any number between **50000** and **2147483647**, and you don't need to stay in the **50000** range.

Adding a custom message is as easy as calling **sp_addmessage** and defining a message number and the message text. The following T-SQL defines the message from the previous section as error message number 50005:

```
EXEC sp_addmessage
    @msgnum = 50005,
    @severity = 16,
    @msgtext = 'Problem with ProductIds %i, %i, %i';
GO
```

Once this T-SQL is executed, an exception can be raised using this error message, by calling **RAISERROR** with the appropriate error number:

```
RAISERROR(50005, 15, 1, 100, 200, 300);
```

This causes the following output to be sent back to the client:

```
Msg 50005, Level 15, State 1, Line 1
Problem with ProductIds 100, 200, 300
```

Note that when calling **RAISERROR** in this case, severity 15 was specified, even though the custom error was originally defined as severity level 16. This brings up an important point about severities of custom errors: whatever severity is specified in the call to **RAISERROR** will override the severity that was defined for the error. However, the default severity will be used if you pass a negative value for that argument to **RAISERROR**:

```
RAISERROR(50005, -1, 1, 100, 200, 300);
```

This produces the following output (notice that **Level** is now 16, as was defined when the error message was created):

```
Msg 50005, Level 16, State 1, Line 1
Problem with ProductIds 100, 200, 300
```

It is recommended that, unless you are overriding the severity for a specific reason, you always use -1 for the severity argument when raising a custom exception.

Changing the text of an exception once defined is also easy using **sp_addmessage**. To do so, pass the optional **@Replace** argument, setting its value to **'Replace'**, as in the following T-SQL:

```
EXEC sp_addmessage
    @msgnum = 50005,
    @severity = 16,
    @msgtext = 'Problem with ProductId numbers %i, %i, %i',
```

```
    @Replace = 'Replace';
GO
```

■ **Note** In addition to being able to add a message and set a severity, **sp_addmessage** supports localization of messages for different languages. The examples here do not show localization; instead, messages will be created for the user's default language. For details on localized messages, refer to SQL Server 2008 Books Online.

Logging User-Thrown Exceptions

Another useful feature of **RAISERROR** is the ability to log messages to SQL Server's error log. This can come in handy especially when working with automated code, such as T-SQL run via a SQL Server agent job. In order to log any exception, use the **WITH LOG** option of the **RAISERROR** function, as in the following T-SQL:

```
RAISERROR('This will be logged.', 16, 1) WITH LOG;
```

Note that specific access rights are required to log an error. The user executing the **RAISERROR** function must either be a member of the **sysadmin** fixed server role or have **ALTER TRACE** permissions.

Monitoring Exception Events with Traces

Some application developers go too far in handling exceptions, and end up creating applications that hide problems by catching every exception that occurs and not reporting it. In such cases it can be extremely difficult to debug issues without knowing whether an exception is being thrown. Should you find yourself in this situation, you can use a Profiler trace to monitor for exceptions occurring in SQL Server.

In order to monitor for exceptions, start a trace and select the **Exception** and **User Error Message** events. For most exceptions with a severity greater than 10, both events will fire. The **Exception** event will contain all of the data associated with the exception except for the actual message. This includes the error number, severity, state, and line number. The **User Error Message** event will contain the formatted error message as it was sent to the client.

For warnings (messages with a severity of less than 11), only the **User Error Message** event will fire. You may also notice error 208 exceptions ("Object not found") without corresponding error message events. These exceptions are used internally by the SQL Server query optimizer during the scope-resolution phase of compilation, and can be safely ignored.

Exception Handling

Understanding when, why, and how SQL Server throws exceptions is great, but the real goal is to actually *do something* when an exception occurs. **Exception handling** refers to the ability to **catch** an exception when it occurs, rather than simply letting it bubble up to the next level of scope.

Why Handle Exceptions in T-SQL?

Exception handling in T-SQL should be thought of as no different from exception handling in any other language. A generally accepted programming practice is to handle exceptions at the *lowest possible scope*, in order to keep them from interacting with higher levels of the application. If an exception can be caught at a lower level and dealt with there, higher-level modules will not require special code to handle the exception, and therefore can concentrate on whatever their purpose is. This means that every routine in the application becomes simpler, more maintainable, and therefore quite possibly more robust.

Put another way, exceptions should be *encapsulated* as much as possible—knowledge of the internal exceptions of other modules is yet another form of coupling, not so different from some of the types discussed in the first chapter of this book.

Keep in mind that encapsulation of exceptions is really something that must be handled on a case-by-case basis. But the basic rule is, if you can "fix" the exception one way or another without letting the caller ever know it even occurred, that is probably a good place to encapsulate.

Exception "Handling" Using @@ERROR

Versions of SQL Server prior to SQL Server 2005 did not have true exception-handling capabilities. Any exception that occurred would be passed back to the caller, regardless of any action taken by the code of the stored procedure or query in which it was thrown. Although for the most part SQL Server 2008 now provides better alternatives, the general method used to "handle" errors in those earlier versions of SQL Server is still useful in some cases—and a lot of legacy code will be around for quite a while—so a quick review is definitely warranted.

■ **Note** If you're following the examples in this chapter in order, make sure that you have turned off the XACT_ABORT setting before trying the following examples.

The @@ERROR function is quite simple: it returns 0 if the last statement in the batch did not throw an error of severity 11 or greater. If the last statement did throw an error, it returns the error number. For example, consider the following T-SQL:

```
SELECT 1/0 AS DivideByZero;
SELECT @@ERROR AS ErrorNumber;
GO
```

The first statement returns the following message:

```
Msg 8134, Level 16, State 1, Line 1
Divide by zero error encountered.
```

---

and the second statement returns a result set containing a single value, containing the error number associated with the previous error:

```
ErrorNumber
8134
```

By checking to see whether the value of **@@ERROR** is nonzero, it is possible to perform some very primitive error handling. Unfortunately, this is also quite error prone due to the nature of **@@ERROR** and the fact that it only operates on the *last statement* executed in the batch. Many developers new to T-SQL are quite surprised by the output of the following batch:

```
SELECT 1/0 AS DivideByZero;
IF @@ERROR <> 0
  SELECT @@ERROR AS ErrorNumber;
GO
```

The first line of this code produces the same error message as before, but on this occasion, the result of **SELECT @@ERROR** is

```
ErrorNumber
0
```

The reason is that the statement executed immediately preceding **@@ERROR** was not the divide by zero, but rather the line **IF @@ERROR <> 0**, which did not generate an error. The solution to this problem is to set a variable to the value of **@@ERROR** after every statement in a batch that requires error handling, and then check that variable rather than the value of **@@ERROR** itself. Of course, if even a single statement is missed, holes may be left in the strategy, and some errors may escape notice.

Even with these problems, **@@ERROR** arguably still has a place in SQL Server 2008. It is a simple, lightweight alternative to the full-blown exception-handling capabilities that have been added more recently to the T-SQL language, and it has the additional benefit of *not* catching the exception. In some cases, full encapsulation is not the best option, and using **@@ERROR** will allow the developer to take some action—for instance, logging of the exception—while still passing it back to the caller.

SQL Server's TRY/CATCH Syntax

The standard error-handling construct in many programming languages, including T-SQL, is known as *try/catch*. The idea behind this construct is to set up two sections (aka **blocks**) of code. The first section, the **try block**, contains exception-prone code to be "tried." The second section contains code that should be executed in the event that the code in the try block fails, and an exception occurs. This is called the **catch block**. As soon as any exception occurs within the try block, code execution immediately jumps into the catch block. This is also known as **catching** an exception.

In T-SQL, try/catch is implemented using the following basic form:

```
BEGIN TRY
    --Code to try here
END TRY
```

```
BEGIN CATCH
    --Catch the exception here
END CATCH
```

Any type of exception—except for connection- or server-level exceptions—that occurs between **BEGIN TRY** and **END TRY** will cause the code between **BEGIN CATCH** and **END CATCH** to be immediately executed, bypassing any other code left in the try block.

As a first example, consider the following T-SQL:

```
BEGIN TRY
    SELECT 1/0 AS DivideByZero;
END TRY
BEGIN CATCH
    SELECT 'Exception Caught!' AS CatchMessage;
END CATCH
```

Running this batch produces the following output:

```
DivideByZero

------------



CatchMessage

-----------------

Exception Caught!
```

The interesting things to note here are that, first and foremost, there is no reported exception. We can see that an exception occurred because code execution jumped to the **CATCH** block, but the exception was successfully handled, and the client is not aware that an exception occurred. Second, notice that an empty result set is returned for the **SELECT** statement that caused the exception. Had the exception not been handled, no result set would have been returned. By sending back an empty result set, the implied contract of the **SELECT** statement is honored (more or less, depending on what the client was actually expecting).

Although already mentioned, it needs to be stressed that when using **TRY/CATCH**, all exceptions encountered within the **TRY** block will immediately abort execution of the remainder of the **TRY** block. Therefore, the following T-SQL has the exact same output as the last example:

```
BEGIN TRY
    SELECT 1/0 AS DivideByZero;
    SELECT 1 AS NoError;
END TRY
BEGIN CATCH
    SELECT 'Exception Caught!' AS CatchMessage;
END CATCH
```

Finally, it is worth noting that parsing and compilation exceptions will not be caught using **TRY/CATCH**, nor will they ever have a chance to be caught—an exception will be thrown by SQL Server before any of the code is ever actually executed.

Getting Extended Error Information in the Catch Block

In addition to the ability to catch an exception, SQL Server 2008 offers a range of additional functions that are available for use within the **CATCH** block. These functions, a list of which follows, enable the developer to write code that retrieves information about the exception that occurred in the **TRY** block.

- ERROR_MESSAGE

- ERROR_NUMBER

- ERROR_SEVERITY

- ERROR_STATE

- ERROR_LINE

- ERROR_PROCEDURE

These functions take no input arguments and are fairly self-explanatory based on their names. However, it is important to point out that unlike **@@ERROR**, the values returned by these functions are not reset after every statement. They are persistent for the entire **CATCH** block. Therefore, logic such as that used in the following T-SQL works:

```
BEGIN TRY
    SELECT CONVERT(int, 'ABC') AS ConvertException;
END TRY
BEGIN CATCH
    IF ERROR_NUMBER() = 123
        SELECT 'Error 123';
    ELSE
        SELECT ERROR_NUMBER() AS ErrorNumber;
END CATCH
```

As expected, in this case the error number is correctly reported:

```
ConvertException

----------------



ErrorNumber

-----------

245
```

These functions, especially **ERROR_NUMBER**, allow for coding of specific paths for certain exceptions. For example, if a developer knows that a certain piece of code is likely to cause an exception that can be programmatically fixed, that exception number can be checked for in the **CATCH** block.

Rethrowing Exceptions

A common feature in most languages that have try/catch capabilities is the ability to **rethrow** exceptions from the catch block. This means that the exception that originally occurred in the try block will be raised again, as if it were not handled at all. This is useful when you need to do some handling of the exception but also let the caller know that something went wrong in the routine.

T-SQL does not include any kind of built-in rethrow functionality. However, it is fairly easy to create such behavior based on the **CATCH** block error functions, in conjunction with **RAISERROR**. The following example shows a basic implementation of rethrow in T-SQL:

```
BEGIN TRY
    SELECT CONVERT(int, 'ABC') AS ConvertException;
END TRY
BEGIN CATCH
    DECLARE
        @ERROR_SEVERITY int = ERROR_SEVERITY(),
        @ERROR_STATE int = ERROR_STATE(),
        @ERROR_NUMBER int = ERROR_NUMBER(),
        @ERROR_LINE int = ERROR_LINE(),
        @ERROR_MESSAGE varchar(245) = ERROR_MESSAGE();

    RAISERROR('Msg %d, Line %d: %s',
        @ERROR_SEVERITY,
        @ERROR_STATE,
        @ERROR_NUMBER,
        @ERROR_LINE,
        @ERROR_MESSAGE);
END CATCH
GO
```

Due to the fact that **RAISERROR** cannot be used to throw exceptions below 13000, in this case "rethrowing" the exception requires raising a user-defined exception and sending back the data in a specially formed error message. As functions are not allowed within calls to **RAISERROR**, it is necessary to define variables and assign the values of the error functions before calling **RAISERROR** to rethrow the exception. Following is the output message of this T-SQL:

```
(0 row(s) affected)


Msg 50000, Level 16, State 1, Line 19

Msg 245, Line 2: Conversion failed when converting the varchar value 'ABC'

to data type int.
```

Keep in mind that, based on your interface requirements, you may not always want to rethrow the same exception that was caught to begin with. It might make more sense in many cases to catch the initial exception, and then throw a new exception that is more relevant (or more helpful) to the caller. For example, if you're working with a linked server and the server is not responding for some reason, your code will throw a timeout exception. It might make more sense to pass back a generic "data not available" exception than to expose the actual cause of the problem to the caller. This is something that should be decided on a case-by-case basis, as you work out optimal designs for your stored procedure interfaces.

When Should TRY/CATCH Be Used?

As mentioned previously, the general use case for handling exceptions in T-SQL routines (such as within stored procedures) is to encapsulate as much as possible at as low a level as possible, in order to simplify the overall code of the application. A primary example of this is logging of database exceptions. Instead of sending an exception that cannot be properly handled back to the application tier where it will be logged back to the database, it probably makes more sense to log it while already in the scope of a database routine.

Another use case involves temporary fixes for problems stemming from application code. For instance, the application—due to a bug—might occasionally pass invalid keys to a stored procedure that is supposed to insert them into a table. It might be simple to *temporarily* "fix" the problem by simply catching the exception in the database rather than throwing it back to the application where the user will receive an error message. Putting quick fixes of this type into place is often much cheaper than rebuilding and redeploying the entire application.

It is also important to consider when *not* to encapsulate exceptions. Make sure not to overhandle security problems, severe data errors, and other exceptions that the application—and ultimately, the user—should probably be informed of. There is definitely such a thing as too much exception handling, and falling into that trap can mean that problems will be hidden until they cause enough of a commotion to make themselves impossible to ignore.

Long-term issues hidden behind exception handlers usually pop into the open in the form of irreparable data corruption. These situations are usually highlighted by a lack of viable backups because the situation has been going on for so long, and inevitably end in lost business and developers getting their resumes updated for a job search. Luckily, avoiding this issue is fairly easy. Just use a little bit of common sense, and don't go off the deep end in a quest to stifle any and all exceptions.

Using TRY/CATCH to Build Retry Logic

An interesting example of where **TRY/CATCH** can be used to fully encapsulate an exception is when dealing with deadlocks. Although it's better to try to find and solve the source of a deadlock than to code around it, this is often a difficult and time-consuming task. Therefore, it's common to deal with deadlocks—at least temporarily—by having the application reissue the request that caused the deadlock. Eventually the deadlock condition will resolve itself (i.e., when the other transaction finishes), and the DML operation will go through as expected. Note that I do not recommend this as a long-term solution to solving recurring deadlock situations!

By using T-SQL's **TRY/CATCH** syntax, the application no longer needs to reissue a request or even know that a problem occurred. A retry loop can be set up, within which the deadlock-prone code can be tried in a **TRY** block and the deadlock caught in a **CATCH** block in order to try again.

A basic implementation of a retry loop follows:

```
DECLARE @Retries int;
SET @Retries = 3;

WHILE @Retries > 0
BEGIN
    BEGIN TRY
        /*
        Put deadlock-prone code here
        */

        --If execution gets here, success
        BREAK;
    END TRY
    BEGIN CATCH
        IF ERROR_NUMBER() = 1205
        BEGIN
            SET @Retries = @Retries - 1;

            IF @Retries = 0
                RAISERROR('Could not complete transaction!', 16, 1);
        END
        ELSE
            RAISERROR('Non-deadlock condition encountered', 16, 1);
            BREAK;
    END CATCH
END;
GO
```

In this example, the deadlock-prone code is retried as many times as the value of **@Retries**. Each time through the loop, the code is tried. If it succeeds without an exception being thrown, the code gets to the **BREAK** and the loop ends. Otherwise, execution jumps to the **CATCH** block, where a check is made to ensure that the error number is 1205 (deadlock victim). If so, the counter is decremented so that the loop can be tried again. If the exception is not a deadlock, another exception is thrown so that the caller knows that something went wrong. It's important to make sure that the wrong exception does not trigger a retry.

Exception Handling and Defensive Programming

Exception handling is extremely useful, and its use in T-SQL is absolutely invaluable. However, I hope that all readers keep in mind that exception handling is no substitute for proper checking of error conditions *before* they occur. Whenever possible, code defensively—proactively look for problems, and if they can be both detected and handled, code around them.

Remember that it's generally a better idea to handle exceptions rather than errors. If you can predict a condition and write a code path to handle it during development, that will usually provide a much more robust solution than trying to trap the exception once it occurs and handle it then.

Exception Handling and SQLCLR

The .NET Framework provides its own exception-handling mechanism, which is quite separate from the mechanism used to deal with exceptions encountered in T-SQL. So, how do the two systems interact when an exception occurs in CLR code executed within the SQLCLR process hosted by SQL Server?

Let's look at an example—the following C# code illustrates a simple CLR user-defined function (UDF) to divide one number by another:

```
[Microsoft.SqlServer.Server.SqlFunction()]
public static SqlDecimal Divide(SqlDecimal x, SqlDecimal y)
{
    return x / y;
}
```

When cataloged and called from SQL Server with a value of **0** for the **y** parameter, the result is as follows:

```
Msg 6522, Level 16, State 2, Line 1

A .NET Framework error occurred during execution of user-defined routine or

aggregate "Divide":

System.DivideByZeroException: Divide by zero error encountered.

System.DivideByZeroException:

    at System.Data.SqlTypes.SqlDecimal.op_Division(SqlDecimal x, SqlDecimal y)

    at ExpertSQLServer.UserDefinedFunctions.Divide(SqlDecimal x, SqlDecimal y)

.
```

SQL Server automatically wraps an exception handler around any managed code executed from within SQL Server. That means that if the managed code throws an exception, it is caught by the wrapper, which then generates an error. The error message contains details of the original exception, together with a stack trace of when it occurred.

In this case, the original CLR exception, **System.DivideByZeroException**, propagated a 6522 error, which is the generic error message for any unhandled exception that occurs within a SQLCLR function.

As previously stated, the best approach to deal with such exceptions is to tackle them at the lowest level possible. In the case of a UDF such as this, the exception should be handled within the CLR code itself (using **try...catch**, for example), in which case it never needs to be caught at the T-SQL level.

One interesting point this raises is how to deal with exceptions arising in system-defined CLR routines, such as any methods defined by the **geometry**, **geography**, or **hierarchyid** types. Consider the following example, which attempts to instantiate variables of the **hierarchyid** and **geography** datatypes with invalid values:

93

```
DECLARE @HierarchyId hierarchyid = '/1/1';
DECLARE @Geography geography = 'POLYGON((0 51, 0 52, 1 52, 1 51 ,0 51))';
GO
```

Both of these statements will lead to CLR exceptions, reported as follows:

Msg 6522, Level 16, State 2, Line 1

A .NET Framework error occurred during execution of user-defined routine or

 aggregate "hierarchyid":

Microsoft.SqlServer.Types.HierarchyIdException: 24001: SqlHierarchyId.Parse

failed because the input string '/1/1' is not a valid string representation of a

SqlHierarchyId node.

Microsoft.SqlServer.Types.HierarchyIdException:

   at Microsoft.SqlServer.Types.SqlHierarchyId.Parse(SqlString input)

.

Msg 6522, Level 16, State 1, Line 2

A .NET Framework error occurred during execution of user-defined routine or

 aggregate "geography":

Microsoft.SqlServer.Types.GLArgumentException: 24205: The specified input does

not represent a valid geography instance because it exceeds a single hemisphere.

Each geography instance must fit inside a single hemisphere. A common reason for

this error is that a polygon has the wrong ring orientation.

Microsoft.SqlServer.Types.GLArgumentException:

   at Microsoft.SqlServer.Types.GLNativeMethods.ThrowExceptionForHr(GL_HResult

errorCode)

   at Microsoft.SqlServer.Types.GLNativeMethods.GeodeticIsValid(GeoData g)

```
   at Microsoft.SqlServer.Types.SqlGeography.IsValidExpensive()

   at Microsoft.SqlServer.Types.SqlGeography.ConstructGeographyFromUserInput(

GeoData g, Int32 srid)

   at Microsoft.SqlServer.Types.SqlGeography.GeographyFromText(OpenGisType type,

SqlChars taggedText, Int32 srid)

   at Microsoft.SqlServer.Types.SqlGeography.STGeomFromText(SqlChars

geometryTaggedText, Int32 srid)

   at Microsoft.SqlServer.Types.SqlGeography.Parse(SqlString s)
```

■ **Note** As demonstrated by the preceding example code, exceptions generated by managed code are statement-level exceptions—the second statement was allowed to run even after the first had generated a 6522 error.

How do we create specific code paths to handle such exceptions? Despite the fact that they relate to very different situations, as both exceptions occurred within managed code, the T-SQL error generated in each case is the same—generic error 6522. This means that we cannot use **ERROR_NUMBER()** to differentiate between these cases. Furthermore, we cannot easily add custom error-handling to the original function code, since these are system-defined methods defined within the precompiled **Microsoft.SqlServer.Types.dll** assembly.

One approach would be to define new custom CLR methods that wrap around each of the system-defined methods in **SqlServer.Types.dll**, which check for and handle any CLR exceptions before passing the result back to SQL Server. An example of such a wrapper placed around the **geography Parse()** method is shown in the following code listing:

```
[Microsoft.SqlServer.Server.SqlFunction()]
public static SqlGeography GeogTryParse(SqlString Input)
{
  SqlGeography result = new SqlGeography();
  try
  {
    result = SqlGeography.Parse(Input);
  }
  catch
  {
    // Exception Handling code here

    // Optionally, rethrow the exception
    // throw new Exception("An exception occurred that couldn't be handled");
```

```
    }

    return result;
}
```

Alternatively, you could create code paths that rely on parsing the contents of `ERROR_MESSAGE()` to identify the details of the original CLR exception specified in the stack trace. The exceptions generated by the system-defined CLR types have five-digit exception numbers in the range 24000 to 24999, so can be distilled from the `ERROR_MESSSAGE()` string using the T-SQL `PATINDEX` function. The following code listing demonstrates this approach when applied to the `hierarchyid` example given previously:

```
DECLARE @errorMsg nvarchar(max);
BEGIN TRY
  SELECT hierarchyid::Parse('/1/1');
END TRY
BEGIN CATCH
  SELECT @errorMsg = ERROR_MESSAGE();
  SELECT SUBSTRING(@errorMsg, PATINDEX('%: 24[0-9][0-9][0-9]%', @errorMsg) + 2,
5);
END CATCH
GO
```

The resulting value, 24001, relates to the specific CLR exception that occurred ("the input string is not a valid string representation of a SqlHierarchyId node"), rather than the generic T-SQL error 6522, and can be used to write specific code paths to deal with such an exception.

Transactions and Exceptions

No discussion of exceptions in SQL Server can be complete without mentioning the interplay between transactions and exceptions. This is a fairly simple area, but one that often confuses developers who don't quite understand the role that transactions play.

SQL Server is a database management system (DBMS), and as such one of its main goals is management and manipulation of data. Therefore, at the heart of every exception-handling scheme within SQL Server must live the idea that these are not mere exceptions—they're also data issues.

The Myths of Transaction Abortion

The biggest mistake that some developers make is the assumption that if an exception occurs during a transaction, that transaction will be aborted. By default, that is almost *never* the case. Most transactions will live on even in the face of exceptions, as running the following T-SQL will show:

```
BEGIN TRANSACTION;
GO
SELECT 1/0 AS DivideByZero;
GO
SELECT @@TRANCOUNT AS ActiveTransactionCount;
GO
```

The output from this T-SQL is as follows:

```
DivideByZero

------------

Msg 8134, Level 16, State 1, Line 1

Divide by zero error encountered.


ActiveTransactionCount

----------------------

1


(1 row(s) affected)
```

Another mistake is the belief that stored procedures represent some sort of atomic unit of work, complete with their own implicit transaction that will get rolled back in case of an exception. Alas, this is also not the case, as the following T-SQL proves:

```
--Create a table for some data
CREATE TABLE SomeData
(
    SomeColumn int
);
GO

--This procedure will insert one row, then throw a divide-by-zero exception
CREATE PROCEDURE NoRollback
AS
BEGIN
    INSERT INTO SomeData VALUES (1);

    INSERT INTO SomeData VALUES (1/0);
END;
GO

--Execute the procedure
EXEC NoRollback;
GO

--Select the rows from the table
```

```
SELECT *
FROM SomeData;
GO
```

The result is that, even though there is an error, the row that didn't throw an exception is still in the table; there is no implicit transaction arising from the stored procedure:

SomeColumn

1

Even if an *explicit* transaction is begun in the stored procedure before the inserts and committed after the exception occurs, this example will still return the same output. By default, unless a rollback is explicitly issued, in most cases an exception will not roll anything back. It will simply serve as a message that something went wrong.

XACT_ABORT: Turning Myth into (Semi-)Reality

As mentioned in the section on **XACT_ABORT** and its effect on exceptions, the setting also has an impact on transactions, as its name might indicate (it is pronounced *transact abort*). In addition to making exceptions act like batch-level exceptions, the setting also causes any active transactions to immediately roll back in the event of an exception. This means that the following T-SQL results in an active transaction count of 0:

```
SET XACT_ABORT ON;
BEGIN TRANSACTION;
GO
SELECT 1/0 AS DivideByZero;
GO
SELECT @@TRANCOUNT AS ActiveTransactionCount;
GO
```

The output is now

ActiveTransactionCount

0

XACT_ABORT does not create an implicit transaction within a stored procedure, but it *does* cause any exceptions that occur within an explicit transaction within a stored procedure to cause a rollback. The following T-SQL shows a much more atomic stored procedure behavior than the previous example:

```
--Empty the table
TRUNCATE TABLE SomeData;
GO

--This procedure will insert one row, then throw a divide-by-zero exception
CREATE PROCEDURE XACT_Rollback
AS
```

```
BEGIN
    SET XACT_ABORT ON;

    BEGIN TRANSACTION;
        INSERT INTO SomeData VALUES (1);

        INSERT INTO SomeData VALUES (1/0);
    COMMIT TRANSACTION;
END;
GO

--Execute the procedure
EXEC XACT_Rollback;
GO

--Select the rows from the table
SELECT *
FROM SomeData;
GO
```

This T-SQL results in the following output, which shows that no rows were inserted:

```
Msg 8134, Level 16, State 1, Procedure XACT_Rollback, Line 10

Divide by zero error encountered.



SomeColumn

-----------



(0 row(s) affected)
```

XACT_ABORT is a very simple yet extremely effective means of ensuring that an exception does not result in a transaction committing with only part of its work done. I recommend turning this setting on in any stored procedure that uses an explicit transaction, in order to guarantee that it will get rolled back in case of an exception.

TRY/CATCH and Doomed Transactions

One interesting outcome of using **TRY/CATCH** syntax is that it is possible for transactions to enter a state in which they can *only* be rolled back. In this case the transaction is not automatically rolled back, as it is with **XACT_ABORT**; instead, SQL Server throws an exception letting the caller know that the transaction cannot be committed, and must be manually rolled back. This condition is known as a **doomed transaction**, and the following T-SQL shows one way of producing it:

```
BEGIN TRANSACTION;

BEGIN TRY
    --Throw an exception on insert
    INSERT INTO SomeData VALUES (CONVERT(int, 'abc'));
END TRY
BEGIN CATCH
    --Try to commit...
    COMMIT TRANSACTION;
END CATCH
GO
```

This results in the following output:

```
Msg 3930, Level 16, State 1, Line 10

The current transaction cannot be committed and cannot support

operations that write to the log file. Roll back the transaction.
```

Should a transaction enter this state, any attempt to either commit the transaction or roll forward (do more work) will result in the same exception. This exception will keep getting thrown until the transaction is rolled back.

In order to determine whether an active transaction can be committed or rolled forward, check the value of the **XACT_STATE** function. This function returns 0 if there are no active transactions, 1 if the transaction is in a state in which more work can be done, and –1 if the transaction is doomed. It is a good idea to always check **XACT_STATE** in any **CATCH** block that involves an explicit transaction.

Summary

It's a fact of life for every developer: sometimes things just go wrong.

A solid understanding of how exceptions behave within SQL Server makes working with them much easier. Especially important is the difference between statement-level and batch-level exceptions, and the implications of exceptions that are thrown within transactions.

SQL Server's **TRY**/**CATCH** syntax makes dealing with exceptions much easier, but it's important to use the feature wisely. Overuse can make detection and debugging of problems exceedingly difficult. And whenever dealing with transactions in **CATCH** blocks, make sure to check the value of **XACT_STATE**.

Errors and exceptions will always occur, but by thinking carefully about how to handle them, you can deal with them easily and effectively.

CHAPTER 5

■ ■ ■

Privilege and Authorization

SQL Server security is a broad subject area, with enough potential avenues of exploration that entire books have been written on the topic. This chapter's goal is not to cover the whole spectrum of security knowledge necessary to create a product that is secure from end to end, but rather to focus on those areas that are most important during the software design and development process.

Broadly speaking, data security can be broken into two areas:

- **Authentication**: The act of verifying the identity of a user of a system

- **Authorization**: The act of giving a user access to the resources that a system controls

These two realms can be delegated separately in many cases; so long as the authentication piece works properly, the user can be handed off to authorization mechanisms for the remainder of a session.

SQL Server authentication on its own is a big topic, with a diverse range of subtopics including network security, operating system security, and so-called surface area control over the server. While production DBAs should be very concerned with these sorts of issues, authentication is an area that developers can mostly ignore. Developers need to be much more concerned with what happens *after* authentication: that is, how the user is authorized for data access and how data is protected from unauthorized users.

This chapter introduces some of the key issues of data privilege and authorization in SQL Server from a development point of view. Included here is an initial discussion on privileges and general guidelines and practices for securing data using SQL Server permissions. A related security topic is that of data encryption, which is covered in detail in the next chapter.

Note that although authentication issues are generally ignored in these pages, you should try to not completely disregard them in your day-to-day development work. Development environments tend to be set up with very lax security in order to keep things simple, but a solid development process should include a testing phase during which full authentication restrictions are applied. This helps to ensure that rollout to a production system does not end in spectacular failure in which users aren't even able to log in!

User VS. Application Logins

The topics covered in this chapter relate to various privilege and authorization scenarios handled within SQL Server itself. However, in many database application designs, authorization is handled in the application layer rather than at the database layer. In such applications, users typically connect and log into the application using their own personal credentials, but the application then connects to the database using a single shared application login. This login is given permission to execute all of the stored procedures in the database related to that application, and it is up to authorization routines in the application itself to determine those actions that can be performed by any given user.

There are some benefits to using this approach, such as being able to take advantage of connection pooling between different sessions. However, it means that any features provided by SQL Server to handle per-user security do not apply. If a bug were to exist in the application, or if the credentials associated with the application login were to become known, it would be possible for users to execute any queries against the database that the application had permission to perform.

For the examples in this chapter, I assume a scenario in which users are connecting to the database using their own personal credentials.

The Principle of Least Privilege

The key to locking down resources in any kind of system—database or otherwise—is quite simple in essence: any given user should have access to only the bare minimum set of resources required, and for only as much time as access to those resources is needed. Unfortunately, in practice this is more of an ideal goal than an actual prescription for data security; many systems do not allow for the set of permissions allocated to a user to be easily escalated dynamically, and the Microsoft Windows family of operating systems have not historically been engineered to use escalation of privilege as a means by which to gain additional access at runtime.

Many multiuser operating systems implement the ability to **impersonate** other users when access to a resource owned by that user is required. Impersonation is slightly different than reauthentication; instead of logging out and resending credentials, thereby forcing any running processes to be stopped, impersonation allows a process to temporarily **escalate** its privileges, taking on the rights held by the impersonated principal. The most common example of this at an operating system level is UNIX's **su** command, which allows a user to temporarily take on the identity of another user, easily reverting back when done. Windows systems can also handle some degree of impersonation, such as provided by the .NET **WindowsIdentity** class.

Permissions in Windows systems are typically provided using **access control lists (ACLs)**. Granting permission to a resource means adding a user to the list, after which the user can access the resource again and again, even after logging in and out of the system. This kind of access control provides no additional security if, for instance, an attacker takes over an account in the system. By taking control of an account, the attacker automatically has full access to every resource that the account has permission to access.

By controlling access with impersonation, the user is required to effectively request access to the resource dynamically, *each time access is required*. In addition, rights to the resource will only be maintained during the course of impersonation. Once the user **reverts** (i.e., turns off impersonation), the additional access rights are no longer granted. In effect, this means that if an account is compromised, the attacker will akso have to compromise the impersonation context in order to gain access to more secure resources.

The idea of security through **least privilege** involves creating users with few or no permissions, and allowing them to briefly escalate their privileges when greater access is required. This is generally implemented using **proxies**—users (or other security principals) that have access to a resource but cannot be authenticated externally. Use of low-privileged external users together with higher-privileged proxy users provides a buffer against attack, due to the fact that the only accounts that an attacker can directly compromise from the outside have no permissions directly associated with them. Accessing more valuable resources requires additional work on the part of the attacker, giving you that much more of a chance to detect problems before they occur.

Creating Proxies in SQL Server

SQL Server 2008 allows creation of security principals at both the server-level and database-level that can be used via proxy.

- At the server level, proxy **logins** can be created that cannot log in.

- At the database level, proxy **users** can be created that are not associated with a login.

The only way to switch into the execution context of either of these types of proxy principals is via impersonation, which makes them ideal for privilege escalation scenarios.

Server-Level Proxies

In order to create a proxy login (which can be used to delegate server-level permissions such as **BULK INSERT** or **ALTER DATABASE**), you must first create a certificate in the **master** database. Certificates are covered in more detail in Chapter 6, but for now think of a certificate as a trusted way to verify the identity of a principal without a password. The following syntax can be used to create a certificate in **master**. (Note that before a certificate can be created in any database, a master key must be created. Again, see Chapter 6.)

```
USE master;
GO

CREATE CERTIFICATE Dinesh_Certificate
ENCRYPTION BY PASSWORD = 'stROn_G paSSWoRdS, pLE@sE!'
WITH SUBJECT = 'Certificate for Dinesh';
GO
```

Once the certificate has been created, a proxy login can be created using the **CREATE LOGIN FROM CERTIFICATE** syntax as follows:

```
CREATE LOGIN Dinesh
FROM CERTIFICATE Dinesh_Certificate;
GO
```

This login can be granted permissions, just like any other login. However, to use the permissions, the login must be mapped to a database user. This is done by creating a user using the same certificate that was used to create the login, using the **CREATE USER FOR CERTIFICATE** syntax. See the section "Stored Procedure Signing Using Certificates" later in this chapter for more information on how to use a proxy login for server-level permissions.

Database-Level Proxies

Proxy principals that operate at the database level can be created by adding a user to the database that is not associated with a server login. This is done using **CREATE USER WITHOUT LOGIN**, as shown in the following code listing:

```
CREATE USER Bob
WITHOUT LOGIN;
GO
```

This user, like any database user, can be assigned ownership and other permissions. However, it is impossible to log into the server and authenticate as Bob. Instead, you must log in using a valid server-level login and authenticate to the database with whatever database user is associated with your login. Only then can you impersonate Bob, taking on whatever permissions the user is assigned. This is discussed in detail in the section "Basic Impersonation Using EXECUTE AS" later in this chapter.

Data Security in Layers: The Onion Model

Generally speaking, the more levels that an attacker must penetrate in order to access a valuable resource, the better the chance of being able to prevent their attack. Developers should strive to construct multiple layers of protection for any sensitive data, in order to ensure that if one security measure is breached, other obstacles will keep an attacker at bay.

The first layer of defense is everything outside of the database server, all of which falls into the realm of authentication. Once a user is authenticated, SQL Server's declarative permissions system kicks in, and a login is authorized to access one or more databases, based on user mappings.

From there, each user is authorized to access specific resources in the database. Another layer that can be added for additional security here is use of stored procedures. By assigning permissions only via stored procedures, it is possible to maintain greater control over when and why escalation should take place—but more on that will be covered later in this chapter.

Of course, the stored procedure itself must have access to whatever tables and columns are required, and these resources can be further locked down if necessary, using encryption or row-level security schemes.

Figure 5-1 shows some of the layers that should be considered when defining a SQL Server security scheme, in order to maximize the protection with which sensitive data is secured. The remainder of this chapter deals primarily with how best to control access to resources using stored procedures as the primary access layer into the data once a user is authenticated.

A stored procedure layer provides an ideal layer of abstraction between data access methods and the data itself, allowing for additional security to be programmed in via parameters or other inline logic. For instance, it is trivial to log every access to sensitive data via a stored procedure, by including logging code in the procedure. Likewise, a stored procedure might be used to force users to access data on a granular basis by requiring parameters that are used as predicates to filter data. These security checks are difficult or impossible to force on callers without using stored procedures to encapsulate the data access logic.

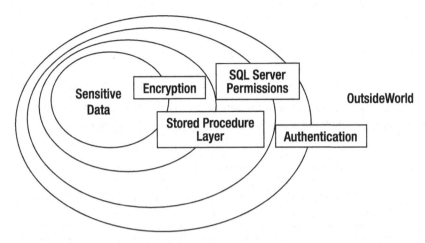

Figure 5-1. Layering security provides multiple levels of protection against attack.

Data Organization Using Schemas

SQL Server 2008 supports ANSI standard schemas, which provide a method by which tables and other objects can be segmented into logical groups. Schemas are essentially containers into which any database object can be placed, and certain actions or rules applied en masse to every item in the schema. This makes tasks such as managing authorization considerably easier since, by dividing your database into schemas, you can easily group related objects and control permissions without having to worry about what objects might be added or removed from that collection in the future. As new objects are added to a schema, existing permissions propagate, thereby allowing you to set up access rights for a given schema once, and not have to manipulate them again as the database changes.

To create a schema, use the **CREATE SCHEMA** command. The following T-SQL creates a schema called **Sales**:

```
CREATE SCHEMA Sales;
GO
```

Optionally you can specify a schema owner by using the **AUTHORIZATION** clause. If an owner is not explicitly specified, SQL Server will assign ownership to the user that creates the schema.

Once a schema is created, you can begin creating database objects within the schema, using two-part naming as follows:

```
CREATE TABLE Sales.SalesData
(
    SaleNumber int,
    SaleDate datetime
);
GO
```

If an object belongs to a schema, then it must be referenced with its associated schema name; so to select from the **SalesData** table, the following SQL is used:

```
SELECT *
FROM Sales.SalesData;
GO
```

■ **Caution** In previous versions of SQL Server, references to tables were prefixed with the name of their owner (e.g., `Owner.SalesData`). This syntax is deprecated, and two-part naming in SQL Server 2008 references a schema rather than an object owner.

The beauty of schemas becomes obvious when it is time to apply permissions to the objects in the schema. Assuming that each object should be treated identically from a permissions point of view, only a single grant is necessary to give a user access to every object within a schema. For instance, after the following T-SQL is run, the **Alejandro** user will have access to select rows from every table in the **Sales** schema, even if new tables are added later:

```
CREATE USER Alejandro
WITHOUT LOGIN;
GO

GRANT SELECT ON SCHEMA::Sales
TO Alejandro;
GO
```

It's important to note that, when initially created, the owner of any object in a schema will be the same as the owner of the schema itself. The individual object owners can be changed later, but in most cases I recommend that you keep everything in any given schema owned by the same user. This is especially important for ownership chaining, covered later in this chapter. To explicitly set the owner of an object requires the **ALTER AUTHORIZATION** command, as shown in the following T-SQL:

```
--Create a user
CREATE USER Javier
WITHOUT LOGIN;
GO

--Create a table
CREATE TABLE JaviersData
(
    SomeColumn int
);
GO

--Set Javier as the owner of the table
ALTER AUTHORIZATION ON JaviersData
TO Javier;
GO
```

As a final note on schemas, there is also a command that can be used to move objects between them. By using **ALTER SCHEMA** with the **TRANSFER** option, you can specify that a table should be moved to another schema:

```
--Create a new schema
CREATE SCHEMA Purchases;
GO

--Move the SalesData table into the new schema
ALTER SCHEMA Purchases
TRANSFER Sales.SalesData;
GO

--Reference the table by its new schema name
SELECT *
FROM Purchases.SalesData;
GO
```

Schemas are a powerful feature, and I recommend that you consider using them any time you're dealing with sets of tables that are tightly related to one another. Legacy database applications that use multiple databases in order to create logical boundaries between objects might also benefit from schemas. The multiple databases can be consolidated to a single database that uses schemas. The benefit is that the same logical boundaries will exist, but because the objects are in the same database, they can participate in declarative referential integrity and can be backed up together.

Basic Impersonation Using EXECUTE AS

Switching to a different user's execution context has long been possible in SQL Server, using the **SETUSER** command, as shown in the following code listing:

```
SETUSER 'Alejandro';
GO
```

To revert back to the previous context, call **SETUSER** again without specifying a username:

```
SETUSER;
GO
```

The **SETUSER** command is only available to members of the **sysadmin** or **db_owner** roles (at the server and database levels, respectively), and is therefore not useful for setting up least-privilege scenarios. Furthermore, although still implemented by SQL Server 2008, the Microsoft Books Online documentation states that **SETUSER** may not be supported in future versions of SQL Server, and recommends usage of the **EXECUTE AS** command instead.

The **EXECUTE AS** command can be used by any user, and access to impersonate a given user or server login is controlled by a permissions setting rather than a fixed role. The other benefit over **SETUSER** is that **EXECUTE AS** automatically reverts to the original context at the end of a module. **SETUSER**, on the other hand, leaves the impersonated context active when control is returned to the caller. This means that it is impossible to encapsulate impersonation within a stored procedure using **SETUSER** and guarantee that the caller will not be able to take control of the impersonated credentials.

To show the effects of **EXECUTE AS**, start by creating a new user and a table owned by the user:

```
CREATE USER Tom
WITHOUT LOGIN;
GO

CREATE TABLE TomsData
(
    AColumn int
);
GO

ALTER AUTHORIZATION ON TomsData TO Tom;
GO
```

Once the user is created, it can be impersonated using **EXECUTE AS**, and the impersonation context can be verified using the **USER_NAME()** function:

```
EXECUTE AS USER = 'Tom';
GO

SELECT USER_NAME();
GO
```

■ **Note** In order to use the EXECUTE AS statement to impersonate another user or login, a user must have been granted IMPERSONATE permissions on the specified target.

The **SELECT** statement returns the value **Tom**, indicating that this is the currently impersonated user. Any action performed after running **EXECUTE AS** will use Tom's credentials. For example, the user can alter the **TomsData** table, since Tom owns the table. However, an attempt to create a new table will fail, since Tom does not have permission to do so:

```
--This statement will succeed
ALTER TABLE TomsData
ADD AnotherColumn datetime;
GO

--This statement will fail with CREATE TABLE PERMISSION DENIED
CREATE TABLE MoreData
(
    YetAnotherColumn int
);
GO
```

Once you have completed working with the database in the context of Tom's permissions, you can return to the outer context by using the **REVERT** command. If you have impersonated another user inside of that context (i.e., called **EXECUTE AS** more than once), **REVERT** will have to be called multiple times in order to return context to your login. The USER_NAME() function can be checked at any time to find out whose context you are executing under.

To see the effects of nested impersonation, first be sure to revert back out of Tom's context, and then create a second user as shown following. The user will be given the right to impersonate Tom, using GRANT IMPERSONATE:

```
CREATE USER Paul
WITHOUT LOGIN;
GO

GRANT IMPERSONATE ON USER::Tom TO Paul;
GO
```

If Paul is impersonated, the session will have no privileges to select rows from the TomsData table. In order to get those permissions, Tom must be impersonated from within Paul's context:

```
EXECUTE AS USER='Paul';
GO

--Fails
SELECT *
FROM TomsData;
GO

EXECUTE AS USER='Tom';
GO

--Succeeds
SELECT *
FROM TomsData;
GO

REVERT;
GO

--Returns 'Paul' -- REVERT must be called again to fully revert
SELECT USER_NAME();
GO

REVERT;
GO
```

The most important thing to understand is that when EXECUTE AS is called, all operations will run as if you are logged in as the impersonated user. You will lose any permissions that the outer user has that the impersonated user does not have, in addition to gaining any permissions that the impersonated user has that the outer user lacks.

For logging purposes, it is sometimes important to record the actual logged-in principal. Since both the USER_NAME() function and the SUSER_NAME() function will return the names associated with the impersonated user, the ORIGINAL_LOGIN() function must be used to return the name of the outermost server login. Use of ORIGINAL_LOGIN() will allow you to get the name of the logged-in server principal, no matter how nested their impersonation scope is.

What is a module?

Each of the privilege escalation examples that follow use stored procedures to demonstrate a particular element of functionality. However, please be aware that these methods work for any kind of module that SQL Server supports, not just stored procedures. A module is defined as any kind of code container that can be created inside of SQL Server: a stored procedure, view, user-defined function, trigger, or CLR assembly.

Ownership Chaining

The most common method of securing SQL Server resources is to deny database users any direct access to SQL Server resources and provide access only via stored procedures or views. If a database user has access to execute a stored procedure, and the stored procedure is owned by the same database user that owns a resource being referenced within the stored procedure, the user executing the stored procedure will be given access to the resource via the stored procedure. This is called an **ownership chain**.

To illustrate, start by creating and switching to a new database:

```
CREATE DATABASE OwnershipChain;
GO

USE OwnershipChain;
GO
```

Now create two database users, Louis and Hugo:

```
CREATE USER Louis
WITHOUT LOGIN;
GO

CREATE USER Hugo
WITHOUT LOGIN;
GO
```

■ **Note** For this and subsequent examples in this chapter, you should connect to SQL Server using a login that is a member of the **sysadmin** server role.

Note that both of these users are created using the **WITHOUT LOGIN** option, meaning that although these users exist in the database, they are not tied to a SQL Server login, and therefore no one can authenticate as one of them by logging into the server. This option is one way of creating the kind of proxy users mentioned previously.

Once the users have been created, create a table owned by Louis:

```
CREATE TABLE SensitiveData
```

```
(
    IntegerData int
);
GO

ALTER AUTHORIZATION ON SensitiveData TO Louis;
GO
```

At this point, Hugo has no access to the table. To create an access path without granting direct permissions to the table, a stored procedure could be created, also owned by Louis:

```
CREATE PROCEDURE SelectSensitiveData
AS
BEGIN
    SET NOCOUNT ON;

    SELECT *
    FROM dbo.SensitiveData;
END;
GO

ALTER AUTHORIZATION ON SelectSensitiveData TO Louis;
GO
```

Hugo still has no permissions on the table at this point; the user needs to be given permission to execute the stored procedure:

```
GRANT EXECUTE ON SelectSensitiveData TO Hugo;
```

At this point Hugo can execute the **SelectSensitiveData** stored procedure, thereby selecting from the **SensitiveData** table. However, this only works when the following conditions are met:

1. The table and the stored procedure are both owned by the same user (in this case, **Louis**).

2. The table and the stored procedure are both in the same database.

If either of those conditions were not true, the ownership chain would break, and Hugo would have to be authorized another way to select from the table. The ownership chain would also fail if the execution context changed within the stored procedure. For example, ownership chaining will not work with dynamic SQL (for more information on dynamic SQL, refer to Chapter 8).

In the case of a stored procedure in one database requesting access to an object in another database, it is possible to maintain an ownership chain, but it gets quite a bit more complex, and security is much more difficult to maintain. To set up **cross-database ownership chaining**, the user that owns the stored procedure and the referenced table(s) must be associated with a server-level login, and each database must have the **DB_CHAINING** property set using the **ALTER DATABASE** command. That property tells SQL Server that either database can participate in a cross-database ownership chain, either as source or target—but there is no way to control the direction of the chain, so setting the option could open up security holes inadvertently.

I recommend that you avoid cross-database ownership chaining whenever possible, and instead call stored procedures in the remote database. Doing so will result in a more secure, more flexible solution. For example, moving databases to separate servers is much easier if they do not depend on one another for authentication. In addition, by using schemas appropriately, splitting objects into multiple databases is no longer as important as it once was. Consider avoiding multiple databases altogether, if at all possible.

Privilege Escalation Without Ownership Chains

Ownership chaining will not work if the object owner does not match the module owner, or if dynamic SQL is used. In these cases, you'll have to use one of the two other kinds of privilege escalation provided by SQL Server: an extension to stored procedures using the **EXECUTE AS** clause, or module signing using certificates.

Using the **EXECUTE AS** clause with stored procedures is an easy and effective method of escalating permissions, but is not nearly as flexible as that which can be achieved using certificates. With certificates, permissions are additive rather than impersonated—the additional permissions provided by the certificate extend rather than replace the permissions of the calling principal. In the following sections, I'll discuss these alternative methods of privilege escalation in more detail.

Stored Procedures and EXECUTE AS

As described in a previous section in this chapter, the **EXECUTE AS** command can be used on its own in T-SQL batches in order to temporarily impersonate other users. However, **EXECUTE AS** is also available for stored procedures, functions, and triggers. The examples in this section only focus on stored procedures, but the same principles can also be applied to the other object types.

To use **EXECUTE AS** to change the impersonation context of an entire stored procedure, add it to the **CREATE PROCEDURE** statement as in the following example:

```
CREATE PROCEDURE SelectSensitiveDataByImpersonation
WITH EXECUTE AS 'Louis'
AS
BEGIN
    SET NOCOUNT ON;

    SELECT *
    FROM dbo.SensitiveData;
END;
GO
```

When this stored procedure is executed by a user, all operations within the procedure will be evaluated as if they are being run by the **Louis** user rather than by the calling user (as is the default behavior). This includes any dynamic SQL operations, or manipulation of data in tables that the **Louis** user has access to. When the stored procedure has completed execution, context will be automatically reverted back to that of the caller.

Keep in mind that use of **EXECUTE AS** does not break ownership chains, but rather can be used to add to them and create additional flexibility. For instance, consider the following two users and associated tables:

```
CREATE USER Kevin
WITHOUT LOGIN;
GO

CREATE TABLE KevinsData
```

```
(
    SomeData int
);
GO

ALTER AUTHORIZATION ON KevinsData TO Kevin;
GO

CREATE USER Hilary
WITHOUT LOGIN;
GO

CREATE TABLE HilarysData
(
    SomeOtherData int
);
GO

ALTER AUTHORIZATION ON HilarysData TO Hilary;
GO
```

Both users, Kevin and Hilary, own tables. A stored procedure might need to be created that accesses both tables, but using ownership chaining will not work; if the procedure is owned by Kevin, ownership chaining would only allow the executing user to access **KevinsData**, and would grant no permissions on **HilarysData**. Likewise, if the procedure was owned by Hilary, then ownership chaining would not permit access to the **KevinsData** table.

One solution in this case is to combine **EXECUTE AS** with ownership chaining and create a stored procedure that is owned by one of the users, but executes under the context of the other. The following stored procedure shows how this might look:

```
CREATE PROCEDURE SelectKevinAndHilarysData
WITH EXECUTE AS 'Kevin'
AS
BEGIN
    SET NOCOUNT ON;

    SELECT *
    FROM KevinsData

    UNION ALL

    SELECT *
    FROM HilarysData;
END;
GO

ALTER AUTHORIZATION ON SelectKevinAndHilarysData TO Hilary;
GO
```

Because Hilary owns the stored procedure, ownership chaining will kick in and allow selection of rows from the **HilarysData** table. But because the stored procedure is executing under the context of the

Kevin user, permissions will also cascade for the **KevinsData** table. In this way, both permission sets can be used, combined within a single module.

Unfortunately, this is about the limit of what can be achieved using **EXECUTE AS**. For more complex permissions scenarios, it is necessary to consider signing stored procedures using certificates.

Stored Procedure Signing Using Certificates

As mentioned previously in the chapter, proxy logins and users can be created based on certificates. Creating a certificate-based proxy is by far the most flexible way of applying permissions using a stored procedure, as permissions granted via certificate are **additive**. One or more certificates can be used to sign a stored procedure, and each certificate will apply its permissions on top of the others already present, rather than replacing the permissions as happens when impersonation is performed using **EXECUTE AS**.

To create a proxy user for a certificate, you must first ensure that your database has a database master key (DMK). If you do not already have a DMK in your database, you can create one using the following code listing:

```
CREATE MASTER KEY ENCRYPTION BY PASSWORD = '5Tr()nG_|)MK_p455woRD';
```

■ **Note** The DMK forms an important part of the SQL Server encryption key hierarchy, which is discussed in the next chapter.

Then create the certificate, followed by the associated user using the **FOR CERTIFICATE** syntax:

```
CREATE CERTIFICATE Greg_Certificate
WITH SUBJECT='Certificate for Greg';
GO

CREATE USER Greg
FOR CERTIFICATE Greg_Certificate;
GO
```

Once the proxy user is created, it can be granted permissions to resources in the database, just like any other database user. But a side effect of having created the user based on a certificate is that the certificate itself can also be used to propagate permissions granted to the user. This is where stored procedure signing comes into play.

To illustrate this concept, create a table and grant **SELECT** access to the **Greg** user, as follows:

```
CREATE TABLE GregsData
(
    DataColumn int
);
GO

GRANT SELECT ON GregsData
TO Greg;
GO
```

A stored procedure can then be created that selects from the **GregsData** table, but for the sake of this example, the stored procedure will be owned by a user called **Steve**, in order to break any possible ownership chain that might result from creating both the table and the stored procedure in the same default schema:

```
CREATE PROCEDURE SelectGregsData
AS
BEGIN
    SET NOCOUNT ON;

    SELECT *
    FROM GregsData;
END;
GO

CREATE USER Steve
WITHOUT LOGIN;
GO

ALTER AUTHORIZATION ON SelectGregsData TO Steve;
GO
```

Note that at this point Steve cannot select from **GregsData**—Steve just owns the stored procedure that attempts to select data from the table. Even if granted permission to execute this stored procedure, any user (other than **Greg**) will be unable to do so successfully, as the stored procedure does not propagate permissions to the **GregsData** table:

```
CREATE USER Linchi
WITHOUT LOGIN;
GO

GRANT EXECUTE ON SelectGregsData TO Linchi;
GO

EXECUTE AS USER='Linchi';
GO

EXEC SelectGregsData;
GO
```

115

This attempt fails with the following error:

```
Msg 229, Level 14, State 5, Procedure SelectGregsData, Line 6

The SELECT permission was denied on the object 'GregsData', database

'OwnershipChain', schema 'dbo'.
```

In order to make the stored procedure work for the **Linchi** user, permissions to the **GregsData** table must be propagated through the stored procedure. This can be done by signing the procedure using the same certificate that was used to create the **Greg** user. Signing a stored procedure is done using the **ADD SIGNATURE** command (be sure to **REVERT** back out of the **Linchi** context before executing the following listing):

```
ADD SIGNATURE TO SelectGregsData
BY CERTIFICATE Greg_Certificate;
GO
```

Once the procedure is signed with the certificate, the procedure has the same permissions that the **Greg** user has; in this case, that means that any user with permission to execute the procedure will be able to select rows from the **GregsData** table when running the stored procedure.

The flexibility of certificate signing becomes apparent when you consider that you can sign a given stored procedure with any number of certificates, each of which can be associated with different users and therefore different permission sets. This means that even in an incredibly complex system with numerous security roles, it will still be possible to write stored procedures to aggregate data across security boundaries.

Keep in mind when working with certificates that any time the stored procedure is altered, all signatures will be automatically revoked by SQL Server. Therefore, it is important to keep signatures scripted with stored procedures, such that when the procedure is modified, the permissions can be easily kept in sync.

It is also important to know how to find out which certificates, and therefore which users, are associated with a given stored procedure. SQL Server's catalog views can be queried to find this information, but getting the right query is not especially obvious. The following query, which returns all stored procedures, the certificates they are signed with, and the users associated with the certificates, can be used as a starting point:

```
SELECT
    OBJECT_NAME(cp.major_id) AS signed_module,
    c.name AS certificate_name,
    dp.name AS user_name
FROM sys.crypt_properties AS cp
INNER JOIN sys.certificates AS c ON c.thumbprint = cp.thumbprint
INNER JOIN sys.database_principals dp
    ON SUBSTRING(dp.sid, 13, 32) = c.thumbprint;
```

This query is somewhat difficult to understand, so it is worth explaining here. The **sys.crypt_properties** view contains information about which modules have been signed by certificates. Each certificate has a 32-byte cryptographic hash, its *thumbprint*, which is used to find out which certificate was used to sign the module, via the **sys.certificates** view. Finally, each database principal has a security identifier, the final 32 bytes of which is the thumbprint if the principal was created from a certificate.

When this query is executed, the results show the signed module just created as follows:

signed_module	certificate_name	user_name
SelectGregsData	Greg_Certificate	Greg

Assigning Server-Level Permissions

The previous example showed only how to assign database-level permissions using a certificate. Signing a stored procedure can also be used to propagate server-level permissions, such as **BULK INSERT** or **ALTER DATABASE**. Doing so requires creation of a proxy login from a certificate, followed by creation of a database user using the same certificate. To accomplish this, the certificate must be backed up after being created, and restored in the database in which you are creating the user. Once the database user is created, the procedure to apply permissions is the same as when propagating database-level permissions.

To begin with, create a certificate in the **master** database. Unlike previous examples, this certificate must be encrypted by a password rather than by the database master key, in order to ensure its private key remains encrypted when removed from the database. Once the certificate has been created, you can use it to create a proxy login as follows:

```
USE MASTER;
GO

CREATE CERTIFICATE alter_db_certificate
    ENCRYPTION BY PASSWORD = 'stR()Ng_PaSSWoRDs are?BeST!'
    WITH SUBJECT = 'ALTER DATABASE permission';
GO

CREATE LOGIN alter_db_login FROM CERTIFICATE alter_db_certificate;
GO
```

This login, in case you can't tell from the name, will be used to propagate **ALTER DATABASE** permissions. The next step is to grant the appropriate permissions to the login:

```
GRANT ALTER ANY DATABASE TO alter_db_login;
GO
```

At this point, you must back up the certificate to a file. The certificate can then be restored from the file into the database of your choosing, and from there it can be used to create a database user that will have the same permissions as the server login, by virtue of having been created using the same certificate.

```
BACKUP CERTIFICATE alter_db_certificate
TO FILE = 'C:\alter_db.cer'
WITH PRIVATE KEY
(
    FILE = 'C:\alter_db.pvk',
```

```
    ENCRYPTION BY PASSWORD = 'YeTanOtHeR$tRoNGpaSSWoRd?',
    DECRYPTION BY PASSWORD = 'stR()Ng_PaSSWoRDs are?BeST!'
);
GO
```

Once backed up, the certificate can be restored to any user database. For the purpose of this example, we'll create a new database specifically for this purpose:

```
CREATE DATABASE alter_db_example;
GO

USE alter_db_example;
GO

CREATE CERTIFICATE alter_db_certificate
FROM FILE = 'C:\alter_db.cer'
WITH PRIVATE KEY
(
    FILE = 'C:\alter_db.pvk',
    DECRYPTION BY PASSWORD = 'YeTanOtHeR$tRoNGpaSSWoRd?',
    ENCRYPTION BY PASSWORD = 'stR()Ng_PaSSWoRDs are?BeST!'
);
GO
```

■ **Note** For more information on the CREATE CERTIFICATE statement, see Chapter 6.

It is worth noting that at this point, the certificate's physical file should probably be either deleted or backed up to a safe storage repository. Although the private key is encrypted with the password, it would certainly be possible for a dedicated attacker to crack it via brute force. And since the certificate is being used to grant **ALTER DATABASE** permissions, such an attack could potentially end in some damage being done—so play it safe with these files.

After the certificate has been created in the database, the rest of the process is just as before. Create a stored procedure that requires the privilege escalation (in this case, the stored procedure will set the database to **MULTI_USER** access mode), create a user based on the certificate, and sign the stored procedure with the certificate:

```
CREATE PROCEDURE SetMultiUser
AS
BEGIN
    ALTER DATABASE alter_db_example
    SET MULTI_USER;
END;
GO

CREATE USER alter_db_user
FOR CERTIFICATE alter_db_certificate;
GO

ADD SIGNATURE TO SetMultiUser
```

```
BY CERTIFICATE alter_db_certificate
WITH PASSWORD = 'stR()Ng_PaSSWoRDs are?BeST!';
GO
```

The permissions can now be tested. In order for propagation of server-level permissions to work, the user executing the stored procedure must be associated with a valid server login, and it is the server-level login that must be impersonated rather than the user. So this time, **CREATE USER WITHOUT LOGIN** will not suffice:

```
CREATE LOGIN test_alter WITH PASSWORD = 'iWanT2ALTER!!';
GO

CREATE USER test_alter FOR LOGIN test_alter;
GO

GRANT EXECUTE ON SetMultiUser TO test_alter;
GO
```

Finally, the **test_alter** login can be impersonated, and the stored procedure executed:

```
EXECUTE AS LOGIN='test_alter';
GO

EXEC SetMultiUser;
GO
```

The command completes successfully, demonstrating that the **test_alter** login had been able to exercise the **ALTER DATABASE** permissions granted via the stored procedure. This example was obviously quite simplistic, but it should serve as a basic template that you can adapt as necessary when you need to provide escalation of server-level privilege to database users.

Summary

SQL Server's impersonation features allow developers to create secure, granular authorization schemes. By keeping authorization layered and following a least-privilege mentality, resources in the database can be made more secure, requiring attackers to do more work in order to retrieve data they are not supposed to access. A stored procedure layer can be used to control security, delegating permissions as necessary based on a system of higher-privileged proxy users.

Schemas should be used when it is necessary to logically break apart a database into groups of objects that are similar in scope. Schemas can also be used to make assignment of permissions an easier task, as permissions may not have to be maintained over time as the objects in the schema change.

The **EXECUTE AS** clause can be a very useful and simple way of propagating permissions based on stored procedures, but certificates provide much more flexibility and control. That said, you should try to keep systems as simple and understandable as possible, in order to avoid creating maintainability nightmares.

A final note along those lines: Try not to go overboard when it comes to security. Many of the techniques laid out in this chapter are probably *not* necessary for the majority of applications. If your application does not store sensitive data, try to not go too far in creating complex privilege escalation schemes; they will only make your application more difficult to deal with.

CHAPTER 6

■ ■ ■

Encryption

Encryption is the process of encoding data in such a way as to render it unusable to anyone except those in possession of the appropriate secret knowledge (the **key**) required to decrypt that data again. The encryption capabilities provided by SQL Server 2008 are powerful features, and you should always consider using them as part of your overall security strategy. If all other security mechanisms fail, encryption can prove to be a very effective last line of defense in protecting confidential data.

Encryption should not be considered lightly, however; it is a complex subject, and the successful implementation of encryption almost invariably requires some degree of consideration at the architecture and design phase of an application. The physical act of encrypting data is relatively straightforward, but without the appropriate procedures in place to securely manage access to that data, and the keys required to decrypt it, any attempt to implement encryption is worthless. A failure to implement encryption properly can actually do more harm than good, as it leads you into a false sense of security believing that your data is safe, when in fact it is exposed to potential hackers.

Furthermore, the additional protection afforded by encryption has an associated performance cost. Typically, the database has to do more work to encrypt written data, and to decrypt it again when that data is required. This means that, particularly in large-scale environments, careful attention must be paid to ensure that encryption does not adversely affect application performance.

In this chapter I do not aim to provide a definitive guide to database encryption. Rather, I will provide a practical guide to using the main encryption features of SQL Server 2008 to create a secure, scalable database application that is capable of working with confidential data. Such a solution clearly assumes that other aspects of security, including user access control and network protection, have already been adequately addressed. I will particularly focus on the two main issues identified in the preceding paragraphs—namely, how to securely store and manage access to encryption keys, and how to design a database application architecture that protects sensitive data while minimizing the negative impact on performance.

Do You Really Need Encryption?

Before addressing the question of how to implement encryption for a given data set, it is necessary to consider whether encryption is required at all. Encryption is a method of protecting data, so the key questions to ask are *what* data are you trying to protect, and *who* (or what) are you trying to protect it from.

What Should Be Protected?

All data is important. If it were not, then we wouldn't bother storing it in a database in the first place. But that doesn't necessarily mean that all data needs to be encrypted.

Most of the encryption methods in SQL Server 2008 provide **cell-level encryption**, which is applied to individual items of data, or columns of a table that contain sensitive information. In contrast, transparent data encryption, a new feature in SQL Server 2008, applies **database-level encryption** to an entire database by encrypting the underlying database files on the file system. Not only do these approaches operate at a different scope, but they have significantly different implications for the design of any application working with encrypted data.

Before deciding on an encryption strategy, it is very important to classify data in order to identify the risk of exposure, and the severity of consequences should that data become exposed. Some examples of the types of data that might require encryption are as follows:

- Many organizations define one or more levels of **sensitive data**—that is, information that could negatively harm the business if it were allowed into the wrong hands. Such information might include pricing information, profit forecasts, or upcoming marketing plans. If a competitor were to get hold of such information, it could have severe consequences on future sales.

- Increasingly, many governments are passing laws and regulatory requirements specifying certain minimum levels of security that must be put in place to protect confidential customer data, and this can include encryption. A failure to meet these standards may result in a company facing severe fines, or even being forced to cease trading.

- Certain clients may specify minimum levels of protection required as part of a customer service level agreement. In some cases, detailed requirements specify exactly those data items that must be encrypted, the type of encryption algorithm used, the minimum length of encryption key, and the schedule by which keys must be rotated.

- In many cases it may be beneficial to encrypt employee records, particularly those that contain payroll information or other personal information, in order to prevent casual snooping by systems administrators or other users who have access to such data.

Conducting a thorough analysis of business requirements to identify all data elements that require protection and determining how that data should be protected are crucial to ensure that any proposed encryption solution adequately addresses security requirements while balancing the need for performance. In addition, the required changes to application design and business processes associated with encryption generally come at a cost, and it is important to be able to justify that cost against the perceived benefits to be gained from encryption.

What Are You Protecting Against?

Perhaps the most basic protection that encryption can offer is against the risk posed to **data at rest**. In SQL Server, *data at rest* refers to the underlying database files stored on the filesystem, including transaction logs and backups. If an unauthorized third party could gain access to those files, it would be possible for them to copy and restore the database onto their own system, allowing them to browse through your data at their leisure. If sensitive data were stored in the database in an encrypted format, however, the attacker would also need to know the relevant keys or passwords to decrypt the stolen data, without which it would be worthless to them.

Besides physical theft of database files, hackers and external threats pose a continuing risk to database security. Hackers are often very knowledgeable, and well-equipped with a range of tools to try to sniff out and exploit any weaknesses in your security systems. By ensuring that all data transmitted over a network is securely encrypted, you can be sure that it can only be understood by its intended recipient, reducing the chance of it being successfully intercepted and used against you.

Many organizations also recognize the threat to data security arising from internal sources. Disgruntled DBAs and developers testing the limits of their authorization can access data they do not require in order to do their jobs. Such information could easily find its way out of the organization and into the wrong hands if the right price were offered. If properly designed and deployed, an encryption strategy can prevent this risk from occurring.

Remember that encryption is not a replacement for other security measures, such as appropriate authentication and authorization procedures. However, if implemented correctly, it can provide an additional level of security that might be the difference between your data becoming exposed and remaining secret as intended.

SQL Server 2008 Encryption Key Hierarchy

All of the encryption methods in SQL Server, as in almost all civilian cryptography, are based on standardized, publicly available encryption algorithms. In many ways, this is a good thing: these algorithms have been developed by some of the world's leading information theorists and, in general, have been proven to withstand concentrated, deliberate attack. However, this use of public knowledge places an interesting assumption on the design of any database application that deals with confidential data, namely, *The enemy knows the system.*

Shannon's maxim, as the preceding statement is commonly known, is a restatement of earlier work by the Dutch cryptographer Auguste Kerchoffs. Kerchoffs proposed a number of principles that, if followed, ensured that military ciphers could remain secure, even when some facts about the system became revealed. Originally published in a French journal, *le Journal des Sciences Militaires*, in 1883, these principles are still very relevant in modern cryptography.

All of the SQL Server encryption methods use an algorithm based on a secret key, or a password from which a key is generated. If we assume that Shannon's maxim holds (i.e., that the details of any encryption algorithm used are public knowledge), then the security of your encrypted data rests *entirely* on protection of the secret key that the algorithm uses to decrypt and encrypt data. Creating a safe environment in which to store your keys must therefore be considered a top priority of any encryption strategy. Indeed, the issues of secure key management and distribution are among the most important areas of modern cryptography, as a failure to properly protect encryption keys compromises your entire security strategy. Before investigating the different types of encryption available in SQL Server, it is first necessary to consider how to manage the keys on which those encryption methods are based.

The Automatic Key Management Hierarchy

The way in which SQL Server addresses the problem of secure key management is to implement a hierarchy of encryption keys, with each key providing protection for those keys below it. The **automatic key management** hierarchy is illustrated in Figure 6-1.

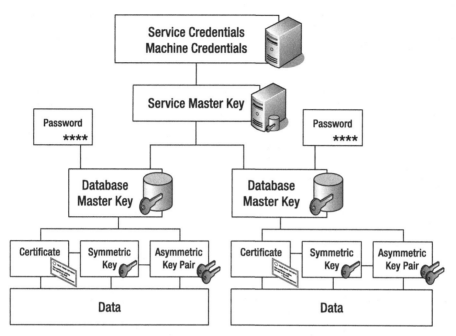

Figure 6-1. The default automatic key management hierarchy in SQL Server 2008

The main features of the automatic key management hierarchy are described under the headings that follow.

Symmetric Keys, Asymmetric Keys, and Certificates

At the lowest level, items of data are encrypted with a **symmetric key**, the public key of an **asymmetric key pair**, or a **certificate**. These keys and certificates are stored in the user database in which they were created. Each of these three methods offers different advantages and disadvantages, which will be discussed later in this chapter.

The syntax for creating each type of key differs slightly, but follows the same basic pattern: listing the name of the key, the encryption algorithm to be used, the name of the database user who will own the key, and the method by which the key will be protected. For example, the following code listing demonstrates the syntax required to create an asymmetric 1,024 bit key using the Rivest, Shamir, and Adleman (RSA) algorithm, owned by the database user **Tom**:

```
CREATE ASYMMETRIC KEY ExampleAsymKey
AUTHORIZATION Tom
WITH ALGORITHM = RSA_1024;
```

In this example, there is no explicitly specified method of protection, so the key will be protected by the automatic key hierarchy. By default, this means that keys and certificates are protected by the **database master key** (DMK) of the database in which they reside.

Database Master Key

Each user database on a server can have its own DMK, which is a symmetric key stored in both the **master** database and the user database. The DMK is protected by two different forms of encryption: an encryption using the Triple DES (Data Encryption Standard) algorithm based on the **service master key** (SMK) of the server, and also encryption by a password.

Even though protected by both the SMK *and* a password, by default SQL Server can automatically open the DMK when required by decrypting with the SMK alone, without needing to be supplied with the password. This means that users of any dependent private keys protected by the DMK do not need to be granted explicit rights to open the DMK. Users only require permissions on the individual dependent keys or certificates, as SQL Server will open the DMK to access those keys as necessary. This has some implications for protecting data from **sysadmin**s and **db_owner**s, which will be discussed later.

A DMK can be created by running the **CREATE MASTER KEY** statement in the database in which the key is to be stored, as follows:

```
CREATE MASTER KEY ENCRYPTION BY PASSWORD = '5Tr()ng_p455woRD_4_dA_DMK!!!';
```

■ **Note** Each database can have only one associated DMK. If you followed the examples in Chapter 5, you may have already created a DMK in order to create a proxy database user from a certificate.

Service Master Key

The SMK is a symmetric key that sits at the top of the SQL Server encryption hierarchy, and is used to encrypt all DMKs stored on the server, as well as protect logins and credentials associated with linked servers.

The SMK is protected by the **Data Protection API** (DPAPI) of the operating system, using the service account credentials and the machine credentials of the SQL Server. If either one of these credentials becomes invalid (such as, for example, if the service account is changed), SQL Server will re-create the invalid key based on the remaining valid key. This ensures that the SMK will remain robust from all but the most severe of failures. There is no command to create an SMK; it is created automatically the first time it is required and stored in the **master** database.

The SMK provides the top level of control over all encryption keys that are contained within the automatic key hierarchy implemented by SQL Server 2008. The hierarchical structure protected by the SMK provides sufficient security for most situations, and makes key access relatively easy: permissions to use individual keys or subtrees of keys within the hierarchy are granted to individuals or groups using the **GRANT** command, and such keys can be opened and used by authorized users as required.

Alternative Encryption Management Structures

There are some occasions where you may want to augment or replace the default automatic key management with alternative methods to protect your encryption keys. The flexible encryption key management structure in SQL Server 2008 provides several ways for doing this, as I'll now discuss.

Symmetric Key Layering and Rotation

Symmetric keys within a database may themselves be **layered** to provide additional levels of hierarchy. For example, a symmetric key may be encrypted by another symmetric key, which is then protected by a certificate protected by the DMK. Layering keys in this way can provide additional control and security, and makes it easier to facilitate **key rotation**, where middle layers of keys can be changed without having to decrypt and reencrypt all of the underlying data.

Key rotation using a flat model, which is based on only a single encryption key, is very cumbersome. To understand why, suppose that you had a very large amount of data encrypted by a single symmetric key. Now suppose that, as a result of a new client requirement, that encryption key had to be rotated every month. Rotation would require decrypting and reencrypting all of the data with a new key, which could require a considerable amount of effort, and may require the data to at least temporarily enter an unencrypted state before reencryption with the new key. In a layered model, you can rotate higher keys very easily, since the only encrypted data they contain is the symmetric key used by the next lower level of encryption.

Not all keys need to be rotated at once; rotation of any key in the hierarchy will reencrypt all dependent keys, which makes it significantly harder for any brute force attacks to break through your encryption hierarchy and obtain access to your sensitive data. However, bear in mind that, although properly handled key rotation generally improves security, key rotation does involve a certain level of inherent risk. Archived encrypted data stored on a tape backup, for example, may be kept safer by being left in a physically secure location than by having the tape retrieved in order to perform reencryption of the data with a new key.

When creating additional layers of keys, you should try to ensure that higher levels of keys have the same or greater encryption strength than the keys that they protect. Protecting a strong key with a weaker key does not add any additional security to the system.

Removing Keys from the Automatic Encryption Hierarchy

When a DMK is protected by both the SMK and a password, as in the default hierarchy, you do not need to explicitly provide the password in order to open the DMK; when a user with appropriate permissions requests a key protected by the DMK, SQL Server opens the DMK automatically using the SMK to access the required dependent keys. One interesting feature of this behavior is that system administrators or DBAs in the **db_owner** role, who have **GRANT** permission on the database, therefore have permission to view *all* dependent keys in the hierarchy.

In cases where you want to restrict access to encrypted data from individuals in these roles, it is necessary to drop the DMK protection by SMK, which will enforce the DMK protection by password instead. The following T-SQL, when run in a database on which the user has **CONTROL** permission, will drop the SMK protection on the DMK associated with that database:

```
ALTER MASTER KEY DROP ENCRYPTION BY SERVICE MASTER KEY;
```

When protected only by a password, a DMK is removed from the default automatic key management hierarchy, and must be explicitly opened by a user with the appropriate password every time it is required:

```
OPEN MASTER KEY DECRYPTION BY PASSWORD = '5Tr()ng_p455woRD_4_dA_DMK!!!';

-- Perform some action on properties dependent on the DMK

CLOSE MASTER KEY;
```

Individual symmetric keys, asymmetric keys, and certificates may also be protected by passwords to prevent them from being opened unless supplied with the appropriate password on every occasion.

The problem with removing keys from the automatic key hierarchy is that it then becomes necessary to have a system that protects the passwords that secure those keys. Unless *this* system is designed with adequate security measures, the encrypted data becomes no more secure (and possibly less secure) with password protected keys than it was when encrypted with keys held under automatic key management.

Extensible Key Management

SQL Server 2008 supports management of encryption keys by extensible key management (EKM) methods. EKM uses an external hardware security module (HSM) to hold symmetric or asymmetric keys outside of SQL Server, and delegates the management of those keys to the HSM.

The following code listing illustrates the syntax required to create an asymmetric key in SQL Server mapped to a key stored on an EKM device:

```
CREATE ASYMMETRIC KEY EKMAsymKey
    FROM PROVIDER EKM_Provider
    WITH
        ALGORITHM = RSA_1024,
        CREATION_DISPOSITION = OPEN_EXISTING,
        PROVIDER_KEY_NAME  = 'EKMKey1';
GO
```

EKM provides a total encryption management solution using dedicated hardware, which means that SQL Server can leave the process of encryption to the HSM and concentrate on other tasks. Implementing EKM involves using vendor-specific libraries to configure the connection between SQL Server and the HSM unit, and is not covered in this chapter.

Figure 6-2 illustrates the different encryption configurations discussed in this section that provide alternatives to the default automatic key management hierarchy.

Each of these possible encryption configurations has different implications on the level of security offered, the ease with which keys can be managed, and the performance impacts for accessing and manipulating the underlying data. To understand more about these differences, it's necessary to have a more detailed look at the various methods by which individual items of data can be encrypted, which will be covered in the next part of this chapter.

Before going any further, run the following code listing to create a new database and associated DMK:

```
CREATE DATABASE ExpertSqlEncryption;
GO
USE ExpertSqlEncryption;
GO
CREATE MASTER KEY ENCRYPTION BY PASSWORD = '-=+I_aM-tH3-DMK_P45sWOrd+=-';
GO
```

This database will be used for all of the examples following in this chapter.

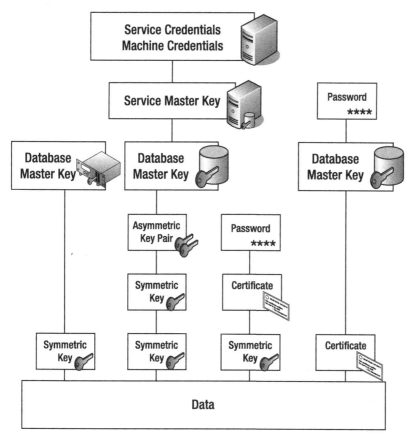

Figure 6-2. Alternative encryption key management structures (from left to right): symmetric key protection by EKM; layered symmetric keys; symmetric key encrypted by password-protected certificate; DMK protected by password rather than SMK

Data Protection and Encryption Methods

SQL Server 2008 provides a range of encryption methods that provide differing levels of protection together with differing associated performance and architecture implications. I will not attempt to describe the full details of every method here; readers who are interested in a detailed description of each method should consult a book dedicated to the subject, such as *Expert SQL Server 2008 Encryption*, by Michael Coles (Apress, 2009). However, I will give a brief overview of the following methods:

- Hashing
- Symmetric key encryption
- Asymmetric key encryption
- Transparent data encryption

Hashing

A hashing function allows you to perform a **one-way** encryption of any data, with deterministic results. By "deterministic," I mean that a given input into the hashing function will always produce the same output. Hashing, in itself, is arguably not a true method of encryption, because once a value has been hashed there is no way to reverse the process to obtain the original input. However, hashing methods are often used in conjunction with encryption, as will be demonstrated later in this chapter.

SQL Server 2008 provides the **HASHBYTES** function, which produces a binary hash of any supplied data using one of a number of standard hashing algorithms. For any given input x, **HASHBYTES(x)** will always produce the same output y, but there is no method provided to retrieve x from the resulting value y. Figure 6-3 illustrates the **HASHBYTES** function in action.

HASHBYTES is useful in situations where you need to compare whether two secure values are the same, but when you are not concerned with what the actual values are: for example, to verify that the password supplied by a user logging into an application matches the stored password for that user. In such cases, instead of comparing the two values directly, you can compare the hashes of each value; if any two given values are equal, then the hashes of those values produced using a given algorithm will also be the same.

Although hash algorithms are deterministic, so that a given input value will always generate the same hash, it is theoretically possible that two different source inputs will share the same hash. Such occurrences, known as **hash collisions**, are relatively rare but important to bear in mind from a security point of view. In a totally secure environment, you cannot be certain that simply because two hashes are equal, the values that generated those hashes were the same.

The **HASHBYTES** function supports the Message Digest (MD) algorithms MD2, MD4, MD5, and the Secure Hash Algorithm (SHA) algorithms SHA, and SHA1. Of these, SHA1 is the strongest, and is the algorithm you should specify in all cases unless you have a good reason otherwise. The following code listing illustrates the result of the **HASHBYTES** function used to hash a plain text string using the SHA1 algorithm:

```
SELECT HASHBYTES('SHA1', 'The quick brown fox jumped over the lazy dog');
GO
```

The hash generated in this case is as follows:

0xF6513640F3045E9768B239785625CAA6A2588842

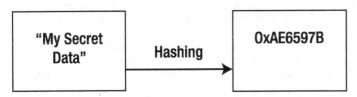

Figure 6-3. The HASHBYTES function in action

This result is entirely repeatable—you can execute the preceding query as many times as you want and you will always receive the same output. This deterministic property of hash functions is both their greatest strength and their greatest weakness.

The advantage of obtaining consistent output is that, from a data architecture point of view, hashed data can be stored, indexed, and retrieved just like any other binary data, meaning that queries of hashed data can be designed to operate efficiently with a minimum amount of query redesign. However, there is a risk that potential attackers can compile a dictionary of known hashes for different algorithms and use these to perform reverse-lookups against your data in order to try to guess the source values. This risk becomes even more plausible in cases where attackers can make reasonable assumptions in order to reduce the list of likely source values. For example, in systems where password strength is not enforced, users who are not security-minded typically choose short, simple passwords or easily predicted variations on common words. If a hacker were to obtain a dataset containing hashes of such passwords generated using the MD5 algorithm, they would only have to search for occurrences of **0x2AC9CB7DC02B3C0083EB70898E549B63** to identify all those users who had chosen to use "Password1" as their password, for example.

Hashes can be made more secure by adding a secret **salt** value to the plain text prior to hashing, as will be shown later in this chapter.

Symmetric Key Encryption

Symmetric key encryption methods use the same single key to perform both encryption and decryption of data. This is illustrated in Figure 6-4.

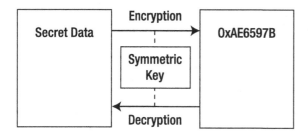

Figure 6-4. Symmetric key encryption

Unlike hashing, which is deterministic, symmetric encryption is a nondeterministic process. That is to say, you will obtain different results from encrypting the same item of data on different occasions, even if it is encrypted with the same key each time.

SQL Server 2008 supports a number of common symmetric encryption algorithms, including Triple DES, and keys with bit lengths of 128, 192, and 256 based on the Advanced Encryption Standard (AES). The strongest symmetric key supported is AES256.

Symmetric keys themselves can be protected either by a certificate, password, asymmetric key, or another symmetric key, or they can be protected outside SQL Server by an EKM provider.

The following example illustrates how to create a new symmetric key, **SymKey1**, that is protected by a password:

```
CREATE SYMMETRIC KEY SymKey1
WITH ALGORITHM = AES_256
ENCRYPTION BY PASSWORD = '5yMm3tr1c_K3Y_P@$$wOrd!';
GO
```

■ **Note** By default, symmetric keys created using the `CREATE SYMMETRIC KEY` statement are randomly generated. If you want to generate a specific, reproduceable key, you must explicitly specify the `KEY_SOURCE` and `IDENTITY_VALUE` options when the key is generated, such as follows: `CREATE SYMMETRIC KEY StaticKey WITH KEY_SOURCE = '#K3y_50urc£#'`, `IDENTITY_VALUE = '-=1d3nt1ty_VA1uE!=-'`, `ALGORITHM = TRIPLE_DES ENCRYPTION BY PASSWORD = 'P@55wOrD'`;

To encrypt data using a symmetric key, you must first open the key. Since **SymKey1** is protected by a password, to open this key you must provide the associated password using the **OPEN SYMMETRIC KEY DECRYPTION BY PASSWORD** syntax. Having opened the key, you can use it to encrypt data by providing the plain text to be encrypted, together with the **GUID** of the symmetric key, to the **ENCRYPTBYKEY** method. Once you are finished using the key, you should close it again using **CLOSE SYMMETRIC KEY** (if you fail to explicitly close any open symmetric keys, they will automatically be closed at the end of a session). These steps are illustrated in the following code listing:

```
-- Open the key
OPEN SYMMETRIC KEY SymKey1
DECRYPTION BY PASSWORD = '5yMm3tr1c_K3Y_P@$$wOrd!';

-- Declare the cleartext to be encrypted
DECLARE @Secret nvarchar(255) = 'This is my secret message';

-- Encrypt the message
SELECT  ENCRYPTBYKEY(KEY_GUID(N'SymKey1'), @secret);

-- Close the key again
CLOSE SYMMETRIC KEY SymKey1;
GO
```

The result of the preceding code listing is an encrypted binary value, such as that shown following:

```
0x007937851F763944BD71F451E4E50D520100000097A76AED7AD1BD77E04A4BE68404AA3B48FF6179A
D9FD74E10EE8406CC489D7CD8407F7EC34A879BB34BA9AF9D6887D1DD2C835A71B760A527B0859D47B3
8EED
```

■ **Note** Remember that encryption is a nondeterministic process, so the results that you obtain will differ from those just shown.

Decrypting data that has been encrypted using a symmetric key follows a similar process as for encryption, but using the **DECRYPTBYKEY** method rather than the **ENCRYPTBYKEY** method. A further difference to note is that the only parameter required by **DECRYPTBYKEY** is the ciphertext to be decrypted;

there is no need to specify the **GUID** of the symmetric key that was used to encrypt the data, as this value is stored as part of the encrypted data itself.

The following code listing illustrates how to decrypt the data encrypted with a symmetric key in the previous example:

```
OPEN SYMMETRIC KEY SymKey1
DECRYPTION BY PASSWORD = '5yMm3tr1c_K3Y_P@$$wOrd!';

DECLARE @Secret nvarchar(255) = 'This is my secret message';
DECLARE @Encrypted varbinary(max);

SET @Encrypted = ENCRYPTBYKEY(KEY_GUID(N'SymKey1'),@secret);

SELECT CAST(DECRYPTBYKEY(@Encrypted) AS nvarchar(255));

CLOSE SYMMETRIC KEY SymKey1;
GO
```

This results in the original plain text message being retrieved:

```
This is my secret message
```

On occasions, you may wish to encrypt data without having to deal with the issues associated with creating and securely storing a permanent symmetric key. In such cases, the **ENCRYPTBYPASSPHRASE** function may prove useful.

ENCRYPTBYPASSPHRASE generates a symmetric key using the Triple DES algorithm based on the value of a supplied password, and uses that key to encrypt a supplied plain text string. The main benefit of this method is that it does not require the creation or storage of any keys or certificates; when the data needs to be decrypted, you simply supply the same password to the **DECRYPTBYPASSPHRASE** method, which enables the identical symmetric key to be generated to decrypt the ciphertext. The key itself is never stored at any point, and is only generated transiently as and when it is required.

To encrypt data using a passphrase, supply a passphrase followed by a clear text string to the **ENCRYPTBYPASSPHRASE** function as follows:

```
SELECT ENCRYPTBYPASSPHRASE('PassPhrase', 'My Other Secret Message');
GO
```

When I ran this code listing, I obtained the binary value shown following. However, remember that **ENCRYPTBYPASSPHRASE** uses nondeterministic symmetric encryption, so you will obtain different results every time you execute this query.

```
0x010000007A65B54B1797E637F3F018C4100468B115CB5B88BEA1A7C36432B0B93B8F616AC8D3BA7307D5005E
```

To decrypt the data again, pass the same passphrase and the encrypted text into the **DECRYPTBYPASSPHRASE** function. As with all the asymmetric and symmetric encryption methods provided by SQL Server, the resulting decrypted data is returned using the **varbinary** datatype, and may need to be converted into the appropriate format for your application. In this case, **CAST**ing the result to a **varchar** returns the original plain text string:

```
SELECT CAST(DECRYPTBYPASSPHRASE('PassPhrase',
0x010000007A65B54B1797E637F3F018C4100468B115CB5B88BEA1A7C36432B0B93B8F616AC8D3BA7307
D5005E) AS varchar(32));
GO
```

My Other Secret Message

As demonstrated, **ENCRYPTBYPASSPHRASE** is a very simple method of implementing symmetric encryption without the issues associated with key management. However, it is not without its drawbacks:

Firstly, ciphertext generated by **ENCRYPTBYPASSPHRASE** can be decrypted only when used in conjunction with the passphrase used to encrypt it. This may seem like an obvious point, but bear in mind that SQL Server provides no mechanism for backing up or recreating the passphrase, so, if it is ever lost, the original data can never be restored. This means that you need to consider strategies for how to backup the passphrase in a secure manner; there is not much point encrypting your data if the passphrase containing the only knowledge required to access that data is stored in an openly accessible place.

Secondly, the **ENCRYPTBYPASSPHRASE** function always encrypts data using the Triple DES algorithm. Although this is a well-recognized and widely used standard, some business requirements or client specifications may require stronger encryption algorithms, such as those based on AES. Although AES symmetric keys of bit lengths 128, 192, and 256 may be created in SQL Server 2008, these cannot be used by **ENCRYPTBYPASSPHRASE**.

The strength of the symmetric key is entirely dependent on the passphrase from which it is generated, but SQL Server does not enforce any degree of password complexity on the passphrase supplied to **ENCRYPTBYPASSPHRASE**. This may lead to weak encryption strength based on a poorly chosen key.

The supplied clear text can only be **varchar** or **nvarchar** type (although this limitation is fairly easily overcome by **CAST**ing any other datatype prior to encryption).

Despite these weaknesses, **ENCRYPTBYPASSPHRASE** can still be a useful choice in certain situations, such as when it is necessary to encrypt data from users in the **sysadmin** and **db_owner** roles. See the sidebar entitled "Protecting Information from the DBA" for more information on this topic.

Protecting Information from the DBA

The recent trend in outsourcing or offshoring of corporate IT departments, combined with ever more stringent regulations about who should be allowed access to sensitive data, has meant that it is an increasingly common requirement to restrict access to sensitive data, even from those users in the `sysadmin` and `db_owner` roles.

DBAs have permissions to view, insert, update, and delete data from any database table, and any DBAs in the `sysadmin` role have control over every key and certificate held on a SQL Server instance. How then do you design database architecture that secures data from these users? Any solution that relies upon the automatic key management hierarchy will not work; the only approach is to rely on a password that is kept secret from these users. This password can either be used with the `ENCRYPTBYPASSPHRASE` function, or it can be used to secure a certificate or asymmetric key that protects the symmetric key with which the data is encrypted.

Even then, there are risks to be aware of; the `sysadmin` can still `DROP` any keys, and you must ensure that whenever the password is supplied, it is done so in a secure manner that cannot be detected as it passes across the network or by profiling of the database.

Asymmetric Key Encryption

Asymmetric encryption is performed using a pair of related keys: the **public key** is used to encrypt data, and the associated **private key** is used to decrypt the resulting ciphertext. The public and private keys of an asymmetric key pair are related, but the mathematical relationship between them is sufficiently complex that it is not feasible to derive one key from knowledge of the other. Figure 6-5 illustrates the asymmetric encryption model.

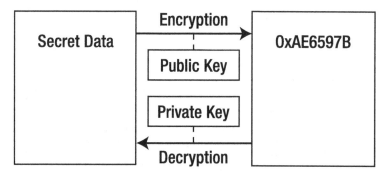

Figure 6-5. Asymmetric key encryption

In addition to asymmetric key pairs, asymmetric encryption may also be implemented using a **certificate**. Certificates based on the X.509 standard are used to bind a public key to a given identity entitled to encrypt data using the associated key. Certificates may be issued by a third-party certification authority (CA), and self-signed certificates can be created within SQL Server 2008 itself. Self-signed certificates were used in the last chapter to demonstrate one method of assigning permissions to stored procedures.

Encryption by certificate and encryption by asymmetric key use the same algorithm and, assuming equal key length, provide exactly the same encryption strength. For every method that deals with asymmetric key encryption in SQL Server, an equivalent method provides the same functionality for certificate encryption.

Asymmetric Keys or Certificates?

Certificate and asymmetric key encryption both use the same widely used RSA algorithm. Assuming equal key length, certificate and asymmetric encryption will provide the same encryption strength, and there are no significant differences between the functionality available with either type. So, which should you choose?

The decision may be influenced by whether you choose to generate the key within SQL Server itself or from an outside source. Self-signed certificates in SQL Server can only have a key length of 1024 bits, whereas stronger asymmetric keys may be created with a private key length of 512, 1024, or 2048 bits. However, asymmetric keys and certificates may both be imported from external sources, in which case the key length may be up to 3456 bits.

I recommend asymmetric encryption using certificates rather than asymmetric key pairs, as certificates allow for additional metadata to be stored alongside the key (such as expiry dates), and certificates can easily be backed up to a CER file using the **BACKUP CERTIFICATE** command, whereas a method to provide the equivalent functionality for an asymmetric key pair is strangely lacking.

As explained previously, by default the private keys of asymmetric key pairs and certificates are protected by the DMK, which is automatically used to open these keys as and when they are required by any users who have been granted permission to the relevant securable.

The following code listing illustrates how to create a 1024-bit asymmetric key using the RSA algorithm:

```
CREATE ASYMMETRIC KEY AsymKey1
WITH Algorithm = RSA_1024;
GO
```

Encrypting data using the asymmetric key follows a slightly different process than for symmetric encryption, as there is no need to explicitly open an asymmetric key prior to encryption or decryption. Instead, you pass the ID of the asymmetric key and the plain text to be encrypted to the **ENCRYPTBYASYMKEY** method, as demonstrated in the following code listing:

```
DECLARE @Secret nvarchar(255) = 'This is my secret message';
DECLARE @Encrypted varbinary(max);

SET @Encrypted = ENCRYPTBYASYMKEY(ASYMKEY_ID(N'AsymKey1'), @Secret);

GO
```

The **DECRYPTBYASYMKEY** (and the equivalent **DECRYPTBYCERT**) functions can be used to return the **varbinary** representation of any asymmetrically encrypted data, by supplying the key ID and encrypted ciphertext, as follows:

```
DECLARE @Secret nvarchar(255) = 'This is my secret message';
DECLARE @Encrypted varbinary(max);

SET @Encrypted = ENCRYPTBYASYMKEY(ASYMKEY_ID(N'AsymKey1'), @secret);

SELECT
  CAST(DECRYPTBYASYMKEY(ASYMKEY_ID(N'AsymKey1'), @Encrypted) AS nvarchar(255));

GO
```

You may have noticed when running the preceding code samples that, even when only dealing with a very small amount of data, asymmetric encryption and decryption methods are much slower than the equivalent symmetric functions. This is one of the reasons that, even though asymmetric encryption provides stronger protection than symmetric encryption, it is not recommended for encrypting any column that will be used to filter rows in a query, or where more than one or two records will be decrypted at a time. Instead, asymmetric encryption is most useful as a method to protect other encryption keys, as will be discussed later in this chapter.

Transparent Data Encryption

Transparent data encryption (TDE) is a new feature available in the Developer and Enterprise editions of SQL Server 2008. It is "transparent" in that, unlike all of the previous methods listed, it requires no explicit change to database architecture, and it doesn't necessitate queries to be rewritten using specific methods to encrypt or decrypt data. In addition, generally speaking, it is not necessary to deal with any key management issues relating to TDE. So how does TDE work?

Rather than operating on chosen values or columns of data, transparent encryption provides automatic symmetric encryption and decryption of *all* data passing from the file system layer to the SQL Server process. In other words, the MDF and LDF files in which database information is saved are stored in an encrypted state. When SQL Server makes a request for data in these files, it is automatically decrypted at the I/O level. The query engine can therefore operate on it just as it does any other kind of data. When the data is written back to disk, TDE automatically encrypts it again.

TDE provides encryption of (almost) all data within any database for which it is enabled, based on the **database encryption key** (DEK) stored in the user database. The DEK is a symmetric key protected by a server certificate stored in the **master** database, which, in turn, is protected by the DMK of the **master** database and the SMK.

To enable TDE on a database, you first need to create a server certificate in the **master** database (assuming that the **master** database already has a DMK):

```
USE MASTER;
GO

CREATE CERTIFICATE TDE_Cert
WITH SUBJECT = 'Certificate for TDE Encryption';
GO
```

Then use the **CREATE DATABASE ENCRYPTION KEY** statement to create the DEK in the appropriate user database:

```
USE ExpertSqlEncryption;
GO

CREATE DATABASE ENCRYPTION KEY
WITH ALGORITHM  = AES_128
ENCRYPTION BY SERVER CERTIFICATE TDE_Cert;
GO
```

■ **Note** The preceding code listing will generate a warning message advising you to make a backup of the server certificate with which the DEK is encrypted. In a production environment, I suggest that you read this message carefully and follow its advice. Should the certificate become unavailable, you will be unable to decrypt the DEK, and all data in the associated database will be lost.

Having created the necessary keys, TDE can be enabled using a single T-SQL statement, as follows:

```
ALTER DATABASE ExpertSqlEncryption
SET ENCRYPTION ON;
GO
```

To check the encryption status of all the databases on a server, you can query the **sys.dm_database_encryption_keys** view, as follows:

```
SELECT
  DB_NAME(database_id) AS database_name,
  CASE encryption_state
    WHEN 0 THEN 'Unencrypted (No database encryption key present)'
    WHEN 1 THEN 'Unencrypted'
    WHEN 2 THEN 'Encryption in Progress'
    WHEN 3 THEN 'Encrypted'
    WHEN 4 THEN 'Key Change in Progress'
    WHEN 5 THEN 'Decryption in Progress'
    END AS encryption_state,
    key_algorithm,
    key_length
  FROM sys.dm_database_encryption_keys;
GO
```

The results indicate that both the **ExpertSqlEncryption** user database and the **tempdb** system database are now encrypted:

database_name	encryption_state	key_algorithm	key_length
tempdb	Encrypted	AES	256
ExpertSqlEncryption	Encrypted	AES	128

This demonstrates an important point: since **tempdb** is a shared system resource utilized by all user databases, if *any* user database on a SQL Server instance is encrypted with TDE, then the **tempdb** database must also be encrypted, as in this case.

Disabling TDE is as simple as the process to enable it:

```
ALTER DATABASE ExpertSqlEncryption
SET ENCRYPTION OFF;
GO
```

Note that, even after TDE has been turned off all user databases, the **tempdb** database will remain encrypted until it is re-created, such as when the server is next restarted.

■ **Note** For more information on the columns available in **sys.dm_database_encryption_keys**, please consult **http://msdn.microsoft.com/en-us/library/bb677274.aspx**.

The benefits of TDE are as follows:

- Data at rest is encrypted (well, not quite *all* data at rest; see the following section). If your primary goal is to prevent physical theft of your data, TDE ensures that your database files (including transaction logs and backups) cannot be stolen and restored onto another machine without the necessary DKM.

- TDE can be applied to existing databases without requiring any application recoding. As a result, TDE can be applied in cases where it would not be viable to redesign existing production applications to incorporate cell-level encryption.

- Performing encryption and decryption at the I/O level is efficient, and the overall impact on database performance is small. Microsoft estimates average performance degradation as a result of enabling TDE to be in the region of 3 to 5 percent.

TDE is certainly a useful addition to the cell-level encryption methods provided by SQL Server, and if used correctly can serve to strengthen protection of your data. However, it would be a gross mistake to believe that merely by enabling TDE your data will be protected. Although on the surface TDE appears to simplify the process of encryption, in practice it hides the complexity that is necessary to ensure a truly secure solution.

There are almost no cases in which it is a business requirement to encrypt every item of data in an entire database. However, the ease with which TDE can be enabled means that, in some cases, it is a simpler option to turn on TDE than perform a proper analysis of each data element. Such actions indicate a lack of planning toward a secure encryption strategy, and are unlikely to provide the level of protection required in a high-security application.

There are also some important differences between TDE and the cell-level methods discussed previously:

- TDE only protects data at rest. When data is requested by SQL Server, it is decrypted, so all in-process data is unencrypted. All data that a user has permission to access will always be presented to the user in an unencrypted state.

- Encryption cannot be controlled at a granular level—either the whole database is encrypted or it is not.

- There is a performance impact on *every* query run against a database that has TDE enabled, whether that query contains "confidential" items of data or not. In fact, because the `tempdb` database must be encrypted when TDE is enabled, there is a performance hit against *every query of every database* on a server that has at least one TDE-enabled database on it.

- TDE negates any reduction in size of database files achieved from using SQL Server 2008's compression options. Compression algorithms only work effectively when there are recognizable patterns in the data, which TDE encryption removes.

- Not all data can be encrypted. For example, the `filestream` datatype stores BLOB data directly to the filesystem. Since this data does not pass through the SQL OS, it cannot be encrypted by TDE.

It is important to realize that TDE provides a totally different model of encryption than the other encryption methods discussed in this chapter. Cell-level encryption methods, such as **ENCRYPTBYKEY** and **ENCRYPTBYASYMKEY**, encrypt an individual item or column of data. TDE, in contrast, applies to the database level. As such, TDE has more in common with encryption methods provided at the operating system level, such as encrypting file system (EFS) technology and Windows BitLocker.

Although useful in some situations, I do not consider TDE to provide sufficient security or control over encrypted data to be relied upon for high-security applications. I will therefore not consider it in the remaining sections in this chapter.

Balancing Performance and Security

Symmetric keys, asymmetric keys, passwords, and certificates . . . each have their own advantages and disadvantages, so how do you choose between them? In this section I'll describe an architecture that means that you don't have to make a compromise between different individual encryption methods; rather, you can combine the best features of each approach into a single hybrid model.

The hybrid model of encryption described in this section is illustrated in Figure 6-6.

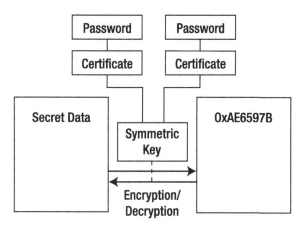

Figure 6-6. A hybrid approach to encryption.

The elements of the hybrid encryption structure can be described as follows:

- Data is encrypted using a symmetric key, which provides the best-performing encryption method. I recommend encryption based on the AES algorithm, and choosing a key length appropriate for your needs. Longer keys provide more protection, but also require more processing overhead.

- The symmetric key is protected by one or more certificates, which provide the strength of asymmetric encryption together with additional benefits, such as the ability to back up and restore certificates from T-SQL, as well as the option to set explicit start and expiration dates for the validity of the certificate. I tend to create one certificate for each user or group of users that need access to the symmetric key. Those same certificates can also be used to encrypt other keys required by that user or group of users.

- Each certificate is protected with a (strong) password, so that it can only be accessed by individuals with knowledge of the password. This means that encrypted information is kept secret from **sysadmin**s, who could otherwise use the DMK to open the certificate and underlying symmetric key.

- Further layers of encryption can be added to this model by protecting the symmetric key with further symmetric keys prior to encryption by the certificate. Each additional layer creates a further barrier for potential hackers to break, and also makes key rotation much easier to facilitate.

To illustrate how to create the hybrid encryption model just described, first create two users:

```
CREATE USER FinanceUser WITHOUT LOGIN;
CREATE USER MarketingUser WITHOUT LOGIN;
GO
```

Then create a certificate for each user, each with their own password:

```
CREATE CERTIFICATE FinanceCertificate
  AUTHORIZATION FinanceUser
  ENCRYPTION BY PASSWORD = '#F1n4nc3_P455w()rD#'
  WITH SUBJECT = 'Certificate for Finance',
  EXPIRY_DATE = '20101031';

CREATE CERTIFICATE MarketingCertificate
  AUTHORIZATION MarketingUser
  ENCRYPTION BY PASSWORD = '-+M@Rket1ng-P@s5wOrD!+-'
  WITH SUBJECT = 'Certificate for Marketing',
  EXPIRY_DATE = '20101105';
GO
```

We'll also create a sample table and give both users permission to select and insert data into the table:

```
CREATE TABLE Confidential (
  EncryptedData varbinary(255)
  );
  GO

GRANT SELECT, INSERT ON Confidential TO FinanceUser, MarketingUser;
GO
```

Now that we have the basic structure set up, we will create a shared symmetric key that will be encrypted by both the finance and marketing certificates. However, you cannot directly create a key in this manner. Instead, we will create the key with protection by the first certificate, and then open and alter the key to add encryption by the second certificate too:

```
-- Create a symmetric key protected by the first certificate
CREATE SYMMETRIC KEY SharedSymKey
WITH ALGORITHM = AES_256
ENCRYPTION BY CERTIFICATE FinanceCertificate;
GO

-- Then OPEN and ALTER the key to add encryption by the second certificate
OPEN SYMMETRIC KEY SharedSymKey
DECRYPTION BY CERTIFICATE FinanceCertificate
WITH PASSWORD = '#F1n4nc3_P455w()rD#';

ALTER SYMMETRIC KEY SharedSymKey
ADD ENCRYPTION BY CERTIFICATE MarketingCertificate;

CLOSE SYMMETRIC KEY SharedSymKey;
GO
```

Finally, we need to grant permissions on the symmetric key for each user:

```
GRANT VIEW DEFINITION ON SYMMETRIC KEY::SharedSymKey TO FinanceUser
GRANT VIEW DEFINITION ON SYMMETRIC KEY::SharedSymKey TO MarketingUser
GO
```

To encrypt data using the shared symmetric key, either user must first open the key by specifying the name and password of their certificate that is protecting it. They can then use the **ENCRYPTBYKEY** function as demonstrated earlier in this chapter. The following listing demonstrates how **FinanceUser** can insert data into the **Confidential** table, encrypted using the shared symmetric key:

```
EXECUTE AS USER = 'FinanceUser';

OPEN SYMMETRIC KEY SharedSymKey
DECRYPTION BY CERTIFICATE FinanceCertificate
WITH PASSWORD = '#F1n4nc3_P455w()rD#';

INSERT INTO Confidential
SELECT ENCRYPTBYKEY(KEY_GUID(N'SharedSymKey'), N'This is shared information
accessible to finance and marketing');

CLOSE SYMMETRIC KEY SharedSymKey;

REVERT;
GO
```

To decrypt this data, either the marketing user or the finance user can explicitly open the **SharedSymKey** key prior to decryption, similar to the pattern used for encryption, or they can take advantage of the **DECRYPTBYKEYAUTOCERT** function, which allows you to automatically open a symmetric key protected by a certificate as part of the inline function that performs the decryption.

To demonstrate the **DECRYPTBYKEYAUTOCERT** function, the following code listing shows how **MarketingUser** can decrypt the value in the **Confidential** table inserted by **FinanceUser**, opening the shared symmetric key using their own certificate name and password protecting the symmetric key:

```
EXECUTE AS USER = 'MarketingUser';

SELECT
  CAST(
    DECRYPTBYKEYAUTOCERT(
      CERT_ID(N'MarketingCertificate'),
      N'-+M@Rket1ng-P@s5w0rD!+-',
      EncryptedData)
  AS nvarchar(255))
FROM Confidential;

REVERT;
GO
```

The result shows that **MarketingUser** can use the **MarketingCertificate** to access data encrypted by **FinanceUser** using the shared symmetric key:

This is shared information accessible to finance and marketing

---

To extend this example a little further, suppose that in addition to storing encrypted data that is shared between finance and marketing, the **Confidential** table also holds data to which only the finance user should be granted access. Using the hybrid model described here, this is very easy to achieve— simply create a new symmetric key that is protected by the existing finance certificate and grant permissions on that key to the finance user.

```
CREATE SYMMETRIC KEY FinanceSymKey
WITH ALGORITHM = AES_256
ENCRYPTION BY CERTIFICATE FinanceCertificate;
GO

GRANT VIEW DEFINITION ON SYMMETRIC KEY::FinanceSymKey TO FinanceUser
GO
```

As this new symmetric key is protected using the existing **FinanceCertificate**, the finance user can open it using exactly the same syntax as for the shared key, and encrypt data using the key by specifying the appropriate **KEY_GUID** to the **ENCRYPTBYKEY** method:

```
EXECUTE AS USER = 'FinanceUser';

OPEN SYMMETRIC KEY FinanceSymKey
DECRYPTION BY CERTIFICATE FinanceCertificate
WITH PASSWORD = '#F1n4nc3_P455w()rD#';

INSERT INTO Confidential
SELECT ENCRYPTBYKEY(
  KEY_GUID(N'FinanceSymKey'),
  N'This information is only accessible to finance');

CLOSE SYMMETRIC KEY FinanceSymKey;
REVERT;
GO
```

The **Confidential** table now contains two rows of data: one row is encrypted using the shared symmetric key, **SharedSymKey**, to which both **MarketingUser** and **FinanceUser** have access; the second row is encrypted using **FinanceSymKey**, which is only accessible by **FinanceUser**.

The beauty of this approach is that, since all of the keys to which a given user has access are protected by a single certificate, the **DECRYPTBYKEYAUTOCERT** method can be used to decrypt the entire column of data, whatever key was used to encrypt the individual values.

For example, the following code listing demonstrates how **FinanceUser** can automatically decrypt all values in the **EncryptedData** column by using **DECRYPTBYKEYAUTOCERT** in conjunction with the **FinanceCertificate**:

```
EXECUTE AS USER = 'FinanceUser';

SELECT
  CAST(
```

```
DECRYPTBYKEYAUTOCERT(
  CERT_ID(N'FinanceCertificate'),
  N'#F1n4nc3_P455w()rD#',
  EncryptedData
  ) AS nvarchar(255))
FROM Confidential;

REVERT;
GO
```

The results show that **FinanceUser** can use **DECRYPTBYKEYAUTOCERT** to decrypt values encrypted by both the **FinanceSymKey** and the **SharedSymKey**, because they are both protected using the same **FinanceCertificate**:

```
This is shared information accessible to finance and marketing
This information is only accessible to finance
```

If **MarketingUser** were to attempt to perform exactly the same query using the **MarketingCertificate**, they would be able to decrypt only those values encrypted using the **SharedSymKey**; the result of attempting to decrypt values that had been encrypted using **FinanceSymKey** would be **NULL**:

```
EXECUTE AS USER = 'MarketingUser';

SELECT
  CAST(
    DECRYPTBYKEYAUTOCERT(
      CERT_ID(N'MarketingCertificate'),
      N'-+M@Rket1ng-P@s5w0rD!+-',
      EncryptedData) AS nvarchar(255))
FROM Confidential;

REVERT;
GO
```

```
This is shared information accessible to finance and marketing
NULL
```

I hope that this has demonstrated how the hybrid model of encryption achieves a balance between security and maintainability for the majority of situations in which encryption is required, and how it can be extended to deal with a range of different use scenarios.

In the following section, I'll show you how to write efficient queries against encrypted data held in such a model.

Implications of Encryption on Query Design

Having discussed the relative merits of different encryption architecture decisions, the remainder of this chapter will focus on methods to optimize the performance of applications that deal with encrypted data.

The security of encryption always comes with an associated performance cost. As previously mentioned, reads and writes of encrypted data are more resource-intensive and typically take longer to perform. However, the special nature of encrypted data has wider-ranging implications than accepting a simple performance hit, and particular attention needs to be paid to any activities that involve ordering, filtering, or performing joins on encrypted data.

Indexing, sorting, and filtering data relies on identifying ordered patterns within that data. Most data can be assigned a logical order: for example, **varchar** or **char** data can be arranged alphabetically; **datetime** data can be ordered chronologically; and **int**, **decimal**, **float**, and **money** data can be arranged in numeric order. The very purpose of encryption, however, is to remove any kind of logical pattern that might expose information about the underlying data, which makes it very tricky to assign order to encrypted data. This creates a number of issues for efficient query design.

To demonstrate these issues, let's create a table containing some example confidential data. The following code listing will create a table and populate it with 100,000 rows of randomly generated 16-digit numbers, representing dummy credit card numbers.

Among the random data, we will also insert one predetermined value representing the credit card number **4005-5500-0000-0019**. It is this known value that we will use to test various methods of searching for values within encrypted data.

```
CREATE TABLE CreditCards (
  CreditCardID int IDENTITY(1,1) NOT NULL,
  CreditCardNumber_Plain nvarchar(32)
  );
GO

WITH RandomCreditCards AS (
  SELECT
    CAST(9E+15 * RAND(CHECKSUM(NEWID())) + 1E+15 AS bigint) AS CardNumber
)
INSERT INTO CreditCards (CreditCardNumber_Plain)
  SELECT TOP 100000
    CardNumber
  FROM
    RandomCreditCards,
    MASTER..spt_values a,
    MASTER..spt_values b
  UNION ALL SELECT
    '4005550000000019' AS CardNumber;
GO
```

■ **Note** Before you rush out on a spending spree, I regret to inform you that the credit card number listed in this example, 4005-5500-0000-0019, is a test card number issued by VISA for testing payment processing systems and cannot be used to make purchases. Of course, the 100,000 randomly generated rows *might* by chance contain valid credit card details, but good luck finding them!

To protect this information, we'll follow the hybrid encryption model described in the previous section. To do so first requires the creation of a certificate encrypted by password:

```
CREATE CERTIFICATE CreditCard_Cert
  ENCRYPTION BY PASSWORD = '#Ch0o53_@_5Tr0nG_P455w0rD#'
  WITH SUBJECT = 'Secure Certificate for Credit Card Information',
  EXPIRY_DATE = '20101031';
GO
```

and then a symmetric key protected by the certificate:

```
CREATE SYMMETRIC KEY CreditCard_SymKey
WITH ALGORITHM = AES_256
ENCRYPTION BY CERTIFICATE CreditCard_Cert;
GO
```

As we're only concerned with testing the performance of different methods, we won't bother creating different users with access to the key this time—we'll do everything as the **dbo** user.

To begin, add a new column to the **CreditCards** table, **CreditCardNumber_Sym**, and populate it with values encrypted using the **CreditCard_SymKey** symmetric key:

```
ALTER TABLE CreditCards ADD CreditCardNumber_Sym varbinary(100);
GO

OPEN SYMMETRIC KEY CreditCard_SymKey
  DECRYPTION BY CERTIFICATE CreditCard_Cert
  WITH PASSWORD = '#Ch0o53_@_5Tr0nG_P455w0rD#';

UPDATE CreditCards
  SET CreditCardNumber_Sym =
  ENCRYPTBYKEY(KEY_GUID('CreditCard_SymKey'),CreditCardNumber_Plain);

CLOSE SYMMETRIC KEY CreditCard_SymKey;
GO
```

Now let's assume that we are designing an application that requires searching for specific credit numbers that have been encrypted in the **CreditCardNumber_Sym** column. Firstly, let's create an index to support the search:

```
CREATE NONCLUSTERED INDEX idxCreditCardNumber_Sym
  ON CreditCards (CreditCardNumber_Sym);
GO
```

Let's try performing a simple search against the encrypted data. We'll search for our chosen credit card number by decrypting the **CreditCardNumber_Sym** column and comparing the result to the search string:

```
DECLARE @CreditCardNumberToSearch nvarchar(32) = '4005550000000019';

SELECT * FROM CreditCards
WHERE DECRYPTBYKEYAUTOCERT(
  CERT_ID('CreditCard_Cert'),
  N'#Ch0o53_@_5Tr0nG_P455w0rD#',
  CreditCardNumber_Sym) = @CreditCardNumberToSearch;
GO
```

A quick glance at the execution plan shown in Figure 6-7 reveals that, despite the index, the query must scan the whole table, decrypting each row in order to see if it satisfies the predicate.

SELECT	Filter	Compute Scalar	Table Scan
Cost: 0%	Cost: 3%	Cost: 1%	[CreditCards]
			Cost: 96%

Figure 6-7. A query scan performed on encrypted data

The need for a table scan is caused by the nondeterministic nature of encrypted data. Since the values in the **CreditCard_Sym** column are encrypted, we cannot tell which rows match the search criteria without decrypting every value. Nor can we simply encrypt the search value **4005550000000019** and search for the corresponding encrypted value in the **CreditCard_Sym** column, because the result is nondeterministic and will differ every time.

Even though we are using symmetric encryption, the faster-performing cell-encryption and -decryption method, the requirement to conduct an entire table scan means that the query does not perform well. We can obtain a quick measure of the overall performance by inspecting **sys.dm_exec_query_stats**, as follows:

```
SELECT
  st.text,
  CAST(qs.total_worker_time AS decimal(18,9)) / qs.execution_count / 1000
    AS Avg_CPU_Time_ms,
  qs.total_logical_reads
FROM
  sys.dm_exec_query_stats qs
    CROSS APPLY sys.dm_exec_sql_text(qs.plan_handle) st

WHERE
  st.text LIKE '%CreditCardNumberToSearch%';
```

The results I obtain are given here:

text	Avg_CPU_Time_ms	total_logical_reads
DECLARE @CreditCardNumberToSearch nvarchar(32)		
= '4005550000000019'; --*SELECT-------------	1389.079	71623

The **SELECT** query is taking nearly 1.5 seconds of CPU time to query only 100,000 rows of encrypted data. Also notice that the query text contained in the **text** column of **sys.dm_exec_sql_text** is blanked out, as it is for all queries that reference encrypted objects.

The appropriate solution to the problem of searching encrypted data differs depending on how the data will be queried—whether it will be searched for a single exact matching row to the search string (an equality match), a pattern match using a wildcard (i.e., **LIKE %**), or a range search (i.e., using the **BETWEEN**, **>**, or **<** operators).

Equality Matching Using Hashed Message Authentication Codes

One method to facilitate the efficient searching and filtering of individual rows of encrypted data is to make use of hashed message authentication codes (HMACs), which are created using a hashing function, as introduced earlier in this chapter. Remember that the output of a hashing function is deterministic—any given input will always lead to the same output, which is a crucial property to allow encrypted data to be efficiently searched for any given search value. Binary hash values stored in a database can be indexed, and filtering data can be performed by creating the hash value of the search criteria and searching for that value in the column containing the precalculated hash values.

However, we don't want to store the simple hash of each credit card number as returned by **HASHBYTES**—as explained previously, hash values can be attacked using dictionaries or rainbow tables, especially if, as in the case of a credit card number, they follow a predetermined format. This would weaken the strength of the existing solution implemented using symmetric encryption.

HMACs, designed to validate the authenticity of a message, overcome this problem by combining a hash function with a secret key (salt). By combining the plain text with a strong salt prior to hashing, the resulting hash can be made virtually invulnerable to a dictionary attack because any lookup would have to combine every possible source value with every possible salt value, leading to an unfeasibly large list of possible hash values against which a hacker would have to compare.

Message Authentication Codes

HMACs are a method of verifying the authenticity of a message to prove that it has not been tampered with in transmission. They work like this:

1. The sender and the receiver agree on a secret value, known only to them. For example, let's say that they agree on the word salt.

2. When the sender creates their message, they append the secret value onto the end of the message. They then create a hash of the combined message with the salt value:

HMAC = HASH("This is the original message" + "salt")

3. The sender transmits the original message to the receiver, together with the HMAC.

4. When the receiver receives the message, they append the agreed salt value to the received message, and then hash the result themselves. They then check to make sure that the result is the same as the supplied HMAC value.

HMACS are a relatively simple but very effective method of ensuring that messages can be verified as authentic by the intended receiver. If somebody had attempted to intercept and tamper with the message, it would no longer match the supplied HMAC value. Nor could the attacker generate a new matching HMAC value, as they would not know the secret salt that had to be applied.

The first step toward implementing an HMAC-based solution is to define a secure way of storing the salt value (or **key**). For the purpose of this example, we'll store the salt in a separate table and encrypt it using a secure asymmetric key.

```
CREATE ASYMMETRIC KEY HMACASymKey
  WITH ALGORITHM = RSA_1024
  ENCRYPTION BY PASSWORD = N'4n0th3r_5tr0ng_K4y!';
GO

CREATE TABLE HMACKeys (
  HMACKeyID int PRIMARY KEY,
  HMACKey varbinary(255)
);
GO

INSERT INTO HMACKeys
SELECT
  1,
  ENCRYPTBYASYMKEY(ASYMKEY_ID(N'HMACASymKey'), N'-->Th15_i5_Th3_HMAC_kEy!');
GO
```

Now we can create an HMAC value based on the key. You could create a simple HMAC in T-SQL by simply using **HASHBYTES** with the salt value appended onto the original message, as follows:

```
DECLARE @HMAC varbinary(max) = HASHBYTES('SHA1', 'PlainText' + 'Salt')
```

However, there are a number of ways in which this method could be improved:

- The **HASHBYTES** function only creates a hash based on the first 8000 bytes of any input. If the message length equals or exceeds this value, then any salt value appended after the message content will be disregarded. It would therefore be better to supply the salt value first, and *then* the message to be hashed.

- The HMAC specification, as defined by the Federal Information Processing Standard (FIPS PUB 198, **http://csrc.share**

nist.gov/publications/fips/fips198/fips-198a.pdf), actually hashes the plain text value twice, as follows:

HMAC = HASH(Key1 + HASH(Key2 + PlainText))

According to the FIPS standard, Key1 and Key2 are calculated by padding the supplied salt value to the size of the block size of the hash function keys. Key1 is padded with the byte **0x5c** and Key2 is padded with the byte **0x36**. These two values are deliberately chosen to have a large **hamming distance**—that is, the resulting padded keys will be significantly different from each other, so that the strengthening effect of hashing with both keys is maximized.

- The HMAC standard does not specify which hashing algorithm is used to perform the hashing, but the strength of the resulting HMAC is directly linked to the cryptographic strength of the underlying hash function on which it is based. The **HASHBYTES** function only supports hashing using the MD2, MD4, MD5, SHA, and SHA1 algorithms. The hashing methods provided by the .NET Framework, in contrast, support the more secure SHA2 family of algorithms, and also the 160-bit RIPEMD160 algorithm.

It seems that SQL Server's basic **HASHBYTES** function leaves a little bit to be desired, but fortunately there is an easy solution. In order to create an HMAC compliant with the FIPS standard, based on a strong hashing algorithm, we can employ a CLR user-defined function that uses methods provided by the .NET **System.Security** namespace instead. The following code listing illustrates the C# required to create a reusable class that can be used to generate HMAC values for all supported hash algorithms for a given key:

```
[SqlFunction(IsDeterministic = true, DataAccess = DataAccessKind.None)]
public static SqlBytes GenerateHMAC
(
  SqlString Algorithm,
  SqlBytes PlainText,
  SqlBytes Key
)
{
  if (Algorithm.IsNull || PlainText.IsNull || Key.IsNull) {
    return SqlBytes.Null;
  }
  HMAC HMac = null;
  switch (Algorithm.Value)
  {
    case "MD5":
      HMac = new HMACMD5(Key.Value);
      break;
    case "SHA1":
      HMac = new HMACSHA1(Key.Value);
      break;
    case "SHA256":
      HMac = new HMACSHA256(Key.Value);
      break;
    case "SHA384":
      HMac = new HMACSHA384(Key.Value);
      break;
```

```
    case "SHA512":
      HMac = new HMACSHA512(Key.Value);
      break;
    case "RIPEMD160":
      HMac = new HMACRIPEMD160(Key.Value);
      break;
    default:
      throw new Exception( "Hash algorithm not recognised" );
  }
  byte[] HMacBytes = HMac.ComputeHash(PlainText.Value);
  return new SqlBytes(HMacBytes);
}
```

■ **Caution** For completeness, the GenerateHMAC function supports all hashing algorithms available within the Security.Cryptography namespace. In practice, it is not recommended to use the MD5 algorithm in production applications, since it has been proven to be vulnerable to hash collisions.

Build the assembly and catalog it in SQL Server. Then create a new column in the **CreditCards** table and populate it with an HMAC-SHA1 value using the **GenerateHMAC** function. I'll create the HMAC column as a **varbinary(255)** type—the actual length of the HMAC values stored in this column will depend on the hashing algorithm used: 128 bits (16 bytes) for MD5; 160 bits (20 bytes) for RIPEMD160 and SHA1, and up to 64 bytes for SHA512. These steps are demonstrated in the following code listing:

```
ALTER TABLE CreditCards
ADD CreditCardNumber_HMAC varbinary(255);
GO

-- Retrieve the HMAC salt value from the MACKeys table
DECLARE @salt varbinary(255);
SET @salt = (
  SELECT DECRYPTBYASYMKEY(
      ASYMKEY_ID('HMACASymKey'),
      HMACKey,
      N'4n0th3r_5tr0ng_K4y!'
    )
FROM HMACKeys
WHERE HMACKeyID = 1);

-- Update the HMAC value using the salt
UPDATE CreditCards
SET CreditCardNumber_HMAC = (
  SELECT dbo.GenerateHMAC(
    'SHA256',
    CAST(CreditCardNumber_Plain AS varbinary(max)),
    @salt
  )
```

```
);
GO
```

■ **Note** If you were implementing the HMAC solution proposed here in a production application, you'd want to create triggers to ensure that the integrity of the `CreditCardNumber_HMAC` column was maintained during INSERTs and UPDATEs to the `CreditCards` table. Because I'm only concentrating on evaluating the performance of HMACs, I won't bother with this step.

We can now issue queries that search for credit cards based on their HMAC; but before we do, let's create an index to help support the search. Queries issued against the **CreditCards** table will filter rows based on **CreditCardNumber_HMAC** column, but we'll want to return the **CreditCardNumber_Sym** column so that we can decrypt the original credit card number.

To ensure that these queries are covered by an index, we'll create a new nonclustered index based on **CreditCardNumber_HMAC**, and we'll include **CreditCard_Sym** in the index as a nonkey column.

```
CREATE NONCLUSTERED INDEX idxCreditCardNumberHMAC
ON CreditCards (CreditCardNumber_HMAC)
INCLUDE (CreditCardNumber_Sym);
GO
```

■ **Note** A **covering** index contains all of the columns required by a query within a single index. This means that the database engine can fulfill the query based on the index alone, without needing to issue additional seeks or lookups on the data page to retrieve additional columns.

Let's test the performance of the new HMAC-based solution by searching for our known credit card in the **CreditCards** table:

```
-- Select a credit card to search for
DECLARE @CreditCardNumberToSearch nvarchar(32) = '4005550000000019';

-- Retrieve the secret salt value
DECLARE @salt varbinary(255);
SET @salt = (
  SELECT DECRYPTBYASYMKEY(
      ASYMKEY_ID('HMACASymKey'),
      MACKey,
      N'4n0th3r_5tr0ng_K4y!'
    )
FROM MACKeys);

-- Generate the HMAC of the credit card to search for
```

```
DECLARE @HMACToSearch varbinary(255);
SET @HMACToSearch = dbo.GenerateHMAC(
  'SHA256',
  CAST(@CreditCardNumberToSearch AS varbinary(max)),
  @salt);

-- Retrieve the matching row from the CreditCards table
SELECT
  CAST(
    DECRYPTBYKEYAUTOCERT(
      CERT_ID('CreditCard_Cert'),
      N'#Choo53_@_5TronG_P455wOrD#',
      CreditCardNumber_Sym) AS nvarchar(32)) AS CreditCardNumber_Decrypted
FROM CreditCards
WHERE CreditCardNumber_HMAC = @HMACToSearch
  AND
  CAST(
    DECRYPTBYKEYAUTOCERT(
      CERT_ID('CreditCard_Cert'),
      N'#Choo53_@_5TronG_P455wOrD#',
      CreditCardNumber_Sym) AS nvarchar(32)) = @CreditCardNumberToSearch;
GO
```

This query generates the HMAC hash of the supplied search value and then uses the **idxCreditCardNumberHMAC** index to search for this value in the **CreditCardNumber_HMAC** column. Having found a matching row, it then decrypts the value contained in the **CreditCardNumber_Sym** column to make sure that it matches the original supplied search value (to prevent the risk of hash collisions, where an incorrect result is returned because it happened to share the same hash as our search string).

The execution plan shown in Figure 6-8 illustrates that the entire query can be satisfied by a single index seek.

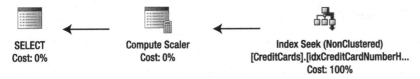

SELECT
Cost: 0%

Compute Scaler
Cost: 0%

Index Seek (NonClustered)
[CreditCards].[idxCreditCardNumberH...
Cost: 100%

Figure 6-8. Performing a clustered index seek on an HMAC hash column

The performance counters contained in **sys.dm_exec_query_stats** reveal that the query is substantially more efficient than direct querying of the **CreditCardNumber_Sym** column, taking only 253ms of CPU time and requiring nine logical reads.

Wildcard Searches Using HMAC Substrings

There are many occasions where a database needs to support queries that require an element of flexibility in the search criteria. This applies to searches of encrypted data just as with any other type of data. For example, perhaps you need to search for all customers whose credit cards expire in a certain month, or perform a search based on the last four digits of their social security number.

The HMAC solution just proposed cannot be used in these cases, since the HMAC hash values are unique to an exact value. The hash generated from a partial string will be completely different from the hash generated from a complete string, as demonstrated here:

```
SELECT
  HASHBYTES('SHA1', 'The quick brown fox jumped over the lazy dog')
UNION SELECT
  HASHBYTES('SHA1', 'The quick brown fox jumped over the lazy dogs');
```

Despite the fact that the input strings differ by only one character, the resulting hash values are substantially different:

```
0xF6513640F3045E9768B239785625CAA6A2588842
0xFBADA4676477322FB3E2AE6353E8BD32B6D0B49C
```

In order to facilitate pattern matching of partial strings, we can still use HMACs, but we need to create a hash based on a section of the string that will remain consistent across all searches. In other words, to support a query to find values LIKE 'The quick brown fox jumped over the lazy%', it would be necessary to search for all rows matching the hash value of the trimmed string The quick brown fox jumped over the lazy. This exact substring must be used consistently across all queries, and it should be sufficiently selective to ensure the query is efficient.

To relate this back to the example used in this chapter, suppose that we wanted to create a method of allowing users to search for a row of data in the CreditCards table based on the last four digits of the credit card number. To do so, we'll add a new column to the table, and populate it by using the GenerateHMAC function to create an HMAC based on the last four digits of each credit card number. This new column, CreditCardNumber_Last4HMAC, will only be used to support wildcard searches, while the existing CreditCardNumber_HMAC column will continue to be used for equality searches on the whole credit card number.

To start, let's add a new key to the HMACKeys table:

```
CREATE ASYMMETRIC KEY HMACSubStringASymKey
  WITH ALGORITHM = RSA_1024
  ENCRYPTION BY PASSWORD = N'~Y3T_an0+h3r_5tR()ng_K4y~';
GO

INSERT INTO HMACKeys
SELECT
  2,
  ENCRYPTBYASYMKEY(
    ASYMKEY_ID(N'HMACSubStringASymKey'),
    N'->Th15_i$_Th3_HMAC_Sub5Tr1ng_k3y');
GO
```

Now let's use the new key to create an HMAC based on the last four characters of each credit card number:

```
ALTER TABLE CreditCards
ADD CreditCardNumber_Last4HMAC varbinary(255);
GO
```

```
-- Retrieve the HMAC salt value from the MACKeys table
DECLARE @salt varbinary(255);
SET @salt = (
  SELECT DECRYPTBYASYMKEY(
      ASYMKEY_ID('HMACSubStringASymKey'),
      HMACKey,
      N'~Y3T_an0+h3r_5tR()ng_K4y~'
    )
FROM HMACKeys
WHERE HMACKeyID = 2);

-- Update the Last4HMAC value using the salt
UPDATE CreditCards
SET CreditCardNumber_Last4HMAC = (SELECT dbo.GenerateHMAC(
  'SHA256',
  CAST(RIGHT(CreditCardNumber_Plain, 4) AS varbinary(max)), @salt));
GO
```

And, to support queries issued against the new substring HMAC, we'll add a new index:

```
CREATE NONCLUSTERED INDEX idxCreditCardNumberLast4HMAC
ON CreditCards (CreditCardNumber_Last4HMAC)
INCLUDE (CreditCardNumber_Sym);
GO
```

Suppose that we wanted to issue a query to find all those credit cards ending in the digits 0019. Such a pattern-matching query could now be issued by comparing the HMAC of these digits with the HMAC value stored in the **CreditCardNumber_Last4HMAC** column, as follows:

```
-- Select the last 4 digits of the credit card to search for
DECLARE @CreditCardLast4ToSearch nchar(4) = '0019';

-- Retrieve the secret salt value
DECLARE @salt varbinary(255);
SET @salt = (
  SELECT DECRYPTBYASYMKEY(
      ASYMKEY_ID('HMACSubStringASymKey'),
      HMACKey,
      N'~Y3T_an0+h3r_5tR()ng_K4y~'
    )
FROM HMACKeys
WHERE HMACKeyID = 2);

-- Generate the HMAC of the last 4 digits to search for
DECLARE @HMACToSearch varbinary(255);
SET @HMACToSearch = dbo.GenerateHMAC(
  'SHA256',
  CAST(@CreditCardLast4ToSearch AS varbinary(max)),
  @salt);
```

```
-- Retrieve the matching row from the CreditCards table
SELECT
    CAST(
      DECRYPTBYKEYAUTOCERT(
        CERT_ID('CreditCard_Cert'),
        N'#ChOo53_@_5TrOnG_P455wOrD#',
        CreditCardNumber_Sym)
    AS nvarchar(32)) AS CreditCardNumber_Decrypted
FROM
  CreditCards
WHERE
  CreditCardNumber_Last4HMAC = @HMACToSearch
  AND
  CAST(
    DECRYPTBYKEYAUTOCERT(
      CERT_ID('CreditCard_Cert'),
      N'#ChOo53_@_5TrOnG_P455wOrD#',
      CreditCardNumber_Sym)
  AS nvarchar(32)) LIKE '%' + @CreditCardLast4ToSearch;
GO
```

The results obtained on my system list the following ten credit cards, including the 4005550000000019 credit card number that we were originally searching for (your list will differ since the records contained in the **CreditCards** table were randomly generated, but you should still find the intended matching value):

6823807913290019

5804462948450019

6742201580250019

7572953718590019

4334945301620019

7859588437020019

3490887629240019

5801804774470019

4005550000000019

2974981474970019

An examination of the query execution plan shown in Figure 6-9 reveals that, so long as the substring chosen is sufficiently selective, as in this case, wildcard searches of encrypted data can be achieved using an efficient index seek.

SELECT	Compute Scaler	Filter	Index Seek (NonClustered)
Cost: 0%	Cost: 0%	Cost: 0%	[CreditCards].[idxCreditCardNumberL...
			Cost: 100%

Figure 6-9. Index seek of an HMAC substring

The performance of this query on my machine is almost identical to the full equality match against the **CreditCard_HMAC** column, taking 301ms of CPU time and requiring nine logical reads.

While this technique demonstrates that it is possible to perform wildcard searches on encrypted data, it is not a very flexible solution. The **CreditCardNumber_Last4HMAC** column used in this example can only be used to satisfy queries that specify the last four digits of a credit card. If you wanted to search on the last six digits of a credit card number, say, you would need to create a whole new HMAC column to support that type of query.

The more flexibility your application demands in its search criteria, the more untenable this solution becomes, and the more additional columns of data must be created. Not only does this become a maintenance headache, it means greater storage requirements, and also increases the risk of your data becoming exposed. Even when storing relatively secure HMAC hash values, every additional column provides a hacker with more information about your data, which can be used to launch a targeted attack.

Range Searches

The last scenario of searching encrypted data I will consider in this chapter is that of the range query. For example, how do we identify those rows of data that contain credit card numbers in the range of 4929100012347890 and 4999100012349999?

These types of searches are perhaps the most difficult to implement with encrypted data, and there are few obvious solutions: The HMAC solution, or its substring derivative, does not help here— sequential plain text numbers clearly do not lead to sequential ciphertext values. In fact, when you're looking at cell-level encryption, there is no way to avoid scanning and decrypting every row in the table to fulfill a range query.

If the range to be searched were very constrained (e.g., +/–10 of a supplied value), it might be possible to forego encryption and store partial plain text values, such as the last two digits of the credit card, in a new column. With some query redesign, queries could be made to facilitate certain range queries based on this column, but this obviously involves a huge amount of risk by disclosing even partial plain text of your sensitive information.

The only other alternative, if range queries absolutely must be supported, is to rely on one of the forms of encryption performed at the I/O level, such as database encryption using TDE, EFS, or Windows BitLocker. In such cases, decryption is performed at such a low level that the database engine can operate on data without consideration of any encryption to which it may have been subjected prior to processing.

Summary

Encryption forms an important part of any security strategy, and can provide the crucial last line of defense in thwarting attackers from gaining access to sensitive or confidential data. However, it comes at a cost—encryption requires carefully planned strategy and security policies, and almost invariably requires design changes to be made at a database or application level in order to be implemented successfully. Added security also has a necessary negative impact on performance.

Encrypted data that results from a nondeterministic algorithm does not exhibit the same structure or patterns as normal data. This means that many standard database tasks, such as sorting, filtering, and joining, must be redesigned in order to work effectively. Although there are methods to work around some of the limitations of dealing with encrypted data, such as searching and matching using HMACs, they are not satisfactory in all cases, and if possible, applications should be designed to avoid direct querying of encrypted data.

CHAPTER 7

■ ■ ■

SQLCLR: Architecture and Design Considerations

When Microsoft first announced that SQL Server would host the .NET Common Language Runtime (CLR) back in SQL Server 2005, it created a lot of excitement in the database world. Some of that excitement was enthusiastic support voiced by developers who envisaged lots of database scenarios that could potentially benefit from the methods provided by the .NET Base Class Library. However, there was also considerable nervousness and resistance from DBAs concerned about the threats posed by the new technology and the rumors that rogue developers would be able to create vast worlds of DBA-impenetrable, compiled in-process data access code.

When it came to it, SQLCLR integration turned out to be neither such a scary nor such a useful idea as many thought. Those hoping to use the SQLCLR features as a wholesale replacement for T-SQL were quickly put off by the fact that writing CLR routines generally requires more code, and performance and reliability suffer due to the continual cost of marshaling data across the CLR boundaries. And for the DBAs who were not .NET developers to begin with, there was a somewhat steep learning curve involved for a feature that really didn't have a whole lot of uses.

We've been living with SQLCLR for over four years now, and although it appears that CLR integration features are still not being used that heavily, their adoption is certainly growing. SQL Server 2008 lifts the previous restriction that constrained CLR User-Defined Types (UDTs) to hold a maximum of only 8KB of data, which seriously crippled many potential usage scenarios; all CLR UDTs may now hold up to a maximum 2GB of data in a single item. This opens up lots of potential avenues for new types of complex object-based data to be stored in the database, for which SQLCLR is better suited than the predominantly set-based T-SQL engine. Indeed, SQL Server 2008 introduces three new system-defined datatypes (**geometry**, **geography**, and **hierarchyid**) that provide an excellent demonstration of the ways in which SQLCLR can extend SQL Server to efficiently store and query types of data beyond the standard numeric and character-based data typically associated with SQL databases.

I will cover the system-defined CLR datatypes in detail in Chapters 10 and 12, which discuss spatial data and hierarchical data, respectively. This chapter, however, concentrates on design and performance considerations for exploiting user-defined functions based on managed code in SQL Server, and discussion of when you should consider using SQLCLR over more traditional T-SQL methods. It is my opinion that the primary strength of SQLCLR integration is in the ability to both move and share code between tiers—so this chapter's primary focus is on maintainability and reuse scenarios.

■ **Note** This chapter assumes that you are already familiar with basic SQLCLR topics, including how to create and deploy functions and catalog new assemblies, in addition to the C# programming language.

Bridging the SQL/CLR Gap: The SqlTypes Library

The native datatypes exposed by the .NET Framework and by SQL Server are in many cases similar, but generally incompatible. A few major issues come up when dealing with SQL Server and .NET interoperability from the perspective of data types:

- First and foremost, all native SQL Server data types are **nullable**—that is, an instance of any given type can either hold a valid value in the domain of the type or represent an unknown (**NULL**). Types in .NET generally do not support this idea (note that C#'s **null** and VB .NET's **nothing** are not the same as SQL Server's **NULL**). Even though the .NET Framework supports nullable types for value type variables, these do not behave in the same way as their SQL Server equivalents.

- The second difference between the type systems has to do with implementation. Format, precision, and scale of the types involved in each system differ dramatically. For example, .NET's **DateTime** type supports a much larger range and much greater precision than does SQL Server's **datetime** type.

- The third major difference has to do with runtime behavior of types in conjunction with operators. For example, in SQL Server, virtually all operations involving at least one **NULL** instance of a type results in **NULL**. However, this is not the same behavior as that of an operation acting on a **null** value in .NET. Consider the following T-SQL:

```
DECLARE @a int = 10;
DECLARE @b int = null;
IF (@a != @b)
  PRINT 'test is true';
ELSE
  PRINT 'test is false';
```

The result of any comparison to a NULL value in T-SQL is undefined, so the preceding code will print "test is false." However, consider the equivalent function implemented using nullable int types in C# (denoted by the ? character after the type declaration):

```
int? a = 10;
int? b = null;
 if (a != b)
   Console.Write("test is true");
 else
   Console.Write("test is false");
```

In .NET, the comparison between 10 and null takes place, resulting in the code printing "test is true." In addition to nullability, differences may result from handling overflows, underflows, and other potential errors inconsistently. For instance, adding 1 to a 32-bit integer with the value of 2147483647 (the maximum 32-bit integer value) in a .NET language may result in the value "wrapping around," producing -2147483648. In SQL Server, this behavior will never occur—instead, an overflow exception will result.

In order to provide a layer of abstraction between the two type paradigms, the .NET Framework ships with a namespace called **System.Data.SqlTypes**. This namespace includes a series of structures that map SQL Server types and behaviors into .NET. Each of these structures implements nullability through the **INullable** interface, which exposes an **IsNull** property that allows callers to determine whether a given instance of the type is **NULL**. Furthermore, these types conform to the same range, precision, and operator rules as SQL Server's native types.

Properly using the **SqlTypes** types is, simply put, the most effective way of ensuring that data marshaled into and out of SQLCLR routines is handled correctly by each type system. It is my recommendation that, whenever possible, all methods exposed as SQLCLR objects use **SqlTypes** types as both input and output parameters, rather than standard .NET types. This will require a bit more development work up front, but it should future-proof your code to some degree and help avoid type incompatibility issues.

Wrapping Code to Promote Cross-Tier Reuse

One of the primary selling points for SQLCLR integration, especially for shops that use the .NET Framework for application development, is the ability to move or share code easily between tiers when it makes sense to do so. It's not so easy, however, to realize that objective.

The Problem

Unfortunately, some of the design necessities of working in the SQLCLR environment do not translate well to the application tier, and vice versa. One such example is use of the **SqlTypes** described in the preceding section; although it is recommended that they be used for all interfaces in SQLCLR routines, that prescription does not make sense in the application tier, because the **SqlTypes** do not support the full range of operators and options that the native .NET types support. Using them in every case might make data access simple, but would rob you of the ability to do many complex data manipulation tasks, and would therefore be more of a hindrance than a helpful change.

Rewriting code or creating multiple versions customized for different tiers simply does not promote maintainability. In the best-case scenario, any given piece of logic used by an application should be coded in exactly one place—regardless of how many different components use the logic or where it's deployed. This is one of the central design goals of object-oriented programming, and it's important to remember that it also applies to code being reused inside of SQL Server.

One Reasonable Solution

Instead of rewriting routines and types to make them compatible with the **SqlTypes** and implement other database-specific logic, I recommend that you get into the habit of designing **wrapper methods** and classes. These wrappers should map the **SqlTypes** inputs and outputs to the .NET types actually used by the original code, and call into the underlying routines via assembly references. Wrappers are also a good place to implement database-specific logic that may not exist in routines originally designed for the application tier.

In addition to the maintainability benefits for the code itself, creating wrappers has a couple of other advantages. First of all, unit tests will not need to be rewritten—the same tests that work in the application tier will still apply in the data tier (although you may want to write secondary unit tests for the wrapper routines). Secondly—and perhaps more importantly—wrapping your original assemblies can help maintain a least-privileged coding model and enhance security, as is discussed later in this chapter in the sections "Working with Code Access Security Privileges" and "Working with Host Protection Privileges."

A Simple Example: E-Mail Address Format Validation

It is quite common for web forms to ask for your e-mail address, and you've no doubt encountered forms that tell you if you've entered an e-mail address that does not comply with the standard format expected. This sort of validation provides a quicker—but less effective—way to test an e-mail address than actually sending an e-mail and waiting for a response, and it gives the user immediate feedback if something is obviously incorrect.

In addition to using this logic for front-end validation, it makes sense to implement the same approach in the database in order to drive a **CHECK** constraint. That way, any data that makes its way to the database—regardless of whether it already went through the check in the application—will be double-checked for correctness.

Following is a simple .NET method that uses a regular expression to validate the format of an e-mail address:

```
public static bool IsValidEmailAddress(string emailAddress)
{
    //Validate the e-mail address
    Regex r =
        new Regex(@"\w+([-+.]\w+)*@\w+([-.]\w+)*\.\w+([-.]\w+)*");

    return (r.IsMatch(emailAddress));
}
```

This code could, of course, be used as-is in both SQL Server and the application tier—using it in SQL Server would simply require loading the assembly and registering the function. But this has some issues, the most obvious of which is the lack of proper **NULL** handling. As-is, this method will return an **ArgumentException** when a **NULL** is passed in. Depending on your business requirements, a better choice would probably be either **NULL** or **false**. Another potential issue occurs in methods that require slightly different logic in the database vs. the application tier. In the case of e-mail validation, it's difficult to imagine how you might enhance the logic for use in a different tier, but for other methods, such modification would present a maintainability challenge.

The solution is to catalog the assembly containing this method in SQL Server, but not directly expose the method as a SQLCLR UDF. Instead, create a wrapper method that uses the **SqlTypes** and internally calls the initial method. This means that the underlying method will not have to be modified in order to create a version that properly interfaces with the database, and the same assembly can be deployed in any tier. Following is a sample that shows a wrapper method created over the **IsValidEmailAddress** method, in order to expose a SQLCLR UDF version that properly supports **NULL** inputs and outputs. Assume that I've created the inner method in a class called **UtilityMethods** and have also included a **using** statement for the namespace used in the **UtilityMethods** assembly.

```
[Microsoft.SqlServer.Server.SqlFunction]
public static SqlBoolean IsValidEmailAddress(
    SqlString emailAddress)
{
    // Return NULL on NULL input
    if (emailAddress.IsNull)
        return (SqlBoolean.Null);

    bool isValid = UtilityMethods.IsValidEmailAddress(emailAddress.Value);
    return (new SqlBoolean(isValid));
}
```

Note that this technique can be used not only for loading assemblies from the application tier into SQL Server, but also for going the other way—migrating logic back out of the data tier. Given the nature of SQLCLR, the potential for code mobility should always be considered, and developers should consider designing methods using wrappers even when creating code specifically for use in the database—this will maximize the potential for reuse later, when or if the same logic needs to be migrated to another tier, or even if the logic needs to be reused more than once inside of the data tier itself.

Cross-assembly references have other benefits as well, when working in the SQLCLR environment. By properly leveraging references, it is possible to create a much more robust, secure SQLCLR solution. The following sections introduce the security and reliability features that are used by SQLCLR, and show how to create assembly references that exploit these features to manage security on a granular level.

SQLCLR Security and Reliability Features

Unlike stored procedures, triggers, UDFs, and other types of code modules that can be exposed within SQL Server, a given SQLCLR routine is not directly related to a database, but rather to an assembly **cataloged** within the database. Cataloging of an assembly is done using SQL Server's **CREATE ASSEMBLY** statement, and unlike their T-SQL equivalents, SQLCLR modules get their first security restrictions not via grants, but rather at the same time their assemblies are cataloged. The **CREATE ASSEMBLY** statement allows the DBA or database developer to specify one of three security and reliability **permission sets** that dictate what the code in the assembly is allowed to do.

The allowed permission sets are **SAFE**, **EXTERNAL_ACCESS**, and **UNSAFE**. Each increasingly permissive level includes and extends permissions granted by lower permission sets. The restricted set of permissions allowed for **SAFE** assemblies includes limited access to math and string functions, along with data access to the host database via the context connection. The **EXTERNAL_ACCESS** permission set adds the ability to communicate outside of the SQL Server instance, to other database servers, file servers, web servers, and so on. And the **UNSAFE** permission set gives the assembly the ability to do pretty much anything—including running unmanaged code.

Although exposed as only a single user-controllable setting, internally each permission set's rights are actually enforced by two distinct methods:

- Assemblies assigned to each permission set are *granted* access to perform certain operations via .NET's **Code Access Security** (CAS) technology.

- At the same time, access is *denied* to certain operations based on checks against a .NET 3.5 attribute called **HostProtectionAttribute** (HPA).

On the surface, the difference between HPA and CAS is that they are opposites: CAS permissions dictate what an assembly can do, whereas HPA permissions dictate what an assembly cannot do. The combination of everything granted by CAS and everything denied by HPA makes up each of the three permission sets.

Beyond this basic difference is a much more important distinction between the two access control methods. Although violation of a permission enforced by either method will result in a runtime exception, the actual checks are done at very different times. CAS grants are checked dynamically at runtime via a stack walk performed as code is executed. On the other hand, HPA permissions are checked at the point of just-in-time compilation—just *before* calling the method being referenced.

To observe how these differences affect the way code runs, a few test cases will be necessary, which are described in the following sections.

■ **Tip** You can download the source code of the examples in this chapter, together with all associated project files and libraries, from the Source Code/Download area of the Apress web site, `www.apress.com`.

Security Exceptions

To begin with, let's take a look at how a CAS exception works. Create a new assembly containing the following CLR stored procedure:

```
[SqlProcedure]
public static void CAS_Exception()
{
    SqlContext.Pipe.Send("Starting...");

    using (FileStream fs =
        new FileStream(@"c:\b.txt", FileMode.Open))
    {
        //Do nothing...
    }

    SqlContext.Pipe.Send("Finished...");

    return;
}
```

Catalog the assembly as **SAFE** and execute the stored procedure. This will result in the following output:

```
Starting...

Msg 6522, Level 16, State 1, Procedure CAS_Exception, Line 0

A .NET Framework error occurred during execution of user-defined routine or

aggregate "CAS_Exception":

System.Security.SecurityException: Request for the permission of type

'System.Security.Permissions.FileIOPermission, mscorlib, Version=2.0.0.0,

Culture=neutral, PublicKeyToken=b77a5c561934e089' failed.

System.Security.SecurityException:

    at System.Security.CodeAccessSecurityEngine.Check(Object demand,
```

```
StackCrawlMark& stackMark, Boolean isPermSet)

   at System.Security.CodeAccessPermission.Demand()

   at System.IO.FileStream.Init(String path, FileMode mode, FileAccess access, Int32

rights, Boolean useRights, FileShare share, Int32 bufferSize, FileOptions options,

SECURITY_ATTRIBUTES secAttrs, String msgPath, Boolean bFromProxy)

   at System.IO.FileStream..ctor(String path, FileMode mode)

   at udf_part2.CAS_Exception()

.
```

The exception thrown in this case is a **SecurityException**, indicating that this was a CAS violation (of the **FileIOPermission** type). But the exception is not the only thing that happened; notice that the first line of the output is the string "Starting..." which was output by the **SqlPipe.Send** method used in the first line of the stored procedure. So before the exception was hit, the method was entered and code execution succeeded until the actual permissions violation was attempted.

■ **Note** File I/O is a good example of access to a resource—local or otherwise—that is not allowed within the context connection. Avoiding this particular violation using the SQLCLR security buckets would require cataloging the assembly using the EXTERNAL_ACCESS permission.

Host Protection Exceptions

To see how HPA exceptions behave, let's repeat the same experiment described in the previous section, this time with the following stored procedure (again, cataloged as **SAFE**):

```
[SqlProcedure]
public static void HPA_Exception()
{
    SqlContext.Pipe.Send("Starting...");

    //The next line will throw an HPA exception...
    Monitor.Enter(SqlContext.Pipe);

    //Release the lock (if the code even gets here)...
    Monitor.Exit(SqlContext.Pipe);

    SqlContext.Pipe.Send("Finished...");
```

```
    return;
}
```

Just like before, an exception occurs. But this time, the output is a bit different:

```
Msg 6522, Level 16, State 1, Procedure HPA_Exception, Line 0
A .NET Framework error occurred during execution of user-defined routine or
aggregate "HPA_Exception":
System.Security.HostProtectionException: Attempted to perform an operation that
was forbidden by the CLR host.

The protected resources (only available with full trust) were: All
The demanded resources were: Synchronization, ExternalThreading

System.Security.HostProtectionException:
   at System.Security.CodeAccessSecurityEngine.ThrowSecurityException(Assembly
asm,
PermissionSet granted, PermissionSet refused, RuntimeMethodHandle rmh,
SecurityAction action, Object demand, IPermission permThatFailed)
   at System.Security.CodeAccessSecurityEngine.ThrowSecurityException(Object
assemblyOrString, PermissionSet granted, PermissionSet refused, RuntimeMethodHandle
rmh, SecurityAction action, Object demand, IPermission permThatFailed)
   at System.Security.CodeAccessSecurityEngine.CheckSetHelper(PermissionSet
grants,
PermissionSet refused, PermissionSet demands, RuntimeMethodHandle rmh, Object
assemblyOrString, SecurityAction action, Boolean throwException)
```

```
   at System.Security.CodeAccessSecurityEngine.CheckSetHelper(CompressedStack
cs,
PermissionSet grants, PermissionSet refused, PermissionSet demands,
RuntimeMethodHandle rmh, Assembly asm, SecurityAction action)
   at udf_part2.HPA_Exception()

.
```

Unlike when executing the **CAS_Exception** stored procedure, this time we do not see the "Starting..." message, indicating that the **SqlPipe.Send** method was not called before hitting the exception. As a matter of fact, the **HPA_Exception** method was not ever entered at all during the code execution phase (you can verify this by attempting to set a breakpoint inside of the function and starting a debug session in Visual Studio). The reason that the breakpoint can't be hit is that the permissions check was performed and the exception thrown immediately after just-in-time compilation.

You should also note that the wording of the exception has a different tone than in the previous case. The wording of the CAS exception is a rather benign "Request for the permission ... failed." On the other hand, the HPA exception carries a much sterner warning: "Attempted to perform an operation that was *forbidden*." This difference in wording is not accidental. CAS grants are concerned with security—to keep code from being able to access something protected because it's not supposed to have access. HPA permissions, on the other hand, are concerned with server reliability and keeping the CLR host running smoothly and efficiently. Threading and synchronization are considered potentially threatening to reliability and are therefore limited to assemblies marked as **UNSAFE**.

■ **Note** Using a .NET disassembler (such as Red Gate Reflector, **www.red-gate.com/products/reflector/**), it is possible to explore the Base Class Library to see which HPA attributes are assigned to various classes and methods. For instance, the **Monitor** class is decorated with the following attributes that control host access: [ComVisible(true), HostProtection(SecurityAction.LinkDemand, Synchronization=true, ExternalThreading=true)].

A full list of what is and is not allowed based on the CAS and HPA models is beyond the scope of this chapter, but is well documented by Microsoft. Refer to the following MSDN topics:

- Host Protection Attributes and CLR Integration Programming (**http://msdn2.microsoft.com/en-us/library/ms403276.aspx**)

- CLR Integration Code Access Security (**http://msdn2.microsoft.com/en-us/library/ms345101.aspx**)

The Quest for Code Safety

You might be wondering why I'm covering the internals of the SQLCLR permission sets and how their exceptions differ, when fixing the exceptions is so easy: simply raise the permission level of the assemblies to **EXTERNAL_ACCESS** or **UNSAFE** and give the code access to do what it needs to do. The fact is, raising the permission levels will certainly work, but by doing so you may be circumventing the security policy, instead of working with it to make your system more secure.

As mentioned in the previous section, code access permissions are granted at the assembly level rather than the method or line level. Therefore, raising the permission of a given assembly in order to make a certain module work can actually affect many different modules contained within the assembly, giving them all enhanced access. Granting additional permissions on several modules within an assembly can in turn create a maintenance burden: if you want to be certain that there are no security problems, you must review each and every line of code in every module in the assembly to make sure it's not doing anything it's not supposed to do—you can no longer trust the engine to check for you.

You might now be thinking that the solution is simple: split up your methods so that each resides in a separate assembly, and then grant permissions that way. Then each method really will have its own permission set. But even in that case, permissions may not be granular enough to avoid code review nightmares. Consider a complex 5,000-line module that requires a single file I/O operation to read some lines from a text file. By giving the entire module **EXTERNAL_ACCESS** permissions, it can now read the lines from that file. But of course, you still have to check all of the 4,999 remaining code lines to make sure they're not doing anything unauthorized.

Then there is the question of the effectiveness of manual code review. Is doing a stringent review every time any change is made enough to ensure that the code won't cause problems that would be detected by the engine if the code was marked **SAFE**? And do you really *want* to have to do a stringent review before deployment every time any change is made? In the following section, I will show you how to eliminate many of these problems by taking advantage of assembly dependencies in your SQLCLR environment.

Selective Privilege Escalation via Assembly References

In an ideal world, SQLCLR module permissions could be made to work like T-SQL module permissions as described in Chapter 5: outer modules would be granted the least possible privileges, but would be able to selectively and temporarily escalate their privileges in order to perform certain operations that require more access. This would lessen the privileged surface area significantly, which would mean that there would be less need to do a stringent security review on outer (less-privileged) module layers, which undoubtedly constitute the majority of code written for a given system—the engine would make sure they behave.

The general solution to this problem is to split up code into separate assemblies based on permissions requirements, but not to do so without regard for both maintenance overhead and reuse. For example, consider the 5,000-line module mentioned in the previous section, which needs to read a few lines from a text file. The entire module could be granted a sufficiently high level of privileges to read the file, or the code to read the file could be taken out and placed into its own assembly. This external assembly would expose a method that takes a file name as input and returns a collection of lines. As I'll show in the following sections, this solution would let you catalog the bulk of the code as **SAFE** yet still do the file I/O operation. Plus, future modules that need to read lines from text files could reference the same assembly, and therefore not have to reimplement this logic.

The encapsulation story is, alas, not quite as straightforward as creating a new assembly with the necessary logic and referencing it. Due to the different behavior of CAS and HPA exceptions, you might have to perform some code analysis in order to properly encapsulate the permissions of the inner modules. In the following sections, I'll cover each of the permission types separately in order to illustrate how to design a solution.

Working with Host Protection Privileges

A fairly common SQLCLR pattern is to create **static** collections that can be shared among callers. However, as with any shared data set, proper synchronization is essential in case you need to update some of the data after its initial load. From a SQLCLR standpoint, this gets dicey due to the fact that threading and synchronization require **UNSAFE** access—granting such an open level of permission is not something to be taken lightly.

For an example of a scenario that might make use of a static collection, consider a SQLCLR UDF used to calculate currency conversions based on exchange rates:

```
[SqlFunction]
public static SqlDecimal GetConvertedAmount(
    SqlDecimal InputAmount,
    SqlString InCurrency,
    SqlString OutCurrency)
{
    //Convert the input amount to the base
    decimal BaseAmount =
        GetRate(InCurrency.Value) *
        InputAmount.Value;

    //Return the converted base amount
    return (new SqlDecimal(
        GetRate(OutCurrency.Value) * BaseAmount));
}
```

The GetConvertedAmount method internally makes use of another method, GetRate:

```
private static decimal GetRate(string Currency)
{
    decimal theRate;
    rwl.AcquireReaderLock(100);

    try
    {
        theRate = rates[Currency];
    }
    finally
    {
        rwl.ReleaseLock();
    }

    return (theRate);
}
```

GetRate performs a lookup in a **static** generic instance of **Dictionary<string, decimal>**, called **rates**. This collection contains exchange rates for the given currencies in the system. In order to protect

169

against problems that will occur if another thread happens to be updating the rates, synchronization is handled using a static instance of **ReaderWriterLock**, called **rwl**. Both the dictionary and the **ReaderWriterLock** are instantiated when a method on the class is first called, and both are marked **readonly** in order to avoid being overwritten after instantiation:

```
static readonly Dictionary<string, decimal>
    rates = new Dictionary<string, decimal>();
static readonly ReaderWriterLock
    rwl = new ReaderWriterLock();
```

If cataloged using either the **SAFE** or **EXTERNAL_ACCESS** permission sets, this code fails due to its use of synchronization (the **ReaderWriterLock**), and running it produces a **HostProtectionException**. The solution is to move the affected code into its own assembly, cataloged as **UNSAFE**. Because the host protection check is evaluated at the moment of just-in-time compilation of a method in an assembly, rather than dynamically as the method is running, the check is done as the assembly boundary is being crossed. This means that an outer method can be marked **SAFE** and temporarily escalate its permissions by calling into an **UNSAFE** core.

■ **Note** You might be wondering about the validity of this example, given the ease with which this system could be implemented in pure T-SQL, which would eliminate the permissions problem outright. I do feel that this is a realistic example, especially if the system needs to do a large number of currency translations on any given day. SQLCLR code will generally outperform T-SQL for even simple mathematical work, and caching the data in a shared collection rather than reading it from the database on every call is a huge efficiency win. I'm confident that this solution would easily outperform any pure T-SQL equivalent.

When designing the **UNSAFE** assembly, it is important from a reuse point of view to carefully analyze what functionality should be made available. In this case, it's not the use of the dictionary that is causing the problem—synchronization via the **ReaderWriterLock** is throwing the actual exception. However, a wrapping method placed solely around a **ReaderWriterLock** would probably not promote very much reuse. A better tactic, in my opinion, is to wrap the **Dictionary** and the **ReaderWriterLock** together, creating a new **ThreadSafeDictionary** class. This class could be used in any scenario in which a shared data cache is required.

Following is my implementation of the **ThreadSafeDictionary**; I have not implemented all of the methods that the generic **Dictionary** class exposes, but rather only those I commonly use—namely, **Add**, **Remove**, and **ContainsKey**:

```
using System;
using System.Collections.Generic;
using System.Text;
using System.Threading;

namespace SafeDictionary
{
    public class ThreadSafeDictionary<K, V>
    {
```

```csharp
private readonly Dictionary<K, V> dict = new Dictionary<K,V>();
private readonly ReaderWriterLock theLock = new ReaderWriterLock();

public void Add(K key, V value)
{
    theLock.AcquireWriterLock(2000);

    try
    {
        dict.Add(key, value);
    }
    finally
    {
        theLock.ReleaseLock();
    }
}

public V this[K key]
{
    get
    {
        theLock.AcquireReaderLock(2000);
        try
        {
            return (this.dict[key]);
        }
        finally
        {
            theLock.ReleaseLock();
        }
    }

    set
    {
        theLock.AcquireWriterLock(2000);
        try
        {
            dict[key] = value;
        }
        finally
        {
            theLock.ReleaseLock();
        }
    }
}

public bool Remove(K key)
{
    theLock.AcquireWriterLock(2000);
    try
    {
        return (dict.Remove(key));
```

```
        }
        finally
        {
            theLock.ReleaseLock();
        }
    }

    public bool ContainsKey(K key)
    {
        theLock.AcquireReaderLock(2000);
        try
        {
            return (dict.ContainsKey(key));
        }
        finally
        {
            theLock.ReleaseLock();
        }
    }
  }
}
```

This class should be placed into a new assembly, which should then be compiled and cataloged in SQL Server as **UNSAFE**. A reference to the **UNSAFE** assembly should be used in the exchange rates conversion assembly, after which a few lines of the previous example code will have to change. First of all, the only static object that must be created is an instance of **ThreadSafeDictionary**:

```
static readonly ThreadSafeDictionary<string, decimal> rates =
    new ThreadSafeDictionary<string, decimal>();
```

Since the **ThreadSafeDictionary** is already thread safe, the **GetRate** method no longer needs to be concerned with synchronization. Without this requirement, its code becomes greatly simplified:

```
private static decimal GetRate(string Currency)
{
    return (rates[Currency]);
}
```

The exchange rates conversion assembly can still be marked **SAFE**, and can now make use of the encapsulated synchronization code without throwing a **HostProtectionException**. And none of the code actually contained in the assembly will be able to use resources that violate the permissions allowed by the **SAFE** bucket—quite an improvement over the initial implementation, from a security perspective.

■ **Note** Depending on whether your database has the TRUSTWORTHY option enabled and whether your assemblies are strongly named, things may not be *quite* as simple as I've implied here. The examples in both this and the next section may fail either at deployment time, if your core assembly doesn't have the correct permissions; or at runtime, if you've decided to go with a strongly named assembly. See the section "Granting Cross-Assembly Privileges" later in this chapter for more information. In the meantime, if you're following along, work in a database with the TRUSTWORTHY option turned on, and forgo the strong naming for now.

Working with Code Access Security Privileges

HPA-protected resources are quite easy to encapsulate, thanks to the fact that permissions for a given method are checked when the method is just-in-time compiled. Alas, things are not quite so simple when working with CAS-protected resources, due to the fact that grants are checked dynamically at runtime via a stack walk. This means that simply referencing a second assembly is not enough—the entire stack is walked each time, without regard to assembly boundaries.

To illustrate this issue, create a new assembly containing the following method, which reads all of the lines from a text file and returns them as a collection of strings:

```
public static string[] ReadFileLines(string FilePath)
{
    List<string> theLines = new List<string>();

    using (System.IO.StreamReader sr =
        new System.IO.StreamReader(FilePath))
    {
        string line;
        while ((line = sr.ReadLine()) != null)
            theLines.Add(line);
    }

    return (theLines.ToArray());
}
```

Catalog the assembly in SQL Server with the EXTERNAL_ACCESS permission set. Now let's revisit the CAS_Exception stored procedure created earlier this chapter, which was contained in a SAFE assembly, and threw an exception when used to access a local file resource. Edit the CAS_Exception assembly to include a reference to the assembly containing the ReadFileLines method, and modify the stored procedure as follows:

```
[SqlProcedure]
public static void CAS_Exception()
{
    SqlContext.Pipe.Send("Starting...");
```

```
string[] theLines =
    FileLines.ReadFileLines(@"C:\b.txt");

SqlContext.Pipe.Send("Finished...");

return;
}
```

Note that I created my **ReadFileLines** method inside a class called **FileLines**; reference yours appropriately depending on what class name you used. Once you've finished the modifications, redeploy the outer assembly, making sure that it is cataloged as **SAFE**.

Running the modified version of this stored procedure, you'll find that even though an assembly boundary is crossed, you will receive the same exception as before. The CAS grant did not change simply because a more highly privileged assembly was referenced, due to the fact that the stack walk does not take into account permissions held by referenced assemblies.

Working around this issue requires taking control of the stack walk within the referenced assembly. Since the assembly has enough privilege to do file operations, it can internally demand that the stack walk discontinue checks for file I/O permissions, even when called from another assembly that does not have the requisite permissions. This is done by using the **Assert** method of the **IStackWalk** interface, exposed in .NET's **System.Security** namespace.

Taking a second look at the CAS violation shown previously, note that the required permission is **FileIOPermission**, which is in the **System.Security.Permissions** namespace. The **FileIOPermission** class—in addition to other "permission" classes in that namespace—implements the **IStackWalk** interface. To avoid the CAS exception, simply instantiate an instance of the **FileIOPermission** class and call the **Assert** method. The following code is a modified version of the **ReadFileLines** method that uses this technique:

```
public static string[] ReadFileLines(string FilePath)
{
    //Assert that anything File IO-related that this
    //assembly has permission to do, callers can do
    FileIOPermission fp = new FileIOPermission(
        PermissionState.Unrestricted);
    fp.Assert();

    List<string> theLines = new List<string>();

    using (System.IO.StreamReader sr =
        new System.IO.StreamReader(FilePath))
    {
        string line;
        while ((line = sr.ReadLine()) != null)
            theLines.Add(line);
    }

    return (theLines.ToArray());
}
```

This version of the method instantiates the **FileIOPermission** class with the **PermissionState.Unrestricted** enumeration, thereby enabling all callers to do whatever file I/O–related activities the assembly has permission to do. The use of the term "unrestricted" in this context is not as dangerous as it sounds; the access is unrestricted in the sense that permission is allowed for only as much access as the assembly already has to the file system. After making the modifications shown here and redeploying both assemblies, the CAS exception will no longer be an issue.

To allow you to control things on a more granular level, the `FileIOPermission` class exposes other constructor overloads with different options. The most useful of these for this example uses an enumeration called `FileIOPermissionAccess` in conjunction with the path to a file, allowing you to limit the permissions granted to the caller to only specific operations on a named file. For instance, to limit access so that the caller can only read the file specified in this example, use the following constructor:

```
FileIOPermission fp = new FileIOPermission(
    FileIOPermissionAccess.Read,
    "C:\b.txt");
```

File I/O is only one of many kinds of permissions for which you might see a CAS exception. The important thing is being able to identify the pattern. In all cases, violations will throw a `SecurityException` and reference a permission class in the `System.Security.Permissions` namespace. Each class follows the same basic pattern outlined here, so you should be able to easily use this technique in order to design any number of privilege escalation solutions.

Granting Cross-Assembly Privileges

The examples in the preceding sections were simplified a bit in order to focus the text on a single issue at a time. There are two other issues you need to be concerned with when working with cross-assembly calls: **database trustworthiness** and **strong naming**.

Database Trustworthiness

The idea of a "trustworthy" database is a direct offshoot of Microsoft's heightened awareness of security issues in recent years. Marking a database as trustworthy is a simple matter of setting an option using `ALTER DATABASE`:

```
ALTER DATABASE AdventureWorks2008
SET TRUSTWORTHY ON;
GO
```

Unfortunately, as simple as enabling this option is, the repercussions of this setting are far from it. Effectively, it comes down to the fact that code running in the context of a trustworthy database can access resources outside of the database more easily than code running in a database not marked as such. This means access to the file system, remote database servers, and even other databases on the same server—all of this access is controlled by this one option, so be careful.

Turning off the **TRUSTWORTHY** option means that rogue code will have a much harder time accessing resources outside of the database, but it also means that, as a developer, you will have to spend more time dealing with security issues. That said, I highly recommend leaving the **TRUSTWORTHY** option turned off unless you really have a great reason to enable it. Dealing with access control in a nontrustworthy database is not too difficult; the module-signing techniques discussed in Chapter 5 should be applied, which puts access control squarely in your hands and does not make life easy for code that shouldn't have access to a given resource.

In the SQLCLR world, you'll see a deploy-time exception if you catalog an assembly that references an assembly using the **EXTERNAL_ACCESS** or **UNSAFE** permission sets in a nontrustworthy database.

Following is the exception I get when trying to catalog the assembly I created that contains the **GetConvertedAmount** method, after setting my database to nontrustworthy mode:

```
CREATE ASSEMBLY for assembly 'CurrencyConversion' failed because
assembly 'SafeDictionary' is not authorized for PERMISSION_SET = UNSAFE.
The assembly is authorized when either of the following is true: the database
owner (DBO) has UNSAFE ASSEMBLY permission and the database has the TRUSTWORTHY
database property on; or the assembly is signed with a certificate or an asymmetric
key that has a corresponding login with UNSAFE ASSEMBLY permission.
If you have restored or attached this database, make sure the database owner is
mapped to the correct login on this server. If not, use sp_changedbowner to fix
 the problem.
```

This rather verbose exception is rare and to be treasured: it describes exactly how to solve the problem! Following the procedure described in Chapter 5, you can grant the **UNSAFE ASSEMBLY** permission by using certificates. To begin, create a certificate and a corresponding login in the **master** database, and grant the login **UNSAFE ASSEMBLY** permission:

```
USE master;
GO

CREATE CERTIFICATE Assembly_Permissions_Certificate
ENCRYPTION BY PASSWORD = 'uSe_a STr()nG PaSSWOrD!'
WITH SUBJECT = 'Certificate used to grant assembly permission';
GO

CREATE LOGIN Assembly_Permissions_Login
FROM CERTIFICATE Assembly_Permissions_Certificate;
GO

GRANT UNSAFE ASSEMBLY TO Assembly_Permissions_Login;
GO
```

Next, back up the certificate to a file:

```
BACKUP CERTIFICATE Assembly_Permissions_Certificate
TO FILE = 'C:\assembly_permissions.cer'
WITH PRIVATE KEY
(
    FILE = 'C:\assembly_permissions.pvk',
    ENCRYPTION BY PASSWORD = 'is?tHiS_a_VeRySTronGP4ssWoR|)?',
    DECRYPTION BY PASSWORD = 'uSe_a STr()nG PaSSWOrD!'
);
GO
```

Now, in the database in which you're working—AdventureWorks2008, in my case—restore the certificate and create a local database user from it:

```
USE AdventureWorks2008;
GO
```

```
CREATE CERTIFICATE Assembly_Permissions_Certificate
FROM FILE = 'C:\assembly_permissions.cer'
WITH PRIVATE KEY
(
    FILE = 'C:\assembly_permissions.pvk',
    DECRYPTION BY PASSWORD = 'is?tHiS_a_VeRySTronGP4ssWoR|)?',
    ENCRYPTION BY PASSWORD = 'uSe_a STr()nG PaSSWOrD!'
);
GO

CREATE USER Assembly_Permissions_User
FOR CERTIFICATE Assembly_Permissions_Certificate;
GO
```

Finally, sign the assembly with the certificate, thereby granting access and allowing the assembly to be referenced:

```
ADD SIGNATURE TO ASSEMBLY::SafeDictionary
BY CERTIFICATE Assembly_Permissions_Certificate
WITH PASSWORD='uSe_a STr()nG PaSSWOrD!';
GO
```

Strong Naming

The other issue you might encounter has to do with strongly named assemblies. Strong naming is a .NET security feature that allows you to digitally sign your assembly, allocating a version number and ensuring its validity to users. For most SQLCLR code, strong naming is probably overkill—code running in secured, managed databases probably doesn't need the additional assurances that strong naming provides. However, vendors looking at distributing applications that include SQLCLR components will definitely want to look at strong naming.

After signing the assembly that contains the **ReadFileLines** method and redeploying both it and the assembly containing the **CAS_Exception** stored procedure, I receive the following error when I call the procedure:

```
Msg 6522, Level 16, State 1, Procedure CAS_Exception, Line 0

A .NET Framework error occurred during execution of user-defined routine or

aggregate "CAS_Exception":

System.Security.SecurityException: That assembly does not allow partially trusted

callers.

System.Security.SecurityException:

    at System.Security.CodeAccessSecurityEngine.ThrowSecurityException(Assembly asm,
```

```
PermissionSet granted, PermissionSet refused, RuntimeMethodHandle rmh,

SecurityAction action, Object demand, IPermission permThatFailed)

   at udf_part2.CAS_Exception()

.
```

The solution is to add an **AllowPartiallyTrustedCallersAttribute** (often referred to merely as APTCA in articles) to the code. This attribute should be added to a single file in the assembly, after the **using** declarations and before definition of any classes or namespaces. In the case of the **FileLines** assembly, the file looks like the following after adding the attribute:

```
using System;
using System.Data;
using System.Data.SqlClient;
using System.Data.SqlTypes;
using Microsoft.SqlServer.Server;
using System.Collections.Generic;
using System.Security.Permissions;

[assembly: System.Security.AllowPartiallyTrustedCallers]

public partial class FileLines
{
```

Once this attribute has been added, any caller can use the methods in the **FileLines** class, without receiving an exception. Keep in mind that this attribute must be specified for a reason, and by using it you may be allowing callers to circumvent security. If the assembly performs operations that not all users should be able to access, make sure to implement other security measures, such as by creating groups of assemblies with different owners, to ensure that nongrouped assemblies cannot reference the sensitive methods.

Performance Comparison: SQLCLR vs. TSQL

Having discussed some of the security and architecture considerations behind implementing a SQLCLR-based solution, you may be wondering about what sort of situations could actually benefit from using SQLCLR.

It is important to realize that SQLCLR is not, and was never intended to be, a replacement for T-SQL as a data manipulation language in SQL Server. In order to read data from the database, and to perform most standard data operations, T-SQL is the only choice. Also, although I've stressed the importance of creating portable code that may be easily moved and shared between tiers, you should not try to use SQLCLR as a way of moving logic that rightly belongs in the application into the database. Although allowing the potential for code reuse between tiers can be beneficial, remember that database servers are typically the most expensive tier to scale, so moving too much logic into the database is an inefficient use of precious database resources, which could have been provided by a much cheaper application server. For a further discussion of the correct placement of data and application logic, refer back to Chapter 1.

Examples of commonly cited situations in which SQLCLR is perhaps a better choice than TSQL include manipulation of string or XML data, certain math functions that are provided by dedicated methods in the .NET Base Class Library, and situations where procedural code is more efficient than set-based logic. In order to test the validity of these claims, I decided to set up some simple test cases to compare the relative performance of T-SQL against SQLCLR, which are described in the following sections.

Creating a "Simple Sieve" for Prime Numbers

For this test, I created two simple procedures that return a list of all prime numbers up to a supplied maximum value—one implemented in T-SQL, and one using SQLCLR. The logic of these tests was made as simple as possible: each is supplied with a maximum value that is decremented in a loop, and in each iteration of the loop, the modulo operator is used to determine the remainder when that value is divided by every lesser number. If the remainder of the division is 0 (in other words, we have found a factor), we know that the current value is not a prime number. The loop therefore moves on to test the next possible value. If the inner loop tests every possible divisor and has not found any factors, then we know the value must be a prime. Using this kind of "simple sieve" algorithm for finding prime numbers relies on basic mathematical functions and procedural logic, which makes it a good test to compare the performance of T-SQL and SQLCLR. Here's the T-SQL implementation:

```
CREATE PROCEDURE ListPrimesTSQL (
  @Limit int
  )
AS BEGIN
DECLARE
  -- @n is the number we're testing to see if it's a prime
  @n int = @Limit,
  --@m is all the possible numbers that could be a factor of @n
  @m int = @Limit - 1;
  -- Loop descending through the candidate primes
  WHILE (@n > 1)
  BEGIN
    -- Loop descending through the candidate factors
    WHILE (@m > 0)
    BEGIN
      -- We've got all the way to 2 and haven't found any factors
      IF(@m = 1)
      BEGIN
        PRINT CAST(@n AS varchar(32)) + ' is a prime'
        BREAK;
      END
      -- Is this @m a factor of this prime?
      IF(@n%@m) <> 0
      BEGIN
        -- Not a factor, so move on to the next @m
        SET @m = @m - 1;
        CONTINUE;
      END
```

```
        ELSE BREAK;
      END
      SET @n = @n-1;
      SET @m = @n-1;
    END
END;
GO
```

And here's the SQLCLR implementation using exactly the same logic:

```
[SqlProcedure]
public static void ListPrimesCLR(SqlInt32 Limit)
{
  int n = (int)Limit;
  int m = (int)Limit - 1;

  while(n > 1)
  {
    while(m > 0)
    {
      if(m == 1)
      {
        SqlContext.Pipe.Send(n.ToString() + " is a prime");
      }

      if(n%m != 0)
      {
        m = m - 1;
        continue;
      }
      else
      {
        break;
      }
    }
    n = n - 1;
    m = n - 1;
  }
}
```

■ **Note** Clearly, if you actually wanted to get a list of the prime numbers, you would NOT use such a naive approach as this. The example used here is intended to provide a simple procedure that can be implemented consistently across both T-SQL and SQLCLR.

I tested each solution several times, supplying different values for the maximum limit from which the loop starts. The average execution time for each solution is shown in the graph illustrated in Figure 7-1.

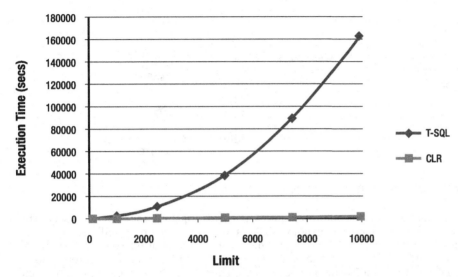

Figure 7-1. Comparison of prime number sieve implemented in T-SQL and SQLCLR

The results should come as no surprise—since the approach taken relies on mathematical operations in an iterative loop, SQLCLR is always likely to outperform set-based T-SQL. However, you might be surprised by the magnitude of the difference between the two solutions, especially as the number of iterations increases. If we were to compare simple inline, or nonprocedural, calculations then there would likely not be such a stark contrast between the two methods.

Calculating Running Aggregates

Few practical database applications need to produce a list of prime numbers—a more common type of mathematical query operation that might benefit from the use of SQLCLR is when you need to calculate a value in a row based on the value of previous rows' data. The most common example of such a linear query is in the calculation of aggregates, such as running sums of columns.

The typical approach using T-SQL is to make use of a self-join on the table, such as follows:

```
SELECT
  T1.x,
  SUM(T2.x) AS running_x
FROM
  T AS T1 INNER JOIN T AS T2
    ON T1.x >= T2.x
GROUP BY
  T1.x;
```

Unfortunately, the process required to satisfy this query is not very efficient. Assuming that an index exists on the **x** column of the table, the preceding query generates the execution plan shown in Figure 7-2.

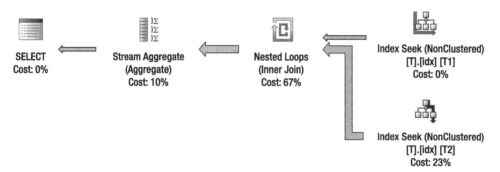

Figure 7-2. A nested index seek used to create a running sum in T-SQL

To sum all of the previous values in the column requires a nested loop containing an index seek. The number of rows returned by this seek increases exponentially as more rows are processed. On the first row, this seek must only sum one value, but to find the running sum over a set of 100 rows, 5,050 total rows need to be read. For a set of 200 rows, the query processor needs to process 20,100 total rows—four times the amount of work required to satisfy the previous query. Thus, the performance of this approach to calculate running aggregates degrades rapidly as more rows are added to the table.

An alternative solution, which can yield some significant performance benefits, is to make use of a cursor. There is a commonly held perception in the SQL Server development world that cursors are a bad thing, but they do have valid use cases, and this might be one of them. However, there are a number of good reasons why many developers are reluctant to use cursors, and I'm certainly not advocating their use in general.

A better approach would be to use SQLCLR to loop through and store the running values using local variables, and then stream the results one row at a time via the **SqlPipe**. An example of such a solution is given in the following code listing:

```
[Microsoft.SqlServer.Server.SqlProcedure]
public static void RunningSum()
{
  using (SqlConnection conn = new SqlConnection("context connection=true;"))
  {
    SqlCommand comm = new SqlCommand();
    comm.Connection = conn;
    comm.CommandText = "SELECT x FROM T ORDER BY x";

    SqlMetaData[] columns = new SqlMetaData[2];
    columns[0] = new SqlMetaData("Value", SqlDbType.Int);
    columns[1] = new SqlMetaData("RunningSum", SqlDbType.Int);

    int RunningSum = 0;

    SqlDataRecord record = new SqlDataRecord(columns);
```

```
    SqlContext.Pipe.SendResultsStart(record);

    conn.Open();

    SqlDataReader reader = comm.ExecuteReader();

    while (reader.Read())
    {
      int Value = (int)reader[0];
      RunningSum += Value;

      record.SetInt32(0, (int)reader[0]);
      record.SetInt32(1, RunningSum);

      SqlContext.Pipe.SendResultsRow(record);
    }

    SqlContext.Pipe.SendResultsEnd();
  }
}
```

I've used this solution on a number of occasions and find it to be very efficient and maintainable, and it avoids the need for any temp tables to be used to hold the running sums as required by the alternatives. When testing against a table containing 100,000 rows, I achieve an average execution time of 2.7 seconds for the SQLCLR query, compared to over 5 *minutes* for the TSQL equivalent.

String Manipulation

To compare the performance of string-handling functions between T-SQL and SQLCLR, I wanted to come up with a fair, practical test. The problem is that there are lots of ingenious techniques for working with string data: in T-SQL, some of the best performing methods use one or more common table expressions (CTEs), **CROSS APPLY** operators, or number tables; or convert text strings to XML in or order to perform nontrivial manipulation of character data. Likewise, in SQLCLR, the techniques available differ considerably depending on whether you use the native **String** methods or those provided by the **StringBuilder** class.

I decided that, rather than try to define a scenario that required a string-handling technique, the only fair test was to perform a direct comparison of two built-in methods that provided the equivalent functionality in either environment. I decided to settle on the T-SQL **CHARINDEX** and .NET's **String.IndexOf()**, each of which searches for and returns the position of one string inside another string. For the purposes of the test, I created **nvarchar(max)** strings of different lengths, each composed entirely of the repeating character **a**. I then appended a single character **x** onto the end of each string, and timed the performance of the respective methods to find the position of that character over 10,000 iterations.

The following code listing demonstrates the T-SQL method:

```
CREATE PROCEDURE SearchCharTSQL
(
  @needle nchar(1),
  @haystack nvarchar(max)
  )
AS BEGIN
  PRINT CHARINDEX(@needle, @haystack);
END;
```

And here's the() CLR equivalent:

```
[SqlProcedure]
public static void SearchCharCLR(SqlString needle, SqlString haystack)
{
  SqlContext.Pipe.Send(
    haystack.ToString().IndexOf(needle.ToString()).ToString()
  );
}
```

Note that the starting position for **CHARINDEX** is 1-based, whereas the index numbering used by **IndexOf()** is 0-based. The results of each method will therefore differ, but they will have done the same amount of work obtaining that result. I tested each procedure as follows, substituting different parameter values for the **REPLICATE** method to change the length of the string to be searched:

```
DECLARE @needle nvarchar(1) = 'x';
DECLARE @haystack nvarchar(max);
SELECT @haystack = REPLICATE(CAST('a' AS varchar(max)), 8000) + 'x';
EXEC dbo.SearchCharTSQL @needle, @haystack;
```

The execution times required for 10,000 runs of each method are shown in Figure 7-3.

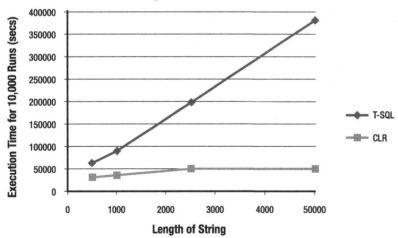

Figure 7-3. Comparing performance of CHARINDEX against String. ( )IndexOf()

As with the prime number sieve example given earlier, the logic required for string searching, matching, and replacing is best suited to the highly efficient routines provided by the .NET Base Class Library. If you currently have code logic that relies heavily on T-SQL string functionality including **CHARINDEX**, **PATINDEX**, or **REPLACE**, I highly recommend that you investigate the alternative options available through SQLCLR—you might be surprised by the performance gain you achieve.

Enhancing Service Broker Scale-Out with SQLCLR

Having discussed some of the theory behind working with the SQLCLR and given some isolated performance comparisons, let's now turn our attention to a more detailed example that puts these ideas into practice. Service Broker is frequently mentioned as an excellent choice for helping to scale out database services. One of the more compelling use cases is a Service Broker service that can be used to asynchronously request data from a remote system. In such a case, a request message would be sent to the remote data service from a local stored procedure, which could do some other work while waiting for the response—the requested data—to come back.

There are many ways to architect such a system, and given that Service Broker allows messages to be sent either as binary or XML, I wondered which would provide the best overall performance and value from a code reuse perspective. In the following sections, I'll guide you through my investigations into XML and binary serialization using SQLCLR.

XML Serialization

I started working with the **HumanResources.Employee** table from the **AdventureWorks2008** database as a sample data set, imagining a remote data service requesting a list of employees along with their attributes. After some experimentation, I determined that the **FOR XML RAW** option is the easiest way to serialize a table in XML format, and I used the **ROOT** option to make the XML valid:

```
DECLARE @x xml;
SET @x = (
   SELECT *
   FROM HumanResources.Employee
   FOR XML RAW, ROOT('Employees')
);
GO
```

XML is, of course, known to be an extremely verbose data interchange format, and I was not surprised to discover that the data size of the resultant XML is 105KB, despite the fact that the **HumanResources.Employee** table itself has only 56KB of data. I experimented with setting shorter column names, but it had very little effect on the size and created what I feel to be unmaintainable code.

Next, I set up a trace to gather some idea of the performance of the XML serialization (for more information on traces, refer to Chapter 3). The trace results revealed that the average execution time for the preceding query on my system, averaged over 1,000 iterations, was a decidedly unimpressive 3.9095 seconds per iteration.

After some trial and error, I discovered that XML serialization could be made to perform better by using the **TYPE** directive, as follows:

```
DECLARE @x xml;
SET @x = (
```

```
    SELECT *
    FROM HumanResources.Employee
    FOR XML RAW, ROOT('Employees'), TYPE
);
GO
```

This change brought the average time per iteration down slightly, to 3.6687 seconds—an improvement, but still not a very good result.

XML Deserialization

Even though XML serialization had not yielded impressive performance, I decided to carry on and test deserialization. The first problem was the code required to deserialize the XML back into a table. In order to get back the same table I started with, I had to explicitly define every column for the result set; this made the code quite a bit more complex than I'd hoped for. Furthermore, since the XQuery **value** syntax does not support the **hierarchyid** datatype, the values in the **OrganizationNode** column must be read as **nvarchar** and then **CAST** to **hierarchyid**. The resulting code is as follows:

```
DECLARE @x xml;
SET @x = (
  SELECT *
  FROM HumanResources.Employee
  FOR XML RAW, ROOT('Employees'), TYPE
);

SELECT
    col.value('@BusinessEntityID', 'int') AS BusinessEntityID,
    col.value('@NationalIDNumber', 'nvarchar(15)') AS NationalIDNumber,
    col.value('@LoginID', 'nvarchar(256)') AS LoginID,
    CAST(col.value('@OrganizationNode', 'nvarchar(256)') AS hierarchyid)
      AS OrganizationNode,
    col.value('@JobTitle', 'nvarchar(50)') AS JobTitle,
    col.value('@BirthDate', 'datetime') AS BirthDate,
    col.value('@MaritalStatus', 'nchar(1)') AS MaritalStatus,
    col.value('@Gender', 'nchar(1)') AS Gender,
    col.value('@HireDate', 'datetime') AS HireDate,
    col.value('@SalariedFlag', 'bit') AS SalariedFlag,
    col.value('@VacationHours', 'smallint') AS VacationHours,
    col.value('@SickLeaveHours', 'smallint') AS SickLeaveHours,
    col.value('@CurrentFlag', 'bit') AS CurrentFlag,
    col.value('@rowguid', 'uniqueidentifier') AS rowguid,
    col.value('@ModifiedDate', 'datetime') AS ModifiedDate
FROM @x.nodes ('/Employees/row') x (col);
GO
```

The next problem was performance. When I tested deserializing the XML using the preceding query, performance went from poor to downright abysmal—averaging 6.8157 seconds per iteration.

At this point, I decided to investigate SQLCLR options for solving the problem, focusing on both reuse potential and performance.

Binary Serialization with SQLCLR

My first thought was to return binary serialized **DataTables**; in order to make that happen, I needed a way to return binary-formatted data from my CLR routines. This of course called for .NET's **BinaryFormatter** class, so I created a class called **serialization_helper**, cataloged in an **EXTERNAL_ACCESS** assembly (required for **System.IO** access):

```
using System;
using System.Data;
using System.Data.SqlClient;
using System.Data.SqlTypes;
using Microsoft.SqlServer.Server;
using System.Security.Permissions;
using System.Runtime.Serialization.Formatters.Binary;

public partial class serialization_helper
{
    public static byte[] getBytes(object o)
    {
        SecurityPermission sp =
            new SecurityPermission(
                SecurityPermissionFlag.SerializationFormatter);
        sp.Assert();

        BinaryFormatter bf = new BinaryFormatter();

        using (System.IO.MemoryStream ms =
            new System.IO.MemoryStream())
        {
            bf.Serialize(ms, o);

            return(ms.ToArray());
        }
    }

    public static object getObject(byte[] theBytes)
    {
        using (System.IO.MemoryStream ms =
            new System.IO.MemoryStream(theBytes, false))
        {
            return(getObject(ms));
        }
    }

    public static object getObject(System.IO.Stream s)
    {
        SecurityPermission sp =
            new SecurityPermission(
                SecurityPermissionFlag.SerializationFormatter);
        sp.Assert();
```

```
        BinaryFormatter bf = new BinaryFormatter();

        return (bf.Deserialize(s));
    }
};
```

Use of this class is fairly straightforward: to serialize an object, pass it into the **getBytes** method. This method first uses an assertion, as discussed previously, to allow **SAFE** callers to use it, and then uses the binary formatter to serialize the object to a **Stream**. The stream is then returned as a collection of bytes. Deserialization can be done using either overload of the **getObject** method. I found that depending on the scenario, I might have ready access to either a **Stream** or a collection of bytes, so creating both overloads made sense instead of duplicating code to produce one from the other. Deserialization also uses an assertion before running, in order to allow calling code to be cataloged as **SAFE**.

My first shot at getting the data was to simply load the input set into a **DataTable** and run it through the **serialization_helper** methods. The following code implements a UDF called **GetDataTable_Binary**, which uses this logic:

```
[Microsoft.SqlServer.Server.SqlFunction(
    DataAccess = DataAccessKind.Read)]
public static SqlBytes GetDataTable_Binary(string query)
{
    SqlConnection conn =
        new SqlConnection("context connection = true;");

    SqlCommand comm = new SqlCommand();
    comm.Connection = conn;
    comm.CommandText = query;

    SqlDataAdapter da = new SqlDataAdapter();
    da.SelectCommand = comm;

    DataTable dt = new DataTable();
    da.Fill(dt);

    //Serialize and return the output
    return new SqlBytes(
        serialization_helper.getBytes(dt));
}
```

This method is used by passing in a query for the table that you'd like to get back in binary serialized form, as in the following example:

```
DECLARE @sql nvarchar(max);
SET @sql = 'SELECT
    BusinessEntityID,
    NationalIDNumber,
    LoginID,
    OrganizationNode.ToString(),
    OrganizationLevel,
    JobTitle,
    BirthDate,
```

```
        MaritalStatus,
        Gender,
        HireDate,
        SalariedFlag,
        VacationHours,
        SickLeaveHours,
        CurrentFlag,
        rowguid,
        ModifiedDate
    FROM HumanResources.Employee';

DECLARE @x varbinary(max);
SET @x = dbo.GetDataTable_Binary(@sql);
GO
```

■ **Note** The `hierarchyid` CLR datatype is not marked as serializable, so in the preceding query I use the `ToString()` method to serialize the string representation of the `OrganizationNode` value.

The results of the initial performance test were very encouraging, revealing that average serialization speed had been reduced to just 0.1437 seconds—a massive improvement over the XML serialization method.

The performance of the binary method could be improved yet further by setting the `RemotingFormat` property of the `DataTable` to `Binary` before serialization:

```
dt.RemotingFormat = SerializationFormat.Binary;
```

Making this change resulted in even faster performance—just 0.0576 seconds. What's more, the resulting binary data was now only 68KB in size.

Encouraged by the success of my first shot, I decided to investigate whether there were other SQLCLR methods that would improve the performance still further. After several more attempts that I won't bore you with the details of, I decided to forgo the `DataTable` in favor of an alternative class: `SqlDataReader`. I worked on pulling the data out into object collections, and initial tests showed serialization performance with `SqlDataReader` to be just as good as the `DataTable`, but with a reduced output size. However, this approach was not without its own difficulties.

The advantage of a `DataTable` is that it's one easy-to-use unit that contains all of the data, as well as the associated metadata. You don't have to be concerned with column names, types, and sizes, as everything is automatically loaded into the `DataTable` for you. Working with a `SqlDataReader` requires a bit more work, since it can't be serialized as a single unit, but must instead be split up into its component parts.

Since the code I implemented is somewhat complex, I will walk you through it section by section. To begin with, I set the `DataAccessKind.Read` property on the `SqlFunctionAttribute` in order to allow the method to access data via the context connection. A generic `List` is instantiated, which will hold one object collection per row of data, in addition to one for the metadata. Finally, the `SqlConnection` is instantiated and the `SqlCommand` is set up and executed:

```
[Microsoft.SqlServer.Server.SqlFunction(
    DataAccess = DataAccessKind.Read)]
```

```
public static SqlBytes GetBinaryFromQueryResult(string query)
{
    List<object[]> theList = new List<object[]>();

    using (SqlConnection conn =
        new SqlConnection("context connection = true;"))
    {
        SqlCommand comm = new SqlCommand();
        comm.Connection = conn;
        comm.CommandText = query;

        conn.Open();

        SqlDataReader read = comm.ExecuteReader();
```

The next step is to pull the metadata for each column out of the **SqlDataReader**. A method called **GetSchemaTable** is used to return a **DataTable** populated with one row per column. The available fields are documented in the MSDN Library, but I'm using the most common of them in the code that follows. After populating the object collection with the metadata, it is added to the output **List**:

```
        DataTable dt = read.GetSchemaTable();

        //Populate the field list from the schema table
        object[] fields = new object[dt.Rows.Count];
        for (int i = 0; i < fields.Length; i++)
        {
            object[] field = new object[5];
            field[0] = dt.Rows[i]["ColumnName"];
            field[1] = dt.Rows[i]["ProviderType"];
            field[2] = dt.Rows[i]["ColumnSize"];
            field[3] = dt.Rows[i]["NumericPrecision"];
            field[4] = dt.Rows[i]["NumericScale"];

            fields[i] = field;
        }

        //Add the collection of fields to the output list
        theList.Add(fields);
```

Finally, the code loops over the rows returned by the query, using the **GetValues** method to pull each row out into an object collection that is added to the output. The **List** is converted into an array of **object[]** (**object[][]**, to be more precise), which is serialized and returned to the caller.

```
        //Add all of the rows to the output list
        while (read.Read())
        {
            object[] o = new object[read.FieldCount];
            read.GetValues(o);
            theList.Add(o);
        }
    }
```

```
//Serialize and return the output
return new SqlBytes(
    serialization_helper.getBytes(theList.ToArray()));
}
```

Once this function is created, calling it is almost identical to calling **GetDataTable_Binary**:

```
DECLARE @sql nvarchar(max);
SET @sql = 'SELECT  BusinessEntityID,
  NationalIDNumber,
  LoginID,
  OrganizationNode.ToString(),
  OrganizationLevel,
  JobTitle,
  BirthDate,
  MaritalStatus,
  Gender,
  HireDate,
  SalariedFlag,
  VacationHours,
  SickLeaveHours,
  CurrentFlag,
  rowguid,
  ModifiedDate FROM HumanResources.Employee'

DECLARE @x varbinary(max);
SET @x = dbo.GetBinaryFromQueryResult(@sql);
GO
```

The result, 57KB worth of binary data, represented a 15 percent reduction in size compared to the **DataTable** method. If using this method to transfer data between broker instances on remote servers, the associated decrease in network traffic could make a big difference to performance. What's more, the serialization performance using **SqlDataReader** was the fastest yet, with an average query execution time of just 0.0490 seconds.

Binary Deserialization

Pleased with the results of binary serialization using SQLCLR, I decided to go ahead with deserialization. Continuing with my stress on reuse potential, I decided that a stored procedure would be a better choice than a UDF. A stored procedure does not have a fixed output as does a UDF, so any input table can be deserialized and returned without worrying about violating column list contracts.

The first part of the stored procedure follows:

```
[Microsoft.SqlServer.Server.SqlProcedure]
public static void GetTableFromBinary(SqlBytes theTable)
{
    //Deserialize the input
    object[] dt = (object[])(
        serialization_helper.getObject(theTable.Value));
```

```
//First, get the fields
object[] fields = (object[])(dt[0]);
SqlMetaData[] cols = new SqlMetaData[fields.Length];

//Loop over the fields and populate SqlMetaData objects
for (int i = 0; i<fields.Length; i++)
{
    object[] field = (object[])(fields[i]);
    SqlDbType dbType = (SqlDbType)field[1];
```

After deserializing the input bytes back into a collection of objects, the first item in the collection—
which is assumed to be the column metadata—is converted into a collection of objects. This collection is
looped over item by item in order to create the output **SqlMetaData** objects that will be used to stream
back the data to the caller.

The trickiest part of setting this up is the fact that each SQL Server data type requires a different
SqlMetaData overload. **decimal** needs a precision and scale setting; character and binary types need a
size; and for other types, size, precision, and scale are all inappropriate inputs. The following **switch**
statement handles creation of the **SqlMetaData** instances:

```
//Different SqlMetaData overloads are required
//depending on the data type
switch (dbType)
{
    case SqlDbType.Decimal:
        cols[i] = new SqlMetaData(
            (string)field[0],
            dbType,
            (byte)field[3],
            (byte)field[4]);
        break;
    case SqlDbType.Binary:
    case SqlDbType.Char:
    case SqlDbType.NChar:
    case SqlDbType.NVarChar:
    case SqlDbType.VarBinary:
    case SqlDbType.VarChar:
        switch ((int)field[2])
        {
            //If it's a MAX type, use -1 as the size
            case 2147483647:
                cols[i] = new SqlMetaData(
                    (string)field[0],
                    dbType,
                    -1);
                break;
            default:
                cols[i] = new SqlMetaData(
                    (string)field[0],
                    dbType,
                    (long)((int)field[2]));
                break;
```

```
            }
            break;
        default:
            cols[i] = new SqlMetaData(
                (string)field[0],
                dbType);
            break;
    }
}
```

Once population of the columns collection has been completed, the data can be sent back to the caller using the **SqlPipe** class's **SendResults** methods. After starting the stream, the remainder of the objects in the input collection are looped over, cast to **object[ ]**, and sent back as **SqlDataRecords**:

```
//Start the result stream
SqlDataRecord rec = new SqlDataRecord(cols);
SqlContext.Pipe.SendResultsStart(rec);

for (int i = 1; i < dt.Length; i++)
{
    rec.SetValues((object[])dt[i]);
    SqlContext.Pipe.SendResultsRow(rec);
}

//End the result stream
SqlContext.Pipe.SendResultsEnd();
}
```

Not only had the binary serialization test yielded positive results, it turns out that deserialization of data prepared in this manner is exceptionally fast compared with the alternatives. The performance test revealed that average time for deserialization of the **SqlDataReader** data was just 0.2666 seconds—an order of magnitude faster than deserialization of similar XML.

The results of the fastest refinements of each of the three methods discussed in this section are shown in Table 7-1.

Table 7-1. Results of different serialization approaches

Method	Average Serialization Time	Average Deserialization Time	Size
XML (with **TYPE**)	3.6687	6.8157	105KB
Binary (**DataTable**)	0.0576		68KB
Binary (**SqlDataReader**)	0.0490	0.2666	57KB

The combination of better network utilization and much faster serialization/deserialization demonstrated in this example shows how SQLCLR can be a great technique for transferring tabular data between Service Broker instances in scale-out and distributed processing scenarios.

Summary

Getting the most out of SQLCLR routines involves a bit of thought investment. Up-front design and architecture considerations will yield great benefits in terms of security, reliability, and performance. You should also consider reuse at every stage, in order to minimize the amount of work that must be done when you need the same functionality six months or a year down the road. If you've already coded it once, why code it again?

To illustrate these concepts, I showed an example that serialized tables using the **BinaryFormatter**, which could be used to extend SQL Server Service Broker. I used a common, core set of more highly privileged utility assemblies in order to limit the outer surface area, and tried to design the solution to promote flexibility and potential for use in many projects throughout the lifetime of the code.

CHAPTER 8

■ ■ ■

Dynamic T-SQL

The general objective of any software application is to provide consistent, reliable functionality that allows users to perform given tasks in an effective manner. The first step in meeting this objective is therefore to keep the application bug-free and working as designed, to expected standards. However, once you've gotten past these basic requirements, the next step is to try to create a great user experience, which raises the question, "What do the users want?" More often than not, the answer is that users want flexible interfaces that let them control the data the way they want to. It's common for software customer support teams to receive requests for slightly different sort orders, filtering mechanisms, or outputs for data, making it imperative that applications be designed to support extensibility along these lines.

As with other data-related development challenges, such requests for flexible data output tend to fall through the application hierarchy, eventually landing on the database (and, therefore, the database developer). This is especially true in web-based application development, where client-side grid controls that enable sorting and filtering are still relatively rare, and where many applications still use a lightweight two-tier model without a dedicated business layer to handle data caching and filtering.

"Flexibility" in the database can mean many things, and I have encountered some very interesting approaches in applications I've worked with over the years, often involving creation of a multitude of stored procedures or complex, nested control-of-flow blocks. These solutions invariably seem to create more problems than they solve, and make application development much more difficult than it needs to be by introducing a lot of additional complexity in the database layer.

In this chapter, I will discuss how dynamic SQL can be used to solve these problems as well as to create more flexible stored procedures. Some DBAs and developers scorn dynamic SQL, often believing that it will cause performance, security, or maintainability problems, whereas in many cases it is simply that they don't understand how to use it properly. Dynamic SQL is a powerful tool that, if used correctly, is a tremendous asset to the database developer's toolbox. There is a lot of misinformation floating around about what it is and when or why it should be used, and I hope to clear up some myths and misconceptions in these pages.

■ **Note** Throughout this chapter, I will illustrate the discussion of various methods with performance measures and timings recorded on my laptop. For more information on how to capture these measures on your own system environment, please refer to the discussion of performance monitoring tools in Chapter 3.

Dynamic T-SQL vs. Ad Hoc T-SQL

Before I begin a serious discussion about how dynamic SQL should be used, it's first important to establish a bit of terminology. Two terms that are often intermingled in the database world with regard to SQL are **dynamic** and **ad hoc**. When referring to these terms in this chapter, I define them as follows:

- Ad hoc SQL is any batch of SQL generated within an application layer and sent to SQL Server for execution. This includes almost all of the code samples in this book, which are entered and submitted via SQL Server Management Studio.

- Dynamic SQL, on the other hand, is a batch of SQL that is generated *within T-SQL* and executed using the **EXECUTE** statement or, preferably, via the **sp_executesql** system stored procedure (which is covered later in this chapter).

Most of this chapter focuses on how to use dynamic SQL effectively using stored procedures. However, if you are one of those working with systems that do not use stored procedures, I advise you to still read the "SQL Injection" and "Compilation and Parameterization" sections at a minimum. Both sections are definitely applicable to ad hoc scenarios and are extremely important.

All of that said, I do not recommend the use of ad hoc SQL in application development, and feel that many potential issues, particularly those affecting application security and performance, can be prevented through the use of stored procedures.

The Stored Procedure vs. Ad Hoc SQL Debate

A seemingly never-ending battle among members of the database development community concerns the question of whether database application development should involve the use of stored procedures. This debate can become quite heated, with proponents of rapid software development methodologies such as test-driven development (TDD) claiming that stored procedures slow down their process, and fans of object-relational mapping (ORM) technologies making claims about the benefits of those technologies over stored procedures. I highly recommend that you search the Web to find these debates and reach your own conclusions. Personally, I heavily favor the use of stored procedures, for several reasons that I will briefly discuss here.

First and foremost, stored procedures create an abstraction layer between the database and the application, hiding details about the schema and sometimes the data. The encapsulation of data logic within stored procedures greatly decreases coupling between the database and the application, meaning that maintenance of or modification to the database will not necessitate changing the application accordingly. Reducing these dependencies and thinking of the database as a data API rather than a simple application persistence layer enables a flexible application development process. Often, this can permit the database and application layers to be developed in parallel rather than in sequence, thereby allowing for greater scale-out of human resources on a given project. For more information on concepts such as encapsulation, coupling, and treating the database as an API, see Chapter 1.

If stored procedures are properly defined, with well-documented and consistent outputs, testing is not at all hindered—unit tests can be easily created, as shown in Chapter 3, in order to support TDD. Furthermore, support for more advanced testing methodologies also becomes easier, not more difficult, thanks to stored procedures. For instance, consider use of **mock objects**—façade methods that return specific known values. Mock objects can be substituted for real methods in testing scenarios so that any given method can be tested in isolation, without also testing any methods that it calls (any calls made from within the method being tested will actually be a call to a mock version of the method). This technique is actually much easier to implement when stored procedures are used, as mock stored procedures can easily be created and swapped in and out without disrupting or recompiling the application code being tested.

Another important issue is security. Ad hoc SQL (as well as dynamic SQL) presents various security challenges, including opening possible attack vectors and making data access security much more difficult to enforce declaratively, rather than programmatically. This means that by using ad hoc SQL, your application may be more vulnerable to being hacked, and you may not be able to rely on SQL Server to secure access to data. The end result is that a greater degree of testing will be required in order to ensure that security holes are properly patched and that users—both authorized and not—are unable to access data they're not supposed to see. See the section "Dynamic SQL Security Considerations" for further discussion of these points.

Finally, I will address the hottest issue that online debates always seem to gravitate toward, which, of course, is the question of performance. Proponents of ad hoc SQL make the valid claim that, thanks to better support for query plan caching in recent versions of SQL Server, stored procedures no longer have a significant performance benefit when compared to ad hoc queries. Although this sounds like a great argument for not having to use stored procedures, I personally believe that it is a nonissue. Given equivalent performance, I think the obvious choice is the more maintainable and secure option (i.e., stored procedures).

In the end, the stored procedure vs. ad hoc SQL question is really one of purpose. Many in the ORM community feel that the database should be used as nothing more than a very simple object persistence layer, and would probably be perfectly happy with a database that only had a single table with only two columns: a GUID to identify an object's ID and an XML column for the serialized object graph.

In my eyes, a database is much more than just a collection of data. It is also an enforcer of data rules, a protector of data integrity, and a central data resource that can be shared among multiple applications. For these reasons, I believe that a decoupled, stored procedure–based design is the best way to go.

Why Go Dynamic?

As mentioned in the introduction for this chapter, dynamic SQL can help create more flexible data access layers, thereby helping to enable more flexible applications, which makes for happier users. This is a righteous goal, but the fact is that dynamic SQL is just one means by which to attain the desired end result. It is quite possible—in fact, often preferable—to do dynamic sorting and filtering directly on the client in many desktop applications, or in a business layer (if one exists) to support either a web-based or client-server–style desktop application. It is also possible not to go dynamic at all, by supporting static stored procedures that supply optional parameters—but that's not generally recommended because it can quickly lead to very unwieldy code that is difficult to maintain, as will be demonstrated in the "Optional Parameters via Static T-SQL" section later in this chapter .

Before committing to any database-based solution, determine whether it is really the correct course of action. Keep in mind the questions of performance, maintainability, and most important, scalability. Database resources are often the most taxed of any used by a given application, and dynamic sorting and filtering of data can potentially mean a lot more load put on the database. Remember that scaling the database can often be much more expensive than scaling other layers of an application.

For example, consider the question of sorting data. In order for the database to sort data, the data must be queried. This means that it must be read from disk or memory, thereby using I/O and CPU time, filtered appropriately, and finally sorted and returned to the caller. Every time the data needs to be resorted a different way, it must be reread or sorted in memory and refiltered by the database engine. This can add up to quite a bit of load if there are hundreds or thousands of users all trying to sort data in different ways, and all sharing resources on the same database server.

Due to this issue, if the same data is resorted again and again (for instance, by a user who wants to see various high or low data points), it often makes sense to do the work in a disconnected cache. A desktop application that uses a client-side data grid, for example, can load the data only once, and then sort and resort it using the client computer's resources rather than the database server's resources. This can take a tremendous amount of strain off the database server, meaning that it can use its resources for other data-intensive operations.

Aside from the scalability concerns, it's important to note that database-based solutions can be tricky and difficult to test and maintain. I offer some suggestions in the section "Going Dynamic: Using EXECUTE," but keep in mind that procedural code may be easier to work with for these purposes than T-SQL.

Once you've exhausted all other resources, *only then* should you look at the database as a solution for dynamic operations. In the database layer, the question of using dynamic SQL instead of static SQL comes down to issues of both maintainability and performance. The fact is, dynamic SQL can be made to perform much better than simple static SQL for many dynamic cases, but more complex (and difficult-to-maintain) static SQL will generally outperform maintainable dynamic SQL solutions. For the best balance of maintenance vs. performance, I always favor the dynamic SQL solution.

Compilation and Parameterization

Any discussion of dynamic SQL and performance would not be complete without some basic background information concerning how SQL Server processes queries and caches their plans. To that end, I will provide a brief discussion here, with some examples to help you get started in investigating these behaviors within SQL Server.

Every query executed by SQL Server goes through a compilation phase before actually being executed by the query processor. This compilation produces what is known as a **query plan**, which tells the query processor how to physically access the tables and indexes in the database in order to satisfy the query. However, query compilation can be expensive for certain queries, and when the same queries or types of queries are executed over and over, there is generally no reason to compile them each time. In order to save on the cost of compilation, SQL Server caches query plans in a memory pool called the **query plan cache**.

The query plan cache uses a simple hash lookup based on the exact text of the query in order to find a previously compiled plan. If the exact query has already been compiled, there is no reason to recompile it, and SQL Server skips directly to the execution phase in order to get the results for the caller. If a compiled version of the query is not found, the first step taken is parsing of the query. SQL Server determines which operations are being conducted in the SQL, validates the syntax used, and produces a **parse tree**, which is a structure that contains information about the query in a normalized form. The parse tree is further validated and eventually compiled into a query plan, which is placed into the query plan cache for future invocations of the query.

The effect of the query plan cache on execution time can be seen even with simple queries. To demonstrate this, first use the **DBCC FREEPROCCACHE** command to empty out the cache:

```
DBCC FREEPROCCACHE;
GO
```

Keep in mind that this command clears out the cache for the entire instance of SQL Server—doing this is not generally recommended in production environments. Then, to see the amount of time spent in the parsing and compilation phase of a query, turn on SQL Server's **SET STATISTICS TIME** option, which causes SQL Server to output informational messages about time spent in parsing/compilation and execution:

```
SET STATISTICS TIME ON;
GO
```

Now consider the following T-SQL, which queries the **HumanResources.Employee** table from the AdventureWorks2008 database:

■ **Note** As of SQL Server 2008, SQL Server no longer ships with any included sample databases. To follow the code listings in this chapter, you will need to download and install the AdventureWorks2008 database from the CodePlex site, available at **http://msftdbprodsamples.codeplex.com**.

```
SELECT *
FROM HumanResources.Employee
WHERE BusinessEntityId IN (1, 2);
GO
```

Executing this query in SQL Server Management Studio on my system produces the following output messages the first time the query is run:

```
SQL Server parse and compile time:

   CPU time = 0 ms, elapsed time = 12 ms.



(2 row(s) affected)



SQL Server Execution Times:

   CPU time = 0 ms,  elapsed time = 1 ms.
```

This query took 12ms to parse and compile. But subsequent runs produce the following output, indicating that the cached plan is being used:

```
SQL Server parse and compile time:

   CPU time = 0 ms, elapsed time = 1 ms.



(2 row(s) affected)



SQL Server Execution Times:

   CPU time = 0 ms,  elapsed time = 1 ms.
```

Thanks to the cached plan, each subsequent invocation of the query takes 11ms less than the first invocation—not bad, when you consider that the actual execution time is less than 1ms (the lowest elapsed time reported by time statistics).

Auto-Parameterization

An important part of the parsing process that enables the query plan cache to be more efficient in some cases involves determination of which parts of the query qualify as parameters. If SQL Server determines that one or more literals used in the query are parameters that may be changed for future invocations of a similar version of the query, it can **auto-parameterize** the query. To understand what this means, let's first take a glance at the contents of the query plan cache, via the **sys.dm_exec_cached_plans** dynamic management view and the **sys.dm_exec_sql_text** function. The following query finds all cached queries that contain the string "HumanResources," excluding those that contain the name of the **sys.dm_exec_cached_plans** view itself—this second predicate is necessary so that the results do not include the plan for this query itself.

```
SELECT
  cp.objtype,
  st.text
FROM sys.dm_exec_cached_plans cp
  CROSS APPLY sys.dm_exec_sql_text(cp.plan_handle) st
WHERE
  st.text LIKE '%HumanResources%'
  AND st.text NOT LIKE '%sys.dm_exec_cached_plans%';
GO
```

■ **Note** I'll be reusing this code several times in this section to examine the plan cache for different types of query, so you might want to keep it open in a separate Management Studio tab.

Running this code listing after executing the previous query against **HumanResources.Employee** gives the following results:

```
objtype  text
Adhoc    SELECT * FROM HumanResources.Employee WHERE BusinessEntityId IN (1, 2);
```

The important things to note here are that the **objtype** column indicates that the query is being treated as **Adhoc**, and that the **Text** column shows the exact text of the executed query. Queries that cannot be auto-parameterized are classified by the query engine as "ad hoc" (note that this is a slightly different definition from the one I use).

The previous example query was used to keep things simple, precisely because it could not be auto-parameterized. The following query, on the other hand, can be auto-parameterized:

```
SELECT *
FROM HumanResources.Employee
WHERE BusinessEntityId = 1;
GO
```

Clearing the execution plan cache, running this query, and then querying **sys.dm_exec_cached_plans** as before results in the output shown following:

```
objtype   text

Adhoc     SELECT * FROM HumanResources.Employee  WHERE BusinessEntityId = 1;

Prepared  (@1 tinyint)SELECT * FROM [HumanResources].[Employee]

          WHERE [BusinessEntityId]=@1
```

In this case, two plans have been generated: an **Adhoc** plan for the query's exact text and a **Prepared** plan for the auto-parameterized version of the query. Looking at the text of the latter plan, notice that the query has been normalized (the object names are bracket-delimited, carriage returns and other extraneous whitespace have been removed, and so on) and that a parameter has been derived from the text of the query.

The benefit of this auto-parameterization is that subsequent queries submitted to SQL Server that can be auto-parameterized to the same normalized form may be able to make use of the prepared query plan, thereby avoiding compilation overhead.

> ■ **Note** The auto-parameterization examples shown here were based on the default settings of the AdventureWorks2008 database, including the "simple parameterization" option. SQL Server 2008 includes a more powerful form of auto-parameterization, called "forced parameterization." This option makes SQL Server work much harder to auto-parameterize queries, which means greater query compilation cost in some cases. This can be very beneficial to applications that use a lot of nonparameterized ad hoc queries, but may cause performance degradation in other cases. See `http://msdn.microsoft.com/en-us/library/ms175037.aspx` for more information on forced parameterization.

Application-Level Parameterization

Auto-parameterization is not the only way that a query can be parameterized. Other forms of parameterization are possible at the application level for ad hoc SQL, or within T-SQL when working with dynamic SQL in a stored procedure. The section "sp_executesql: A Better EXECUTE," later in this chapter, describes how to parameterize dynamic SQL, but I will briefly discuss application-level parameterization here.

Every query framework that can communicate with SQL Server supports the idea of remote procedure call (RPC) invocation of queries. In the case of an RPC call, parameters are bound and strongly typed, rather than encoded as strings and passed along with the rest of the query text. Parameterizing queries in this way has one key advantage from a performance standpoint: the application tells SQL Server what the parameters are; SQL Server does not need to (and will not) try to find them itself.

To see application-level parameterization in action, the following code listing demonstrates the C# code required to issue a parameterized query via ADO.NET, by populating the **Parameters** collection on the **SqlCommand** object when preparing a query.

```
SqlConnection sqlConn = new SqlConnection(
  "Data Source=localhost;
  Initial Catalog=AdventureWorks2008;
  Integrated Security=SSPI");
sqlConn.Open();
SqlCommand cmd = new SqlCommand(
  "SELECT * FROM HumanResources.Employee WHERE BusinessEntityId IN (@Emp1,
  @Emp2)", sqlConn);

SqlParameter param = new SqlParameter("@Emp1", SqlDbType.Int);
param.Value = 1;
cmd.Parameters.Add(param);

SqlParameter param2 = new SqlParameter("@Emp2", SqlDbType.Int);
param2.Value = 2;
cmd.Parameters.Add(param2);

cmd.ExecuteNonQuery();

sqlConn.Close();
```

Notice that the underlying query is the same as the first query shown in this chapter, which, when issued as a T-SQL query via Management Studio, was unable to be auto-parameterized by SQL Server. However, in this case, the literal employee IDs have been replaced with the variables `@EmpId1` and `@EmpId2`.

Executing this code listing and then examining the `sys.dm_exec_cached_plans` view once again using the query from the previous section gives the following results:

objtype	text
Prepared	(@Emp1 int,@Emp2 int)SELECT * FROM HumanResources.Employee WHERE BusinessEntityId IN (@Emp1, @Emp2)

Just like with auto-parameterized queries, the plan is prepared and the text is prefixed with the parameters. However, notice that the text of the query is not normalized. The object name is not bracket-delimited, and although it may not be apparent, whitespace has not been removed. This fact is extremely important! If you were to run the same query, but with slightly different formatting, you would get a second plan—so when working with parameterized queries, make sure that the application generating the query produces the exact same formatting every time. Otherwise, you will end up wasting both the CPU cycles required for needless compilation and memory for caching the additional plans.

■ **Note** Whitespace is not the only type of formatting that can make a difference in terms of plan reuse. The cache lookup mechanism is nothing more than a simple hash on the query text and is case sensitive. So the exact same query submitted twice with different capitalization will be seen by the cache as two different queries—even on a case-insensitive server. It's always a good idea when working with SQL Server to try to be consistent with your use of capitalization and formatting. Not only does it make your code more readable, but it may also wind up improving performance!

Performance Implications of Parameterization and Caching

Now that all of the background information has been covered, the burning question can be answered: why should you care, and what does any of this have to do with dynamic SQL? The answer, of course, is that this has everything to do with dynamic SQL if you care about performance (and other issues, but we'll get to those shortly).

Suppose, for example, that we placed the previous application code in a loop—calling the same query 2,000 times and changing only the supplied parameter values on each iteration:

```
SqlConnection sqlConn = new SqlConnection(
  "Data Source=localhost;
  Initial Catalog=AdventureWorks2008;
  Integrated Security=SSPI");
sqlConn.Open();

for (int i = 1; i <= 2000; i++)
{
  SqlCommand cmd = new SqlCommand(
    "SELECT * FROM HumanResources.Employee
    WHERE BusinessEntityId IN (@Emp1, @Emp2)",
    sqlConn);

  SqlParameter param = new SqlParameter("@Emp1", SqlDbType.Int);
  param.Value = i;
  cmd.Parameters.Add(param);

  SqlParameter param2 = new SqlParameter("@Emp2", SqlDbType.Int);
  param2.Value = i + 1;
  cmd.Parameters.Add(param2);

  cmd.ExecuteNonQuery();
}

sqlConn.Close();
```

Once again, return to SQL Server Management Studio and query the **sys.dm_exec_cached_plans** view, and you will see that the results have not changed. There is only one plan in the cache for this form of the query, even though it has just been run 2,000 times with different parameter values:

objtype	text
Prepared	(@Emp1 int,@Emp2 int)SELECT * FROM HumanResources.Employee
	WHERE BusinessEntityId IN (@Emp1, @Emp2)

This result indicates that parameterization is working, and the server does not need to do extra work to compile the query every time a slightly different form of it is issued.

Now that a positive baseline has been established, let's investigate what happens when queries are *not* properly parameterized. Consider what would happen if we had instead designed the application code loop as follows:

```
SqlConnection sqlConn = new SqlConnection(
  "Data Source=localhost;
  Initial Catalog=AdventureWorks2008;
  Integrated Security=SSPI");
sqlConn.Open();

for (int i = 1; i < 2000; i++)
```

```
{
  SqlCommand cmd = new SqlCommand(
    "SELECT * FROM HumanResources.Employee
     WHERE BusinessEntityId IN (" + i + ", " + (i+1) + ")",
    sqlConn);

  cmd.ExecuteNonQuery();
}

sqlConn.Close();
```

The abridged results of querying the query plan cache after running this code are shown here:

objtype	text
Adhoc	SELECT * FROM HumanResources.Employee WHERE BusinessEntityId IN (1, 2)
Adhoc	SELECT * FROM HumanResources.Employee WHERE BusinessEntityId IN (2, 3)
Adhoc	SELECT * FROM HumanResources.Employee WHERE BusinessEntityId IN (3, 4)
...1,995 rows later...	
Adhoc	SELECT * FROM HumanResources.Employee WHERE BusinessEntityId IN (1998...
Adhoc	SELECT * FROM HumanResources.Employee WHERE BusinessEntityId IN (1999...

Running 2,000 nonparameterized ad hoc queries with different parameters resulted in 2,000 additional cached plans. That means that not only will the query execution experience slowdown resulting from the additional compilation, but also quite a bit of RAM will be wasted in the query plan cache. In SQL Server 2008, queries are aged out of the plan cache on a least-recently-used basis, and depending on the server's workload, it can take quite a bit of time for unused plans to be removed.

In large production environments, a failure to use parameterized queries can result in gigabytes of RAM being wasted caching query plans that will never be used again. This is obviously not a good thing! So please—for the sake of all of that RAM—learn to use your connection library's parameterized query functionality and avoid falling into this trap.

Supporting Optional Parameters

The most commonly cited use case for dynamic SQL is the ability to write stored procedures that can support optional parameters for queries in an efficient, maintainable manner. Although it is quite easy to write static stored procedures that handle optional query parameters, these are generally grossly inefficient or highly unmaintainable—as a developer, you can take your pick.

Optional Parameters via Static T-SQL

Before presenting the dynamic SQL solution to the optional parameter problem, a few demonstrations are necessary to illustrate why static SQL is *not* the right tool for the job. There are a few different methods of creating static queries that support optional parameters, with varying complexity and effectiveness, but each of these solutions contains flaws.

As a baseline, consider the following query, which selects one row of data from the **HumanResources.Employee** table in the **AdventureWorks2008** database:

```
SELECT
  BusinessEntityID,
  LoginID,
  JobTitle
FROM
  HumanResources.Employee
WHERE
  BusinessEntityID = 28
  AND NationalIDNumber = N'14417807';
GO
```

This query uses predicates to filter on both the **BusinessEntityID** and **NationalIDNumber** columns. Executing the query produces the execution plan shown in Figure 8-1, which has an estimated cost of 0.0032831, and which requires two logical reads. This plan involves a seek of the table's clustered index, which uses the **BusinessEntityID** column as its key.

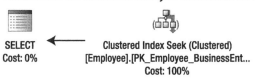

SELECT ◄─── Clustered Index Seek (Clustered)
Cost: 0%   [Employee].[PK_Employee_BusinessEnt...
                      Cost: 100%

Figure 8-1. Base execution plan with seek on BusinessEntityID clustered index

Since the query uses the clustered index, it does not need to do a lookup to get any additional data. Furthermore, since **BusinessEntityID** is the primary key for the table, the **NationalIDNumber** predicate is not used when physically identifying the row. Therefore, the following query, which uses only the **BusinessEntityId** predicate, produces the exact same query plan with the same cost and same number of reads:

```
SELECT
  BusinessEntityID,
  LoginID,
  JobTitle
FROM
  HumanResources.Employee
WHERE
  BusinessEntityID = 28;
GO
```

Another form of this query involves removing **BusinessEntityID** and querying based only on **NationalIDNumber**:

```
SELECT
   BusinessEntityID,
   LoginID,
   JobTitle
FROM
   HumanResources.Employee
WHERE
   NationalIDNumber = N'14417807';
GO
```

This query results in a very different plan from the other two, due to the fact that a different index must be used to satisfy the query. Figure 8-2 shows the resultant plan, which involves a seek on a nonclustered index on the **NationalIDNumber** column, followed by a lookup to get the additional rows for the **SELECT** list. This plan has an estimated cost of 0.0065704, and performs four logical reads.

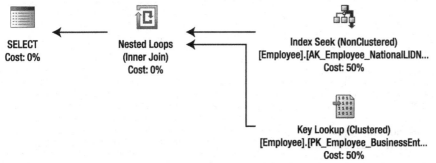

Figure 8-2. Base execution plan with seek on NationalIDNumber nonclustered index followed by a lookup into the clustered index

The final form of the base query has no predicates at all:

```
SELECT
   BusinessEntityID,
   LoginID,
   JobTitle
FROM
   HumanResources.Employee;
GO
```

As shown in Figure 8-3, the query plan in this case is a simple clustered index scan, with an estimated cost of 0.0080454, and nine logical reads. Since all of the rows need to be returned and no index covers every column required, a clustered index scan is the most efficient way to satisfy this query.

SELECT
Cost: 0%

Clustered Index Scan (Clustered)
[Employee].[PK_Employee_BusinessEnt...
Cost: 100%

Figure 8-3. Base execution plan with scan on the clustered index

These baseline figures will be used to compare the relative performance of various methods of creating a dynamic stored procedure that returns the same columns, but that optionally filters the rows returned based on one or both predicates of **BusinessEntityID** and **NationalIDNumber**. To begin with, the query can be wrapped in a stored procedure:

```
CREATE PROCEDURE GetEmployeeData
  @BusinessEntityID int = NULL,
  @NationalIDNumber nvarchar(15) = NULL
AS
BEGIN
  SET NOCOUNT ON;

  SELECT
    BusinessEntityID,
    LoginID,
    JobTitle
  FROM
    HumanResources.Employee
  WHERE
    BusinessEntityID = @BusinessEntityID
    AND NationalIDNumber = @NationalIDNumber;

END;
GO
```

This stored procedure uses the parameters **@BusinessEntityID** and **@NationalIDNumber** to support the predicates. Both of these parameters are optional, with **NULL** default values. However, this stored procedure does not really support the parameters optionally; not passing one of the parameters will mean that no rows will be returned by the stored procedure at all, since any comparison with **NULL** in a predicate will not result in a **true** answer.

As a first shot at making this stored procedure enable the optional predicates, a developer might try to rewrite the procedure using control-of-flow statements as follows:

```
ALTER PROCEDURE GetEmployeeData
  @BusinessEntityID int = NULL,
 @NationalIDNumber nvarchar (15) = NULL
AS
BEGIN
  SET NOCOUNT ON;

  IF (@BusinessEntityID IS NOT NULL AND @NationalIDNumber IS NOT NULL)
    BEGIN
      SELECT
        BusinessEntityID,
```

```
      LoginID,
      JobTitle
    FROM
      HumanResources.Employee
    WHERE
      BusinessEntityID = @BusinessEntityID
      AND NationalIDNumber = @NationalIDNumber;
  END

  ELSE IF (@BusinessEntityID IS NOT NULL)
  BEGIN
    SELECT
      BusinessEntityID,
      LoginID,
      JobTitle
    FROM
      HumanResources.Employee
    WHERE
      BusinessEntityID = @BusinessEntityID;
  END

  ELSE IF (@NationalIDNumber IS NOT NULL)
  BEGIN
    SELECT
      BusinessEntityID,
      LoginID,
      JobTitle
    FROM
      HumanResources.Employee
    WHERE
      NationalIDNumber = @NationalIDNumber;
  END

  ELSE
  BEGIN
    SELECT
      BusinessEntityID,
      LoginID,
      JobTitle
    FROM
      HumanResources.Employee;
  END

END;
GO
```

Although executing this stored procedure produces the exact same query plans—and, therefore, the exact same performance—as the equivalent individual query created in the test batch, it has an unfortunate problem. Namely, taking this approach turns what was a very simple 10-line stored procedure into a 42-line monster.

Adding one more column to the **SELECT** list for this procedure would require a change to be made in four places. Now consider what would happen if a third predicate were needed—the number of cases would jump from four to eight, meaning that any change such as adding or removing a column would have to be made in eight places. Now consider 10 or 20 predicates, and it's clear that this method has no place in the SQL Server developer's toolbox. It is simply not a manageable solution.

The next most common technique is one that has appeared in articles on several SQL Server web sites over the past few years. As a result, a lot of code has been written against it by developers who don't seem to realize that they're creating a performance time bomb. This technique takes advantage of the **COALESCE** function, as shown in the following rewritten version of the stored procedure:

```
ALTER PROCEDURE GetEmployeeData
  @BusinessEntityID int = NULL,
  @NationalIDNumber nvarchar(15) = NULL
AS
BEGIN
  SET NOCOUNT ON;

  SELECT
    BusinessEntityID,
    LoginID,
    JobTitle
  FROM
    HumanResources.Employee
  WHERE
    BusinessEntityID = COALESCE(@BusinessEntityID, BusinessEntityID)
    AND NationalIDNumber = COALESCE(@NationalIDNumber, NationalIDNumber);

END;
GO
```

This version of the stored procedure looks great and is easy to understand. The **COALESCE** function returns the first non-**NULL** value passed into its parameter list. So if either of the arguments to the stored procedure are **NULL**, the **COALESCE** will "pass through," comparing the value of the column to itself—and at least in theory, that seems like it should not require any processing since it will always be true.

Unfortunately, because the **COALESCE** function uses a column from the table as an input, it cannot be evaluated deterministically before execution of the query. The result is that the function is evaluated once for every row of the table, whatever combination of parameters is supplied. This means *consistent* performance results, but probably not in a good way; all four combinations of parameters result in the same query plan: a clustered index scan with an estimated cost of 0.0080454 and nine logical reads. This is over four times the I/O for the queries involving the **BusinessEntityID** column—quite a performance drain.

Similar to the version that uses **COALESCE** is a version that uses **OR** to conditionally set the parameter only if the argument is not **NULL**:

```
ALTER PROCEDURE GetEmployeeData
  @BusinessEntityID int = NULL,
  @NationalIDNumber nvarchar(15) = NULL
AS
BEGIN
  SET NOCOUNT ON;
```

```
SELECT
  BusinessEntityID,
  LoginID,
  JobTitle
FROM
  HumanResources.Employee
WHERE
  (@BusinessEntityID IS NULL OR BusinessEntityID = @BusinessEntityID)
  AND (@NationalIDNumber IS NULL OR @NationalIDNumber = NationalIDNumber);

END;
GO
```

This version, while similar in idea to the version that uses **COALESCE**, has some interesting performance traits. Depending on which parameters you use the first time you call it, you'll see vastly different results. If you're lucky enough to call it the first time with no arguments, the result will be an index scan, producing nine logical reads—and the same number of reads will result for any combination of parameters passed in thereafter. If, however, you first call the stored procedure using only the **@BusinessEntityID** parameter, the resultant plan will use only four logical reads—until you happen to call the procedure with no arguments, which will produce a massive 582 reads.

Given the surprisingly huge jump in I/O that the bad plan can produce, as well as the unpredictable nature of what performance characteristics you'll end up with, this is undoubtedly the worst possible choice.

The final method that can be used is a bit more creative, and also can result in somewhat better results. The following version of the stored procedure shows how it is implemented:

```
ALTER PROCEDURE GetEmployeeData
  @BusinessEntityID int = NULL,
  @NationalIDNumber nvarchar(15) = NULL
AS
BEGIN
  SET NOCOUNT ON;

  SELECT
    BusinessEntityID,
    LoginID,
    JobTitle
  FROM
    HumanResources.Employee
  WHERE
    BusinessEntityID BETWEEN COALESCE(@BusinessEntityID, -2147483648) AND
      COALESCE(@BusinessEntityID, 2147483647)
    AND NationalIDNumber LIKE COALESCE(@NationalIDNumber, N'%');

END;
GO
```

If you're a bit confused by the logic of this stored procedure, you're now familiar with the first reason that I don't recommend this technique: it's relatively unmaintainable if you don't understand exactly how it works. Using it almost certainly guarantees that you will produce stored procedures that will stump others who attempt to maintain them in the future. And while that might be good for job security, using it for that purpose is probably not a virtuous goal.

This stored procedure operates by using **COALESCE** to cancel out **NULL** arguments by substituting in minimum and maximum conditions for the integer predicate (**BusinessEntityID**) and a **LIKE** expression that will match anything for the string predicate (**NationalIDNumber**). This approach works as follows:

> If **@BusinessEntityID** is **NULL**, the **BusinessEntityID** predicate effectively becomes
> **BusinessEntityID BETWEEN -2147483648 AND 2147483647**—in other words, all
> possible integers. If **@BusinessEntityID** is not **NULL**, the predicate becomes
> **BusinessEntityID BETWEEN @BusinessEntityID AND @BusinessEntityID**. This is
> equivalent to **BusinessEntityID=@BusinessEntityID**.

> The same basic logic is true for the **NationalIDNumber** predicate, although because
> it's a string instead of an integer, **LIKE** is used instead of **BETWEEN**. If
> **@NationalIDNumber** is **NULL**, the predicate becomes **NationalIDNumber LIKE N'%'**.
> This will match any string in the **NationalIDNumber** column. On the other hand, if
> **@NationalIDNumber** is not **NULL**, the predicate becomes **NationalIDNumber LIKE**
> **@NationalIDNumber**, which is equivalent to **NationalIDNumber=@NationalIDNumber**—
> assuming that **@NationalIDNumber** contains no string expressions. This predicate
> can also be written using **BETWEEN** to avoid the string expression issue (for instance,
> **BETWEEN N'' AND REPLICATE(nchar(1000), 15)**). However, that method is both
> more difficult to read than the **LIKE** expression and fraught with potential problems
> due to collation issues (which is why I only went up to **nchar(1000)** instead of
> **nchar(65535)** in the example).

The real question, of course, is one of performance. Unfortunately, this stored procedure manages to confuse the query optimizer, resulting in the same plan being generated for every invocation. The plan, in every case, involves a clustered index seek on the table, with an estimated cost of 0.0033107, as shown in Figure 8-4. Unfortunately, this estimate turns out to be highly inconsistent, as the number of actual logical reads varies widely based on the arguments passed to the procedure.

SELECT ← Clustered Index Seek (Clustered)
Cost: 0% [Employee].[PK_Employee_BusinessEnt...
Cost: 100%

Figure 8-4. Every set of arguments passed to the stored procedure results in the same execution plan.

If both arguments are passed, or **@BusinessEntityID** is passed but **@NationalIDNumber** is not, the number of logical reads is three. While this is much better than the nine logical reads required by the previous version of the stored procedure, it's still 50 percent more I/O than the two logical reads required by the baseline in both of these cases. This estimated plan really breaks down when passing only **@NationalIDNumber**, since there is no way to efficiently satisfy a query on the **NationalIDNumber** column using the clustered index. In both that case and when passing no arguments, nine logical reads are reported. For the **NationalIDNumber** predicate this is quite a failure, as the stored procedure does over twice as much work for the same results as the baseline.

Going Dynamic: Using EXECUTE

The solution to all of the aforementioned static SQL problems is, of course, to go dynamic. Building dynamic SQL inside of a stored procedure is simple, the code is relatively easy to understand and, as I'll show, it can provide excellent performance. However, there are various potential issues to note, not the least of which being security concerns. I'll explain how to deal with these as the examples progress.

The real benefit of dynamic SQL is that the execution plans generated for each invocation of the query will be optimized for only the predicates that are actually being used at that moment. The main issue with the static SQL solutions, aside from maintainability, was that the additional predicates confused the query optimizer, causing it to create inefficient plans. Dynamic SQL gets around this issue by not including anything extra in the query.

The simplest way to implement dynamic SQL in a stored procedure is with the **EXECUTE** statement. This statement takes a string input and executes whatever SQL the string contains. The following batch shows this in its simplest—and least effective—form:

```
EXEC('SELECT
    BusinessEntityID,
    LoginID,
    JobTitle
FROM HumanResources.Employee');
GO
```

Note that in this example (and all other examples in this chapter), I use the truncated form of **EXECUTE**. This seems to be a de facto standard for SQL Server code; I very rarely see code that uses the full form with the added "UTE." Although this is only a savings of three characters, I am very used to seeing it, and for some reason it makes a lot more sense to me when reading SQL than seeing the full **EXECUTE** keyword.

In this case, a string literal is passed to **EXECUTE**, and this doesn't really allow for anything very "dynamic." For instance, to add a predicate on **BusinessEntityID** to the query, the following would not work:

```
DECLARE @BusinessEntityID int = 28;

EXEC('SELECT
    BusinessEntityID,
    LoginID,
    JobTitle
FROM HumanResources.Employee
WHERE BusinessEntityID = ' + CONVERT(varchar, @BusinessEntityID));
GO
```

This fails (with an "incorrect syntax" exception) because of the way **EXECUTE** is parsed by the SQL Server engine. SQL Server performs only one pass to parse the syntax, and then tries to concatenate and execute the SQL in a second step. But due to the fact that the first step does not include a stage for inline expansion, the **CONVERT** is still a **CONVERT**, rather than a literal, when it's time for concatenation.

The solution to this issue is quite simple. Define a variable and assign the dynamic SQL to it, and *then* call **EXECUTE**:

```
DECLARE @BusinessEntityID int = 28;

DECLARE @sql nvarchar(max);

SET @sql = 'SELECT
    BusinessEntityID,
    LoginID,
```

```
    JobTitle
FROM HumanResources.Employee
WHERE BusinessEntityID = ' + CONVERT(VARCHAR, @BusinessEntityID);

EXEC (@sql);
GO
```

The string variable, **@sql**, can be manipulated in any way in order to form the desired dynamic SQL string, and since it's a variable, various code paths can be created using control-of-flow statements. In other words, forming the dynamic SQL is now limited only by the tools available within the T-SQL language for string manipulation.

A first shot at optional inclusion of both the **BusinessEntityID** and **NationalIDNumber** predicates follows:

```
DECLARE @BusinessEntityID int = 28;
DECLARE @NationalIDNumber nvarchar(15) = N'14417807';

DECLARE @sql nvarchar(max);

SET @sql = 'SELECT
    BusinessEntityID,
    LoginID,
    JobTitle
FROM HumanResources.Employee ';

IF (@BusinessEntityID IS NOT NULL AND @NationalIDNumber IS NOT NULL)
BEGIN
  SET @sql = @sql +
    'WHERE BusinessEntityID = ' + CONVERT(nvarchar, @BusinessEntityID) +
    ' AND NationalIDNumber = N''' + @NationalIDNumber + '''';
END

ELSE IF (@BusinessEntityID IS NOT NULL)
BEGIN
  SET @sql = @sql +
    'WHERE BusinessEntityID = ' +
    CONVERT(nvarchar, @BusinessEntityID);
END

ELSE IF (@NationalIDNumber IS NOT NULL)
BEGIN
  SET @sql = @sql +
    'WHERE NationalIDNumber = N''' + @NationalIDNumber + '''';
END

EXEC(@sql);
GO
```

If this looks sickeningly familiar, you've been doing a good job of paying attention as the chapter has progressed; this example has the same maintenance issues as the first shot at a static SQL stored procedure. Adding additional parameters will create a combinatorial explosion, making this solution completely unmaintainable. In addition, the SQL statement has been broken up into two component parts, making it lack a good sense of flow. Think about how bad this might get if you had to add **ORDER BY** or **GROUP BY** clauses.

To solve this problem, I like to concatenate my dynamic SQL in one shot, using **CASE** expressions instead of control-of-flow statements in order to optionally concatenate sections. The following example should serve to illustrate how this works:

```
DECLARE @BusinessEntityID int = 28;
DECLARE @NationalIDNumber nvarchar(15) = N'14417807';

DECLARE @sql nvarchar(max);

SET @sql = 'SELECT
    BusinessEntityID,
    LoginID,
    JobTitle
FROM HumanResources.Employee
WHERE 1=1' +
CASE
  WHEN @BusinessEntityID IS NULL THEN ''
  ELSE 'AND BusinessEntityID = ' + CONVERT(nvarchar, @BusinessEntityID)
END +
CASE
  WHEN @NationalIDNumber IS NULL THEN ''
  ELSE 'AND NationalIDNumber = N''' + @NationalIDNumber + ''''
END;

EXEC(@sql);
GO
```

In this example, the **CASE** expressions concatenate an empty string if one of the parameters is **NULL**. Otherwise, the parameter is formatted as a string and concatenated to the predicate.

Thanks to the **CASE** expressions, the code is much more compact, and the query is still generally formatted like a query instead of like procedural code. But the real trick here is the addition of **1=1** to the **WHERE** clause, in order to avoid the combinatorial explosion problem. The query optimizer will "optimize out" (i.e., discard) **1=1** in a **WHERE** clause, so it has no effect on the resultant query plan. What it does do is allow the optional predicates to use **AND** without having to be aware of whether other optional predicates are being concatenated. Each predicate can therefore be listed only once in the code, and combinations are not a problem.

The final maintainability issue with this code is one of formatting, and this is an area that I feel is extremely important when working with dynamic SQL. Careful, consistent formatting can mean the difference between quick changes to stored procedures and spending several hours trying to decipher messy code.

To see the problem with the way the code is currently formatted, add **PRINT @sql** to the end of the batch to see the final string:

```
SELECT
  BusinessEntityID,
  LoginID,
  JobTitle
```

```
FROM HumanResources.Employee
WHERE 1=1AND BusinessEntityID = 28AND NationalIDNumber = N'14417807'
```

Although this SQL is valid and executes as-is without exception, it has the potential for problems due to the lack of spacing between the predicates. Debugging spacing issues in dynamic SQL can be maddening, so I recommend adopting a consistent formatting standard to combat the issue. When I am working with dynamic SQL, I concatenate every line separately, ensuring that each line is terminated with a space. This adds a bit more complexity to the code, but I've found that it makes it much easier to debug. Following is an example of how I like to format my dynamic SQL:

```
DECLARE @BusinessEntityID int = 28;
DECLARE @NationalIDNumber nvarchar(15) = N'14417807';

DECLARE @sql nvarchar(max);

SET @sql = '' +
 'SELECT ' +
   'BusinessEntityID, ' +
   'LoginID, ' +
   'JobTitle ' +
 'FROM HumanResources.Employee ' +
   'WHERE 1=1 ' +
   CASE
     WHEN @BusinessEntityID IS NULL THEN ''
     ELSE 'AND BusinessEntityID = ' + CONVERT(nvarchar, @BusinessEntityID) + ' '
   END +
   CASE
     WHEN @NationalIDNumber IS NULL THEN ''
     ELSE 'AND NationalIDNumber = N''' + @NationalIDNumber + ''' '
   END;

EXEC(@sql);
GO
```

■ **Note** I developed this style when working with older versions of SQL Server, which did not have the **max** data types and therefore had stringent variable size limitations. Cutting everything up into individual tokens greatly reduced the amount of whitespace, meaning that I could fit a lot more code in each variable. Removal of extraneous whitespace is not necessary in SQL Server 2008, but I still feel that this technique is great for ensuring proper spacing, which both improves readability and ensures consistency to enable reuse of cached plans.

Now that the code fragment is properly formatted, it can be transferred into a new version of the GetEmployeeData stored procedure:

```
ALTER PROCEDURE GetEmployeeData
  @BusinessEntityID int = NULL,
  @NationalIDNumber nvarchar(15) = NULL
```

```
AS
BEGIN
  SET NOCOUNT ON;

  DECLARE @sql nvarchar(max);

  SET @sql = '' +
  'SELECT ' +
    'BusinessEntityID, ' +
    'LoginID, ' +
    'JobTitle ' +
  'FROM HumanResources.Employee ' +
  'WHERE 1=1 ' +
    CASE
     WHEN @BusinessEntityID IS NULL THEN ''
     ELSE 'AND BusinessEntityID = ' + CONVERT(nvarchar, @BusinessEntityID) + ' '
    END +
    CASE
     WHEN @NationalIDNumber IS NULL THEN ''
     ELSE 'AND NationalIDNumber = N''' + @NationalIDNumber + ''' '
    END

    EXEC(@sql);
END;
GO
```

So that's it—a dynamic stored procedure with optional parameters. At first glance, this might look like a great solution, but it is still fraught with problems.

From a performance point of view, this procedure appears to be great when taken for a few test runs. Each set of input parameters produces the same execution plan as the baseline examples, with the same estimated costs and number of reads. However, under the covers, a major issue still exists: parameterization is not occurring. To illustrate this, execute the following T-SQL, which clears the query plan cache and then runs the procedure with the same optional parameter, for three different input values:

```
DBCC FREEPROCCACHE;
GO

EXEC GetEmployeeData
  @BusinessEntityID = 1;
GO

EXEC GetEmployeeData
  @BusinessEntityID = 2;
GO
EXEC GetEmployeeData
  @BusinessEntityID = 3;
GO
```

Now, query the **sys.dm_exec_cached_plans** view using the query introduced earlier this chapter, and you will see the output as follows:

objtype	text
Proc	CREATE PROCEDURE GetEmployeeData @BusinessEntityID int = NULL ...
Adhoc	SELECT BusinessEntityID, LoginID, JobTitle FROM HumanResources.Employee
	WHERE 1=1 AND BusinessEntityID = 3
Adhoc	SELECT BusinessEntityID, LoginID, JobTitle FROM HumanResources.Employee
	WHERE 1=1 AND BusinessEntityID = 2
Adhoc	SELECT BusinessEntityID, LoginID, JobTitle FROM HumanResources.Employee
	WHERE 1=1 AND BusinessEntityID = 1

Notice that there is one **Proc** cached plan for the procedure itself—which is expected for any stored procedure—and an additional ad hoc plan cached for each invocation of the stored procedure. This means that every time a new argument is passed, a compilation occurs, which is clearly going to kill performance.

The other issue with this stored procedure, as it currently stands, is a serious security hole. A stored procedure implemented similarly to this one but with a minor modification would open a simple attack vector that a hacker could exploit to easily pull information out of the database, or worse.

SQL Injection

Concatenating string parameters such as **@NationalIDNumber** directly onto queries can open your applications to considerable problems. The issue is a hacking technique called a **SQL injection attack**, which involves passing bits of semiformed SQL to the database, typically via values entered in web forms, in order to try to manipulate dynamic or ad hoc SQL on the other side.

The example **GetEmployeeData** stored procedure doesn't actually have much of a problem as-is, because **@NationalIDNumber** is only 15 characters long—this doesn't give a hacker much room to work with (although bear in mind that it only takes 8 characters to issue the **SHUTDOWN** command). But what if you were working with another stored procedure that had to be a bit more flexible? The following example procedure, which might be used to search for addresses in the AdventureWorks2008 database, gives an attacker more than enough characters to do some damage:

```
CREATE PROCEDURE FindAddressByString
  @String nvarchar(60)
AS
BEGIN
  SET NOCOUNT ON;

  DECLARE @sql nvarchar(max);

  SET @sql = '' +
    'SELECT AddressID ' +
```

```
    'FROM Person.Address ' +
    'WHERE AddressLine1 LIKE ''%' + @String + '%'''

  EXEC(@sql);

END;
GO
```

This stored procedure can be executed with a string such as "Stone" used for the parameter value:

```
EXEC FindAddressByString
  @String = 'Stone';
GO
```

This outputs the result set you might expect, with all of the address IDs that use that string in the **AddressLine1** column. The abridged list of results is as follows:

AddressID
16475
21773
23244
23742
16570
6
...
1042

Consider what actually happened inside of the stored procedure. The **WHERE** clause for the query was concatenated, such that it literally became **WHERE AddressLine1 LIKE '%Stone%'**. But nothing is stopping someone from passing a string into the stored procedure that has a more profound effect. For instance, consider what happens in the following case:

```
EXEC FindAddressByString
  @String = ''' ORDER BY AddressID --';
GO
```

After concatenation, the **WHERE** clause reads, **WHERE AddressLine1 LIKE '%' ORDER BY AddressID --%'**. The effect is that filtering is no longer applied, and an **ORDER BY** clause—which was not there before—has been added to the query. When supplied with this input, the results of the query now list every **AddressID** in the **Person.Address** table, in order, as follows:

AddressID
1
2
3
6
...
32521

This is, of course, a fairly mundane example. How about something a bit more interesting, such as getting back the full pay history for every employee in the database?

```
EXEC FindAddressByString
  @String = 'Fake address'; SELECT * FROM HumanResources.EmployeePayHistory --';
GO
```

Assuming that the account used for the query has access to the **HumanResources.EmployeePayHistory** table, running the stored procedure now produces two result sets—the first is an empty result set from the **Person.Address** table, but the second lists all details from the **EmployeePayHistory** table:

BusinessEntityID	RateChangeDate	Rate	PayFrequency	ModifiedDate
1	1999-02-15	125.50	2	2004-07-31
...				
290	2002-07-01	23.0769	2	2004-07-31

The fact is the attacker can do anything in the database that the authenticated account has access to do and that can be done in 60 characters (the size of the string parameter). This includes viewing data, deleting data, and inserting fake data. Such an attack can often be waged from the comfort of a web browser, and intrusion can be incredibly difficult to detect.

The solution is not to stop using dynamic SQL. Rather, it's to make sure that your dynamic SQL is always parameterized. Let me repeat that for effect: *always, always, always parameterize your dynamic SQL!* The next section shows you how to use **sp_executesql** to do just that.

sp_executesql: A Better EXECUTE

In the previous sections, I identified two major problems with building dynamic SQL statements and executing them using **EXECUTE**: first, there is the issue of extraneous compilation and query plan caching, which makes performance drag and uses up valuable system resources. Second, and perhaps more important, is the threat of SQL injection attacks.

Query parameterization, mentioned earlier in this chapter in the context of application development, is the key to fixing both of these problems. Parameterization is a way to build a query such that any parameters are passed as strongly typed variables, rather than formatted as strings and appended to the query. In addition to the performance benefits this brings by reducing the amount of work to process the query, parameterization also has the benefit of virtually eliminating SQL injection attacks.

The first step in parameterizing a query is to replace literals with variable names. For instance, the injection-vulnerable query from the previous section could be rewritten in a parameterized manner as follows (I've removed the stored procedure–creation code for simplicity):

```
DECLARE @String nvarchar(60) = 'Stone';

DECLARE @sql nvarchar(max);

SET @sql = '' +
    'SELECT AddressID ' +
    'FROM Person.Address ' +
    'WHERE AddressLine1 LIKE ''%'' + @String + ''%''';
```

The only thing that has changed about this query compared to the version in the last section is that two additional single quotes have been added such that the literal value of **@String** is no longer concatenated with the rest of the query. Previously, the literal value of **@sql** after concatenation would have been as follows:

```
SELECT AddressID FROM Person.Address WHERE AddressLine1 LIKE '%Stone%'
```

As a result of this change, the literal value after concatenation is now the following:

```
SELECT AddressID FROM Person.Address WHERE AddressLine1 LIKE '%' + @String + '%'
```

Trying to execute this SQL using **EXECUTE** results in the following exception:

```
Msg 137, Level 15, State 2, Line 1
Must declare the scalar variable "@String".
```

The reason for this is that **EXECUTE** runs the SQL in a different context than that in which it was created. In the context in which the statement is run, the variable **@String** has not been declared and is therefore unknown. Since the value of the variable is not concatenated directly into the query, the type of SQL injection described in the previous section is impossible in this scenario. However, we need to find an alternative way to pass legitimate, strongly typed parameters to the query.

The solution to this problem is to use the **sp_executesql** system stored procedure, which allows you to pass parameters to dynamic SQL, much as you can to a stored procedure. The parameters for **sp_executesql** are a Unicode (**nvarchar** or **nchar**) string containing a dynamic SQL batch, a second Unicode string that defines the data types of the variables referenced in the dynamic SQL, and a list of values or variables from the calling scope that correspond to the variables defined in the data type list. The following T-SQL shows how to execute the **Person.Address** query using **sp_executesql**:

```
DECLARE @String nvarchar(60) = 'Stone'

DECLARE @sql nvarchar(max);
```

```
SET @sql = '' +
    'SELECT AddressID ' +
    'FROM Person.Address ' +
    'WHERE AddressLine1 LIKE ''%'' + @String + ''%'''

EXEC sp_executesql
    @sql,
    N'@String nvarchar(60)',
    @String;
GO
```

Running this batch will produce the same results as calling **FindAddressByString** and passing the string "Stone." The parameters to **sp_executesql** serve to map the **@String** variable from the outer scope into the new scope spawned when the dynamic SQL is executed—without having to concatenate the literal value of the variable.

For an example that uses multiple parameters, consider again the **GetEmployeeData** stored procedure, now rewritten to use **sp_executesql** instead of **EXECUTE**:

```
ALTER PROCEDURE GetEmployeeData
  @BusinessEntityID int = NULL,
  @NationalIDNumber nvarchar(15) = NULL
AS
BEGIN
  SET NOCOUNT ON;

  DECLARE @sql nvarchar(max);

  SET @sql = '' +
    'SELECT ' +
      'BusinessEntityID, ' +
      'LoginID, ' +
      'JobTitle ' +
    'FROM HumanResources.Employee ' +
    'WHERE 1=1 ' +
      CASE
        WHEN @BusinessEntityID IS NULL THEN ''
          ELSE 'AND BusinessEntityID = @BusinessEntityID '
      END +
      CASE
        WHEN @NationalIDNumber IS NULL THEN ''
        ELSE 'AND NationalIDNumber = @NationalIDNumber '
      END

  EXEC sp_executesql
    @sql,
    N'@BusinessEntityID int, @NationalIDNumber nvarchar(60)',
    @BusinessEntityID,
    @NationalIDNumber;

END;
GO
```

For multiple parameters, simply comma-delimit their data type definitions in the second parameter, and then pass as many outer parameters as necessary to define every variable listed in the second parameter. Note that you can use a string variable for the second parameter, which might make sense if you are defining a long list—but I usually keep the list in a string literal so that I can easily match the definitions with the variables passed in from the outer scope.

Another important thing to note here is that even though both parameters are optional, they will both get passed to the query every time it is executed. This is perfectly OK! There is very little overhead in passing parameters into sp_executesql, and trying to work around this issue would either bring back the combinatorial explosion problem or require some very creative use of nested dynamic SQL. Neither solution is maintainable or worth the time required, so save your energy for more interesting pursuits.

To verify that sp_executesql really is reusing query plans as expected, run the same code that was used to show that the EXECUTE method was not reusing plans:

```
DBCC FREEPROCCACHE;
GO

EXEC GetEmployeeData
    @BusinessEntityID = 1;
GO

EXEC GetEmployeeData
    @BusinessEntityID = 2;
GO

EXEC GetEmployeeData
    @BusinessEntityID = 3;
GO
```

After running this code, query the sys.dm_exec_cached_plans view as before. The results should show two rows, as follows:

objtype	text
Proc	CREATE PROCEDURE GetEmployeeData @BusinessEntityID int = NULL...
Prepared	(@BusinessEntityID INT, @NationalIDNumber nvarchar(60))SELECT ...

One plan is cached for the procedure itself, and one is cached for the invocation of the dynamic query with the @BusinessEntityID parameter. Invoking the query with a different combination of parameters will result in creation of more cached plans, because the resultant query text will be different. However, the maximum number of plans that can be cached for the stored procedure is five: one for the procedure itself and one for each possible combination of parameters.

Performance Comparison

Having considered the implications for maintenance and cache plan reuse, let's now conduct some simple load testing to see how the three different approaches (static, EXECUTE, and sp_executesql) compare in terms of actual performance.

To begin, create a renamed version of the best-performing (but hardest-to-maintain) static SQL version of the stored procedure. Call it **GetEmployeeData_Static**:

```
CREATE PROCEDURE GetEmployeeData_Static
  @BusinessEntityID int = NULL,
  @NationalIDNumber nvarchar(15) = NULL
AS
BEGIN
  SET NOCOUNT ON;

  IF (@BusinessEntityID IS NOT NULL AND @NationalIDNumber IS NOT NULL)
    BEGIN
      SELECT
        LoginID,
        JobTitle
      FROM HumanResources.Employee
      WHERE
        BusinessEntityID = @BusinessEntityID
        AND NationalIDNumber = @NationalIDNumber;
    END

    ELSE IF (@BusinessEntityID IS NOT NULL)
    BEGIN
      SELECT
        LoginID,
        JobTitle
      FROM HumanResources.Employee
      WHERE
        BusinessEntityID = @BusinessEntityID;
    END

    ELSE IF (@NationalIDNumber IS NOT NULL)
    BEGIN
      SELECT
        LoginID,
        JobTitle
      FROM HumanResources.Employee
      WHERE
        NationalIDNumber = @NationalIDNumber;
    END

    ELSE
    BEGIN
      SELECT
        LoginID,
        JobTitle
      FROM HumanResources.Employee;
    END

END;
GO
```

This version produces the best possible query plans, but of course has the issue of being very difficult to maintain. It also has no additional overhead associated with context switching, which may make it slightly faster than a dynamic SQL solution if the queries are very simple. For more complex queries that take longer to run, any context switching overhead will be overshadowed by the actual runtime of the query.

To test the performance of the **GetEmployeeData_Static** stored procedure, we'll call it from a simple C# application via ADO.NET. But first we need to obtain a set of values to supply for the **@NationalIDNumber** and **@BusinessEntityID** parameters. For each row in the **HumanResources.Employee** table, we'll call the procedure with every combination of those two parameters: once supplying just the **BusinessEntityID**, once supplying just the **NationalIDNumber**, once supplying both, and once providing **NULL** for both parameters. There are 290 rows in the **HumanResources.Employee** table, so this provides (290 x 3) + 1 = 871 combinations. To increase the sample size, we'll place the procedure call in a loop that will call every combination ten times—leading to 8,710 iterations of the query.

The following code listing illustrates the C# code required to perform the test just described. It first fills a **DataTable** with the possible set of parameter values, and then steps through the rows of the table, calling the **GetEmployeeData_static** with each combination:

```
SqlConnection sqlConn = new SqlConnection(
  "Data Source=localhost;
  Initial Catalog=AdventureWorks2008;
  Integrated Security=SSPI");

sqlConn.Open();

/* Grab every combination of parameters */
SqlCommand cmd = new SqlCommand(@"
  SELECT BusinessEntityId, NationalIDNumber FROM HumanResources.Employee
  UNION ALL SELECT NULL, NationalIDNumber FROM HumanResources.Employee
  UNION ALL SELECT BusinessEntityId, NULL FROM HumanResources.Employee
  UNION ALL SELECT NULL, NULL", sqlConn);

SqlDataAdapter da = new SqlDataAdapter();
da.SelectCommand = cmd;
DataTable dt = new DataTable();
da.Fill(dt);

for (int i = 0; i < 10; i++)
{
  foreach (DataRow r in dt.Rows)
  {

    SqlCommand cmd2 = new SqlCommand("GetEmployeeData_static", sqlConn);
    cmd2.CommandType = CommandType.StoredProcedure;

    SqlParameter param = new SqlParameter("@BusinessEntityID", SqlDbType.Int);
    param.Value = r[0];
    cmd2.Parameters.Add(param);

    SqlParameter param2 = new SqlParameter("@NationalIDNumber",
      SqlDbType.NVarChar, 16);
    param2.Value = r[1];
```

```
        cmd2.Parameters.Add(param2);

        cmd2.ExecuteNonQuery();

    }
}
sqlConn.Close();
```

Before running the code, be sure to clear out the stored procedure cache by issuing the following command:

```
DBCC FREEPROCCACHE;
GO
```

Then execute the C# code to call the static procedure in a loop. Once it's run, we'll investigate the performance by once again interrogating the system DMVs. This time, we'll amend our original cache plan query to add in performance counter columns from the **sys.dm_exec_query_stats** view as follows:

```
SELECT
  cp.objtype AS type,
  COUNT(DISTINCT st.text) AS plans,
  SUM(qs.execution_count) AS execution_count,
  CAST(SUM(qs.total_worker_time) AS decimal(18,9)) / SUM(qs.execution_count)
    / 1000 AS avg_CPU_ms
FROM sys.dm_exec_query_stats qs
  JOIN sys.dm_exec_cached_plans cp ON cp.plan_handle = qs.plan_handle
  CROSS APPLY sys.dm_exec_sql_text(qs.sql_handle) st
WHERE
  st.text LIKE '%HumanResources.Employee%'
  AND st.text NOT LIKE '%sys.dm_exec_sql_text%'
GROUP BY
  cp.objtype
```

The results obtained when I run this on my laptop are as follows:

type	plans	execution_count	avg_CPU_ms
Adhoc	1	1	3.00000000000000000000000000000
Proc	1	8710	0.08829402985074626865671641791

As expected, the cache contains a single execution plan, which was compiled once and then reused for all 8,710 queries. Each static query took, on average, 0.08829ms to run. Not bad.

Next, create a renamed version of the **EXECUTE** solution, called **GetEmployeeData_Execute**:

```
CREATE PROCEDURE GetEmployeeData_Execute
  @BusinessEntityID int = NULL,
  @NationalIDNumber nvarchar(15) = NULL
```

```
AS
BEGIN
  SET NOCOUNT ON;

  DECLARE @sql nvarchar(max);

  SET @sql = '' +
    'SELECT ' +
      'LoginID, ' +
      'JobTitle ' +
    'FROM HumanResources.Employee ' +
    'WHERE 1=1 ' +
      CASE
        WHEN @BusinessEntityID IS NULL THEN ''
        ELSE
          'AND BusinessEntityID = ' +
          CONVERT(nvarchar, @BusinessEntityID) + ' '
      END +
      CASE
        WHEN @NationalIDNumber IS NULL THEN ''
        ELSE
          'AND NationalIDNumber = N''' +
          @NationalIDNumber + ''' '
      END;

  EXEC(@sql);

END
```

Testing this stored procedure against the static solution, and later, the **sp_executesql** solution, will create a nice means by which to compare static SQL against both parameterized and nonparameterized dynamic SQL, and will show the effects of parameterization on performance. Back in the C# application, change the **SqlCommand** to reflect the name of the new procedure, as follows:

```
SqlCommand cmd2 = new SqlCommand("GetEmployeeData_execute", sqlConn);
```

Once you've made this change, clear the stored procedure cache with another call to **DBCC FREEPROCCACHE**, and then run the tests again. Interrogating the DMV tables after the test runs on my system gives the following results:

type	plans	execution_count	avg_CPU_ms
Adhoc	872	8711	0.1120422454368040408678821260

Using the **EXECUTE** method, the cache contains 872 different **Adhoc** plans—one for the original creation of the stored procedure, and one for each time it is called with a different set of parameters. The overall average CPU time for this method is 0.112ms per query—over ten times slower than the static solution.

The final stored procedure to test is, of course, the **sp_executesql** solution. Once again, create a renamed version of the stored procedure in order to differentiate it. This time, call it **GetEmployeeData_sp_executesql**:

```
CREATE PROCEDURE GetEmployeeData_sp_executesql
  @BusinessEntityID int = NULL,
  @NationalIDNumber nvarchar(15) = NULL
AS
BEGIN
  SET NOCOUNT ON;

  DECLARE @sql nvarchar(max);

  SET @sql = '' +
    'SELECT ' +
      'LoginID, ' +
      'JobTitle ' +
    'FROM HumanResources.Employee ' +
    'WHERE 1=1 ' +
      CASE
        WHEN @BusinessEntityID IS NULL THEN ''
        ELSE 'AND BusinessEntityID = @BusinessEntityID '
      END +
      CASE
        WHEN @NationalIDNumber IS NULL THEN ''
        ELSE 'AND NationalIDNumber = @NationalIDNumber '
      END;

  EXEC sp_executesql
    @sql,
    N'@BusinessEntityID int, @NationalIDNumber nvarchar(15)',
    @BusinessEntityID,
    @NationalIDNumber;

END
```

In the C# code, change the **SqlCommand** text to the following:

```
SqlCommand cmd2 = new SqlCommand("GetEmployeeData_sp_executesql", sqlConn);
```

Clear the query plan cache and run the tests. When finished, check the performance results one last time. The results from my system are as follows:

type	plans	execution_count	avg_CPU_ms
Adhoc	1	1	3.0000000000000000000000000000
Prepared	4	8710	0.0954129735935706084959816303

Interestingly, the results of the two dynamic SQL solutions are very close, with the **sp_executesql** solution only just beating the **EXECUTE** solution, even given the benefits of parameterization for performance. Runs with fewer iterations or against stored procedures that are more expensive for SQL Server to compile will highlight the benefits more clearly.

The static SQL version, as expected, still wins from a performance point of view (although all three are extremely fast). Again, more complex stored procedures with longer runtimes will naturally overshadow the difference between the dynamic SQL and static SQL solutions, leaving the dynamic SQL vs. static SQL question purely one of maintenance.

■ **Note** When running these tests on my system, I restarted my SQL Server service between each run in order to ensure absolute consistency. Although this may be overkill for this case, you may find it interesting to experiment on your end with how restarting the service affects performance. This kind of test can also be useful for general scalability testing, especially in clustered environments. Restarting the service before testing is a technique that you can use to simulate how the application will behave if a failover occurs, without requiring a clustered testing environment.

Output Parameters

Although it is somewhat of an aside to this discussion, I would like to point out one other feature that sp_executesql brings to the table as compared to EXECUTE—one that is often overlooked by users who are just getting started using it. sp_executesql allows you to pass parameters to dynamic SQL just like to a stored procedure—and this includes output parameters.

Output parameters become quite useful when you need to use the output of a dynamic SQL statement that perhaps only returns a single scalar value. An output parameter is a much cleaner solution than having to insert the value into a table and then read it back into a variable.

To define an output parameter, simply append the OUTPUT keyword in both the parameter definition list and the parameter list itself. The following T-SQL shows how to use an output parameter with sp_executesql:

```
DECLARE @SomeVariable int;

EXEC sp_executesql
    N'SET @SomeVariable = 123',
    N'@SomeVariable int OUTPUT',
    @SomeVariable OUTPUT;
```

As a result of this T-SQL, the @SomeVariable variable will have a value of 123.

Since this is an especially contrived example, I will add that in practice I often use output parameters with sp_executesql in stored procedures that perform searches with optional parameters. A common user interface requirement is to return the number of total rows found by the selected search criteria, and an output parameter is a quick way to get the data back to the caller.

Dynamic SQL Security Considerations

To finish up this chapter, a few words on security are important. Aside from the SQL injection example shown in a previous section, there are a couple of other security topics that are important to consider. In this section, I will briefly discuss permissions issues and a few interface rules to help you stay out of trouble when working with dynamic SQL.

Permissions to Referenced Objects

As mentioned a few times throughout this chapter, dynamic SQL is invoked in a different scope than static SQL. This is extremely important from an authorization perspective, because upon execution, permissions for all objects referenced in the dynamic SQL will be checked. Therefore, in order for the dynamic SQL to run without throwing an authorization exception, the user executing the dynamic SQL must either have access directly to the referenced objects or be impersonating a user with access to the objects.

This creates a slightly different set of challenges from those you get when working with static SQL stored procedures, due to the fact that the change of context that occurs when invoking dynamic SQL breaks any ownership chain that has been established. If you need to manage a permissions hierarchy such that users should have access to stored procedures that use dynamic SQL, but not to the base tables they reference, make sure to become intimately familiar with certificate signing and the **EXECUTE AS** clause, both described in detail in Chapter 4.

Interface Rules

This chapter has focused on optional parameters of the type you might pass to enable or disable a certain predicate for a query. However, there are other types of optional parameters that developers often try to use with dynamic SQL. These parameters involve passing table names, column lists, **ORDER BY** lists, and other modifications to the query itself into a stored procedure for concatenation.

If you've read Chapter 1 of this book, you know that these practices are incredibly dangerous from a software development perspective, leading to tight coupling between the database and the application, in addition to possibly distorting stored procedures' implied output contracts, therefore making testing and maintenance extremely arduous.

As a general rule, you should never pass any database object name from an application into a stored procedure (and the application should not know the object names anyway). If you absolutely must modify a table or some other object name in a stored procedure, try to encapsulate the name via a set of parameters instead of allowing the application to dictate.

For instance, assume you were working with the following stored procedure:

```
CREATE PROC SelectDataFromTable
  @TableName nvarchar(200)
AS
BEGIN
  SET NOCOUNT ON;

  DECLARE @sql nvarchar(max);

  SET @sql = '' +
    'SELECT ' +
```

```
        'ColumnA, ' +
        'ColumnB, ' +
        'ColumnC ' +
      'FROM ' + @TableName;

    EXEC(@sql);

END;
GO
```

Table names cannot be parameterized, meaning that using **sp_executesql** in this case would not help in any way. However, in virtually all cases, there is a limited subset of table names that can (or will) realistically be passed into the stored procedure. If you know in advance that this stored procedure will only ever use tables **TableA**, **TableB**, and **TableC**, you can rewrite the stored procedure to keep those table names out of the application while still providing the same functionality.

The following code listing provides an example of how you might alter the previous stored procedure to provide dynamic table functionality while abstracting the names somewhat to avoid coupling issues:

```
ALTER PROC SelectDataFromTable
  @UseTableA bit = 0,
  @UseTableB bit = 0,
  @UseTableC bit = 0
AS
BEGIN
  SET NOCOUNT ON;

  IF (
    CONVERT(tinyint, COALESCE(@UseTableA, 0)) +
    CONVERT(tinyint, COALESCE(@UseTableB, 0)) +
    CONVERT(tinyint, COALESCE(@UseTableC, 0))
  ) <> 1
  BEGIN
    RAISERROR('Must specify exactly one table', 16, 1);
    RETURN;
  END

  DECLARE @sql nvarchar(max);

  SET @sql = '' +
    'SELECT ' +
      'ColumnA, ' +
      'ColumnB, ' +
      'ColumnC ' +
    'FROM ' +
      CASE
        WHEN @UseTableA = 1 THEN 'TableA'
        WHEN @UseTableB = 1 THEN 'TableB'
        WHEN @UseTableC = 1 THEN 'TableC'
      END
```

```
  EXEC(@sql);

END;
GO
```

This version of the stored procedure is obviously quite a bit more complex, but it is still relatively easy to understand. The **IF** block validates that exactly one table is selected (i.e., the value of the parameter corresponding to the table is set to 1), and the **CASE** expression handles the actual dynamic selection of the table name.

If you find yourself in a situation in which even this technique is not possible, and you *absolutely must* support the application passing in object names dynamically, you can at least do a bit to protect from the possibility of SQL injection problems. SQL Server includes a function called **QUOTENAME**, which bracket-delimits any input string such that it will be treated as an identifier if concatenated with a SQL statement. For instance, **QUOTENAME('123')** returns the value **[123]**.

By using **QUOTENAME**, the original version of the dynamic table name stored procedure can be modified such that there will be no risk of SQL injection:

```
ALTER PROC SelectDataFromTable
  @TableName nvarchar(200);
AS
BEGIN
  SET NOCOUNT ON;

  DECLARE @sql nvarchar(max);

  SET @sql = '' +
    'SELECT ' +
      'ColumnA, ' +
      'ColumnB, ' +
      'ColumnC ' +
    'FROM ' + QUOTENAME(@TableName);

  EXEC(@sql);

END;
GO
```

Unfortunately, this does nothing to fix the interface issues, and modifying the database schema may still necessitate a modification to the application code.

Summary

Dynamic SQL can be an extremely useful tool for working with stored procedures that require flexibility. However, it is important to make sure that you are using dynamic SQL properly in order to ensure the best balance of performance, maintainability, and security. Make sure to *always* parameterize queries and *never* trust any input from a caller, lest a nasty payload is waiting, embedded in an otherwise innocent search string.

Summary

Dynamic SQL can be an extremely useful tool for working with stored procedures that require flexibility. However, it is important to make sure that you are using dynamic SQL properly in order to ensure the best balance of performance, maintainability, and security. Make sure to *always* parameterize queries and *never* trust any input from a caller, lest a nasty payload is waiting, embedded in an otherwise innocent search string.

CHAPTER 9

■ ■ ■

Designing Systems for Application Concurrency

It is hardly surprising how well applications tend to both behave and scale when they have only one concurrent user. Many developers are familiar with the wonderful feeling of checking in complex code at the end of an exhaustingly long release cycle and going home confident in the fact that everything works and performs according to specification. Alas, that feeling can be instantly ripped away, transformed into excruciating pain, when the multitude of actual end users start hammering away at the system, and it becomes obvious that just a bit more testing of concurrent utilization might have been helpful. Unless your application will be used by only one user at a time, it simply can't be designed and developed as though it will be.

Concurrency can be one of the toughest areas in application development, because the problems that occur in this area often depend on extremely specific timing. An issue that causes a test run to end with a flurry of exceptions on one occasion may not fire any alarms on the next run because some other module happened to take a few milliseconds longer than usual, lining up the cards just right. Even worse is when the opposite happens, and a concurrency problem pops up seemingly out of nowhere, at odd and irreproducible intervals (but *always* right in the middle of an important demo).

While it may be difficult or impossible to completely eliminate these kinds of issues from your software, proper up-front design can help you greatly reduce the number of incidents you see. The key is to understand a few basic factors:

- What kinds of actions can users perform that might interfere with the activities of others using the system?

- What features of the database (or software system) will help or hinder your users performing their work concurrently?

- What are the business rules that must be obeyed in order to make sure that concurrency is properly handled?

This chapter delves into the different types of application concurrency models you might need to implement in the database layer, the tools SQL Server offers to help you design applications that work properly in concurrent scenarios, and how to go beyond what SQL Server offers out of the box.

The Business Side: What Should Happen When Processes Collide?

Before getting into the technicalities of dealing with concurrency in SQL Server, it's important to define both the basic problem areas and the methods by which they are commonly handled. In the context of a database application, problems arising as a result of concurrent processes generally fall into one of three categories:

- **Overwriting** of data occurs when two or more users edit the same data simultaneously, and the changes made by one user are lost when replaced by the changes from another. This can be a problem for several reasons: first of all, there is a loss of effort, time, and data (not to mention considerable annoyance for the user whose work is lost). Additionally, a more serious potential consequence is that, depending on what activity the users were involved in at the time, overwriting may result in data corruption at the database level. A simple example is a point-of-sale application that reads a stock number from a table into a variable, adds or subtracts an amount based on a transaction, and then writes the updated number back to the table. If two sales terminals are running and each processes a sale for the same product at exactly the same time, there is a chance that both terminals will retrieve the initial value and that one terminal will overwrite instead of update the other's change.

- **Nonrepeatable reading** is a situation that occurs when an application reads a set of data from a database and performs some calculations on it, and then needs to read the same set of data again for another purpose—but the original set has changed in the interim. A common example of where this problem can manifest itself is in drill-down reports presented by analytical systems. The reporting system might present the user with an aggregate view of the data, calculated based on an initial read. As the user clicks summarized data items on the report, the reporting system might return to the database in order to read the corresponding detail data. However, there is a chance that another user may have changed some data between the initial read and the detail read, meaning that the two sets will no longer match.

- **Blocking** may occur when one process is writing data and another tries to read or write the same data. Blocking can be (and usually is) a good thing—it prevents many types of overwriting problems and ensures that only consistent data is read by clients. However, excessive blocking can greatly decrease an application's ability to scale, and therefore it must be carefully monitored and controlled.

There are several ways of dealing with these issues, with varying degrees of ease of technical implementation. But for the sake of this section, I'll ignore the technical side for now and keep the discussion focused on the business rules involved. There are four main approaches to addressing database concurrency issues that should be considered:

- **Anarchy**: Assume that collisions and inconsistent data do not matter. Do not block readers from reading inconsistent data, and do not worry about overwrites or repeatable reads. This methodology is often used in applications in which users have little or no chance of editing the same data point concurrently, and in which repeatable read issues are unimportant.

- **Pessimistic concurrency control**: Assume that collisions will be frequent; stop them from being able to occur. Block readers from reading inconsistent data, but do not necessarily worry about repeatable reads. To avoid overwrites, do not allow anyone to begin editing a piece of data that's being edited by someone else.

- **Optimistic concurrency control**: Assume that there will occasionally be some collisions, but that it's OK for them to be handled when they occur. Block readers from reading inconsistent data, and let the reader know what version of the data is being read. This enables the reader to know when repeatable read problems occur (but not avoid them). To avoid overwrites, do not allow any process to overwrite a piece of data if it has been changed in the time since it was first read for editing by that process.

- **Multivalue concurrency control (MVCC)**: Assume that there will be collisions, but that they should be treated as new versions rather than as collisions. Block readers both from reading inconsistent data and encountering repeatable read problems by letting the reader know what version of the data is being read and allowing the reader to reread the same version multiple times. To avoid overwrites, create a new version of the data each time it is saved, keeping the old version in place.

Each of these methodologies represents a different user experience, and the choice must be made based on the necessary functionality of the application at hand. For instance, a message board application might use a more-or-less anarchic approach to concurrency, since it's unlikely or impossible that two users would be editing the same message at the same time—overwrites and inconsistent reads are acceptable.

On the other hand, many applications cannot bear overwrites. A good example of this is a source control system, where overwritten source code might mean a lot of lost work. However, the best way to handle the situation for source control is up for debate. Two popular systems, Subversion and Visual SourceSafe, each handle this problem differently. Subversion uses an optimistic scheme in which anyone can edit a given file, but you receive a collision error when you commit if someone else has edited it in the interim. Visual SourceSafe, on the other hand, uses a pessimistic model where you must check out a given file before editing it, thereby restricting anyone else from doing edits until you check it back in.

Finally, an example of a system that supports MVCC is a wiki. Although some wiki packages use an optimistic model, many others allow users to make edits at any time, simply incrementing the version number for a given page to reflect each change, but still saving past versions. This means that if two users are making simultaneous edits, some changes might get overwritten. However, users can always look back at the version history to restore overwritten content—in an MVCC system, nothing is ever actually deleted.

In later sections of this chapter I will describe solutions based on each of these methodologies in greater detail.

Isolation Levels and Transactional Behavior

This chapter assumes that you have some background in working with SQL Server transactions and isolation levels, but in case you're not familiar with some of the terminology, this section presents a very basic introduction to the topic.

Isolation levels are set in SQL Server in order to tell the database engine how to handle locking and blocking when multiple transactions collide, trying to read and write the same data. Selecting the correct isolation level for a transaction is extremely important in many business cases, especially those that require consistency when reading the same data multiple times.

SQL Server's isolation levels can be segmented into two basic classes: those in which readers are blocked by writers, and those in which blocking of readers does not occur. The **READ COMMITTED**, **REPEATABLE READ**, and **SERIALIZABLE** isolation levels are all in this first category, whereas **READ UNCOMMITTED** and **SNAPSHOT** fall into the latter group. A special subclass of the **SNAPSHOT** isolation level, **READ COMMITTED SNAPSHOT**, is also included in this second, nonblocking class.

All transactions, regardless of the isolation level used, take exclusive locks on data being updated. Transaction isolation levels do not change the behavior of locks taken at write time, but rather only those taken or honored by readers.

In order to see how the isolation levels work, create a table that will be accessed by multiple concurrent transactions. The following T-SQL creates a table called **Blocker** in **TempDB** and populates it with three rows:

```
USE TempDB;
GO

CREATE TABLE Blocker
(
  Blocker_Id int NOT NULL PRIMARY KEY
);
GO

INSERT INTO Blocker VALUES (1), (2), (3);
GO
```

Once the table has been created, open two SQL Server Management Studio query windows. I will refer to the windows hereafter as the **blocking window** and the **blocked window**, respectively.

In each of the three blocking isolation levels, readers will be blocked by writers. To see what this looks like, run the following T-SQL in the blocking window:

```
BEGIN TRANSACTION;

UPDATE Blocker
SET Blocker_Id = Blocker_Id + 1;
```

Now run the following in the blocked window:

```
SELECT *
FROM Blocker;
```

This second query will not return any results until the transaction started in the blocking window is either committed or rolled back. In order to release the locks, roll back the transaction by running the following in the blocking window:

```
ROLLBACK;
```

In the following section, I'll demonstrate the effects of specifying different isolation levels on the interaction between the blocking query and the blocked query.

■ **Note** Complete coverage of locking and blocking is out of the scope of this book. Refer to the topic "Locking in the Database Engine" in SQL Server 2008 Books Online for a detailed explanation.

Blocking Isolation Levels

Transactions using the blocking isolation levels take shared locks when reading data, thereby blocking anyone else trying to update the same data during the course of the read. The primary difference between these three isolation levels is in the granularity and behavior of the shared locks they take, which changes what sort of writes will be blocked and when.

READ COMMITTED Isolation

The default isolation level used by SQL Server is **READ COMMITTED**. In this isolation level, a reader will hold its locks only for the duration of the statement doing the read, even inside of an explicit transaction. To illustrate this, run the following in the blocking window:

```
BEGIN TRANSACTION;

SELECT *
FROM Blocker;
```

Now run the following in the blocked window:

```
BEGIN TRANSACTION;

UPDATE Blocker
SET Blocker_Id = Blocker_Id + 1;
```

In this case, the update runs without being blocked, even though the transaction is still active in the blocking window. The reason is that as soon as the **SELECT** ended, the locks it held were released. When you're finished observing this behavior, don't forget to roll back the transactions started in both windows by executing the **ROLLBACK** statement in each.

REPEATABLE READ Isolation

Both the **REPEATABLE READ** and **SERIALIZABLE** isolation levels hold locks for the duration of an explicit transaction. The difference is that **REPEATABLE READ** transactions take locks at a level of granularity that ensures that data already read cannot be updated by another transaction, but that allows other transactions to insert data that would change the results. On the other hand, **SERIALIZABLE** transactions take locks at a higher level of granularity, such that no data can be either updated or inserted within the locked range.

To observe the behavior of a **REPEATABLE READ** transaction, start by running the following T-SQL in the blocking window:

```
SET TRANSACTION ISOLATION LEVEL REPEATABLE READ;
```

```
BEGIN TRANSACTION;

SELECT *
FROM Blocker;
GO
```

Running the following update in the blocked window will result in blocking behavior—the query will wait until the blocking window's transaction has completed:

```
BEGIN TRANSACTION;

UPDATE Blocker
SET Blocker_Id = Blocker_Id + 1;
```

Both updates and deletes will be blocked by the locks taken by the query. However, inserts such as the following will not be blocked:

```
BEGIN TRANSACTION;

INSERT INTO Blocker VALUES (4);

COMMIT;
```

Rerun the **SELECT** statement in the blocking window, and you'll see the new row. This phenomenon is known as a **phantom row**, because the new data seems to appear like an apparition—out of nowhere. Once you're done investigating the topic of phantom rows, make sure to issue a **ROLLBACK** in both windows.

SERIALIZABLE Isolation

The difference between the **REPEATABLE READ** and **SERIALIZABLE** isolation levels is that while the former allows phantom rows, the latter does not. Any key—existent or not at the time of the **SELECT**—that is within the range predicated by the **WHERE** clause will be locked for the duration of the transaction if the **SERIALIZABLE** isolation level is used. To see how this works, first run the following in the blocking window:

```
SET TRANSACTION ISOLATION LEVEL SERIALIZABLE;

BEGIN TRANSACTION;

SELECT *
FROM Blocker;
```

Next, try either an **INSERT** or **UPDATE** in the blocked window. In either case, the operation will be forced to wait for the transaction in the blocking window to commit, since the transaction locks all rows in the table—whether or not they exist yet. To lock only a specific range of rows, add a **WHERE** clause to the blocking query, and all DML operations within the key range will be blocked for the duration of the transaction. When you're done, be sure to issue a **ROLLBACK**.

■ **Tip** The **REPEATABLE READ** and **SERIALIZABLE** isolation levels will hold shared locks for the duration of a transaction on whatever tables are queried. However, you might wish to selectively hold locks only on specific tables within a transaction in which you're working with multiple objects. To accomplish this, you can use the **HOLDLOCK** table hint, applied only to the tables that you want to hold the locks on. In a **READ COMMITTED** transaction, this will have the same effect as if the isolation level had been escalated just for those tables to **REPEATABLE READ**. For more information on table hints, see SQL Server 2008 Books Online.

Nonblocking Isolation Levels

The nonblocking isolation levels, **READ UNCOMMITTED** and **SNAPSHOT**, each allow readers to read data without waiting for writing transactions to complete. This is great from a concurrency standpoint—no blocking means that processes spend less time waiting and therefore users get their data back faster—but can be disastrous for data consistency.

READ UNCOMMITTED Isolation

READ UNCOMMITTED transactions do not apply shared locks as data is read and do not honor locks placed by other transactions. This means that there will be no blocking, but the data being read might be inconsistent (not yet committed). To see what this means, run the following in the blocking window:

```
BEGIN TRANSACTION;

UPDATE Blocker
SET Blocker_Id = 10
WHERE Blocker_Id = 1;
GO
```

This operation will place an exclusive lock on the updated row, so any readers should be blocked from reading the data until the transaction completes. However, the following query will not be blocked if run in the blocked window:

```
SET TRANSACTION ISOLATION LEVEL READ UNCOMMITTED;

SELECT *
FROM Blocker;
GO
```

The danger here is that because the query is not blocked, a user may see data that is part of a transaction that later gets rolled back. This can be especially problematic when users are shown aggregates that do not add up based on the leaf-level data when reconciliation is done later. I recommend that you carefully consider these issues before using **READ UNCOMMITTED** (or the **NOLOCK** table hint) in your queries.

SNAPSHOT Isolation

An alternative to **READ UNCOMMITTED** is SQL Server 2008's **SNAPSHOT** isolation level. This isolation level shares the same nonblocking characteristics as **READ UNCOMMITTED**, but only consistent data is shown. This is achieved by making use of a row-versioning technology that stores previous versions of rows in **TempDB** as data modifications occur in a database.

SNAPSHOT almost seems like the best of both worlds: no blocking, yet no danger of inconsistent data. However, this isolation level is not without its problems. First and foremost, storing the previous row values in **TempDB** can create a huge amount of load, causing many problems for servers that are not properly configured to handle the additional strain. And secondly, for many apps, this kind of nonblocking read does not make sense. For example, consider an application that needs to read updated inventory numbers. A **SNAPSHOT** read might cause the user to receive an invalid quantity, because the user will not be blocked when reading data, and may therefore see previously committed data rather than the latest updated numbers.

If you do decide to use either nonblocking isolation level, make sure to think carefully through the issues. There are many possible caveats with both approaches, and they are not right for every app, or perhaps even most apps.

■ **Note** SNAPSHOT isolation is a big topic, out of the scope of this chapter, but there are many excellent resources available that I recommend readers investigate for a better understanding of the subject. One place to start is the MSDN Books Online article "Understanding Row Versioning-Based Isolation Levels," available at http://msdn.microsoft.com/en-us/library/ms189050.aspx.

From Isolation to Concurrency Control

Some of the terminology used for the business logic methodologies mentioned in the previous section—particularly the adjectives *optimistic* and *pessimistic*—are also often used to describe the behavior of SQL Server's own locking and isolation rules. However, you should understand that the behavior of the SQL Server processes described by these terms is not quite the same as the definition used by the associated business process. From SQL Server's standpoint, the only concurrency control necessary is between two transactions that happen to hit the server at the same time—and from that point of view, its behavior works quite well. However, from a purely business-based perspective, there are no transactions (at least not in the sense of a database transaction)—there are only users and processes trying to make modifications to the same data. In this sense, a purely transactional mindset fails to deliver enough control.

SQL Server's default isolation level, **READ COMMITTED**, as well as its **REPEATABLE READ** and **SERIALIZABLE** isolation levels, can be said to support a form of pessimistic concurrency. When using these isolation levels, writers are not allowed to overwrite data in the process of being written by others. However, the moment the blocking transaction ends, the data is fair game, and another session can overwrite it without even knowing that it was modified in the interim. From a business point of view, this falls quite short of the pessimistic goal of keeping two end users from ever even beginning to edit the same data at the same time.

The **SNAPSHOT** isolation level is said to support a form of optimistic concurrency control. This comparison is far easier to justify than the pessimistic concurrency of the other isolation levels: with **SNAPSHOT** isolation, if you read a piece of data in order to make edits or modifications to it, and someone else updates the data after you've read it but before you've had a chance to write your edits, you will get an exception when you try to write. This is almost a textbook definition of optimistic concurrency, with one slight problem: SQL Server's isolation levels are *transactional*—so in order to make this work, you would have to have held a transaction open for the entire duration of the read, edit, and rewrite attempt. This doesn't scale especially well if, for instance, the application is web-enabled and the user wants to spend an hour editing the document.

Another form of optimistic concurrency control supported by SQL Server is used with updateable cursors. The **OPTIMISTIC** options support a very similar form of optimistic concurrency to that of **SNAPSHOT** isolation. However, given the rarity with which updateable cursors are actually used in properly designed production applications, this isn't an option you're likely to see very often.

Although both **SNAPSHOT** isolation and the **OPTIMISTIC WITH ROW VERSIONING** cursor options work by holding previous versions of rows in a version store, these should not be confused with MVCC. In both the case of the isolation level and the cursor option, the previous versions of the rows are only held temporarily in order to help support nonblocking reads. The rows are not available later—for instance, as a means by which to merge changes from multiple writers—which is a hallmark of a properly designed MVCC system.

Yet another isolation level that is frequently used in SQL Server application development scenarios is **READ UNCOMMITTED**. This isolation level implements the anarchy business methodology mentioned in the previous section, and does it quite well—readers are not blocked by writers, and writers are not blocked by readers, whether or not a transaction is active.

Again, it's important to stress that although SQL Server does not really support concurrency properly from a business point of view, it wouldn't make sense for it to do so. The goal of SQL Server's isolation levels is to control concurrency at the transactional level, ultimately helping to keep data in a consistent state in the database.

Regardless of its inherent lack of provision for business-compliant concurrency solutions, SQL Server provides all of the tools necessary to easily build them yourself. The following sections discuss how to use SQL Server in order to help define concurrency models within database applications.

Preparing for the Worst: Pessimistic Concurrency

Imagine for a moment that you are tasked with building a system to help a life insurance company input data from many years of paper-based customer profile update forms. The company sent out the forms to each of its several hundred thousand customers on a biannual basis, in order to get the customers' latest information.

Most of the profiles were filled in by hand, so OCR is out of the question—they must be keyed in manually. To make matters worse, a large percentage of the customer files were removed from the filing system by employees and incorrectly refiled. Many were also photocopied at one time or another, and employees often filed the photocopies in addition to the original forms, resulting in a massive amount of duplication. The firm has tried to remove the oldest of the forms and bring the newer ones to the top of the stack, but it's difficult because many customers didn't always send back the forms each time they were requested—for one customer, 1994 may be the newest year, whereas for another, the latest form may be from 2009.

Back to the challenge at hand—building the data input application is fairly easy, as is finding students willing to do the data input for fairly minimal rates. The workflow is as follows: for each profile update form, the person doing the data input will bring up the customer's record based on that customer's Social Security number or other identification number. If the date on the profile form is more recent than the last updated date in the system, the profile needs to be updated with the newer data. If the dates are the same, the firm has decided that the operator should scan through the form and make sure all of the data already entered is correct—as in all cases of manual data entry, the firm is aware that typographical errors will be made. Each form is several pages long, and the larger ones will take hours to type in.

As is always the case in projects like this, time and money are of the essence, and the firm is concerned about the tremendous amount of profile form duplication as well as the fact that many of the forms are filed in the wrong order. It would be a huge waste of time for the data input operators if, for instance, one entered a customer's 1996 update form at the same time another happened to be entering the same customer's 2002 form.

Progressing to a Solution

This situation all but cries out for a solution involving pessimistic concurrency control. Each time a customer's Social Security number is entered into the system, the application can check whether someone else has entered the same number and has not yet persisted changes or sent back a message saying there are no changes (i.e., hit the cancel button). If another operator is currently editing that customer's data, a message can be returned to the user telling him or her to try again later—this profile is locked.

The problem then becomes a question of how best to implement such a solution. A scheme I've seen attempted several times is to create a table along the lines of the following:

```
CREATE TABLE CustomerLocks
(
  CustomerId int NOT NULL PRIMARY KEY
    REFERENCES Customers (CustomerId),
  IsLocked bit NOT NULL DEFAULT (0)
);
GO
```

The **IsLocked** column could instead be added to the existing **Customers** table, but that is not recommended in a highly transactional database system. I generally advise keeping locking constructs separate from actual data in order to limit excessive blocking on core tables.

In this system, the general technique employed is to populate the table with every customer ID in the system. The table is then queried when someone needs to take a lock, using code such as the following:

```
DECLARE @LockAcquired bit = 0;

IF
  (
    SELECT IsLocked
    FROM CustomerLocks
    WHERE CustomerId = @CustomerId
  ) = 0
BEGIN
  UPDATE CustomerLocks
  SET IsLocked = 1
  WHERE CustomerId = @CustomerId;

  SET @LockAcquired = 1;
END
```

Unfortunately, this approach is fraught with issues. The first and most serious problem is that between the query in the IF condition that tests for the existence of a lock and the UPDATE, the row's value can be changed by another writer. If two sessions ask for the lock at the same moment, the result may be that both writers will believe that they hold the exclusive lock. In order to remedy this issue, the IF condition should be eliminated; instead, check for the ability to take the lock at the same time as you're taking it, in the UPDATE's WHERE clause:

```
DECLARE @LockAcquired bit;

UPDATE CustomerLocks
SET IsLocked = 1
WHERE
  CustomerId = @CustomerId
  AND IsLocked = 0;

SET @LockAcquired = @@ROWCOUNT;
```

This pattern fixes the issue of two readers requesting the lock at the same time, but leaves open a maintenance issue: my recommendation to separate the locking from the actual table used to store customer data means that you must now ensure that all new customer IDs are added to the locks table as they are added to the system.

To solve this issue, avoid modeling the table as a collection of lock statuses per customer. Instead, define the existence of a row in the table as indication of a lock being held. Then the table becomes as follows:

```
CREATE TABLE CustomerLocks
(
  CustomerId int NOT NULL PRIMARY KEY
    REFERENCES Customers (CustomerId)
);
GO
```

To take a lock with this new table, you can attempt an INSERT, using a TRY/CATCH block to find out whether you've caused a primary key violation:

```
DECLARE @LockAcquired bit;

BEGIN TRY
  INSERT INTO CustomerLocks
  (
    CustomerId
  )
  VALUES
  (
    @CustomerId
  )

  --No exception: Lock acquired
  SET @LockAcquired = 1;
END TRY
BEGIN CATCH
```

```
  --Caught an exception: No lock acquired
  SET @LockAcquired = 0;
END CATCH
GO
```

Releasing the lock is a simple matter of deleting the row:

```
DELETE FROM CustomerLocks
WHERE CustomerId = @CustomerId;
GO
```

We are now getting closer to a robust solution, but we haven't quite gotten there yet. Imagine that a buggy piece of code exists somewhere in the application, and instead of calling the stored procedure to take a lock, it's occasionally calling the other stored procedure, which releases the lock. In the system as it's currently designed, there is no protection against this kind of issue—anyone can request a lock release at any time, whatever user holds the current lock on the record. This is very dangerous, as it will invalidate the entire locking scheme for the system. In addition, the way the system is implemented as shown, the caller will not know that a problem occurred and that the lock didn't exist. Both of these problems can be solved with some additions to the framework in place.

In order to help protect the locks from being prematurely invalidated, a **lock token** can be issued. This token is nothing more than a randomly generated unique identifier for the lock, and will be used as the key to release the lock instead of the customer ID. To implement this solution, the table's definition can be changed as follows:

```
CREATE TABLE CustomerLocks
(
  CustomerId int NOT NULL PRIMARY KEY
    REFERENCES Customers (CustomerId),
  LockToken uniqueidentifier NOT NULL UNIQUE
);
GO
```

With this table in place, the insert routine to request a lock becomes the following:

```
DECLARE @LockToken uniqueidentifier

BEGIN TRY
  --Generate the token
  SET @LockToken = NEWID();

  INSERT INTO CustomerLocks
  (
    CustomerId,
    LockToken
  )
  VALUES
  (
    @CustomerId,
    @LockToken
  )
END TRY
```

```
BEGIN CATCH
  --Caught an exception: No lock acquired
  SET @LockToken = NULL;
END CATCH
GO
```

Now, rather than checking whether **@LockAcquired** is **1** to find out if the lock was successfully taken, check whether **@LockToken** is **NULL**. By using a GUID, this system greatly decreases the chance that a buggy piece of application code will cause the lock to be released by a process that does not hold it.

After taking the lock, the application should remember the lock token, passing it instead of the customer ID when it comes time to release the lock:

```
DELETE FROM CustomerLocks
WHERE LockToken = @LockToken;
GO
```

Even better, the code used to release the lock can check to find out whether the lock was not successfully released (or whether there was no lock to release to begin with) and return an exception to the caller:

```
DELETE FROM CustomerLocks
WHERE LockToken = @LockToken;

IF @@ROWCOUNT = 0
  RAISERROR('Lock token not found!', 16, 1);

GO
```

The caller should do any updates to the locked resources and request the lock release in the same transaction. That way, if the caller receives this exception, it can take appropriate action—rolling back the transaction—ensuring that the data does not end up in an invalid state.

Almost all of the issues have now been eliminated from this locking scheme: two processes will not erroneously be granted the same lock, there is no maintenance issue with regard to keeping the table populated with an up-to-date list of customer IDs, and the tokens greatly eliminate the possibility of lock release issues.

One final, slightly subtle problem remains: what happens if a user requests a lock, forgets to hit the save button, and leaves for a two-week vacation? Or in the same vein, what should happen if the application takes a lock and then crashes 5 minutes later, thereby losing its reference to the token?

Solving this issue in a uniform fashion that works for all scenarios is unfortunately not possible, and one of the biggest problems with pessimistic schemes is that there will always be administrative overhead associated with releasing locks that for some reason did not get properly handled. The general method of solving this problem is to add an audit column to the locks table to record the date and time the lock was taken:

```
CREATE TABLE CustomerLocks
(
  CustomerId int NOT NULL PRIMARY KEY
    REFERENCES Customers (CustomerId),
  LockToken uniqueidentifier NOT NULL UNIQUE,
```

```
  LockGrantedDate datetime NOT NULL DEFAULT (GETDATE())
);
GO
```

None of the code already listed needs to be modified in order to accommodate the **LockGrantedDate** column, since it has a default value. An external job must be written to poll the table on a regular basis, "expiring" locks that have been held for too long. The code to do this is simple; the following T-SQL deletes all locks older than 5 hours:

```
DELETE FROM CustomerLocks
WHERE LockGrantedDate < DATEADD(hour, -5, GETDATE());
GO
```

This code can be implemented in a SQL Server agent job, set to run occasionally throughout the day. The actual interval depends on the amount of activity your system experiences, but once every 20 or 30 minutes is sufficient in most cases.

Although this expiration process works in most cases, it's also where things can break down from both administrative and business points of view. The primary challenge is defining a timeout period that makes sense. If the average lock is held for 20 minutes, but there are certain long-running processes that might need to hold locks for hours, it's important to define the timeout to favor the later processes, even providing padding to make sure that their locks will never automatically expire when not appropriate. Unfortunately, no matter what timeout period you choose, it will never work for everyone. There is virtually a 100 percent chance that at some point, a user will be working on a very high-profile action that must be completed quickly, and the application will crash, leaving the lock in place. The user will have no recourse available but to call for administrative support or wait for the timeout period—and of course, if it's been designed to favor processes that take many hours, this will not be a popular choice.

Although I have seen this problem manifest itself in pessimistic concurrency solutions, it has generally not been extremely common and hasn't caused any major issues aside from a few stressed-out end users. I am happy to say that I have never received a panicked call at 2:00 a.m. from a user requesting a lock release, although I could certainly see it happening. If this is a concern for your system, the solution is to design the application such that it sends "heartbeat" notifications back to the database on a regular basis as work is being done. These notifications should update the lock date/time column:

```
UPDATE CustomerLocks
SET LockGrantedDate = GETDATE()
WHERE LockToken = @LockToken;
```

The application can be made to send a heartbeat as often as necessary—for instance, once every 5 minutes—during times it detects user activity. This is easy even in web applications, thanks to AJAX and similar asynchronous techniques. If this design is used, the timeout period can be shortened considerably, but keep in mind that users may occasionally become temporarily disconnected while working; buffer the timeout at least a bit in order to help keep disconnection-related timeouts at bay.

■ **Tip** As an alternative to keeping the LockGrantedDate in the locks table, you could instead model the column as a LockExpirationDate. This might improve the flexibility of the system a bit by letting callers request a maximum duration for a lock when it is taken, rather than being forced to take the standard expiration interval. Of course, this has its downside: users requesting locks to be held for unrealistically large amounts of time. Should you implement such a solution, carefully monitor usage to make sure that this does not become an issue.

Enforcing Pessimistic Locks at Write Time

A problem with the solution proposed previously, and other programmatic pessimistic concurrency schemes, is the fact that the lock is generally not enforced outside of the application code. While that's fine in many cases, it is important to make sure that every data consumer follows the same set of rules with regard to taking and releasing locks. These locks do not *prevent* data modification, but rather only serve as a means by which to tell calling apps whether they are allowed to modify data. If an application is not coded with the correct logic, violation of core data rules may result.

It may be possible to avoid some or all of these types of problems by double-checking locks using triggers at write time, but this can be difficult to implement because you may not be able to tell which user has taken which lock for a given row, let alone make a determination about which user is doing a particular update, especially if your application uses only a single database login.

I have come up with a technique that can help get around some of these issues. To begin with, a new candidate key should be added to the CustomerLocks table, based on the CustomerId and LockToken columns:

```
ALTER TABLE CustomerLocks
ADD CONSTRAINT UN_Customer_Token
    UNIQUE (CustomerId, LockToken);
GO
```

This key can then be used as a reference in the Customers table once a LockToken column is added there:

```
ALTER TABLE Customers
ADD
  LockToken uniqueidentifier NULL,
  CONSTRAINT FK_CustomerLocks
    FOREIGN KEY (CustomerId, LockToken)
    REFERENCES CustomerLocks (CustomerId, LockToken);
GO
```

Since the LockToken column in the Customers table is nullable, it is not required to reference a valid token at all times. However, when it is actually set to a certain value, that value must exist in the CustomerLocks table, and the combination of customer ID and token in the Customers table must coincide with the same combination in the CustomerLocks table.

Once this is set up, enforcing the lock at write time, for all writers, can be done using a trigger:

```
CREATE TRIGGER tg_EnforceCustomerLocks
ON Customers
```

```
FOR UPDATE
AS
BEGIN
  SET NOCOUNT ON;

  IF EXISTS
  (
    SELECT *
    FROM inserted
    WHERE LockToken IS NULL
  )
  BEGIN
    RAISERROR('LockToken is a required column', 16, 1);
    ROLLBACK;
  END

  UPDATE Customers
  SET LockToken = NULL
  WHERE
    LockToken IN
    (
      SELECT LockToken
      FROM inserted
    );
END
GO
```

The foreign key constraint enforces that any non-**NULL** value assigned to the **LockToken** column must be valid. However, it does not enforce **NULL** values; the trigger takes care of that, forcing writers to set the lock token at write time. If all rows qualify, the tokens are updated back to **NULL** so that the locks can be released—holding a reference would mean that the rows could not be deleted from the **CustomerLocks** table.

This technique adds a bit of overhead to updates, as each row must be updated twice. If your application processes a large number of transactions each day, make sure to test carefully in order to ensure that this does not cause a performance issue.

Application Locks: Generalizing Pessimistic Concurrency

The example shown in the previous section can be used to pessimistically lock rows, but it requires some setup per entity type to be locked and cannot easily be generalized to locking of resources that span multiple rows, tables, or other levels of granularity supported within a SQL Server database.

Recognizing the need for this kind of locking construct, Microsoft included a feature in SQL Server called **application locks**. Application locks are programmatic, named locks, which behave much like other types of locks in the database: within the scope of a session or a transaction, a caller attempting to acquire an incompatible lock with a lock already held by another caller causes blocking and queuing.

Application locks are acquired using the **sp_getapplock** stored procedure. By default, the lock is tied to an active transaction, meaning that ending the transaction releases the lock. There is also an option to tie the lock to a session, meaning that the lock is released when the user disconnects. To set a transactional lock, begin a transaction and request a lock name (**resource**, in application lock parlance). You can also specify a lock mode, such as **shared** or **exclusive**. A caller can also set a wait timeout period, after which the stored procedure will stop waiting for other callers to release the lock. The following T-SQL acquires an exclusive transactional lock on the **customers** resource, waiting up to 2 seconds for other callers to release any locks they hold on the resource:

```
BEGIN TRAN;

EXEC sp_getapplock
    @Resource = 'customers',
    @LockMode = 'exclusive',
    @LockTimeout = 2000;
```

sp_getapplock does not throw an exception if the lock is not successfully acquired, but rather sets a return value. The return will be **0** if the lock was successfully acquired without waiting, **1** if the lock was acquired after some wait period had elapsed, and any of a number of negative values if the lock was not successfully acquired. As a consumer of **sp_getapplock**, it's important to know whether or not you actually acquired the lock you asked for—so the preceding example call is actually incomplete. The following call checks the return value to find out whether the lock was granted:

```
BEGIN TRAN;

DECLARE @ReturnValue int;

EXEC @ReturnValue = sp_getapplock
    @Resource = 'customers',
    @LockMode = 'exclusive',
    @LockTimeout = 2000;

IF @ReturnValue IN (0, 1)
    PRINT 'Lock granted';
ELSE
    PRINT 'Lock not granted';
```

To release the lock, you can commit or roll back the active transaction, or use the **sp_releaseapplock** stored procedure, which takes the lock resource name as its input value:

```
EXEC sp_releaseapplock
    @Resource = 'customers';
```

SQL Server's application locks are quite useful in many scenarios, but they suffer from the same problems mentioned previously concerning the discrepancy between concurrency models offered by SQL Server and what the business might actually require. Application locks are held only for the duration of a transaction or a session, meaning that to lock a resource and perform a long-running business transaction based on the lock, the caller would have to hold open a connection to the database the entire time. This is clearly not a scalable option, so I set out to write a replacement, nontransactional application lock framework.

My goal was to mimic most of the behavior of **sp_getapplock**, but for exclusive locks only—pessimistic locking schemes do not generally require shared locks on resources. I especially wanted callers to be able to queue and wait for locks to be released by other resources. Since this would not be a transactional lock, I also wanted to handle all of the caveats I've discussed in this section, including making sure that multiple callers requesting locks at the same time would not each think they'd been granted the lock, returning tokens to avoid invalid lock release scenarios, and adding lock timeout periods to ensure that orphaned locks would not be stranded until an admin removed them.

When considering the SQL Server 2008 features that would help me create this functionality, I immediately thought of Service Broker. Service Broker provides asynchronous queuing that can cross transactional and session boundaries, and the **WAITFOR** command allows callers to wait on a message without having to continually poll the queue.

■ **Note** For a thorough background on SQL Server Service Broker, see *Pro SQL Server 2008 Service Broker*, by Klaus Aschenbrenner (Apress, 2008).

The architecture I developed to solve this problem begins with a central table used to keep track of which locks have been taken:

```
CREATE TABLE AppLocks
(
  AppLockName nvarchar(255) NOT NULL,
  AppLockKey uniqueidentifier NULL,
  InitiatorDialogHandle uniqueidentifier NOT NULL,
  TargetDialogHandle uniqueidentifier NOT NULL,
  LastGrantedDate datetime NOT NULL DEFAULT(GETDATE()),
  PRIMARY KEY (AppLockName)
);
GO
```

The **AppLockName** column stores the names of locks that users have requested, and the **AppLockKey** functions as a lock token. This token also happens to be the conversation handle for a Service Broker dialog, but I'll get to that shortly. The **InitiatorDialogHandle** and **TargetDialogHandle** columns are conversation handles for another Service Broker dialog, which I will also explain shortly. Finally, the **LastGrantedDate** column is used just as in the examples earlier, to keep track of when each lock in the table was used. As you'll see, this column is even more important than it was in the previous case, because locks are reused instead of deleted in this scheme.

To support the Service Broker services, I created one message type and one contract:

```
CREATE MESSAGE TYPE AppLockGrant
VALIDATION = EMPTY;
GO

CREATE CONTRACT AppLockContract (
  AppLockGrant SENT BY INITIATOR
);
GO
```

If you're wondering why there is a message used to grant locks but none used to request them, it's because this solution does not use a lock request service. Service Broker is used only because it happens to provide the queuing, waiting, and timeout features I needed—a bit different from most Service Broker samples.

I created two queues to support this infrastructure, along with two services. Here is where we get closer to the meat of the system:

```
CREATE QUEUE AppLock_Queue;
GO

CREATE SERVICE AppLock_Service
ON QUEUE AppLock_Queue (AppLockContract);
GO

CREATE QUEUE AppLockTimeout_Queue;
GO

CREATE SERVICE AppLockTimeout_Service
ON QUEUE AppLockTimeOut_Queue;
GO
```

The **AppLock_Queue** queue and its associated service are used as follows: when a lock on a given resource is requested by a caller, if no one has ever requested a lock on that resource before, a dialog is started between the **AppLock_Service** service and itself. Both the initiator and target conversation handles for that dialog are used to populate the **InitiatorDialogHandle** and **TargetDialogHandle** columns, respectively. Later, when that caller releases its lock, an **AppLockGrant** message is sent on the queue from the initiator dialog handle stored in the table. When another caller wants to acquire a lock on the same resource, it gets the target dialog handle from the table and waits on it. This way callers can wait for the lock to be released without having to poll, and will be able to pick it up as soon as it is released if they happen to be waiting at that moment.

The **AppLockTimeout_Queue** is used a bit differently. You might notice that its associated service uses the default contract. This is because no messages—except perhaps Service Broker system messages—will ever be sent from or to it. Whenever a lock is granted, a new dialog is started between the service and itself, and the initiator conversation handle for the dialog becomes the lock token.

In addition to being used as the lock token, the dialog serves another purpose: when it is started, a lifetime is set. A dialog lifetime is a timer that, after its set period, sends a message to all active parties involved in the conversation—in this case, since no messages will have been sent, only the initiator will receive the message. Upon receipt, an activation procedure is used to release the lock. I found this to be a more granular way of controlling lock expirations than using a SQL Server agent job, as I did in the example in the previous section. Whenever a lock is released by a caller, the conversation is ended, thereby clearing its lifetime timer.

To allow callers to request locks, I created a stored procedure called **GetAppLock**. As this stored procedure is quite long, I will walk through it in sections in order to explain the details more thoroughly. To begin with, the stored procedure exposes three parameters, each required: the name of the resource to be locked, how long to wait for the lock in case someone else already has it, and an output parameter—the lock key to be used later to release the lock. Following are the first several lines of the stored procedure, ending where the transactional part of the procedure begins:

```
CREATE PROC GetAppLock
  @AppLockName nvarchar(255),
  @LockTimeout int,
  @AppLockKey uniqueidentifier = NULL OUTPUT
AS
BEGIN
  SET NOCOUNT ON;
```

```
SET XACT_ABORT ON;

--Make sure this variable starts NULL
SET @AppLockKey = NULL;

DECLARE @LOCK_TIMEOUT_LIFETIME int = 18000; --5 hours

DECLARE @startWait datetime = GETDATE();

DECLARE @init_handle uniqueidentifier;
DECLARE @target_handle uniqueidentifier;

BEGIN TRAN;
```

The stored procedure defines a couple of important local variables. The **@LOCK_TIMEOUT_LIFETIME** is the amount of time to wait until expiring an orphaned lock. It is currently hard-coded, but could easily be converted into a parameter in order to allow callers to specify their own estimated times of completion. This might be a more exact way of handling the lock expiration problem. The **@startWait** variable is used in order to track lock wait time, so that the procedure does not allow callers to wait longer than the requested lock timeout value.

Next, the stored procedure makes use of the very feature that I was attempting to supersede: SQL Server's native transactional application locks. There is a bit of a backstory to why I had to use them. During development of this technique, I discovered that Service Broker waits are processed according to last-in first-out (LIFO) rules: the most recent process waiting is the first to get a message off the queue. This is counterintuitive if you're used to working with first-in first-out (FIFO) queues, but is designed to allow the minimum number of activation stored procedures to stay alive after bursts of activity. By giving the message to the newest waiting process, the older processes are forced to eventually time out and expire.

Obviously such a scheme, while useful in the world of activation stored procedures, does not follow the requirements of a queued lock, so I made use of a transactional application lock in order to force serialization of the waits. Following is the code used to take the lock:

```
--Get the app lock -- start waiting
DECLARE @RETURN int;
EXEC @RETURN = sp_getapplock
  @resource = @AppLockName,
  @lockmode = 'exclusive',
  @LockTimeout = @LockTimeout;

IF @RETURN NOT IN (0, 1)
BEGIN
  RAISERROR(
    'Error acquiring transactional lock for %s', 16, 1, @AppLockName);
  ROLLBACK;
  RETURN;
END
```

If the lock is successfully granted, the code will keep going; otherwise, it will roll back and the caller will receive an error so that it knows it did not acquire the requested lock. Once inside the scope of the transactional lock, it's finally time to start thinking about the Service Broker queues. The next thing the stored procedure does is get the target conversation handle, if one exists. If so, the stored procedure starts a wait on the queue for a message:

```
--Find out whether someone has requested this lock before
SELECT
  @target_handle = TargetDialogHandle
FROM AppLocks
WHERE AppLockName = @AppLockName;

--If we're here, we have the transactional lock
IF @target_handle IS NOT NULL
BEGIN
  --Find out whether the timeout has already expired...
  SET @LockTimeout = @LockTimeout - DATEDIFF(ms, @startWait, GETDATE());

  IF @LockTimeout > 0
  BEGIN
    --Wait for the OK message
    DECLARE @message_type nvarchar(255);

    --Wait for a grant message
    WAITFOR
    (
      RECEIVE
        @message_type = message_type_name
      FROM AppLock_Queue
      WHERE conversation_handle = @target_handle
    ), TIMEOUT @LockTimeout;
```

One thing to make note of in this section of the code is that the input lock timeout is decremented by the length of time the stored procedure has already been waiting, based on the **@startWait** variable. It's possible that a caller could specify, say, a 2500ms wait time, and wait 2000ms for the transactional lock. At that point, the caller should only be made to wait up to 500ms for the message to come in on the queue. Therefore, the reduced timeout is used as the **RECEIVE** timeout on the **WAITFOR** command.

The procedure next checks the received message type. If it is an **AppLockGrant** message, all is good—the lock has been successfully acquired. The timeout conversation is started, and the lock token is set. If an unexpected message type is received, an exception is thrown and the transaction is rolled back:

```
IF @message_type = 'AppLockGrant'
BEGIN
  BEGIN DIALOG CONVERSATION @AppLockKey
  FROM SERVICE AppLockTimeout_Service
  TO SERVICE 'AppLockTimeout_Service'
  WITH
    LIFETIME = @LOCK_TIMEOUT_LIFETIME,
    ENCRYPTION = OFF;

  UPDATE AppLocks
  SET
    AppLockKey = @AppLockKey,
    LastGrantedDate = GETDATE()
```

```
        WHERE
            AppLockName = @AppLockName;
    END

    ELSE IF @message_type IS NOT NULL
    BEGIN
        RAISERROR('Unexpected message type: %s', 16, 1, @message_type);
        ROLLBACK;
    END

  END
END
```

The next section of code deals with the branch that occurs if the target handle acquired before entering the **IF** block was **NULL**, meaning that no one has ever requested a lock on this resource before. The first thing this branch does is begin a dialog on the **AppLock_Service** service. Since the target conversation handle is required for others to wait on the resource, and since the target handle is not generated until a message is sent, the first thing that must be done is to send a message on the dialog. Once the message has been sent, the target handle is picked up from the **sys.conversation_endpoints** catalog view, and the sent message is picked up so that no other callers can receive it:

```
ELSE
BEGIN
  --No one has requested this lock before
  BEGIN DIALOG @init_handle
  FROM SERVICE AppLock_Service
  TO SERVICE 'AppLock_Service'
  ON CONTRACT AppLockContract
  WITH ENCRYPTION = OFF;

  --Send a throwaway message to start the dialog on both ends
  SEND ON CONVERSATION @init_handle
  MESSAGE TYPE AppLockGrant;

  --Get the remote handle
  SELECT
    @target_handle = ce2.conversation_handle
  FROM sys.conversation_endpoints ce1
  JOIN sys.conversation_endpoints ce2 ON
    ce1.conversation_id = ce2.conversation_id
  WHERE
    ce1.conversation_handle = @init_handle
    AND ce2.is_initiator = 0;

  --Receive the throwaway message
  RECEIVE
    @target_handle = conversation_handle
  FROM AppLock_Queue
  WHERE conversation_handle = @target_handle;
```

After starting the lock grant dialog and initializing the target conversation handle, the timeout/token dialog can finally be started and the lock inserted into the **AppLocks** table. Once that's taken care of, the stored procedure checks to find out whether the **@AppLockKey** variable was populated. If it was, the transaction is committed. Otherwise, a timeout is assumed to have occurred, and all work is rolled back.

```
BEGIN DIALOG CONVERSATION @AppLockKey
FROM SERVICE AppLockTimeout_Service
TO SERVICE 'AppLockTimeout_Service'
WITH
  LIFETIME = @LOCK_TIMEOUT_LIFETIME,
  ENCRYPTION = OFF;

INSERT INTO AppLocks
(
  AppLockName,
  AppLockKey,
  InitiatorDialogHandle,
  TargetDialogHandle
)
VALUES
(
  @AppLockName,
  @AppLockKey,
  @init_handle,
  @target_handle
);
END

IF @AppLockKey IS NOT NULL
  COMMIT;
ELSE
BEGIN
  RAISERROR(
    'Timed out waiting for lock on resource: %s', 16, 1, @AppLockName);
  ROLLBACK;
END
END;
GO
```

The bulk of the work required to set up these locks is done in the **GetAppLock** stored procedure. Luckily, the accompanying **ReleaseAppLock** procedure is much simpler:

```
CREATE PROC ReleaseAppLock
  @AppLockKey uniqueidentifier
AS
BEGIN
  SET NOCOUNT ON;
  SET XACT_ABORT ON;

  BEGIN TRAN;
```

```
    DECLARE @dialog_handle uniqueidentifier;

    UPDATE AppLocks
    SET
      AppLockKey = NULL,
      @dialog_handle = InitiatorDialogHandle
    WHERE
      AppLockKey = @AppLockKey;

    IF @@ROWCOUNT = 0
    BEGIN
      RAISERROR('AppLockKey not found', 16, 1);
      ROLLBACK;
    END

    END CONVERSATION @AppLockKey;

    --Allow another caller to acquire the lock
    SEND ON CONVERSATION @dialog_handle
    MESSAGE TYPE AppLockGrant;

    COMMIT;
END;
GO
```

The caller sends the acquired lock's token to this procedure, which first tries to nullify its value in the **AppLocks** table. If the token is not found, an error is raised and the transaction rolled back. Otherwise, the conversation associated with the token is ended. Finally—and most importantly—an **AppLockGrant** message is sent on the grant conversation associated with the lock. This message will be picked up by any other process waiting for the lock, thereby granting it.

One final stored procedure is required to support this infrastructure: an activation stored procedure that is used in case of dialog lifetime expirations on the **AppLockTimeout_Queue** queue. The following T-SQL creates the procedure and enables activation on the queue:

```
CREATE PROC AppLockTimeout_Activation
AS
BEGIN
  SET NOCOUNT ON;
  SET XACT_ABORT ON;

  DECLARE @dialog_handle uniqueidentifier;

  WHILE 1=1
  BEGIN
    SET @dialog_handle = NULL;

    BEGIN TRAN;

    WAITFOR
    (
      RECEIVE @dialog_handle = conversation_handle
```

```
      FROM AppLockTimeout_Queue
    ), TIMEOUT 10000;

    IF @dialog_handle IS NOT NULL
    BEGIN
      EXEC ReleaseAppLock @AppLockKey = @dialog_handle;
    END

    COMMIT;
  END
END;
GO

ALTER QUEUE AppLockTimeout_Queue
WITH ACTIVATION
(
  STATUS = ON,
  PROCEDURE_NAME = AppLockTimeout_Activation,
  MAX_QUEUE_READERS = 1,
  EXECUTE AS OWNER
);
GO
```

This procedure waits, on each iteration of its loop, up to 10 seconds for a message to appear on the queue. Since no messages are expected other than timeout notifications, any message received is assumed to be one, and spawns a call to the **ReleaseAppLock** stored procedure. If no message is received within 10 seconds, the activation procedure exits.

Once this system is in place, application locks can be requested using the **GetAppLock** stored procedure, as in the following example:

```
DECLARE @AppLockKey uniqueidentifier
EXEC GetAppLock
    @AppLockName = 'customers',
    @LockTimeout = 2000,
    @AppLockKey = @AppLockKey OUTPUT;
GO
```

In this example, the stored procedure will wait up to 2 seconds for the resource to become available before returning an error. Just as with other pessimistic schemes, it's important for the application to keep the returned key in order to release the lock later, using the **ReleaseAppLock** stored procedure.

Note that ongoing maintenance of this approach to locks is somewhat different from the method described for row-based pessimistic locks. After a lock has been requested once, its row in the **AppLocks** table as well as its associated grant dialog will not expire. I designed the system this way in order to minimize setup and break down a large number of dialogs in a system using and reusing a lot of locks, but it is possible that due to this architecture, the number of dialogs could get quite large over time. If this should become an issue, use the **LastGrantedDate** column to find locks that have not been recently requested, and call **END CONVERSATION** for both the initiator and target handles.

Hoping for the Best: Optimistic Concurrency

Compared with the complexity and overhead of pessimistic concurrency solutions, optimistic schemes feel like a wonderful alternative. Indeed, even the word *optimistic* evokes a much nicer feeling, and the name is quite appropriate to the methodology. Optimistic schemes use no read-time or edit-time locks, instead only checking for conflicts just before the data is actually written to the table. This means none of the administrative overhead of worrying about orphans and other issues that can occur with pessimistic locks, but it also means that the system may not be as appropriate to many business situations.

Consider the life insurance firm described in the section "Preparing for the Worst: Pessimistic Concurrency." For that firm, an optimistic scheme would mean many hours of lost time and money—not a good idea. However, suppose that the firm had a new project: this time, instead of updating many years' worth of lengthy personal information forms, the firm merely wants some address change cards input into the system. Just like with the personal information forms, these cards have not been well managed by the employees of the insurance firm, and there is some duplication. Luckily, however, the cards were filed using a much newer system, and the repetition of data is not nearly as serious as it was for the personal information forms.

In this scenario, the management overhead associated with a pessimistic scheme is probably not warranted. The chance for collision is much lower than in the personal information form scenario, and should an operator's input happen to collide with another's, it will only cost a few minutes' worth of lost work, instead of potentially hours.

The basic setup for optimistic concurrency requires a column that is updated whenever a row gets updated. This column is used as a version marker and retrieved along with the rest of the data by clients. At update time, the retrieved value is sent back along with updates, and its value is checked to ensure that it did not change between the time the data was read and the time of the update.

There are a few different choices for implementing this column, but to begin with I'll discuss a popular option: SQL Server's **rowversion** type. The **rowversion** type is an 8-byte binary string that is automatically updated by SQL Server every time a row is updated in the table. For example, consider the following table:

```
CREATE TABLE CustomerNames
(
  CustomerId int NOT NULL PRIMARY KEY,
  CustomerName varchar(50) NOT NULL,
  Version rowversion NOT NULL
);
GO
```

The following T-SQL inserts two rows and then retrieves all rows from the table:

```
INSERT INTO CustomerNames
(
  CustomerId,
  CustomerName
)
VALUES
  (123, 'Mickey Mouse'),
  (456, 'Minnie Mouse');
GO
```

```
SELECT *
FROM CustomerNames;
GO
```

The output of this query is as follows:

CustomerId	CustomerName	Version
123	Mickey Mouse	0x00000000000007E3
456	Minnie Mouse	0x00000000000007E4

Updating either row automatically updates the **rowversion** column. The following T-SQL updates one of the rows and then retrieves all of the rows in the table:

```
UPDATE CustomerNames
SET CustomerName = 'Pluto'
WHERE CustomerId = 456;
GO

SELECT *
FROM CustomerNames;
GO
```

The output of this query reveals the values in the table to be now as follows:

CustomerId	CustomerName	Version
123	Mickey Mouse	0x00000000000007E3
456	Pluto	0x00000000000007E5

It's important to note that any committed update operation on the table will cause the **Version** column to get updated—even if you update a column with the same value. Do not assume that the version is tracking changes to the data; instead, it's tracking actions on the row.

Using a column such as this to support an optimistic scheme is quite straightforward. An effective first pass involves pulling back the **Version** column along with the rest of the data in the row when reading, and checking it at write time:

```
DECLARE
  @CustomerIdToUpdate int = 456,
  @Version rowversion;

SET @Version =
(SELECT Version
FROM CustomerNames
WHERE CustomerId = @CustomerIdToUpdate);
```

```
UPDATE CustomerNames
SET CustomerName = 'Pluto'
WHERE
  CustomerId = @CustomerIdToUpdate
  AND Version = @Version;
IF @@ROWCOUNT = 0
RAISERROR('Version conflict encountered', 16, 1);
```

This is a simple method of handling optimistic concurrency, but it has a couple of problems. First of all, every update routine in the system must be made to comply with the requirements of checking the version. As with the pessimistic schemes described in the previous section, even one buggy module will cause the entire system to break down—not a good thing. Secondly, this setup does not leave you with many options when it comes to providing a nice user experience. Getting a conflict error without any means of fixing it is not especially fun—when possible, I prefer to send back enough data so that users can perform a merge if they feel like it (and only if the application provides that capability, of course).

The solution to both of these problems starts with a change to the version column's data type. Since columns that use the **rowversion** type are not updateable by anything except SQL Server, it makes the system difficult to control. Therefore, my first suggestion is to switch to either **uniqueidentifier** or **datetime**. Following is an updated version of **CustomerNames**, which uses a **uniqueidentifier** column:

```
-- Recreate the CustomerNames table
CREATE TABLE CustomerNames
(
  CustomerId int NOT NULL PRIMARY KEY,
  CustomerName varchar(50) NOT NULL,
  Version uniqueidentifier NOT NULL
    DEFAULT (NEWID())
);
GO


-- Populate the new table
INSERT INTO CustomerNames
(
  CustomerId,
  CustomerName
)
VALUES
  (123, 'Mickey Mouse'),
  (456, 'Minnie Mouse');
GO
```

To solve the potential problem of routines not following the rules, a trigger can be used to enforce the optimistic scheme. This is done by requiring that any updates to the table include an update to the **Version** column, which is enforced by checking the **UPDATE** function in the trigger. The column should be set to the value of whatever version was returned when the data was read. This way, the trigger can check the value present in the **inserted** table against the value in the **deleted** table for each row updated. If the two don't match, there is a version conflict. Finally, the trigger can set a new version value for the updated rows, thereby marking them as changed for anyone who has read the data. Following is the definition for the trigger:

```
CREATE TRIGGER tg_UpdateCustomerNames
ON CustomerNames
FOR UPDATE AS
BEGIN
  SET NOCOUNT ON;

  IF NOT UPDATE(Version)
  BEGIN
    RAISERROR('Updating the Version column is required', 16, 1);
    ROLLBACK;
  END

  IF EXISTS
  (
    SELECT *
    FROM inserted i
    JOIN deleted d ON i.CustomerId = d.CustomerId
    WHERE i.Version <> d.Version
  )
  BEGIN
    RAISERROR('Version conflict encountered', 16, 1);
    ROLLBACK;
  END

  ELSE
    --Set new versions for the updated rows
    UPDATE CustomerNames
    SET Version = NEWID()
    WHERE
      CustomerId IN
      (
        SELECT CustomerId
        FROM inserted
      );
END;
GO
```

This trigger solves the problem of version control in an optimistic model, but it takes quite a blunt approach—simply raising an error and rolling back the transaction if a version conflict is encountered. Perhaps it would be better to extend this trigger to help provide users with more options when they get a conflict. This is one place I find SQL Server's XML capabilities to be useful. To create an output document similar to an ADO.NET XML DiffGram, modify the **IF** block of the trigger as highlighted in the following code listing:

```
ALTER TRIGGER tg_UpdateCustomerNames
ON CustomerNames
FOR UPDATE AS
BEGIN
  SET NOCOUNT ON;
```

```
IF NOT UPDATE(Version)
BEGIN
  RAISERROR('Updating the Version column is required', 16, 1);
  ROLLBACK;
END
IF EXISTS
(
  SELECT *
  FROM inserted i
  JOIN deleted d ON i.CustomerId = d.CustomerId
  WHERE i.Version <> d.Version
)
BEGIN
  SELECT
  (
    SELECT
      ROW_NUMBER() OVER (ORDER BY CustomerId) AS [@row_number],
      *
    FROM inserted
    FOR XML PATH('customer_name'), TYPE
  ) new_values,
  (
    SELECT
    ROW_NUMBER() OVER (ORDER BY CustomerId) AS [@row_number],
    *
    FROM deleted
    FOR XML PATH('customer_name'), TYPE
  ) old_values
  FOR XML PATH('customer_name_rows');
END

ELSE
  --Set new versions for the updated rows
  UPDATE CustomerNames
  SET Version = NEWID()
  WHERE
    CustomerId IN
    (
      SELECT CustomerId
      FROM inserted
    );
END;
GO
```

After making this modification, let's try updating the table with an invalid version value, as shown in the following T-SQL:

```
DECLARE
  @CustomerId int = 123,
  @Version uniqueidentifier;
```

```sql
-- Retrieve the current version value
SELECT @Version = Version
FROM CustomerNames
WHERE CustomerId = @CustomerId

-- Do something with the retrieved data here

-- Meanwhile, something else updates the version number
UPDATE CustomerNames
SET CustomerName = 'Popeye',
Version = @Version
WHERE CustomerId = @CustomerId;


-- Now try to write the changes back to the table
UPDATE CustomerNames
SET CustomerName = 'Top Cat',
Version = @Version
WHERE CustomerId = @CustomerId;
GO
```

Executing this code will produce output similar to that shown here:

```xml
<customer_name_rows>

  <new_values>

    <customer_name  row_number="1">

      <CustomerId>123</CustomerId>

      <CustomerName>Top Cat</CustomerName>

      <Version>10E83AAD-B966-4250-A66D-FE0085706F9E</Version>

    </customer_name>

  </new_values>

  <old_values>

    <customer_name row_number="1">

      <CustomerId>123</CustomerId>

      <CustomerName>Popeye</CustomerName>

      <Version>DDEDE0D4-44FE-42EA-B605-7431098D8A24</Version>

    </customer_name>

  </old_values>

</customer_name_rows>
```

Although this doesn't exactly write the merge routine for you, I find that the XML format is very easy to work with when it comes to doing these kinds of operations.

Since the document contains the newer version value that caused the conflict, you can let the end user perform a merge or choose to override the other user's change without having to go back to the database to get the new rows a second time.

A Note on Triggers and Performance

Throughout the previous two sections, update triggers were employed as a mechanism by which to control workflows around locking. Triggers are a great tool because the caller has no control over them—they will fire on any update to the table, regardless of whether it was made in a stored procedure or an ad hoc batch, and regardless of whether the caller has bothered to follow the locking rules. Unfortunately, triggers also cause problems: most notably, they can have an acute effect on performance.

The major performance problems caused by triggers generally result from lengthened transactions and the resultant blocking that can occur when low-granularity locks are held for a long period. In the case of these triggers, that's not much of an issue since they use the same rows that were already locked anyway by the updates themselves. However, these triggers will slow down updates a bit. In SQL Server 2008, the inserted and deleted tables are actually hidden temporary tables; the population of these tables does not come for free—the data must be transferred into `TempDB`. In addition, each of these triggers incurs additional index operations against the base table that are not necessary for a simple update.

In my testing, I've found that these triggers slow down updates by a factor of 2. However, that's generally the difference between a few milliseconds and a few more milliseconds—certainly not a big deal, especially given the value that they bring to the application. It's worth testing to make sure that these triggers don't cause severe performance issues for your application, but at the same time remember that nothing is free—and if it's a question of data integrity vs. performance, I personally would always choose the former.

Embracing Conflict: Multivalue Concurrency Control

While optimistic and pessimistic concurrency are focused on enabling long-running business processes to work together without mangling data that happens to be getting modified concurrently, MVCC is based around the idea that performance is king.

MVCC is not concerned with making sure you can't overwrite someone else's data, because in an MVCC scheme there is no overwriting of data—period. Instead of updating existing rows, every change is done as an insert. This means that there's no reason to check for data collisions; no data can get lost if nothing is being updated. In an MVCC system, new rows are marked with a version number—generally a date/time column or ascending key—so that newer versions can be readily identified and queried by users.

Generally speaking, to benefit from MVCC, the cost of blocking for a given set of transactions must outweigh all other resource costs, particularly with regard to disk I/O. Since new versions of rows will be inserted as entirely new rows, the potential for massive amounts of disk utilization is quite huge. However, due to the fact that no updates are taking place, blocking becomes almost nonexistent.

Illustrating the performance gains possible from an insert-only architecture is fairly simple using a load tool. To begin with, create a table and populate it with some sample data, as shown in the following T-SQL:

```
CREATE TABLE Test_Updates
(
  PK_Col int NOT NULL PRIMARY KEY,
  Other_Col varchar(100) NOT NULL
);
GO

INSERT INTO Test_Updates (
  PK_Col,
  Other_Col)
SELECT DISTINCT
  Number,
  'Original Value'
FROM master..spt_values
WHERE number BETWEEN 1 AND 10;
```

Next, enter the following code into a new query window:

```
-- Choose an abitrary row to update
DECLARE @PK_Col int = CEILING(RAND() * 10)

BEGIN TRAN;

-- Update the table
UPDATE Test_Updates
SET Other_Col = 'new value set at ' + CAST(SYSDATETIME() AS varchar(32))
WHERE PK_Col = @PK_Col;

-- Add a delay
WAITFOR DELAY '00:00:00.25';

COMMIT;
```

This code simulates an **UPDATE** followed by a quarter of a second of other actions taking place in the same transaction. It doesn't matter what the other actions are; the important thing is that this is a somewhat long-running transaction, and that the **UPDATE** will hold its locks for the duration of the transaction, which is necessary in order to guarantee consistency of the updated data.

To simulate a concurrent environment, we will execute the preceding query simultaneously across several parallel threads. To do this, we'll use the ostress tool, which is available as part of the Microsoft Replay Markup Language (RML) utilities for SQL Server, downloadable from **http://support.microsoft.com/default.aspx/kb/944837**. Before using the ostress tool, save the preceding query to a new file—I'll assume that you'll save it as **c:\update_test.sql**. To test the performance of this query in a concurrent environment, open up the RML command prompt and enter the following:

```
ostress.exe -Slocalhost -dtempDB -i"c:\update_test.sql" -n25 -100 -q
```

This will execute the contents of the **update_test.sql** file across 25 threads, each running the query 100 times. If necessary, you should change the ostress parameters supplied as follows:

- **-S**: Server name

- **-d**: Database name against which to execute the query

- **-U**: Login ID (only required if not using Windows Authentication)

- **-P**: password (only required if not using Windows Authentication)

After execution, the ostress tool reports the elapsed time on my system as 00:01:42.514. To compare this performance with the relative performance of inserts in a highly concurrent scenario, create a similar table to **Test_Updates**, this time designed to hold—and version—inserted rows:

```
CREATE TABLE Test_Inserts
(
  PK_Col int NOT NULL,
  Other_Col varchar(100) NOT NULL,
  Version int IDENTITY(1,1) NOT NULL,
  PRIMARY KEY (PK_Col, Version)
);
GO
```

Edit the previous query so that, rather than updating records, it inserts records into the new table as follows:

```
DECLARE @PK_Col int = CEILING(RAND() * 10);

BEGIN TRAN;

-- Insert the values into a new table
INSERT INTO Test_Inserts (
  PK_Col,
  Other_Col
)
SELECT
  @PK_Col,
  'new value set at ' + CAST(SYSDATETIME() AS varchar(32));

-- Add a delay
WAITFOR DELAY '00:00:00.25';

COMMIT;
```

Save this query as **insert_test.sql** and execute it using the same ostress settings as before. The elapsed time of this test when run on my laptop is 00:00:29.184—less than a third of the time taken for the equivalent update test.

The results are fairly clear: when simulating a massive blocking scenario, inserts are the clear winner over updates, thanks to the fact that processes do not block each other trying to write the same rows. Admittedly, this example is contrived, but it should serve to illustrate the purported benefit of MVCC as a concurrency technique.

Of course, there is a bit more to MVCC than the idea of using inserts instead of updates. You still need to be able to retrieve a consistent view of the data. A query such as the following can be used to get the latest version of every row in the **Test_Inserts** table:

```
SELECT
  ti.PK_Col,
  ti.Other_Col,
  ti.Version
FROM Test_Inserts ti
WHERE
  Version =
  (
    SELECT MAX(ti1.Version)
    FROM Test_Inserts ti1
    WHERE
      ti1.PK_Col = ti.PK_Col
);
```

I will not cover MVCC queries extensively in this section—instead, I will refer you to Chapter 11, which covers temporal data. The bitemporal techniques discussed in that chapter share many similarities with MVCC, but with a greater overall value proposition thanks to the fact that they take advantage of time as well as versioning, allowing you to pull back consistent views of the data based on time rather than just version.

As you might guess, MVCC, while an interesting concept, cannot be applied as described here to many real-world applications. Merging the MVCC concept with bitemporal data models can help make this a much more interesting technique for highly concurrent applications in which versioning of data collisions makes sense.

Sharing Resources Between Concurrent Users

So far in this chapter, we've looked at the business rules for protecting the integrity of data—preventing overwrites and minimizing occurrences of blocking—and a brief consideration of performance implications of different concurrent models. However, I have yet to address the important issue of how to balance competing demand for limited resources in a concurrent environment.

By default, when multiple requests are made to a SQL Server instance, the database engine shares resources between all concurrent users equally. As a result, every request will face more contention for CPU, memory, and I/O resources, leading to longer average query times and greater risk of blocking scenarios occurring. In practice, however, it is rare for all queries to be of equal importance. Some requests may be classified as high-priority based on the urgency with which the data is needed, or on the seniority of the user asking for that data. Maintenance tasks, in contrast, should sometimes run only in the background, when there is idle resource to fulfill them. By using **Resource Governor**, a new feature introduced in the Developer and Enterprise editions of SQL Server 2008, it is possible to classify and prioritize incoming connections into categories to determine how resources are allocated between them.

I don't intend to cover every aspect of Resource Governor in these pages: for readers not familiar with the topic, I recommend reading the introduction to Resource Governor on Books Online, at **http://msdn.microsoft.com/en-us/library/bb895232.aspx**. In this section, I'll concentrate only on demonstrating some of the ways in which Resource Governor can be applied to benefit performance in high-concurrency environments.

Before continuing, create a new database and add two new users to that database that will be used in the upcoming examples:

```
-- Create and switch to a new database
CREATE DATABASE ResourceGovernor;
GO
USE ResourceGovernor;
GO

-- Create two users and a DB login based on each
CREATE LOGIN UserA
WITH
  PASSWORD = 'password',
  CHECK_POLICY = OFF;
CREATE USER UserA FROM LOGIN UserA;
GO

CREATE LOGIN UserB WITH
  PASSWORD='password',
  CHECK_POLICY = OFF;
CREATE USER UserB FROM LOGIN UserB;
GO

-- For simplicity, make both users db_owners
EXEC sp_addrolemember 'db_owner', 'UserA';
EXEC sp_addrolemember 'db_owner', 'UserB';
GO
```

To keep the example simple, requests from each of these database users will be mapped to their own workload group, which in turn has its own dedicated resource pool, as follows:

```
USE master;
GO

ALTER RESOURCE GOVERNOR RECONFIGURE;
GO

-- Create two resource pools with default settings
CREATE RESOURCE POOL PoolA;
CREATE RESOURCE POOL PoolB;
GO

-- Create two workload groups
CREATE WORKLOAD GROUP GroupA USING PoolA;
CREATE WORKLOAD GROUP GroupB USING PoolB;
GO
```

Next, we must create the classifier function that will be used to assign the workload group into which incoming requests are placed. For this example, we will classify all requests from **UserA** into the **GroupA** workload group, and all requests from **UserB** into the **GroupB** workload group, as follows:

```
CREATE FUNCTION dbo.RGClassifier()
RETURNS sysname WITH SCHEMABINDING
AS
BEGIN
  DECLARE @grp_name AS sysname = N'default';
  DECLARE @login_name AS sysname = SUSER_NAME();

  IF @login_name = N'UserA'
    SET @grp_name = N'GroupA';
  ELSE IF @login_name = N'UserB'
    SET @grp_name = N'GroupB';
  RETURN @grp_name;
END;
GO
```

For the purposes of this demonstration, I've simply classified each incoming connection request based on the login name of the user making the request. All requests from **UserA** are classified into the **GroupA** workgroup, and all requests from **UserB** will be classified into the **GroupB** workgroup. All other requests will use the default group.

You can also make classification decisions based on other factors, including the name of the host or application supplied in the connection string (retrieved using **HOST_NAME()** and **APP_NAME()**, respectively), and whether the user is a member of a particular role or group.

It is important to note that once Resource Governor is activated, the classifier function will be run to classify *every* incoming connection to the server, and govern the resources available for that session. It is therefore crucially important to make sure that this function is thoroughly tested and optimized or else you risk potentially crippling your system.

■ **Tip** All queries issued via a dedicated administrator connection (DAC) are run using the internal workload group and resource pool, and are not subject to classification. You may find that you need to connect to SQL Server 2008 via DAC in order to investigate and repair issues if a classifier function goes awry.

Finally, Resource Governor will be bound to the classifier function and activated as follows:

```
ALTER RESOURCE GOVERNOR
  WITH ( CLASSIFIER_FUNCTION = dbo.RGClassifier );
GO

ALTER RESOURCE GOVERNOR RECONFIGURE;
GO
```

Now that we have set up the basic resource governor infrastructure, we need some way of monitoring the effects on performance in high-concurrency environments. To do so, open up the system performance monitor console (**perfmon.exe**). Right-click the performance graph and select the Add Counters menu option. Scroll down the list of available counters, and, when you get to the SQL

Server:Workload Group Stats heading, click to add the CPU Usage % measure for both GroupA and GroupB. These steps are illustrated in Figure 9-1.

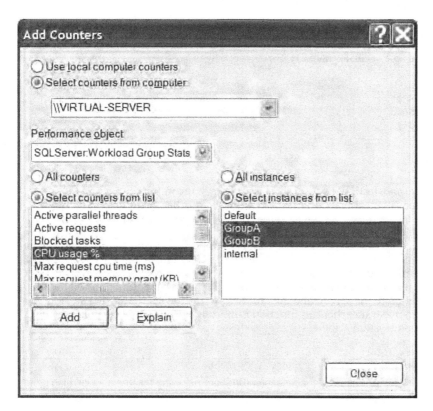

Figure 9-1. Adding performance counters for GroupA and GroupB CPU usage percentage

Controlling Resource Allocation

One of the most fundamental uses of Resource Governor is to set explicit minimum and maximum levels for CPU and server memory allocated to different resource pools. To demonstrate the effect of applying these limits, we first need to place some load on the server. Open the RML command prompt and use the ostress tool to set up a query issued by UserA, as follows:

```
ostress -U"UserA" -P"password" -Q"WHILE(1=1) SELECT REPLICATE('a',4000);" -n5 -q
```

Next, open a second RML command prompt and enter the following request issued by UserB:

```
ostress -U"UserB" -P"password" -Q"WHILE(1=1) SELECT REPLICATE('b',4000);" -n5 -q
-o"C:\UserB"
```

Each of these queries will issue a recurring, relatively CPU-intensive query that will repeat indefinitely across five separate threads. We can confirm that the classifier function is working correctly by checking the **sys.dm_resource_governor_workload_groups** DMV, as shown in the following code listing:

```
SELECT
  name,
  total_request_count
FROM
  sys.dm_resource_governor_workload_groups
WHERE
  name IN ('GroupA', 'GroupB');
```

The results show that there are five requests running under each workload group. Now check on the performance monitor graph. On my system, this appears as shown in Figure 9-2.

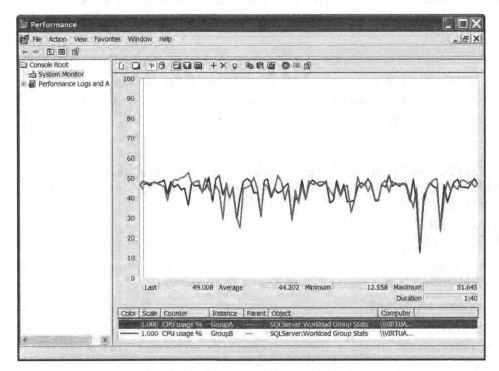

Figure 9-2. Balanced performance of two default workload groups

Perhaps unsurprisingly, as we have left all resource governor settings at their default values, the graph shows an approximately equal split of CPU usage percentage between the two workloads. So now let's try to change things around a bit. Firstly, we'll try to limit the CPU resources given to both resource pools:

```
ALTER RESOURCE POOL PoolA
WITH ( MAX_CPU_PERCENT = 10 );
```

```
ALTER RESOURCE POOL PoolB
WITH ( MAX_CPU_PERCENT = 10 );

ALTER RESOURCE GOVERNOR RECONFIGURE;
GO
```

Executing this code, you might be surprised to find, makes no difference to the graph. So how come the Resource Governor is seemingly ignoring our specified MAX_CPU_PERCENT and has failed to limit both resource pools to 10 percent of CPU? This illustrates an important point concerning the way in which resources are allocated by the Resource Governor—rather than prescribing a hard limit on CPU usage, the MAX_CPU_PERCENT value is used to balance competing requests *when there is contention for resources*. In this case, since the combined stated MAX_CPU_PERCENT of all resource pools is less than 100 percent, there is no contention. The SQL Server OS will always attempt to maximize CPU resource usage, so if there is spare CPU available, it will be assigned between the available pools. The MAX_CPU_PERCENT of a resource pool is only enforced in situations where exceeding that limit would prevent another resource pool from being granted its requested maximum CPU settings.

■ **Note** When testing applications that execute using resource pools limited to a MAX_CPU_PERCENT, it is important to remember that that limit will only be enforced if there is contention for that CPU resource from other resource pools. You should therefore always test in environments with competing concurrent processes.

With this in mind, let's now try another example. For this example, we'll ensure that the total MAX_CPU_PERCENT of the two resource pools adds up to 100 percent so that neither will be allowed to exceed that limit (lest the other would be denied CPU resources):

```
ALTER RESOURCE POOL PoolA
WITH ( MAX_CPU_PERCENT = 90 );

ALTER RESOURCE POOL PoolB
WITH ( MAX_CPU_PERCENT = 10 );

ALTER RESOURCE GOVERNOR RECONFIGURE;
GO
```

Following the rules explained previously, you would perhaps now expect the CPU usage between PoolA and PoolB to be split in the ratio 90:10, and depending on your system, this might be the outcome that you now observe on the performance monitor graph. However, the graph on my system *still* shows little discernible difference between the two workload groups, as shown in Figure 9-3.

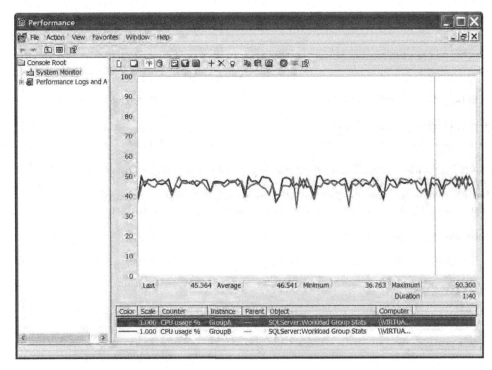

Figure 9-3. CPU usage percentage

The explanation of the behavior shown in Figure 9-3 is that the **MAX_CPU_PERCENT** limit (and other resource pool options) used by the Resource Governor are specified at a *per scheduler* level. In other words, the **MAX_CPU_PERCENT** setting is used to allocate the amount of CPU resource granted to a resource pool, as a percent of the CPU on which the process is running. I'm running these tests on a multiprocessor computer, which means that the queries under each workload group are split across separate CPUs. I can confirm this by executing the following:

```
SELECT
  rgwg.name AS group_name,
  est.text AS SQL,
  ot.scheduler_id,
  cpu_id,
  er.status
FROM
  sys.dm_exec_requests er
  JOIN sys.dm_os_tasks ot on er.task_address = ot.task_address
  JOIN sys.dm_resource_governor_workload_groups rgwg
      ON er.group_id = rgwg.group_id
  JOIN sys.dm_os_schedulers os ON ot.scheduler_id = os.scheduler_id
  CROSS APPLY sys.dm_exec_sql_text(er.sql_handle) est
WHERE
  rgwg.name IN ('GroupA', 'GroupB');
```

The results indicate that the two queries are being executed under different schedulers executing on different CPUs:

group_name	SQL	scheduler_id	cpu_id	status
GroupA	WHILE(1=1) SELECT REPLICATE('a'...	0	0	running
GroupB	WHILE(1=1) SELECT REPLICATE('b'...	1	1	runnable

Since each query is executing against a separate scheduler, once again there is no contention for CPU resource, and so the **MAX_CPU_PERCENT** limit is not enforced.

In order to be able to demonstrate the effects of the Resource Governor more clearly, it is necessary to constrain the execution of SQL Server threads to a single CPU by setting the affinity mask as follows:

```
sp_configure 'show advanced options', 1;
RECONFIGURE;
GO

sp_configure 'affinity mask', 1;
RECONFIGURE;
GO
```

■ **Caution** Calling sp_configure 'affinity mask' with the bitmask value 1 will assign all SQL Server threads to Processor 0, irrespective of how many CPU cores are present on the system. You should exercise extreme caution when setting this option, even in testing environments.

The results of changing the CPU affinity mask on my system are shown in Figure 9-4.

Finally, it appears that we are close to the result we were expecting, but rather than seeing the split between the resource pools as 90:10, it appears to be 45:5—this is the correct ratio between the pools, but what has happened to the other 50 percent of resource?

The reason for this is that the "CPU usage %" performance counter is normalized based on the number of CPUs on the server. In this case, I am running the tests on a dual-processor machine, but I've just set the SQL Server affinity mask to only allow SQL Server processor threads on one processor. As a result, all measurements for CPU usage percentage are half their expected value, with a maximum CPU usage figure of 50 percent.

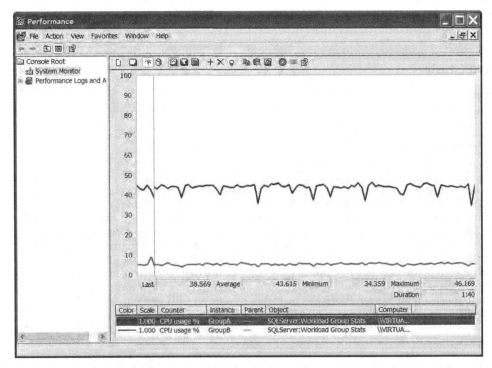

Figure 9-4. CPU usage between resource pools after setting CPU affinity to a single processor

Calculating Effective and Shared Maximum Resource Allocation

In a highly concurrent environment, it is rare for every request to be treated equally. In many cases, it is a business requirement to ensure that certain defined groups of users or specific sets of queries receive preferential treatment to guarantee fast response times. Special treatment may be required for queries from high-priority users or queries that must be completed within a certain timeframe in order to ensure that customer service level agreements are met.

So far, I have demonstrated how the Resource Governor can be used to limit the maximum server resource usage in certain scenarios, but a more practical situation involves guaranteeing the *minimum* resource available to a query. By setting appropriate limits on the MAX_CPU_USAGE and MIN_CPU_USAGE of different resource pools (and the corresponding MIN_MEMORY_PERCENT and MAX_MEMORY_PERCENT), it is easy to classify preferential requests to a dedicated resource pool that receives a guaranteed minimum share of the server CPU and memory resource while capping the resource given to other pools.

To understand the interplay between settings of different pools, suppose that we want PoolA to be our preferential pool and PoolB to be our normal pool. To achieve this, we will state that PoolA should have a minimum CPU resource of 30 percent and a maximum of 90 percent. We will state a minimum of 0 percent CPU for PoolB, and a maximum CPU limit of 50 percent. These changes can be made using the following T-SQL:

```
ALTER RESOURCE POOL PoolA
WITH (
```

```
  MIN_CPU_PERCENT = 30,
  MAX_CPU_PERCENT = 90
);

ALTER RESOURCE POOL PoolB
WITH (
  MIN_CPU_PERCENT = 0,
  MAX_CPU_PERCENT = 50
);

ALTER RESOURCE GOVERNOR RECONFIGURE;
GO
```

Now, how do these settings affect the way in which resources are allocated between the pools? Remember that the MAX_CPU_PERCENT limit is only enforced when there is contention for resource. PoolA specifies a minimum server CPU usage of 30 percent. However, since PoolB only requests a maximum of 50 percent of CPU, both of these requests can be granted without contention. The **effective maximum** CPU usage of each pool in this case is therefore the same as the requested max: 90 percent for PoolA and 50 percent for PoolB.

For PoolA, 30 percent of the effective maximum CPU comes from dedicated resource, while the remaining 60 percent comes from the shared resource pool, and is therefore dependent on other demands of other requests on the server. PoolB has no stated minimum CPU percent, so all of the effective maximum CPU usage of 50 percent comes from the shared resource pool.

▪ **Note** For more information on effective maximum limits, see the following Books Online page: http://msdn.microsoft.com/en-us/library/bb934084.aspx.

Let's now see what would happen if we were to create a third resource pool, as follows:

```
CREATE RESOURCE POOL PoolC
WITH (
  MIN_CPU_PERCENT = 15,
  MAX_CPU_PERCENT = 100
);
```

The effect of creating this new resource pool is as follows:

- PoolA now has an effective maximum CPU usage of 85 percent. The previous effective maximum of 90 percent must be reduced to ensure that PoolC's MIN_CPU_PERCENT request of 15 percent can be granted. PoolA now receives 55 percent of its maximum effective CPU resource from the shared resource pool.

- PoolB remains unchanged, with an effective maximum of 50 percent of CPU resource, all of which is taken from the shared resource pool.

- **PoolC** has an effective maximum of 70 percent of CPU resource (since **PoolA**'s minimum request of 30 percent must be granted), with 55 percent of this resource coming from the shared resource pool.

Note that in this section I have only demonstrated the allocation of CPU resource using **MIN_CPU_PERCENT** and **MAX_CPU_PERCENT**, but the same resource-balancing rules can be applied to memory resource assigned to resource pools using **MIN_MEMORY_PERCENT** and **MAX_MEMORY_PERCENT**. By setting appropriate limits for each resource pool, it is possible to balance the requirements of different categories of requests when there is competition for limited resources on the server. Always remember that these are not hard limits, but are used to calculate how resources are allocated when there is contention. When there is no contention, a resource pool may consume all of the available resources on the server, even if other resource pools have specified minimum values.

Controlling Concurrent Request Processing

Whereas the previous section discussed changing the amount of resources available to various resource pools used by the Resource Governor, it is also important to consider the configuration of workload groups into which query requests are placed. One option of particular interest in a highly concurrent environment is the **GROUP_MAX_REQUESTS** setting, which limits the number of concurrent requests that will be processed in a given workload group. Once the maximum request limit has been reached, any additional requests for this workload group will be placed into a wait state until capacity becomes available.

Before going any further, cancel any running ostress windows that you might still have running. Then reset the query plan cache, the Resource Governor statistics, and wait statistics held in the DMV tables by issuing the following T-SQL:

```
ALTER RESOURCE GOVERNOR RESET STATISTICS;
DBCC FREEPROCCACHE;
DBCC SQLPERF('sys.dm_os_wait_stats', CLEAR);
GO
```

Now open a new RML command prompt and use the ostress tool to execute a simple query 100 times each across 500 threads, creating a total of 50,000 requests:

```
ostress -U"UserA" -P"password" -Slocalhost -Q"DECLARE @table TABLE (x varchar(4000));
 INSERT INTO @table SELECT REPLICATE('a',4000);" -n500 -r100 -q
```

When ostress is finished, you will see the total elapsed time required to complete all of the queries. On my laptop, the time reported is 00:03:23.255.

Back in SQL Server Management Studio, we can examine the performance of these queries using the following T-SQL:

```
SELECT
  total_request_count AS requests,
  total_queued_request_count AS queued,
  total_lock_wait_count AS locks,
  CAST(total_cpu_usage_ms AS decimal(18,9)) / total_request_count
    AS avg_cpu_time,
  max_request_cpu_time_ms AS max_cpu_time
```

```
FROM
  sys.dm_resource_governor_workload_groups
WHERE
  name = N'GroupA';
```

requests	queued	locks	avg cpu_time	max_cpu_time
50500	0	627216	3.5299801980198019801980198	80

Now let's alter the resource governor settings to limit the maximum allowed number of concurrent requests for this workload group to three. This will create a queue.

```
ALTER WORKLOAD GROUP GroupA
WITH (  GROUP_MAX_REQUESTS = 3  )
USING PoolA;

ALTER RESOURCE GOVERNOR RECONFIGURE
GO
```

Before running the tests again, reset the tables:

```
ALTER RESOURCE GOVERNOR RESET STATISTICS;
DBCC FREEPROCCACHE;
DBCC SQLPERF('sys.dm_os_wait_stats', CLEAR);
GO
```

Then rerun the ostress test exactly as before. This time the final execution time for all the queries on my system is 00:03:03.257. By limiting the maximum number of concurrent requests for the workgroup, the total time taken to process a queue of 50,000 queries in this example has been reduced by approximately 10 percent.

Although at first this result may surprise you, it actually makes perfect sense. To understand what's occurring, rerun the previous query against the **sys.dm_resource_governor_workload_groups** DMV. The results on my system are shown following:

requests	queued	locks	avg cpu_time	max_cpu_time
50500	48372	36727	3.4667128712871287128712871	54

Since we set **GROUP_MAX_REQUESTS** to **3**, requests issued to the **GroupA** workload group are forced to wait as expected, while overall average CPU time required to fulfill each request remains largely similar.

However, when there are fewer concurrent requests, each query experiences substantially fewer waits on resources that are locked by other threads. In this particular example, the benefit of reduced lock waits outweighs the cost of waiting time enforced by Resource Governor throttling. As a result, not only was the overall elapsed time to process a queue of requests reduced, but the consistency between the time taken to fulfill each query was increased (with the maximum CPU time of 54ms when there were only three concurrent requests, compared to 80ms in the previous example).

■ **Tip** If you are interested in finding further statistics about the waits enforced by Resource Governor, try looking for rows in the `sys.dm_os_wait_stats` DMV where `wait_type` is `RESMGR_THROTTLED`.

Summary

Concurrency is a complex topic with many possible solutions. In this chapter, I introduced the various concurrency models that should be considered from a business process and data collision point of view, and explained how they differ from the similarly named concurrency models supported by the SQL Server database engine. Pessimistic concurrency is probably the most commonly used form, but it can be complex to set up and maintain. Optimistic concurrency, while more lightweight, might not be so applicable to many business scenarios, and multivalue concurrency control, while a novel technique, might be difficult to implement in such a way that allowing collisions will help deliver value other than a performance enhancement.

Finally, I covered an overview of how Resource Governor can balance the way in which limited resources are allocated between different competing requests in a concurrent environment. The discussion here only scratched the surface of the potential for this technique, and I recommend that readers interested in the subject dedicate some time to further research this powerful feature.

■ ■ ■

CHAPTER 10

Working with Spatial Data

The addition of spatial capabilities was one of the most exciting new features introduced in SQL Server 2008. Although generally a novel concept for many SQL developers, the principles of working with spatial data have been well established for many years. Dedicated geographic information systems (GISs), such as ARC/INFO from ESRI, have existed since the 1970s. However, until recently, spatial data analysis has been regarded as a distinct, niche subject area, and knowledge and usage of spatial data has remained largely confined within its own realm rather than being integrated with mainstream development.

The truth is that there is hardly any corporate database that does not store spatial information of some sort or other. Customers' addresses, sales regions, the area targeted by a local marketing campaign, or the routes taken by delivery and logistics vehicles all represent spatial data that can be found in many common applications.

In this chapter, I'll first describe some of the fundamental principles involved in working with spatial data, and then discuss some of the important features of the **geometry** and **geography** datatypes, which are the specific datatypes used to represent and perform operations on spatial data in SQL Server. After demonstrating how to use these methods to answer some common spatial questions, I'll then concentrate on the elements that need to be considered to create high-performance spatial applications.

■ **Note** Working with spatial data presents a unique set of challenges, and in many cases requires the adoption of specific techniques and understanding compared to other traditional datatypes. If you're interested in a more thorough introduction to spatial data in SQL Server, I recommend reading *Beginning Spatial with SQL Server 2008*, one of my previous books (Apress, 2008).

Modeling Spatial Data

Spatial data describes the position, shape, and orientation of objects in space. These objects might be tangible, physical things, like an office building, railroad, or mountain, or they might be abstract features such as the imaginary line marking the political boundary between countries or the area served by a particular store.

SQL Server adopts a vector model of spatial data, in which every object is represented using one or more **geometries**—primitive shapes that approximate the shape of the real-world object they represent. There are three basic types of geometry that may be used with the **geometry** and **geography** datatypes: Point, LineString, and Polygon:

- A **Point** is the most fundamental type of geometry, representing a singular location in space. A Point geometry is zero-dimensional, meaning that it has no associated area or length.

- A **LineString** is comprised of a series of two or more distinct points, together with the line segments that connect those points together. LineStrings have a length, but no associated area. A **simple** LineString is one in which the path drawn between the points does not cross itself. A **closed** LineString is one that starts and ends at the same point. A LineString that is both simple and closed is known as a **ring**.

- A **Polygon** consists of an **exterior ring**, which defines the perimeter of the area of space contained within the polygon. A polygon may also specify one or more **internal rings**, which define areas of space contained within the external ring but excluded from the Polygon. Internal rings can be thought of as "holes" cut out of the Polygon. Polygons are two-dimensional—they have a length measured as the total length of all defined rings, and also an area measured as the space contained within the exterior ring (and not excluded by any interior rings).

■ **Note** The word *geometry* has two distinct meanings when dealing with spatial data in SQL Server. To make the distinction clear, I will use the word *geometry* (regular font) as the generic name to describe Points, LineStrings, and Polygons, and `geometry` (code font) to refer to the `geometry` datatype.

Sometimes, a single feature may be represented by more than one geometry, in which case it is known as a **GeometryCollection**. GeometryCollections may be homogenous or heterogeneous. For example, the Great Wall of China is not a single contiguous wall; rather, it is made up of several distinct sections of wall. As such, it could be represented as a MultiLineString—a homogenous collection of LineString geometries. Similarly, many countries, such as Japan, may be represented as a MultiPolygon—a GeometryCollection consisting of several polygons, each one representing a distinct island. It is also possible to have a heterogeneous GeometryCollection, such as a collection containing a Point, three LineStrings, and two Polygons.

Figure 10-1 illustrates the three basic types of geometries used in SQL Server 2008 and some examples of situations in which they are commonly used.

Having chosen an appropriate type of geometry to represent a given feature, we need some way of relating each point in the geometry definition to the relevant real-world position it represents. For example, to use a Polygon geometry to represent the US Department of Defense Pentagon building, we need to specify that the five points that define the boundary of the Polygon geometry relate to the location of the five corners of the building. So how do we do this?

You are probably familiar with the terms *longitude* and *latitude*, in which case you may be thinking that it is simply a matter of listing the relevant latitude and longitude coordinates for each point in the geometry. Unfortunately, it's not quite that simple.

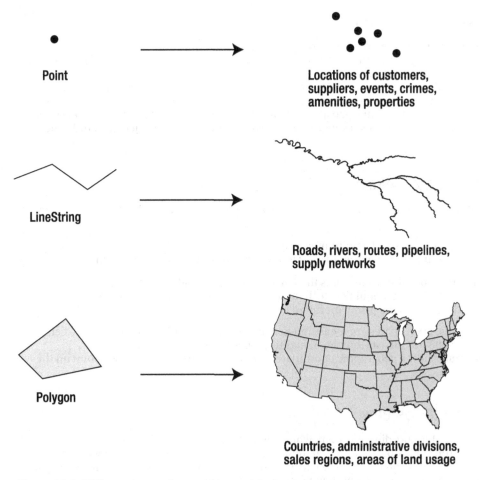

Figure 10-1. Different types of geometries and their common uses

What many people don't realize is that any particular point on the earth's surface does not have only one unique latitude or longitude associated with it. There are, in fact, many different systems of latitude and longitude, and the coordinates of a given point on the earth will vary depending on which system is used. Furthermore, latitude and longitude coordinates are not the only way of expressing positions on the earth—there are other types of coordinates that define the location of an object without using latitude and longitude at all.

In order to understand how to specify the coordinates of a geometry, we first need to examine how different spatial reference systems work.

Spatial Reference Systems

A spatial reference system is a system designed to unambiguously identify and describe the location of any point in space. This ability is essential to enable spatial data to store the coordinates of geometries used to represent features on the earth.

To describe the positions of points in space, every spatial reference system is based on an underlying coordinate system. There are many different types of coordinate systems used in various fields of mathematics, but when defining geospatial data in SQL Server 2008, you are most likely to use a spatial reference system based on either a **geographic coordinate system** or a **projected coordinate system**.

Geographic Coordinate Systems

In a geographic coordinate system, any position on the earth's surface can be defined using two angular coordinates:

- The **latitude** coordinate of a point measures the angle between the plane of the equator and a line drawn perpendicular to the surface of the earth at that point.

- The **longitude** coordinate measures the angle in the equatorial plane between a line drawn from the center of the earth to the point and a line drawn from the center of the earth to the **prime meridian**.

Typically, geographic coordinates are measured in degrees. As such, latitude can vary between −90° (at the South Pole) and +90° (at the North Pole). Longitude values extend from −180° to +180°.

Figure 10-2 illustrates how a geographic coordinate system can be used to identify a point on the earth's surface.

Projected Coordinate Systems

In contrast to the geographic coordinate system, which defines positions on a three-dimensional, round model of the earth, a projected coordinate system describes positions on the earth's surface on a flat, two-dimensional plane (i.e., a **projection** of the earth's surface). In simple terms, a projected coordinate system describes positions on a map rather than positions on a globe.

If we consider all of the points on the earth's surface to lie on a flat plane, we can define positions on that plane using familiar Cartesian coordinates of **x** and **y** (sometimes referred to as Easting and Northing), which represent the distance of a point from an origin along the x axis and y axis, respectively. Figure 10-3 illustrates how the same point illustrated in Figure 10-2 could be defined using a projected coordinate system.

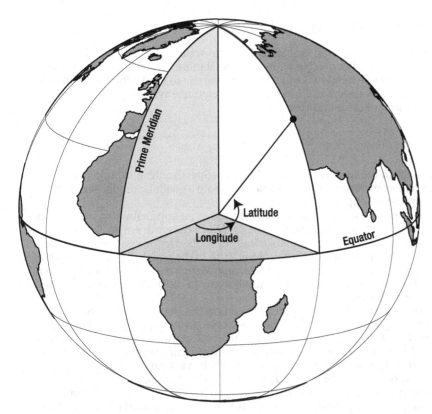

Figure 10-2. Describing a position on the earth using a geographic coordinate system

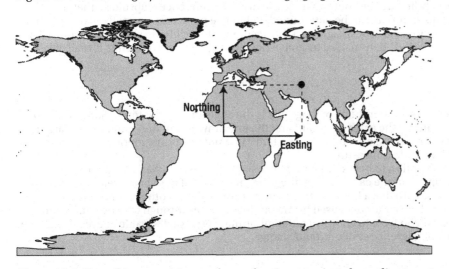

Figure 10-3. Describing a position on the earth using a projected coordinate system

Applying Coordinate Systems to the Earth

A set of coordinates from either a geographic or projected coordinate system does not, on its own, uniquely identify a position on the earth. We need to know additional information, such as where to measure those coordinates from and in what units, and what shape to use to model the earth. Therefore, in addition to specifying the coordinate system used, every spatial reference system must also contain a **datum**, a **prime meridian**, and a **unit of measurement**.

Datum

A datum contains information about the size and shape of the earth. Specifically, it contains the details of a **reference ellipsoid** and a **reference frame**, which are used to create a geodetic model of the earth onto which a coordinate system can be applied.

The reference ellipsoid is a three-dimensional shape that is used as an approximation of the shape of the earth. Although described as a reference *ellipsoid*, most models of the earth are actually an oblate spheroid—a squashed sphere that can be exactly mathematically described by two parameters—the length of the semimajor axis (which represents the radius of the earth at the equator) and the length of the semiminor axis (the radius of the earth at the poles), as shown in Figure 10-4. The degree by which the spheroid is squashed may be stated as a ratio of the semimajor axis to the difference between the two axes, which is known as the **inverse-flattening ratio**.

Different reference ellipsoids provide different approximations of the shape of the earth, and there is no single reference ellipsoid that provides a best fit across the whole surface of the globe. For this reason, spatial applications that operate at a regional level tend to use a spatial reference system based on whatever reference ellipsoid provides the best approximation of the earth's surface for the area in question. In Britain, for example, this is the Airy 1830 ellipsoid, which has a semimajor axis of 6,377,563m and a semiminor axis of 6,356,257m. In North America, the NAD83 ellipsoid is most commonly used, which has a semimajor axis of 6,378,137m and a semiminor axis of 6,356,752m.

The reference frame defines a set of locations in the real world that are assigned known coordinates relative to the reference ellipsoid. By establishing a set of points with known coordinates, these points can then be used to correctly line up the coordinate system with the reference ellipsoid so that the coordinates of other, unknown points can be determined. Reference points are normally places on the earth's surface itself, but they can also be assigned to the positions of satellites in stationary orbit around the earth, which is how the WGS84 datum used by global positioning system (GPS) units is realized.

Prime Meridian

As defined earlier, the geographic coordinate of longitude is the angle in the equatorial plane between the line drawn from the center of the earth to a point and the line drawn from the center of the earth to the prime meridian. Therefore, any spatial reference system must state its prime meridian—the axis from which the angle of longitude is measured.

It is a common misconception to believe that there is a single prime meridian based on some inherent fundamental property of the earth. In fact, the prime meridian of any spatial reference system is arbitrarily chosen simply to provide a line of zero longitude from which all other coordinates of longitude can be measured. One commonly used prime meridian passes through Greenwich, London, but there are many others. If you were to choose a different prime meridian, the value of every longitude coordinate in a given spatial reference system would change.

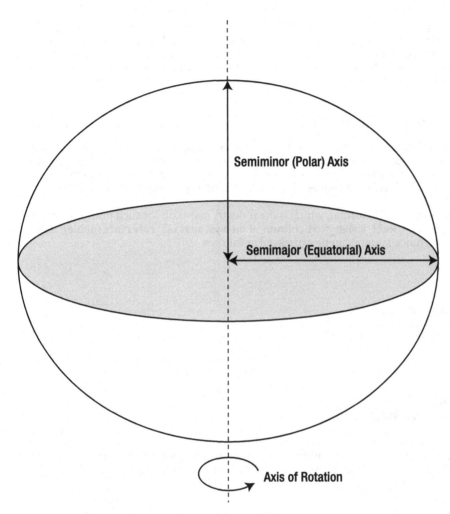

Figure 10-4. Properties of a reference ellipsoid

Projection

A projected coordinate reference system allows you to describe positions on the earth on a flat, two-dimensional image of the world, created as a result of projection. There are many ways of creating such map projections, and each one results in a different image of the world. Some common map projections include Mercator, Bonne, and equirectangular projections, but there are many more.

It is very important to realize that, in order to represent a three-dimensional model of the earth on a flat plane, *every* map projection distorts the features of the earth in some way. Some projections attempt to preserve the relative area of features, but in doing so distort their shape. Other projections preserve the properties of features that are close to the equator, but grossly distort features toward the poles. Some compromise projections attempt to balance distortion in order to create a map in which no one aspect is distorted too significantly. The magnitude of distortion of features portrayed on the map is normally related to the extent of the area projected. For this reason, projected spatial reference systems tend to work best when only applied to a single country or smaller area, rather than a full world view.

Since the method of projection affects the features on the resulting map image, coordinates from a projected coordinate system are only valid for a given projection.

Spatial Reference Identifiers

The most common spatial reference system in global usage uses a geographic coordinate based on the WGS84 datum, which has a reference ellipsoid of radius 6,378,137m and an inverse-flattening ratio of 298.257223563. Coordinates are measured in degrees, based on a prime meridian of Greenwich. This system is used by handheld GPS devices, as well as many consumer mapping products, including Google Earth and Bing Maps APIs.

Using the Well-Known Text (WKT) format, which is the industry standard for such information (and the system SQL Server uses in the **well_known_text** column of the **sys.spatial_references** table), the properties of this spatial reference system can be expressed as follows:

```
GEOGCS[
  "WGS 84",
  DATUM[
    "World Geodetic System 1984",
    ELLIPSOID[
      "WGS 84",
        6378137,
        298.257223563
      ]
    ],
  PRIMEM["Greenwich", 0],
  UNIT["Degree", 0.0174532925199433]
]
```

Returning to the example at the beginning of this chapter, using this spatial reference system, we can describe the approximate location of each corner of the US Pentagon building as a pair of latitude and longitude coordinates as follows:

```
38.870, -77.058
38.869, -77.055
38.871, -77.053
38.873, -77.055
38.872, -77.058
```

Note that, since we are describing points that lie to the west of the prime meridian, the longitude coordinate in each case is negative.

Now let's consider another spatial reference system—the Universal Transverse Mercator (UTM) Zone 18N system, which is a projected coordinate system used in parts of North America. This spatial reference system is based on the 1983 North American datum, which has a reference ellipsoid of 6,378,137m and an inverse-flattening ratio of 298.257222101. This geodetic model is projected using a transverse Mercator projection, centered on the meridian of longitude 75°W, and coordinates based on the projected image are measured in meters. The full properties of this system are expressed in WKT format as follows:

```
PROJCS[
  "NAD_1983_UTM_Zone_18N",
  GEOGCS[
    "GCS_North_American_1983",
    DATUM[
      "D_North_American_1983",
      SPHEROID[
        "GRS_1980",
        6378137,
        298.257222101
        ]
      ],
    PRIMEM["Greenwich",0],
    UNIT["Degree", 0.0174532925199433]
  ],
  PROJECTION["Transverse_Mercator"],
  PARAMETER["False_Easting", 500000.0],
  PARAMETER["False_Northing", 0.0],
  PARAMETER["Central_Meridian", -75.0],
  PARAMETER["Scale_Factor", 0.9996],
  PARAMETER["Latitude_of_Origin", 0.0],
  UNIT["Meter", 1.0]
]
```

Using this spatial reference system, the same five points of the Pentagon building can instead be described using the following coordinates:

```
321460, 4304363
321718, 4304246
321896, 4304464
321728, 4304690
321465, 4304585
```

Comparing these results clearly demonstrates that any coordinate pair only describes a unique location on the earth when stated with the details of the coordinate system from which they were obtained. However, it would be quite cumbersome if we had to write out the full details of the datum, prime meridian, unit of measurement, and projection details every time we wanted to quote a pair of coordinates. Fortunately, there is an established set of **spatial reference identifiers** (SRIDs) that provide a unique integer code associated with each spatial reference system. The two spatial reference systems used in the preceding examples are represented by SRID 4326 and SRID 26918, respectively.

Every time you state an item of spatial data using the **geography** or **geometry** types in SQL Server 2008, you *must* state the corresponding SRID from which the coordinate values were obtained. What's more, since SQL Server does not provide any mechanism for converting between spatial reference systems, if you want to perform any calculations involving two or more items of spatial data, each one must be defined using the same SRID.

If you don't know the SRID associated with a set of coordinates—say, you looked up some latitude and longitude coordinates from a web site that didn't state the system used—the chances are more than likely that they are geographic coordinates based on SRID 4326, the system used by GPSs.

■ **Note** To find out the SRID associated with any given spatial reference system, you can use the search facility provided at **www.epsg-registry.org**.

Geography vs. Geometry

Early Microsoft promotional material for SQL Server 2008 introduced the **geography** datatype as suitable for "round-earth" data, whereas the **geometry** datatype was for "flat-earth" data. These terms have since been repeated verbatim by a number of commentators, with little regard for explaining the practical meaning of "flat" or "round." A simple analogy might be that, in terms of geospatial data, the **geometry** datatype operates on a map, whereas the **geography** datatype operates on a globe.

With that distinction in mind, one obvious difference between the datatypes concerns the types of coordinates that can be used with each:

- The **geography** datatype requires data to be expressed using latitude and longitude coordinates, obtained from a geographic coordinate system. Furthermore, since SQL Server needs to know the parameters of the ellipsoidal model onto which those coordinates should be applied, all **geography** data must be based on one of the spatial reference systems listed in the **sys.spatial_reference_systems** system table.

- The **geometry** datatype operates on a flat plane, which makes it ideal for dealing with geospatial data from projected coordinate systems, including Universal Transverse Mercator (UTM) grid coordinates, national grid coordinates, or state plane coordinates. However, there are occasions when you may wish to store latitude and longitude coordinates using the **geometry** datatype, as I'll demonstrate later this chapter. The **geometry** datatype can also be used to store any abstract nonspatial data that can be modeled as a pair of floating point x, y coordinates, such as the nodes of a graph.

This distinction between coordinate types is not the only property that distinguishes the two datatypes. In the following sections I'll analyze some of the other differences in more detail.

■ **Note** Both the flat plane used by the **geometry** datatype and the curved ellipsoidal surface of the **geography** datatype are two-dimensional surfaces, and a position on those surfaces can be described using exactly two coordinates (latitude and longitude for the **geography** datatype, or x and y for the **geometry** datatype). SQL Server 2008 also allows you to store Z and M coordinates, which can represent two further dimensions associated with each point (typically, Z is elevation above the surface, and M is a measure of time). However, while these values can be stored and retrieved, none of the methods provided by the **geography** or **geometry** datatypes account for the value of Z and M coordinates in their calculations.

Standards Compliance

The **geometry** datatype operates on a flat plane, where the two coordinate values for each point represent the x and y position from a designated origin on the plane. As a result, many of the standard methods provided by the **geometry** datatype can be performed using elementary trigonometry and geometry. For example, the following code listing demonstrates how to calculate the distance between a Point located at (50,100) and a Point at (90,130) using the **STDistance()** method of the **geometry** datatype:

```
DECLARE @point1 geometry = geometry::Point(50, 100, 0);
DECLARE @point2 geometry = geometry::Point(90, 130, 0);
SELECT @point1.STDistance(@point2);
```

The result, **50**, could have been obtained without using the **geometry** datatype, using basic knowledge of the Pythagorean theorem, as in the following equivalent T-SQL query:

```
DECLARE
  @x1 int = 50, @y1 int = 100,
  @x2 int = 90, @y2 int = 130;

SELECT
  SQRT(
    POWER(@x2 - @x1, 2) +
    POWER(@y2 - @y1, 2)
  );
```

Of course, other **geometry** operations, such as finding whether a Point lies within a Polygon, or the area created by the intersection of two Polygons, become more involved than the simple example given here, but they are still generally achievable using alternative methods in T-SQL or SQLCLR. So why the fuss about the **geometry** datatype?

One key benefit of implementing such functionality using the **geometry** datatype instead of rolling your own code is that all the methods implemented by the **geometry** datatype conform to the Open Geospatial Consortium (OGC) Simple Features for SQL Specification v1.1.0. This is the industry standard format for the interchange and implementation of spatial functionality. By using the **geometry** datatype, you can be sure that the results of any spatial methods will be the same as those obtained from any other system based on the same standards.

Note that although OGC compliance ensures *consistency* of results, the OGC methods do not necessarily give predictable results, at least not in the sense that you can reasonably guess the behavior of a method based on its name alone. For example, consider the two LineStrings illustrated in Figure 10-5.

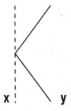

Figure 10-5. Two LineStrings that cross but do not touch

In normal English language, most people would describe these two LineStrings as *touching*, but not *crossing*. However, according to the OGC definitions, the reverse is true. You can test this for yourself by examining the results of the **STTouches()** and **STCrosses()** methods, as shown in the following code listing:

```
DECLARE @x geometry = geometry::STLineFromText('LINESTRING(0 0, 0 10)', 0);
DECLARE @y geometry = geometry::STLineFromText('LINESTRING(10 0, 0 5, 10 10)', 0);
SELECT
  @x.STCrosses(@y),
  @x.STTouches(@y);
```

The result of the **STCrosses()** method is **1**, indicating that the LineString x crosses over the LineString y. According to the OGC standards, two LineStrings cross each other if the geometry created by their intersection is zero-dimensional. In this case, the two LineStrings intersect at a single point (5,5), so they are deemed to cross. In contrast, two LineStrings only touch each other if the points at which they intersect lie in the boundary (i.e., the ends) of the LineString. In this case, the point (5,5) lies in the interior of both LineStrings rather than in their boundary, so the result of **STTouches()** is **0** (i.e., false). Be careful to check the documentation of any methods to ensure that the behavior is exactly as you expect!

Accuracy

The world is round. The **geometry** datatype, however, operates on a flat plane. By definition, therefore, any geospatial calculations performed using the **geometry** datatype will involve a degree of error. This is not a limitation of the **geometry** datatype in itself, but rather of the inevitable distortions introduced when using a projected coordinate system to represent a round model of the earth.

Generally speaking, the effects of distortion become greater as the area of projection is increased. For this reason, results obtained using the **geometry** datatype will become less accurate than results obtained using the **geography** datatype over large distances.

In global spatial applications, the **geography** datatype is a more suitable choice, as there are few projected systems that can be used for general global purposes with sufficient accuracy. For storing spatial data contained within a single country or smaller area, the **geometry** datatype will generally provide sufficient accuracy, and comes with the benefits of additional functionality over the **geography** type.

Technical Limitations and Performance

The ellipsoidal calculations used by the **geography** datatype are by their nature more complex than the planar calculations of the **geometry** datatype. This means that applications using the **geography** datatype may experience slightly slower performance than those based on the **geometry** datatype, although the impact is not normally significant. Additionally, the indexes created on columns of **geometry** data may specify an explicit bounding box, creating a more granular grid, which leads to more efficient filtering of results than a **geography** index, which is assumed to span the entire globe (but more on that later).

However, there are other more important implications arising between the different models on which the two datatypes are based. The first of these differences is that currently, no **geography** instance may exceed a single hemisphere. In this context, the term *hemisphere* means one-half of the surface of the earth, centered about any point on the globe. Thus, it is not possible to have a **geography** MultiPoint instance containing one Point at the North Pole and one at the South Pole. Nor is it possible to have a **geography** LineString that extends from London to Auckland and then on to Los Angeles. In order to work around this limitation, you must break down large **geography** objects into several smaller objects that each fit within a hemisphere. In contrast, there is no limit to the size of a **geometry** instance, which may extend indefinitely on an infinite plane.

The second technical difference arises from the conceptual differences of working on a curved surface rather than a flat plane. As defined earlier, the external ring of a Polygon defines an area of space contained within the Polygon, and may also contain one or more internal rings that define "holes"—areas of space cut out from the Polygon. This is fairly straightforward to visualize when drawing Polygons on a flat piece of paper. However, a problem occurs when you try to apply this definition on a continuous round surface such as used by the **geography** datatype, because it becomes ambiguous as to which area of space is contained *inside* a Polygon ring, and which is *outside*.

To demonstrate this problem, consider Figure 10-6, which illustrates a Polygon whose exterior ring is a set of points drawn around the equator. Does the area contained within the Polygon represent the Northern Hemisphere or the Southern Hemisphere?

Figure 10-6. Polygon ring orientation is significant for the geography datatype

The solution used by SQL Server (and in common with some other spatial systems) is to consider the **ring orientation** of the Polygon—i.e., the order in which the points of the ring are specified. When defining a **geography** Polygon, SQL Server treats the area on the "left" of the path drawn between the points as contained within the ring, whereas the points on the "right" side are excluded. Thus, the Polygon depicted in Figure 10-6 represents the Northern Hemisphere. Whenever you define **geography** polygons, you must ensure that you specify the correct ring orientation or else your polygons will be "inside-out"—excluding the area they were intended to contain, and including everything else. In **geometry**, data ring orientation is not significant, as there is no ambiguity as to the area contained within a Polygon ring on a flat plane.

A final technical difference concerns **invalid geometries**. In an ideal world, we would always want our spatial data to be "valid"—that is, it meeting all the OGC specifications for that type of geometry. However, as developers we have to reluctantly accept that spatial data, like any other data, is rarely as perfect as we would like. This means that you will frequently encounter invalid data where, for example, Polygons do self-intersect.

Rather perversely, perhaps, the **geometry** datatype, which conforms to OGC standards, is also the datatype that provides options for dealing with data that fails to meet those standards. For example, not only can the **geometry** datatype be used to store invalid geometries, but it also provides the **STIsValid()** method to identify whether a geometry is valid or not, and the **MakeValid()** method to attempt to "fix" invalid geometries. All **geography** data, in contrast, is assumed to be valid at all times. Although this means that once **geography** data is in SQL Server, you can work with it comfortable in the knowledge that it is always valid, it can provide an obstacle to importing that data in the first place. Since SQL Server cannot import invalid **geography** data, you may have to rely on external tools to validate and fix any erroneous data prior to importing it.

Creating Spatial Data

The first challenge presented to many users new to the spatial features in SQL Server 2008 is how to get spatial data into the database. Unfortunately, the most commonly used spatial format, the ESRI shapefile format (SHP), is not directly supported by any of the **geography** or **geometry** methods, nor by any of the file data sources available in SQL Server Integration Services (SSIS). What's more, internally, **geography** and **geometry** data is stored using a proprietary binary format, which is quite complex. For readers who are interested, the structure is documented at **http://msdn.microsoft.com/en-us/library/ee320529.aspx**, but in general you do not need to worry about the specifics involved, as SQL Server instead provides static methods to create spatial data from three different alternative spatial formats: WKT, Well-Known Binary (WKB), and Geography Markup Language (GML).

Well-Known Text

WKT is a simple, text-based format defined by the OGC for the exchange of spatial information. Owing to its easy readability and relative conciseness, the WKT format is a popular way of storing and sharing spatial data, and is the format used in most of the examples in this chapter. It is also the format used in the spatial documentation in SQL Server 2008 Books Online, at **http://msdn.microsoft.com/en-us/library/ms130214.aspx**.

The following code listing demonstrates the WKT string used to represent a Point geometry located at an x coordinate of 258647 and a y coordinate of 665289:

```
POINT(258647 665289)
```

Based on the National Grid of Great Britain, which is a projected coordinate system denoted by the SRID 27700, these coordinates represent the location of Glasgow, Scotland. Once we know the WKT string and the relevant SRID, we can create a **geometry** Point instance representing the city using the **STPointFromText** method as follows:

```
DECLARE @Glasgow geometry;
SET @Glasgow = geometry::STPointFromText('POINT(258647 665289)', 27700);
GO
```

In order to create more complex geometries from WKT, simply specify the individual coordinate pairs of each point in a comma-delimited list, as shown in the following example, which creates a LineString between two points representing Sydney Harbor Bridge:

```
DECLARE @SydneyHarbourBridge geography;
SET @SydneyHarbourBridge = geography::STLineFromText(
  'LINESTRING(151.209 -33.855, 151.212 -33.850)', 4326);
GO
```

Note that when using WKT to express coordinates for use in the **geography** datatype, as in the last example, the longitude coordinate must be listed first in each coordinate pair, followed by the latitude coordinate. This is in contrast to the expression of a "latitude, longitude" coordinate pair, which most people are familiar with using in everyday speech.

One disadvantage of the WKT format is that, as with any text-based representation, it is not possible to precisely state the value of certain floating-point coordinate values obtained from binary methods. The inevitable rounding errors introduced when attempting to do so will lead to a loss of precision. Additionally, since SQL Server must parse the text in a WKT representation to create the relevant spatial object, instantiating objects from WKT can be slower than when using other methods.

Well-Known Binary

The WKB format, like the WKT format, is a standardized way of representing spatial data defined by the OGC. In contrast to the text-based WKT format, WKB represents a **geometry** or **geography** object as a contiguous stream of bytes in binary format. Every WKB representation begins with a header section that specifies the order in which the bytes are listed (big-endian or little-endian), a value defining the type of geometry being represented, and a stream of 8-byte values representing the coordinates of each point in the geometry.

The following code demonstrates how to construct a Point geometry from WKB representing the city of Warsaw, Poland, located at latitude 52.23 and longitude 21.02, using the **geography** STPointFromWKB() method:

```
DECLARE @Warsaw geography;
SET @Warsaw = geography::STPointFromWKB(
  0x010100000085EB51B81E0535403D0AD7A3701D4A40,
  4326);
```

One advantage of using WKB is that it can be more efficiently processed than either of the text-based (GML or WKT) formats. Additionally, since it is a binary format, WKB maintains the precision of floating-point coordinate values calculated from binary operations, without the rounding errors introduced in a text-based format. It is therefore the best choice of format for transmission of spatial data directly between system interfaces, where the speed and precision of this format are beneficial and the lack of human readability is not significant.

■ **Note** Although SQL Server stores spatial data in a binary format similar to WKB, it is not the same. In order to create items of spatial data from WKB, you must supply it to the appropriate STxxxxFromWKB() method.

Geography Markup Language

GML is an XML-based language for representing spatial information. Like all XML formats, GML is a very explicit and highly structured hierarchical format. The following code demonstrates an example of the GML representation of a point located at latitude –33.86 and longitude 151.21:

```
<Point xmlns="http://www.opengis.net/gml">
  <pos>-33.86 151.21</pos>
</Point>
```

GML, like WKT, has the advantages of being easy to read and understand. Additionally, the XML structure makes it is easy to assess and query the structure of complex spatial objects by examining the structure of the associated GML document. However, it is very verbose—the GML representation of an object occupies substantially more space than the equivalent WKT representation and, like WKT, it too suffers from precision issues caused by rounding when expressing binary floating-point coordinate values. GML is most commonly used for representing spatial information in an XML-based environment, including the syndication of spatial data over the Internet.

Importing Data

It is very common to want to analyze custom-defined spatial data, such as the locations of your customers, in the context of commonly known geographical features, such as political boundaries, the locations of cities, or the paths of roads and railways. There are lots of places to obtain such generic spatial data, from a variety of commercial and free sources.

SQL Server doesn't provide any specific tools for importing predefined spatial data, but there are a number of third-party tools that can be used for this purpose. It is also possible to use programmatic techniques based on the functionality provided by the **SqlServer.Types.dll** library, which contains the methods used by the **geography** and **geometry** datatypes themselves. To demonstrate one method of importing spatial data, and to provide some sample data for use in the remaining examples in this chapter, we'll import a dataset from the Geonames web site (**www.geonames.org**) containing the geographic coordinates of locations around the world.

To begin, download and unzip the main dataset from the Geonames web site, available from **http://download.geonames.org/export/dump/allCountries.zip.** This archive contains a tab-delimited text file containing nearly 7 million rows, and when unzipped, occupies nearly 800MB. If you would like to use a smaller dataset, you can alternatively download the **http://download.geonames.org/export/dump/cities1000.zip** archive, which uses the same schema but contains a subset of approximately 80,000 records, representing only those cities with a population exceeding 1,000 inhabitants.

■ **Caution** The Geonames `allCountries.zip` export is a large file (approximately 170MB), and may take some time to download.

To store the Geonames information in SQL Server, first create a new table as follows:

```
CREATE TABLE allCountries(
  [geonameid] int NOT NULL,
  [name] nvarchar(200) NULL,
  [asciiname] nvarchar(200) NULL,
  [alternatenames] nvarchar(4000) NULL,
  [latitude] real NULL,
  [longitude] real NULL,
  [feature class] nvarchar(1) NULL,
  [feature code] nvarchar(10) NULL,
  [country code] nvarchar(2) NULL,
  [cc2] nvarchar(60) NULL,
  [admin1 code] nvarchar(20) NULL,
  [admin2 code] nvarchar(80) NULL,
  [admin3 code] nvarchar(20) NULL,
  [admin4 code] nvarchar(20) NULL,
  [population] int NULL,
  [elevation] smallint NULL,
  [gtopo30] smallint NULL,
  [timezone] nvarchar(80) NULL,
  [modification date] datetime NULL
);
GO
```

I've kept all the column names and datatypes exactly as they are defined in the Geonames schema, but you may want to adjust them. I personally dislike column names that include spaces, such as "modification date," but I also think that when importing data from an external source, it is very important to clearly reference how the columns are mapped, and the easiest way of doing this is to keep the column names the same as in the source.

There are a variety of methods of importing the Geonames text file into the **allCountries** table—for this example, however, we'll keep things as simple as possible by using the Import and Export Wizard. Start the wizard from Management Studio by right-clicking in the Object Explorer pane on the name of the database in which you created the **allCountries** table, and select Tasks → Import Data. When prompted to choose a data source, select the Flat File Source option, click the Browse button, and navigate to and select the **allCountries.txt** file that you downloaded earlier. From the 'Code page' drop-down, scroll down and highlight 65001 (UTF-8), and then click the Columns tab in the left pane.

On the Columns page, change the Column delimiter to Tab {t}, and then select Refresh to preview the data in the file, which should appear as shown in Figure 10-7. Then click Advanced from the left pane.

On the Advanced pane, click each column name in turn, and configure the column properties to match the values shown in Table 10-1.

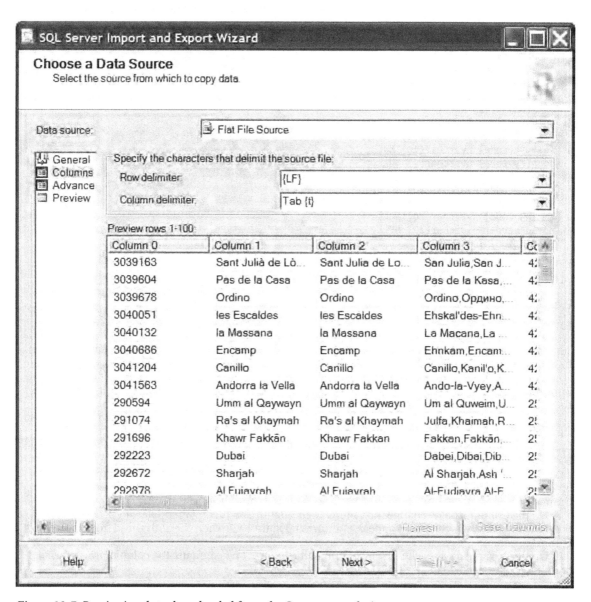

Figure 10-7. Previewing data downloaded from the Geonames web site

Table 10-1. Column Properties for Geonames Data

Column	Name	DataType	OutputColumnWidth
0	geonameid	Four-byte signed integer [DT_I4]	
1	name	Unicode string [DT_WSTR]	200
2	asciiname	Unicode string [DT_WSTR]	200
3	alternatenames	Unicode string [DT_WSTR]	4000
4	latitude	Float [DT_R4]	
5	longitude	Float [DT_R4]	
6	feature class	Unicode string [DT_WSTR]	1
7	feature code	Unicode string [DT_WSTR]	10
8	country code	Unicode string [DT_WSTR]	2
9	cc2	Unicode string [DT_WSTR]	60
10	admin1 code	Unicode string [DT_WSTR]	20
11	admin2 code	Unicode string [DT_WSTR]	80
12	admin3 code	Unicode string [DT_WSTR]	20
13	admin4 code	Unicode string [DT_WSTR]	20
14	population	Four-byte signed integer [DT_I4]	
15	elevation	Two-byte signed integer [DT_I2]	
16	gtopo30	Two-byte signed integer [DT_I2]	
17	timezone	Unicode string [DT_WSTR]	80
18	modification date	Date [DT_DATE]	

■ **Note** For a full description of the columns available from the Geonames export data listed in Table 10-1, please consult `http://download.geonames.org/export/dump/readme.txt`.

Once the columns are set up, click Next to proceed, and check that the destination database is correctly configured to import the records to the **allCountries** table. Click Next again to finish the import wizard.

On my laptop, the import takes about 10 minutes, so take this opportunity to stretch your legs and get a coffee, if you wish. After the import wizard successfully completes the import operation, every column from the Geonames dataset will be imported into the **allCountries** table, but we are not yet making use of the spatial capabilities of SQL Server 2008. Every record in the table has an associated latitude and longitude coordinate value, but these are currently held in separate, floating point, columns. Since the Geonames coordinates are measured using a geographic coordinate system of SRID 4326, the best way of modeling this data is to add a new **geography** column to the table and populate it with individual Point instances representing each location. The following code listing illustrates the T-SQL required to add a **geography** column called **location**, and update it using the **Point()** method based on the coordinate values held in the **latitude** and **longitude** columns for each row:

```
ALTER TABLE allCountries
ADD location geography;
GO

UPDATE allCountries
SET location = geography::Point(latitude, longitude, 4326);
GO
```

The approach described here can be used to load spatial data from a variety of tabular formats such as gazetteers of place names. A similar method could also be adopted in an SSIS package, whereby the **location** column could be calculated as a derived column as part of the load, rather than added afterward as in this case.

■ **Tip** Having populated the **location** column, the **latitude** and **longitude** columns could be dropped from the **allCountries** table if so desired—the individual coordinate values associated with each point can be obtained using the **Lat** and **Long** properties of the **location** column instead.

Querying Spatial Data

Now that we've imported a good-sized set of sample data, we can start to write some spatial queries against it, but there are a few important considerations when writing queries that involve **geometry** or

geography data. Because spatial data types are not comparable, there are certain restrictions placed on the types of query in which they can be used—for example:

- You can't **ORDER BY** a **geometry** or **geography** column.

- You can't **SELECT DISTINCT** spatial data, nor can you **UNION** two result sets containing **geography** or **geometry** data. However, you can **UNION ALL** two datasets.

- You can't use regular query comparison operators, such as **WHERE t1.shape = t2.shape**, but you can test whether two shapes are equal by using a predicate based on the **STEquals()** method, such as **WHERE t1.shape.STEquals(t2.shape) = 1**.

In terms of actually performing operations on spatial data itself, the **geography** and **geometry** datatypes both provide a range of methods for performing common calculations, including intersections, measuring distances, and addition and subtraction of geometries.

It is important to notice that the methods available in a given situation are dependent on the datatype being used. Although in most cases there are methods to provide equivalent functionality for all operations performed on both the **geometry** and **geography** datatypes, there are some methods that can only be applied to one or the other. The most noticeable example is that, although both **geometry** and **geography** support the ability to test whether two geometries intersect (using the **STIntersects()** method), only the **geometry** datatype provides the methods required to test the specific *sort* of intersection—whether one geometry crosses, overlaps, touches, or is contained within another. Some other methods provide equivalent functionality for the two types under a different name: for example, **Lat** and **Long**, which return the coordinate values of a **geography** instance, provide equivalent functionality to **STY** and **STX** in the **geometry** datatype.

In general, the methods available using either type can be classified into one of two categories:

> Methods that adhere to the OGC specifications are prefixed by the letters **ST** (an abbreviation for *spatiotemporal*). In general, these methods provide basic functionality for working with spatial instances, such a **STIntersects()**, used to determine whether one instance intersects another; **STDistance()**, used to calculate the shortest distance between two instances; and **STArea()**, used to calculate the area contained within a polygon instance.

> SQL Server also provides a number of **extended methods**, which provide additional functionality on top of the OGC standard. These include **Reduce()**, which simplifies a geometry; **BufferWithTolerance()**, which applies a buffer within a given tolerance limit; and **Filter()**, which performs an approximate test of intersection based on a spatial index.

In this section, I won't discuss every available method—you can look these up on SQL Server Books Online (or in *Beginning Spatial with SQL Server 2008*). Instead, I'll examine a couple of common scenarios and illustrate how you can combine one or more methods to solve them. Before we begin, let's create a clustered primary key and a basic spatial index on the **allCountries** table to support any queries executed against it:

```
ALTER TABLE allCountries
  ADD CONSTRAINT PK_geonameid
  PRIMARY KEY (geonameid );
GO
CREATE SPATIAL INDEX idxallCountries
ON allCountries(location) USING GEOGRAPHY_GRID
```

```
WITH (
  GRIDS =(
    LEVEL_1 = MEDIUM,
    LEVEL_2 = MEDIUM,
    LEVEL_3 = MEDIUM,
    LEVEL_4 = MEDIUM),
  CELLS_PER_OBJECT = 16);
```

I'll cover spatial indexes later in this chapter, so don't worry if you're not familiar with the syntax used here—it will become clear soon!

Nearest-Neighbor Queries

Perhaps the most commonly asked question regarding spatial data is, "Where is the closest *x* to a given location?" or in the more general case, "How do we identify the nearest *n* features to a location?" This type of query is generally referred to as a **nearest-neighbor** query, and there are a number of ways of performing such a query in SQL Server 2008.

The simplest method that springs to mind is to order a dataset based on the result of the `STDistance()` method, sorting all records in ascending order of distance from the given point, so that the top *n* records can be easily identified. This approach is demonstrated in the following query:

```
DECLARE @Point geography;
SET @Point = geography::STPointFromText('POINT(0 52)', 4326);
SELECT TOP 3
  name,
  location.STAsText() AS WKT,
  location.STDistance(@Point) AS Distance
FROM
  allCountries
ORDER BY
  location.STDistance(@Point) ASC;
```

■ **Caution** This query is perfectly valid and will lead to the correct results being obtained. However, it will take a very long time to execute, as will be explained in the following section. Rather than wasting time and server resources, you might want to just take my word for it and try the next example instead!

The preceding query defines a **geography** Point instance located at latitude 52 degrees and longitude 0 degrees, using the spatial reference system SRID 4326. It then orders the results of the query from the **allCountries** table based on their distance from this point, and returns the top three results as follows:

Name	WKT	Distance
Periwinkle Hill	POINT (-0.00112 52.0055)	616.78524720001
Barkway	POINT (0.0166667 52)	1144.6358911887
Reed	POINT (-0.0166667 52)	1144.6358911887

Although this query correctly identifies and returns the nearest *n* results, there is a fundamental problem with this approach; **STDistance()** is a computationally expensive method, and the preceding query must evaluate the result of this method on every one of the rows in the result set to order them and select the closest *n* records. This results in a table scan of 6.9 million rows, and the spatial index doesn't provide any help here because every row must be evaluated before the results can ordered. Performing a nearest-neighbor search like this on a table containing many rows is very slow and costly, as you will no doubt have discovered if you tried executing the example yourself!

An alternative method for finding nearest neighbors involves a two-stage approach. The first stage is to use the index to identify a set of likely nearest-neighbor candidates, based on those records that lie within a predetermined buffer around the feature in question. The size of the buffer is chosen to be large enough so that it contains the required number of nearest neighbors, but not so large that it includes lots of additional rows of data that exceed the desired number of results. The second stage of this method uses the **STDistance()** method as before, but only to calculate the distance of those candidate records lying within the buffer area, rather than processing and sorting the whole table. By being selective in choosing the candidate records to sort, we can take advantage of the spatial index.

The following listing demonstrates this approach, using **STBuffer(25000)** to identify candidate records that lie within a 25km search area:

```
DECLARE @Point geography;
SET @Point = geography::STPointFromText('POINT(0 52)', 4326);

DECLARE @SearchArea geography;
SET @SearchArea = @Point.STBuffer(25000);   --25km search radius

DECLARE @Candidates table (
  Name varchar(200),
  Location geography,
  Distance float
);
INSERT INTO @Candidates
SELECT
  name,
  location,
  location.STDistance(@Point) AS Distance
FROM
  allCountries
  WITH(INDEX(idxallCountries))
WHERE
  location.Filter(@SearchArea) = 1;

SELECT TOP 3 * FROM @Candidates ORDER BY Distance;
```

> ■ **Note** Notice that in the preceding example query, I explicitly included an index hint,
> `WITH(INDEX(idxallCountries))`, to ensure that the query optimizer chooses a plan using the `idxallCountries`
> spatial index. The cost-based estimates for spatial queries are not always accurate, which means that SQL Server
> 2008 does not always pick the optimal plan for a query. SQL Server 2008 SP1 improves the situation, but there are
> still occasions when an explicit hint is required to ensure that a spatial index is used.

As in the last example, this approach correctly identifies the three closest cities. The advantage of
the buffer approach is that, by first filtering the set of candidate results to only that lie within the
vicinity of the feature, the number of times that **STDistance()** needs to be called is reduced, and the
dataset to be sorted becomes much smaller, making the query significantly faster than the basic nearest-
neighbor approach described previously. The locations lying within the buffer zone can be identified
using a spatial index seek, as illustrated in the execution plan shown in Figure 10-8. On my laptop, the
top three nearest neighbors are now obtained in just 33ms, whereas the time taken to execute the first
query was over an hour!

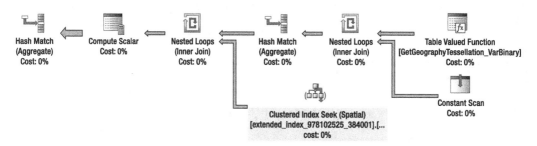

*Figure 10-8. A query to identify nearest-neighbor candidates within a buffer zone can utilize a clustered
spatial index seek.*

However, the main problem with this approach is that it relies on an appropriate buffer size in
which to search for candidate results. If you set the buffer too large, then there will be too many possible
candidates returned and the filter will not be efficient. If you set the buffer size too small, then there is a
risk that the search area will not contain *any* candidates, resulting in the query failing to identify any
nearest neighbors at all.

The buffer search zone approach is most useful in situations where you are able to reliably set an
appropriate buffer size in which to select a set of candidate nearest neighbors. This might be based on a
known, uniform distribution of your data—for example, you know that any item in the dataset will never
lie more than 25km from its nearest neighbor. Alternatively, you might want to obtain nearest neighbors
in combination with an additional distance constraint—for example, "Show me the three closest gas
stations to this location, but only if they are within 10 miles."

Rather than identifying candidates that lie within a fixed search zone (which faces the risk of failing
to find any nearest neighbors at all), a better approach is to create a query that identifies candidates
within an expanding search range. The search for candidate results can be initially limited to a close
vicinity to the chosen location, but gradually increased until at least the required number of nearest

neighbors is found. These candidate results can then be sorted in the second stage to find the true n nearest neighbors.

A query that identifies nearest neighbors based on expanding search ranges requires the use of a **numbers table**. If you don't already have a numbers table, you can create one and populate it with the integers between 0 and 1,000 using the following code:

```
CREATE TABLE Numbers (
  Number int PRIMARY KEY CLUSTERED
);

DECLARE @i int = 0;
WHILE @i <= 1000
  BEGIN
    INSERT INTO Numbers VALUES (@i);
    SET @i = @i + 1;
  END;
GO
```

The **Numbers** table will be joined to the **allCountries** table to create a series of expanding search ranges. The distance to which each successive search extends increases exponentially until a search area of sufficient size is found that contains the requisite number of nearest neighbors. All of the features in this search area are returned as candidates, and then the **TOP 3** syntax is used to select the three true nearest neighbors. This approach is demonstrated in the following code listing:

```
DECLARE @Point geography;
SET @Point = geography::STPointFromText('POINT(0 52)', 4326);

DECLARE @Candidates table (
  Name varchar(200),
  Location geography,
  Distance float,
  Range int
);

INSERT INTO @Candidates
SELECT TOP 3 WITH TIES
  Name,
  Location,
  Location.STDistance(@Point) AS Distance,
  1000*POWER(2, Number) AS Range
FROM
  allCountries
  WITH(INDEX(idxallCountries))
INNER JOIN Numbers
ON allCountries.Location.STDistance(@Point) < 1000*POWER(2,Numbers.Number)
ORDER BY Number;

SELECT TOP 3 * FROM @Candidates ORDER BY Range DESC, Distance ASC;
```

This code might not seem that intuitive, so let's step through it. Remember that the **Numbers** table contains consecutive integers, starting at zero. So the condition **allCountries.Location.STDistance(@Point)** < **1000*POWER(2,Numbers.Number)** specifies that the initial criterion for a feature to be considered a nearest-neighbor candidate is that the distance between that feature and **@Point** is less than **1000 * 2^0**. Since the EPSG:4326 spatial reference system defines distances in meters, this equates to a 1km search area—if you want to specify an alternative starting search radius, you may do so by changing the value of **1000** to another value (remember to use the unit of measure appropriate to the datatype and SRID of the data in question).

If the requisite number of neighbors (in this case, we are searching for the top three) is not found within the specified distance, then the search range is increased in size. Successive search ranges are obtained by raising 2 to the power of the next number in the **Numbers** table. Thus, the first range extends to 1km around the point, the second range extends to 2km—then 4km, 8km, 16km, and so on. By adopting an exponential growth model, this method is guaranteed to find the nearest neighbor within a relatively short number of iterations, however dispersed the distribution of the underlying features is.

Once the search range has been sufficiently increased to contain at least the required number of candidate nearest neighbors, *all* of the features lying within that range are selected as candidates, by using a **SELECT** statement with the **WITH TIES** argument. Finally, the candidates are sorted by ascending distance from the point, and the **TOP 3** records are selected as the true nearest neighbors. The **Range** column returned in the results states the distance to which the search range was extended to find the nearest neighbor.

On my laptop, this approach identifies the three nearest neighbors in 45ms. While it is slightly more complex, this last approach provides the most flexible solution for implementing a nearest-neighbor query. It is significantly faster than the basic approach, and although not quite as fast as the fixed search area technique, it does not suffer from the limitations associated with having to specify a fixed search radius. To enhance the performance of this query further, we'll need to look at the matter of spatial indexes, which is covered later in this chapter.

Finding Locations Within a Given Bounding Box

Over the past few years, there has been a huge growth in the adoption of web-mapping services, including Google Maps, Yahoo Maps, and Microsoft Bing Maps. Whereas once considered gimmicks and eye candy with little real value, these tools are now being used in increasingly important applications, including for disaster response planning, logistics, epidemiology, and other health-reporting scenarios.

Typically, these web-mapping applications are used as dynamic front-end interfaces to spatial data held in a database. Users pan and zoom the map to display a particular area of interest, and any data contained within the visible map view is retrieved from the database to be plotted on the map. In this section, we'll look at a scenario that uses Microsoft Bing Maps as an interface to spatial data held in SQL Server 2008, although the same approach could be applied to most map interfaces.

The first requirement is to identify the area visible within a given map view—in other words, the **bounding box** of the map. Typically, the bounding box of a map view can be described using only two pairs of coordinate values, representing the points at opposite corners of the map. Unfortunately, these is no standardized view of which two corners to use: the **GetMapView()** method in Bing Maps returns the coordinates of the points at the top-left and bottom-right corners of the map, whereas the equivalent **getBounds()** method used by Google Maps returns the points at the southwest and northeast corners. Although these differences are easily handled, it's something to be aware of as you develop your code.

Having identified the coordinate of two opposing points, we next need to construct a Polygon representing the bounding box enclosed by those points. To illustrate this, consider the map view shown in Figure 10-9, which is centered on the state of Colorado. The coordinate values of the top-left and bottom-right corners of the map are (41,–109) and (37,–102), respectively.

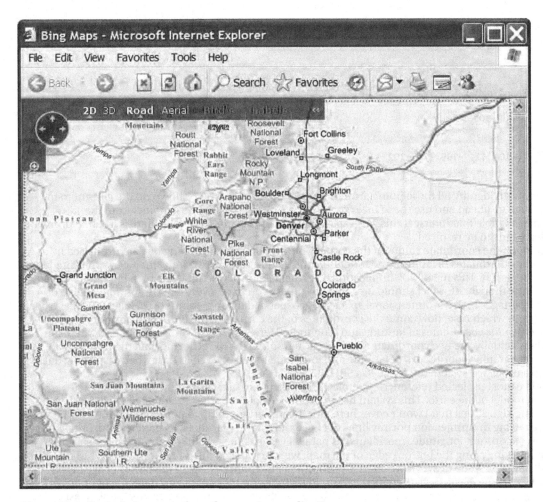

Figure 10-9. Typical viewport of a web-mapping application

The coordinates of the bounding box returned from Bing Maps/Google Maps are expressed using latitude/longitude values measured using the SRID 4326. Therefore, it seems to makes sense to use the **geography** datatype to represent the bounding box. A first shot at doing so might look something like this:

```
DECLARE @TopLeft geography = geography::Point(41, -109, 4326);
DECLARE @BotRight geography = geography::Point(37, -102, 4326);

DECLARE @BoundingBox geography;
SET @BoundingBox = geography::STPolyFromText('POLYGON((' 
+ CAST(@TopLeft.Long AS varchar(32)) + ' '+ CAST(@TopLeft.Lat AS varchar(32)) + ','
+ CAST(@TopLeft.Long AS varchar(32)) + ' '+ CAST(@BotRight.Lat AS varchar(32)) + ','
+ CAST(@BotRight.Long AS varchar(32)) + ' '+ CAST(@BotRight.Lat AS varchar(32)) +','
```

```
+ CAST(@BotRight.Long AS varchar(32)) +' ' + CAST(@TopLeft.Lat AS varchar(32)) + ','
+ CAST(@TopLeft.Long AS varchar(32)) + ' ' + CAST(@TopLeft.Lat AS varchar(32))
+ '))',
4326);
```

```
SELECT @BoundingBox.STAsText();
```

The result looks good:

```
POLYGON ((-109 41, -109 37, -102 37, -102 41, -109 41))
```

So now, to identify all those points from the database that should be shown on the current map view, we can go ahead and use the **STIntersects()** method to select all those points from the **allCountries** table that intersect this **geography** Polygon, right? Unfortunately, there is a subtle problem here that needs to be resolved.

Although the coordinate values of the corner points of the map bounding box are expressed in geographic coordinates of latitude and longitude, the default two-dimensional map view presented in the browser is flat. This means, by implication, that the data displayed on the screen has been *projected*. Given a little thought, this fact should be obvious—unless you have a very clever monitor capable of displaying images in three-dimensional space, all geospatial data on a computer display must have been projected. In which case, how come the coordinates of the corners of the bounding box were stated using *geographic* coordinates of latitude and longitude? Here's the twist: Google Maps and Microsoft Bing Maps actually use two coordinate systems—when supplying or retrieving data through the API, they use geographic coordinates of latitude and longitude based on WGS84, but when displaying data, they use a projected system referenced as SRID 3785.

Unlike most projected reference systems, SRID 3785 uses a Mercator projection based on a perfectly spherical model of the earth. This system has many beneficial properties that enable efficient tile referencing algorithms that I won't cover here, but the important thing to note is that it means that maps displayed using this projection portray lines of constant latitude (**parallels**) as parallel horizontal lines, and lines of constant longitude (**meridians**) as parallel vertical lines. In this example, this means that every point lying along the bottom edge of the map, which connects the points at (37,–109) and (37,–102), all have a latitude of 37. However, this is not true of the points lying on the bottom edge of the **geography** Polygon **@BoundingBox** created earlier. Remember that the **geography** datatype operates on an ellipsoidal model, so the edge between the points (37,–109) and (37,–102) represents the shortest distance between those two points on the surface of the reference ellipsoid in question (SRID 4326, in this case). The line connecting any two points in the **geography** datatype therefore represents the **great elliptic arc** between those two points, and does not follow the straight line portrayed on a projection.

What does this all mean for the application in this example? Consider a point located at latitude 37.0281 and longitude –107.419. These are the coordinates stored in the **allCountries** tables for the community of Arboles (**geonameid** 5412070), located at the northwest edge of Navajo Lake. Since the latitude of 37.0281 lies between 37 and 41, and the longitude value of –107.419 lies between –102 and –109, this point is contained in the map view used in this example, and we would expect it to be included in the result set retrieved from the database. However, this is not the result implied by the **STIntersects()** method of the **geography** datatype:

```
DECLARE @BoundingBox geography;
SET @BoundingBox = geography::STPolyFromText(
  'POLYGON ((-109 41, -109 37, -102 37, -102 41, -109 41))',
  4326);
```

```
SELECT
  name,
  location.STAsText(),
  location.STIntersects(@BoundingBox)
FROM
  allCountries
WHERE
  geonameid = 5412070;
```

The result **0** indicates that, despite being contained within the map window, the location of Arboles is not contained within the **geography** Polygon defined by the coordinates at the corners of the map. The reason might become more obvious if we take a visual look at what's happening here. Execute the following code listing and then switch to the Spatial Results tab in Management Studio:

```
DECLARE @BoundingBox geography;
SET @BoundingBox = geography::STPolyFromText(
  'POLYGON ((-109 41, -109 37, -102 37, -102 41, -109 41))',
  4326);

SELECT location
FROM allCountries
WHERE geonameid = 5412070
UNION ALL SELECT @BoundingBox;
```

The result is illustrated in Figure 10-10.

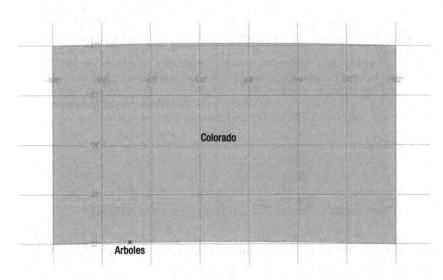

Figure 10-10. The Spatial Results tab displaying the bounding box of Colorado and the location of Arboles

Notice how the top and bottom edges of the **geography** Polygon follow the great elliptic arc that bends north away from the line of constant latitude between the two points. The result is that the point representing Arboles falls outside the Polygon, and is not included in the results of the **geography** **STIntersects()** method.

While the **geography** datatype gives the correct behavior in terms of the area drawn on an ellipsoidal surface, it does not give us the result we want in this case, which was to define a rectangle with "straight" lines representing the bounding box of the map. One solution to this problem is to create additional anchor points along the bottom and top edges of the Polygon, which will lead to a closer approximation of the projected map view, but will make our Polygon more complex and potentially slower to use in spatial queries.

An alternative solution could be to not use the spatial datatypes at all, but rather to create a simple numerical bounded query based on the limits defined by the map window. In other words, execute a query directly on the **latitude** and **longitude** columns as follows:

```
SELECT *
FROM allCountries
WHERE
  latitude > 37 AND latitude < 41
  AND
  longitude > -109 AND longitude < -102;
```

Not only will this avoid the problem of mixing flat/round data, but it will also perform significantly faster than the previous solution using the **geography** datatype if we were to add an index to the **longitude** and **latitude** columns. Of course, the problem with this solution is that it is only going to be of use in the very specific scenario used in this case—namely, when searching for *points* that lie within a *rectangular* search area. If we wanted to extend the application so that users could draw an irregular search area on the map, or if we wanted to search for LineStrings or Polygons that intersected the area, this approach would not work since we could no longer perform a query based on simple search criteria.

A better solution in this case is to store geometries using geographic coordinates of latitude and longitude, as before, but using the **geometry** datatype rather than the **geography** datatype. The **latitude** coordinate is mapped directly to the y coordinate, and the **longitude** coordinate is mapped to the x coordinate. Using this approach, the "straight" line between two points at equal latitude will follow the constant line of latitude between them, rather than the great elliptic arc as defined by the **geography** datatype. To implement this approach, execute the following code listing:

```
ALTER TABLE allCountries
ADD locationgeom geometry;
GO

UPDATE allCountries
SET locationgeom = geometry::STGeomFromWKB(location.STAsBinary(), location.STSrid);
GO
```

Selecting those **geometry** records that intersect the Polygon **POLYGON ((-109 41, -109 37, -102 37, -102 41, -109 41))** now gives the results expected. This is one example of a situation in which it is sometimes beneficial to break the general rule of always only using the **geography** datatype for geographic coordinates and the **geometry** datatype for projected coordinates. Other situations in which this can occur are when you need to rely on a function that is only available within the **geometry** datatype, such as **STConvexHull()** or **STRelate()**. If the distances involved are not great, the effect of distortion caused by the curvature of the earth can be ignored, and the greater functionality afforded by the **geometry** datatype offsets its associated loss of accuracy.

However, you should exercise great caution when using the **geometry** datatype to store geographic data in this way, because you may receive surprising results from certain operations. Consider the fact that the **STArea()** and **STLength()** methods of the **geometry** datatype return results in the unit of measurement in which coordinate values were defined. If using the **geometry** datatype to store coordinate values expressed in geographic coordinates of latitude and longitude, this means that lengths will be measured in degrees, and areas in degrees squared, which is almost certainly not what you want.

Spatial Indexing

Developers and DBAs alike know that a good index can make a significant amount of difference to the performance of a database application. Nowhere is this truer than in the realm of spatial indexes, where it is not uncommon to witness performance improvements exceeding 1,000 percent by creating a spatial index on even a small table of data. Of course, you can also get performance deterioration at the same rate by using a poorly chosen or nonexistent index, so it pays well to have an understanding of how spatial indexes work.

Spatial indexes operate very differently compared to the clustered and nonclustered indexes used for more conventional datatypes. In fact, columns of **geometry** and **geography** data can only be added to a spatial index, and spatial indexes can only be used for those two types of data. To understand why, in this section I'll first provide an overview of spatial indexing, and then look at some of the ways of optimizing a spatial index to provide optimal performance for your spatial applications.

How Does a Spatial Index Work?

When you execute a query involving a spatial predicate, such as **STIntersects()**, the SQL Server database engine applies that predicate in two stages:

- The **primary filter** identifies a set of candidate results that may fulfill the required criteria. The result set obtained from the primary filter is a superset—while it is guaranteed to contain all of the true results, it may also contain false positives.

- The **secondary filter** analyzes each of the records selected by the primary filter to determine whether they truly meet the criteria of the query. The secondary filter is more accurate, but slower than the primary filter.

The role of a spatial index is to provide an approximation of the location and shape of geometries so that they can be identified quickly in a primary filter. To do this, spatial indexes in SQL Server utilize a multilevel grid model, with four levels of grid nested inside each other, as illustrated in Figure 10-11.

The grid is overlaid on the area of space covered by the index, and every geometry lying in that area is then **tessellated** according to the grid. Rather than describing the detailed shape of the associated geometry, each entry in a spatial index comprises a reference to a grid cell, together with the primary key of the geometry that intersects that cell. Note that not *every* cell intersected by the geometry is included in the index—optimizations such as the **deepest-cell rule** and the **covering rule** are applied to ensure every entry in the spatial index describes the associated geometry in the greatest amount of detail while requiring the least amount of grid cells. For more information on these topics, please refer to a book dedicated to the subject, or refer to Books Online.

To see how the database engine uses the grid to satisfy a spatial query, consider the example from the previous section to retrieve all those points contained within the bounding box of a map:

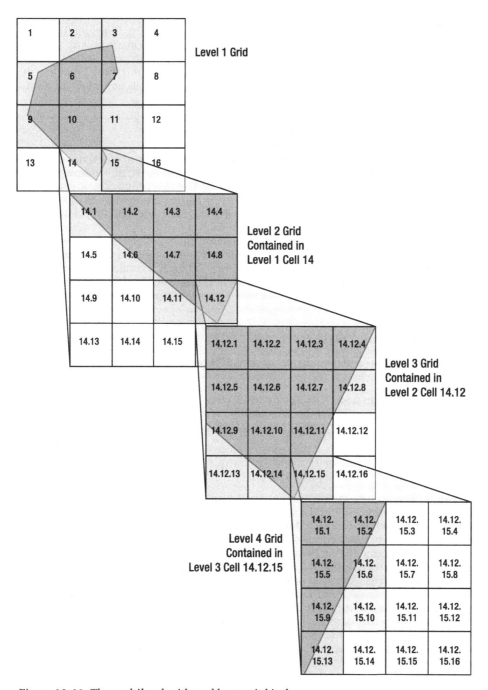

Figure 10-11. The multilevel grid used by spatial indexes

```
DECLARE @BoundingBox geography;
SET @BoundingBox = geography::STPolyFromText(
  'POLYGON ((-109 41, -109 37, -102 37, -102 41, -109 41))',
  4326);

SELECT
  name,
  location.STAsText()
FROM
  allCountries
WHERE
  location.STIntersects(@BoundingBox) = 1;
```

The **location** column is included in the **idxallCountries geography** index, and the predicate **location.STIntersects(@BoundingBox) = 1** supports the use of a spatial index, so the execution plan for this query can take advantage of a primary filter based on the index. To do so, the **@BoundingBox** parameter is first tessellated according to the same grid as the **idxallCountries** index on the **location** column. The grid cells occupied by each cell in the index can then be compared to the grid cells occupied by the **@BoundingBox**. The outcome of the primary filter can lead to one of three results:

- If a geometry in the **location** column has no index cells in common with the cells occupied by **@BoundingBox**, it can be discarded by the primary filter, since the geometries themselves cannot intersect.

- If the geometry occupies the whole of a grid cell in the index occupied by **@BoundingBox**, it is certain to intersect the **@BoundingBox** geometry itself. This row can therefore definitely be included in the result set without need to call the secondary filter. This is known as internal filtering.

- If the geometry only partially occupies a grid cell occupied by **@BoundingBox**, it cannot be determined for certain whether that cell intersects the **@BoundingBox**. In these cases, the geometries must be passed to the secondary filter, which involves calling the **STIntersects()** method itself.

To get the best performance from a spatial query, the ideal goal is to get as much of the processing done by the primary filter, and reduce the number of times that the secondary filter needs to be called. This means ensuring that as many rows as possible are either discarded completely by the primary filter or definitely included based on the primary filter alone. Achieving this goal requires tuning the grid properties to best match the data in the underlying dataset and the type of queries run against that data.

Optimizing the Grid

If a spatial index is to be effective in acting as a primary filter for the results of a spatial query, not only must it be fast, but it must also minimize the number of false positive results returned. How well an index succeeds in meeting these two aims is largely determined by the values chosen for the grid resolution, the bounding box, and the cells per object parameters of the index.

The optimum value for each of these parameters depends very much on the exact distribution of the underlying dataset in question. However, in the following section I'll give you some general ideas to bear in mind when determining the settings for a spatial index.

> ■ **Tip** You can have up to 249 spatial indexes on the same table, and you may create multiple spatial indexes on the same column, using different settings for each index. You may find this useful in order to index unevenly distributed data.

Grid resolution: Choosing the correct grid resolution—the number of cells contained at each level of the grid—is a matter of balancing the degree of precision offered by the index (the "tightness of fit" around features) with the number of grid cells required to obtain that precision. The resolution at each level of the grid may be set independently to one of three resolutions: `LOW` corresponds to a 4×4 grid, `MEDIUM` corresponds to an 8×8 grid, and `HIGH` corresponds to a 16×16 grid. If you set a low grid resolution (i.e., the index contains a small number of relatively large grid cells), then the primary filter may return more false positives—features that intersect the grid cell that don't actually intersect the geometry in question. These false positives will lead to more work having to be done by the secondary filter, leading to query degradation. However, if you set a high grid resolution (i.e., the index contains a large number of grid cells, but each one is individually small), then the resulting index will contain more grid cell entries for each geometry, which may mean that it will take longer to query the index, also degrading query performance. Another effect of a high resolution may be that the number of cells required to fully tessellate the geometry exceeds the `CELLS_PER_OBJECT` limit, in which case tessellation will not be fully complete.

Bounding box: The bounding box of a spatial index specifies the area of space that will be tessellated by the grid. Specifying a smaller bounding box but maintaining the same number of grid cells will lead to each individual grid cell being smaller, creating a more precise fit around any features and making the primary filter more accurate. However, if you restrict the extent of the bounding box too much, you may find that you exclude some outlying features from the index altogether. For the **geography** datatype, there is no explicit bounding box, as every **geography** index is assumed to cover the whole globe.

Cells per object: The `CELLS_PER_OBJECT` parameter allows you to explicitly state the maximum number of grid cells that will be stored to describe each feature in the spatial index. The optimum number of cells per object is intricately linked to the resolution of the cells used at each level; a higher-resolution grid will contain smaller cells, which may mean that more cells are required to fully cover the object at a given level of the grid. If the `CELLS_PER_OBJECT` limit is set too low, then each index entry might not be allowed to contain the total number of cells required to describe a geometry, based on the deepest-cell rule and the covering rule. In such cases, the grid cells will not be fully subdivided and the index entry will not be as accurate as it can be. If the `CELLS_PER_OBJECT` limit is set too high, then each index entry will be allowed to grow to contain a large number of cells. This may lead to a more accurate index, but a slower query, thereby negating the purpose of using a spatial index in the first place.

To understand the interaction between these different parameters, let's consider the `idxallCountries` index created earlier this chapter. This index used the default parameters of `MEDIUM` grid resolution at all four levels, and 16 cells per object. Indexes that are tessellated using the **geography** grid do not have an explicit bounding box, as they implicitly cover the whole globe.

To assess the effectiveness of the **idxallCountries** index, we could simply obtain some performance timings using queries with different index settings. However, rather than rely on this trial-and-error approach, SQL Server 2008 comes with two very helpful stored procedures— **sp_help_spatial_geometry_index** and **sp_help_spatial_geography_index**—which provide a variety of useful information to help diagnose how a spatial index is working.

To use either of these procedures, you supply parameters for the table and index name to be tested, together with a **query sample**—a **geography** or **geometry** instance that will be tessellated according to the settings used by the index. Since the **idxallCountries** index uses the **location** column of the **geography** datatype, we will use the corresponding **sp_help_geography_index** procedure, supplying the **geography** bounding box created earlier as a query sample, as shown in the following code listing:

```
EXEC sp_help_spatial_geography_index
@tabname = allCountries,
@indexname = idxallCountries,
@verboseoutput = 1,
@query_sample = 'POLYGON ((-109 41, -109 37, -102 37, -102 41, -109 41))';
```

There are lots of rows of detail in the output, but let's just focus on some of the important ones from a performance point of view:

Base_Table_Rows 6906119

This value very simply tells us the total number of rows in the base table, just as would be reported by `SELECT COUNT(*) FROM allCountries`. The important thing to bear in mind is that, without a spatial index on this table, a query to find out which rows lie within the chosen query sample would have to call the `STIntersects()` method on every one of these 6.9 million rows. Fortunately, this is not the case, because the spatial index can provide a primary filter of these records, as shown in the following rows returned by the procedure:

Number_Of_Rows_Selected_By_Primary_Filter   49018

Number_Of_Rows_Selected_By_Internal_Filter   38913

Number_Of_Times_Secondary_Filter_Is_Called   10105

Based on the primary filter of the table, 49,018 records were selected as candidates for this query sample. This is less than 0.71 percent of the total number of rows in the table. Of these candidate rows, 38,913 rows could be selected as certain results straight away without need to call the secondary filter. For example, in the case of an intersection predicate, if a point lies in a grid cell that is completely covered by the query sample, the point is certain to be intersected by that geometry, and so the `STIntersects()` method need never be used. The inclusion of output rows that can be selected based on the primary filter alone is known as an **internal filter**. In this case, 79.385 percent of the primary filter rows could be selected by the internal filter.

The remaining 10,105 records selected by the primary filter lay in index cells that were only partially intersected by the geometry specified in the query sample, and so had to rely on the secondary filter to confirm whether they should be selected or not.

After applying both the primary and secondary filters, the confirmed **Number_Of_Rows_Output** was 44,840. Note that the final number-of-rows output is less than the number of rows initially selected by the primary filter, as some of those rows would have been false positives that were then eliminated by the secondary filter.

Number_Of_Rows_Output	44840
Internal_Filter_Efficiency	86.7818911685995
Primary_Filter_Efficiency	91.4766004324942

The important thing to bear in mind is that, whatever index settings you have (including none), you will always get the same final results from a given spatial query. The only difference is in how those rows are identified. In this case, the **Primary_Filter_Efficiency** measure indicates that 91.476 percent of rows selected by the primary filter were included in the final results. The **Internal_Filter_Efficiency** was 86.78 percent, indicating the percentage of output rows selected just from the internal filter. The objective when tuning a spatial index is to maximize both of these measures.

Now let's consider what happens when we create a new index, using **HIGH** resolution at all four grid levels:

```
CREATE SPATIAL INDEX idxallCountriesHigh
ON allCountries(location) USING GEOGRAPHY_GRID
WITH (
  GRIDS =(
    LEVEL_1 = HIGH,
    LEVEL_2 = HIGH,
    LEVEL_3 = HIGH,
    LEVEL_4 = HIGH),
  CELLS_PER_OBJECT = 16);
```

Once again, we'll examine the properties of this index using the **sp_help_spatial_geography_index** procedure:

```
EXEC sp_help_spatial_geography_index
@tabname = allCountries,
@indexname = idxallCountriesHigh,
@verboseoutput = 1,
@query_sample = 'POLYGON ((-109 41, -109 37, -102 37, -102 41, -109 41))';
```

Unsurprisingly, the **Base_Table_Rows** value remains unchanged at 6,906,119, as does the total number-of-rows output from the query, 44,840. The number of rows selected by the primary filter remains very similar at 49,157, and the primary filter efficiency barely changes—from 91.4766 to 91.21793. However, there is a very important distinction between the indexes, as shown in the following rows:

Number_Of_Rows_Selected_By_Internal_Filter	25333
Number_Of_Times_Secondary_Filter_Is_Called	23824
Percentage_Of_Primary_Filter_Rows_Selected_By_Internal_Filter	51.5348780438188
Internal_Filter_Efficiency	56.4964317573595

When using a MEDIUM grid resolution, 79.385 percent of the candidate rows selected by the primary filter could be automatically included in the result set. The secondary filter therefore only needed to be called on the remaining 10,105 rows. However, when set to HIGH resolution, only 51.53 percent of the primary filter could be preselected by the internal filter. Thus, the expensive secondary filter had to be called twice as many times.

At first consideration, this may seem illogical. One would assume that when indexing a table of Points, in which each geometry can only intersect a single cell (or at most four cells, if the Point were placed on a corner where cells meet), the HIGH grid resolution must provide the best fit. Each Point geometry would only require a single cell in the index, and by using the HIGH resolution, that cell would be as granular as possible.

However, the important thing to realize is that, in order to satisfy a spatial query, the spatial predicate against which the geometries are being compared (the query sample, as defined by the stored procedure) must also be tessellated using the same index settings as the base table itself. In this case, @BoundingBox is quite a large Polygon representing the state of Colorado, which requires a great number of cells to fully cover. Since this exceeds the CELLS_PER_OBJECT limit, tessellation is stopped and the fit is not as good as it could have been. In this example, the MEDIUM resolution grid provides a more accurate index, and hence better performance, than the HIGH resolution grid.

Unfortunately, there are very few general rules to follow with regard to determining optimum spatial index settings, since they are very much dependent on the exact distribution of the data in question, together with the nature of the queries run against that data. Tuning spatial indexes requires a large degree of trial and error, but the stored procedures introduced here can provide valuable statistics to assess the performance of an index to help the process.

Summary

Spatial data is an exciting and growing area of database development. As more applications and services become location-aware, there is a requirement for all types of data to be stored with associated spatial information in a structured, searchable manner.

The **geography** and **geometry** datatypes in SQL Server 2008 provide a powerful, standards-compliant way of storing, retrieving, and performing calculations against spatial data using either a flat or ellipsoidal model. However, the complexity and uniqueness of spatial data means that specific approaches must be taken to ensure that spatial queries remain performant. Spatial indexes can be used to provide a primary filter of data to satisfy a spatial query, reducing the amount of processing required to perform expensive accurate spatial operations such as **STIntersects()**.

■ ■ ■

CHAPTER 11

Working with Temporal Data

It's probably fair to say that time is a critical piece of information in almost every useful database. Imagining a database that lacks a time component is tantamount to imagining life without time passing; it simply doesn't make sense. Without a time axis, it is impossible to describe the number of purchases made last month, the average overnight temperature of the warehouse, or the maximum duration that callers were required to hold the line when calling in for technical support.

Although utterly important to our data, few developers commit to really thinking in depth about the intricacies required to process temporal data successfully, which in many cases require more thought than at first you might imagine.

In this chapter, I will delve into the ins and outs of dealing with time in SQL Server. I will explain some of the different types of temporal requirements you might encounter and describe how best to tackle some common—and surprisingly complex—temporal queries.

Modeling Time-Based Information

When thinking of "temporal" data in SQL Server, the scenario that normally springs to mind is a `datetime` column representing the time that some action took place, or is due to take place in the future. However, a `datetime` column is only one of several possible ways that temporal data can be implemented. Some of the categories of time-based information that may be modeled in SQL Server are as follows:

- **Instance-based data** is concerned with recording the instant in time at which an event occurs. As in the example described previously, instance-based data is typically recorded using a single column of `datetime` values, although alternative datatypes, including the `datetime2` and `datetimeoffset` types introduced in SQL Server 2008, may also be used to record instance data at different levels of granularity. Scenarios in which you might model an instance include the moment a user logs into a system, the moment a customer makes a purchase, and the exact time any other kind of event takes place that you might need to record in the database. The key factor to recognize is that you're describing a specific instant in time, based on the precision of the data type you use.

- **Interval-based data** extends on the idea of an instance by describing the period of time between a specified start point and an endpoint. Depending on your requirements, intervals may be modeled using two temporal columns (for example, using the `datetime` type), or a single temporal column together with another column (usually numeric) that represents the amount of time that passed since that time. A subset of interval-based data is the idea of **duration**, which records only the length of time for which an event lasts, irrespective of when it occurred. Durations may be modeled using a single numeric column.

- **Period-based data** is similar to interval-based data, but it is generally used to answer slightly different sorts of questions. When working with an interval or duration, the question is "How long?" whereas for a period, the question is "When?" Examples of periods include "next month," "yesterday," "New Year's Eve," and "the holiday season." Although these are similar to—and can be represented by—intervals, the mindset of working with periods is slightly different, and it is therefore important to realize that other options exist for modeling them. For more information on periods, see the section "Defining Periods Using Calendar Tables" later in this chapter.

- **Bitemporal data** is temporal data that falls into any of the preceding categories, but also includes an additional time component (known as a **valid time**, or more loosely, an **as-of date**) indicating when the data was considered to be valid. This data pattern is commonly used in data warehouses, both for slowly changing dimensions and for updating semiadditive fact data. When querying the database bitemporally, the question transforms from "On a certain day, what happened?" to "As of a certain day, what did we think happened on a certain (other) day?" The question might also be phrased as "What is the most recent idea we have of what happened on a certain day?" This mindset can take a bit of thought to really get; see the section "Managing Bitemporal Data" later in this chapter for more information.

SQL Server's Date/Time Data Types

The first requirement for successfully dealing with temporal data in SQL Server is an understanding of what the DBMS offers in terms of native date/time data types. Prior to SQL Server 2008, there wasn't really a whole lot of choice when it came to storing temporal data in SQL Server—the only temporal datatypes available were **datetime** and **smalldatetime** and, in practice, even though it required less storage, few developers used **smalldatetime** owing to its reduced granularity and range of values.

SQL Server 2008 still supports both **datetime** and **smalldatetime**, but also offers a range of new temporal data types. The full list of supported temporal datatypes is listed in Table 11-1.

Table 11-1. Date/Time Datatypes Supported by SQL Server 2008

Datatype	Range	Resolution	Storage
datetime	January 1, 1753, 00:00:00.000– December 31, 9999, 23:59:59.997	3.33ms	8 bytes
datetime2	January 1, 0001, 00:00:00.0000000–December 31, 9999, 23:59:59.9999999	100 nanoseconds (ns)	6–8 bytes
smalldatetime	January 1, 1900, 00:00–June 6, 2079, 23:59	1 minute	4 bytes

datetimeoffset	January 1, 0001, 00:00:00.0000000–December 31, 9999, 23:59:59.9999999	100ns	8–10 bytes
date	January 1, 0001–December 31, 9999	1 day	3 bytes
time	00:00:00.0000000–23:59:59.9999999	100ns	3–5 bytes

Knowing the date ranges and storage requirements of each datatype is great; however, working with temporal data involves quite a bit more than that. What developers actually need to understand when working with SQL Server's date/time types is what input and output formats should be used, and how to manipulate the types in order to create various commonly needed queries. This section covers both of these issues.

Input Date Formats

There is really only one rule to remember when working with SQL Server's date/time types: when accepting data from a client, *always* avoid ambiguous date formats! The unfortunate fact is that, depending on how it is written, a given date can be interpreted differently by different people.

As an example, by a remarkable stroke of luck, I happen to be writing this chapter on August 7, 2009. It's nearly 12:35 p.m. Why is this of particular interest? Because if I write the current time and date, it forms an ascending numerical sequence as follows:

12:34:56 07/08/09

I live in England, so I tend to write and think of dates using the dd/mm/yy format, as in the preceding example. However, people in the United States would have already enjoyed this rather neat time pattern last month, on July 8. And if you're from one of various Asian countries (Japan, for instance), you might have seen this sequence occur nearly two years ago, on August 9, 2007. Much like the inhabitants of these locales, SQL Server tries to follow local format specifications when handling input date strings, meaning that on occasion users do not get the date they expect from a given input.

Luckily, there is a solution to this problem. Just as with many other classes of problems in which lack of standardization is an issue, the International Standards Organization (ISO) has chosen to step in. **ISO 8601** is an international standard date/time format, which SQL Server (and other software) will automatically detect and use, independent of the local server settings. The full ISO format is specified as follows:

yyyy-mm-ddThh:mi:ss.mmm

yyyy is the four-digit year, which is key to the format; any time SQL Server sees a four-digit year first, it assumes that the ISO format is being used. **mm** and **dd** are month and day, respectively, and **hh**, **mi**, **ss**, and **mmm** are hours, minutes, seconds, and milliseconds. According to the standard, the hyphens and the **T** are both optional, but if you include the hyphens, you must also include the **T**.

The **datetime**, **datetime2**, **smalldatetime**, and **datetimeoffset** datatypes store both a date and time component, whereas the **date** and **time** datatypes store only a date or a time, respectively. However, one important point to note is that whatever datatype is being used, both the time and date elements of any input are optional. If no time portion is provided to a datatype that records a time component, SQL Server will use midnight as the default; if the date portion is not specified in the input to one of the datatypes that records a date, SQL Server will use January 1, 1900. In a similar vein, if a time component is provided as an input to the **date** datatype, or a date is supplied to the **time** datatype, that value will simply be ignored.

Each of the following are valid, unambiguous date/time formats that can be used when supplying inputs for any of the temporal datatypes:

```
--Unseparated date and time
20090501 13:45:03
```

```
--Date with dashes, and time specified with T (ISO 8601)
2009-05-01T13:45:03
```

```
--Date only
20090501
```

```
--Time only
13:45:03
```

■ **Caution** If you choose to use a dash separator between the year, month, and day values in the ISO 8601 format, you *must* include the T character before the time component. To demonstrate the importance of this character, compare the results of the following: SET LANGUAGE British; SELECT CAST('2003-12-09 00:00:00' AS datetime), CAST('2003-12-09T00:00:00' AS datetime).

By always using one of the preceding formats—and always making sure that clients send dates according to that format—you can ensure that the correct dates will always be used by SQL Server. Remember that SQL Server does not store the original input date string; the date is converted and stored internally in a binary format. So if invalid dates do end up in the database, there will be no way of reconstituting them from just the data.

Unfortunately, it's not always possible to get data in exactly the right format before it hits the database. SQL Server provides two primary mechanisms that can help when dealing with nonstandard date/time formats: an extension to the **CONVERT** function that allows specification of a date "style," and a runtime setting called **DATEFORMAT**.

To use **CONVERT** to create an instance of date/time data from a nonstandard date, use the third parameter of the function to specify the date's format. The following code block shows how to create a **date** for the British/French and US styles:

```
--British/French style
SELECT CONVERT(date, '01/02/2003', 103);
```

```
--US style
SELECT CONVERT(date, '01/02/2003', 101);
```

Style 103 produces the date "February 1, 2003," whereas style 101 produces the date, "January 2, 2003." By using these styles, you can more easily control how date/time input is processed, and explicitly tell SQL Server how to handle input strings. There are over 20 different styles documented; see the topic "CAST and CONVERT (Transact-SQL)" in SQL Server 2008 Books Online for a complete list.

The other commonly used option for controlling the format of input date strings is the **DATEFORMAT** setting. **DATEFORMAT** allows you to specify the order in which day, month, and year appear in the input date format, using the specifiers **D**, **M**, and **Y**. The following T-SQL is equivalent to the previous example that used **CONVERT**:

```
--British/French style
SET DATEFORMAT DMY;
SELECT CONVERT(date, '01/02/2003');

--US style
SET DATEFORMAT MDY;
SELECT CONVERT(date, '01/02/2003');
```

There is really not much of a difference between using **DATEFORMAT** and **CONVERT** to correct nonstandard inputs. **DATEFORMAT** may be cleaner in some cases as it only needs to be specified once per connection, but **CONVERT** offers slightly more control due to the number of styles that are available. In the end, you should choose whichever option makes the particular code you're working on more easily readable, testable, and maintainable.

■ **Note** Using **SET DATEFORMAT** within a stored procedure will cause a recompile to occur whenever the procedure is executed. This may cause a performance problem in some cases, so make sure to test carefully before deploying solutions to production environments.

Output Date Formatting

The **CONVERT** function is not only useful for specification of input date/time string formats. It is also commonly used to format dates for output.

Before continuing, I feel that a quick disclaimer is in order: it's generally not a good idea to do formatting work in the database. By formatting dates into strings in the data layer, you may reduce the ease with which stored procedures can be reused. This is because it may force applications that require differing date/time formats to convert the strings back into native date/time objects, and then reformat them as strings again. Such additional work on the part of the application is probably unnecessary, and there are very few occasions in which it really makes sense to send dates back to an application formatted as strings. One example that springs to mind is when doing data binding to a grid or other object that doesn't support the date format you need—but that is a rare situation.

Just like when working with input formatting, the main T-SQL function used for date/time output formatting is **CONVERT**. The same set of styles that can be used for input can also be used for output formats; the only difference is that the function is converting from an instance of a date/time type into a string, rather than the other way around. The following T-SQL shows how to format the current date as a string in both US and British/French styles:

```
--British/French style
SELECT CONVERT(varchar(50), GETDATE(), 103);

--US style
SELECT CONVERT(varchar(50), GETDATE(), 101);
```

The set of styles available for the **CONVERT** function is somewhat limited, and may not be enough for all situations. Fortunately, SQL Server's CLR integration provides a solution to this problem. The .NET **System.DateTime** class includes extremely flexible string-formatting capabilities that can be harnessed using a CLR scalar user-defined function (UDF). The following method exposes the necessary functionality:

```
public static SqlString FormatDate(
    SqlDateTime Date,
    SqlString FormatString)
{
    DateTime theDate = Date.Value;
    return new SqlString(theDate.ToString(FormatString.ToString()));
}
```

This UDF converts the **SqlDateTime** instance into an instance of **System.DateTime**, and then uses the overloaded **ToString** method to format the date/time as a string. The method accepts a wide array of formatting directives, all of which are fully documented in the Microsoft MSDN Library. As a quick example, the following invocation of the method formats the current date/time with the month part first, followed by a four-digit year, and finally the day:

```
SELECT dbo.FormatDate(GETDATE(), 'MM yyyy dd');
```

Keep in mind that the **ToString** method's formatting overload is case sensitive. **MM**, for instance, is not the same as **mm**, and you may get unexpected results if you are not careful.

Efficiently Querying Date/Time Columns

Knowing how to format dates for input and output is a good first step, but the real goal of any database system is to allow the user to query the data to answer business questions. Querying date/time data in SQL Server has some interesting pitfalls, but for the most part they're easily avoidable if you understand how the DBMS treats temporal data.

To start things off, create the following table:

```
CREATE TABLE VariousDates
(
    ADate datetime NOT NULL,
    PRIMARY KEY (ADate) WITH (IGNORE_DUP_KEY = ON)
);
GO
```

Now we'll insert some data into the table. The following T-SQL will insert 85,499 rows into the table, with dates spanning from February through November of 2010:

```
WITH Numbers
AS
(
    SELECT DISTINCT number
    FROM master..spt_values
    WHERE number BETWEEN 1001 AND 1256
)
INSERT INTO VariousDates ( ADate )
SELECT
    CASE x.n
        WHEN 1 THEN
            DATEADD(millisecond,
                POWER(a.number, 2) * b.number,
                DATEADD(day, a.number-1000, '20100201'))
        WHEN 2 THEN
            DATEADD(millisecond,
                b.number-1001,
                DATEADD(day, a.number-1000, '20100213'))
    END
FROM Numbers a, Numbers b
CROSS JOIN
(
    SELECT 1
    UNION ALL
    SELECT 2
) x (n);
GO
```

Once the data has been inserted, the next logical step is of course to query it. You might first want to ask the question "What is the minimum date value in the table?" The following query uses the **MIN** aggregate to answer that question:

```
SELECT MIN(ADate)
FROM VariousDates;
GO
```

This query returns one row, with the value **2010-02-13 14:36:43.000**. But perhaps you'd like to know what other times from February 13, 2010 are in the table. A first shot at that query might be something like the following:

```
SELECT *
FROM VariousDates
WHERE ADate = '20100213';
GO
```

If you run this query, you might be surprised to find out that instead of seeing all rows for February 13, 2010, zero rows are returned. The reason for this is that the **ADate** column uses the **datetime** type, which, as stated earlier, includes both a date and a time component. When this query is evaluated and the search argument **ADate = '20100213'** is processed, SQL Server sees that the **datetime ADate** column is being compared to the **varchar** string **'20100213'**. Based on SQL Server's rules for data type precedence, the string is converted to **datetime** before being compared; and because the string includes no time portion, the default time of **00:00:00.000** is used. To see this conversion in action, try the following T-SQL:

```
SELECT CONVERT(datetime, '20100213');
GO
```

When this code is run, the default time portion is automatically added, and the output of this **SELECT** is the value **2010-02-13 00:00:00.000**. Clearly, querying based on the implicit conversion between this string and the **datetime** type is ineffective—unless you only want values for midnight.

There are many potential solutions to this problem. We could of course alter the table schema to use the **date** datatype for the **ADate** column rather than **datetime**. Doing so would facilitate easy queries on a particular date, but would lose the time element associated with each record. This solution is therefore only really suitable in situations where you never need to know the time associated with a record, but just the date on which it occurred.

A better solution is to try to control the conversion from **datetime** to **date** in a slightly different way. Many developers' first reaction is to try to avoid the conversion of the string to an instance of **datetime** altogether, by converting the **ADate** column itself and using a conversion style that eliminates the time portion. The following query is an example of one such way of doing this:

```
SELECT *
FROM VariousDates
WHERE CONVERT(varchar(20), ADate, 112) = '20100213';
```

Running this query, you will find that the correct data is returned; you'll see all rows from February 13, 2010. While getting back correct results is a wonderful thing, there is unfortunately a major problem that might not be too obvious with the small sample data used in this example. The table's index on the **ADate** column is based on **ADate** as it is natively typed—in other words, as **datetime**. The table does not have an index for **ADate** converted to **varchar(20)** using style **112** (or any other style, for that matter). As a result, this query is unable to seek an index, and SQL Server is forced to scan every row of the table, convert each **ADate** value to a string, and then compare it to the date string. This produces the execution plan shown in Figure 11-1, which has an estimated cost of 0.229923.

SELECT
Cost: 0%

Clustered Index Scan (Clustered)
[VariousDates].[PK_VariousD_B5C54...
Cost: 100%

Figure 11-1. Converting the date/time column to a string does not result in a good execution plan.

Similar problems arise with any method that attempts to use string manipulation functions to truncate the time portion from the end of the **datetime** string.

Generally speaking, performing a calculation or conversion of a column in a query precludes any index on that column from being used. However, there is an exception to this rule: in the special case of a query predicate of **datetime**, **datetime2**, or **datetimeoffset** type that is converted (or **CAST**) to a **date**, the query optimizer can still rely on index ordering to satisfy the query.

To demonstrate this unusual but surprisingly useful behavior, we can rewrite the previous query as follows:

```
SELECT *
```

```
FROM VariousDates
WHERE CAST(ADate AS date) = '20100213';
```

This query performs much better, producing the execution plan shown in Figure 11-2, which has a clustered index seek with an estimated cost of 0.0032831 (1/68 the estimated cost of the previous version!)

SELECT ⟵————— Clustered Index Seek (Clustered)
Cost: 0%   [VariousDates].[PK_VariousD_B5C54...
                            Cost: 100%

Figure 11-2. Querying date/time columns CAST to date type allows the query engine to take advantage of an index seek.

CASTing a **datetime** to **date** is all very well for querying distinct dates within a **datetime** range, but what if we wanted to query a range of time that did not represent a whole number of days? Suppose, for instance, that we were to divide each day into two 12-hour shifts: one from midnight to midday, and the other from midday to midnight. A query based on this data might look like this:

```
SELECT *
FROM VariousDates
WHERE ADate BETWEEN '20100213 12:00:00' AND '20100214 00:00:00';
```

This query, like the last, is able to use an efficient clustered index seek, but it has a problem. The **BETWEEN** operator is inclusive on either end, meaning that X **BETWEEN** Y **AND** Z expands to X **>=** Y **AND** X **<=** Z. If there happens to be a row for February 14, 2010 at midnight (and the data in the sample table does indeed include such a row), that row will be included in the results of both this query and the query to return data for the following shift. Luckily, solving this problem is easy; when performing range queries of time data, don't use **BETWEEN**. Instead, always use the fully expanded version, inclusive of the start of the interval, and *exclusive* of the end value:

```
SELECT *
FROM VariousDates
WHERE
    ADate >= '20100213 12:00:00'
    AND ADate < '20100214 00:00:00';
```

This pattern can be used to query any kind of date and time range and is actually quite flexible. In the next section, you will learn how to extend this pattern to find all of "today's" rows, "this month's" rows, and other similar requirements.

Date/Time Calculations

The query pattern presented in the previous section to return all rows for a given date works and returns the correct results, but is rather overly static as-is. Expecting all date range queries to have hard-coded values for the input dates is neither a realistic expectation nor a very maintainable solution. By using

SQL Server's date calculation functions, input dates can be manipulated in order to dynamically come up with whatever ranges are necessary for a given query.

The two primary functions that are commonly used to perform date/time calculations are **DATEDIFF** and **DATEADD**. The first returns the difference between two dates; the second adds (or subtracts) time from an existing date. Each of these functions takes granularity as a parameter and can operate at any level between milliseconds and years.

DATEDIFF takes three parameters: the time granularity that should be used to compare the two input dates, the start date, and the end date. For example, to find out how many hours elapsed between midnight on February 13, 2010, and midnight on February 14, 2010, the following query could be used:

```
SELECT DATEDIFF(hour, '20100113', '20100114');
```

The result, as you might expect, is **24**. Note that I mentioned that this query compares the two dates, both at midnight, even though neither of the input strings contains a time. Again, I want to stress that any time you use a string as an input where a date/time type is expected, it will be implicitly converted by SQL Server.

It's also important to note that **DATEDIFF** maintains the idea of "start" and "end" times, and the result will change if you reverse the two. Changing the previous query so that February 14 is passed before February 13 results in the output of **-24**.

The **DATEADD** function takes three parameters: the time granularity, the amount of time to add, and the input date. For example, the following query adds 24 hours to midnight on February 13, 2010, resulting in an output of **2010-01-14 00:00:00.000**:

```
SELECT DATEADD(hour, 24, '20100113');
```

DATEADD will also accept negative amounts, which will lead to the relevant amount of time being subtracted rather than added, as in this case.

Truncating the Time Portion of a datetime Value

In versions of SQL Server prior to SQL Server 2008, the limited choice of only **datetime** and **smalldatetime** temporal datatypes meant that it was not possible to store a date value without an associated time component. As a result, developers came up with a number of methods to "truncate" **datetime** values so that, without changing the underlying datatype, they could be interrogated as dates without consideration of the time component. These methods generally involve rounding the time portion of a **datetime** value down to 00:00:00 (midnight), so that the only remaining significant figures of the result represent the day, month, and year of the associated value.

Although, with the introduction of the **date** datatype, it is no longer necessary to perform such truncation, the "rounding" approach taken is still very useful as a basis for other temporal queries. To demonstrate, let me first break down the truncation process into its component parts:

1. First, you must decide on the level of granularity to which you'd like to round the result. For instance, if you want to remove the seconds and milliseconds of a time value, you'd round down using minutes. Likewise, to remove the entire time portion, you'd round down using days.

2. Once you've decided on a level of granularity, pick a reference date/time. I generally use midnight on **1900-01-01**, but you can use any date/time within the range of the data type you're working with.

3. Using the **DATEDIFF** function, find the difference between the reference date/time and the date/time you want to truncate, at the level of granularity you've chosen.

4. Finally, use **DATEADD** to add the output from the **DATEDIFF** function to the same reference date/time that you used to find the difference. The result will be the truncated value of the original date/time.

Walking through an example should make this a bit clearer. Assume that you want to start with **2010-04-23 13:45:43.233** and truncate the time portion (in other words, come out with **2010-04-23** at midnight). The granularity used will be days, since that is the lowest level of granularity above the units of time (milliseconds, seconds, minutes, and hours). The following T-SQL can be used to determine the number of days between the reference date of **1900-01-01** and the input date:

```
DECLARE @InputDate datetime = '20100423 13:45:43.233';
SELECT DATEDIFF(day, '19000101', @InputDate);
```

Running this T-SQL, we discover that **40289** days passed between the reference date and the input date. Using **DATEADD**, that number can be added to the reference date:

```
SELECT DATEADD(day, 40289, '19000101');
```

The result of this operation is the desired truncation: **2010-04-23 00:00:00.000**. Because only the number of days was added back to the reference date—with no time portion—the date was rounded down and the time portion eliminated. Of course, you don't have to run this T-SQL step by step; in a real application, you'd probably combine everything into one inline statement:

```
SELECT DATEADD(day, DATEDIFF(day, '19000101', @InputDate), '19000101');
```

Because it is a very common requirement to round down date/time values to different levels of granularity—to find the first day of the week, the first day of the month, and so on—you might find it helpful to encapsulate this logic in a reusable function with common named units of time, as follows:

```
CREATE FUNCTION DateRound (
  @Unit varchar(32),
  @InputDate datetime
) RETURNS datetime
AS
BEGIN
  DECLARE @RefDate datetime = '19000101';
  SET @Unit = UPPER(@Unit);
RETURN
    CASE(@Unit)
      WHEN 'DAY' THEN
  DATEADD(day, DATEDIFF(day, @RefDate, @InputDate), @RefDate)
      WHEN 'MONTH' THEN
        DATEADD(month, DATEDIFF(month, @RefDate, @InputDate), @RefDate)
      WHEN 'YEAR' THEN
        DATEADD(year, DATEDIFF(year, @RefDate, @InputDate), @RefDate)
      WHEN 'WEEK' THEN
        DATEADD(week, DATEDIFF(week, @RefDate, @InputDate), @RefDate)
      WHEN 'QUARTER' THEN
        DATEADD(quarter, DATEDIFF(quarter, @RefDate, @InputDate), @RefDate)
```

```
    END
END;
GO
```

The following code illustrates how the **DateRound()** function can be used with a date/time value representing 08:48 a.m. on August 20, 2009:

```
SELECT
dbo.DateRound('Day', '20090820 08:48'),
dbo.DateRound('Month', '20090820 08:48'),
dbo.DateRound('Year', '20090820 08:48'),
dbo.DateRound('Week', '20090820 08:48'),
dbo.DateRound('Quarter', '20090820 08:48');
```

This code returns the following results:

2009-08-20 00:00:00.000
2009-08-01 00:00:00.000
2009-01-01 00:00:00.000
2009-08-17 00:00:00.000
2009-07-01 00:00:00.000

■ **Note** Developers who have experience with Oracle databases may be familiar with the Oracle PL/SQL TRUNC() method, which provides similar functionality to the DateRound function described here.

Finding Relative Dates

Once you understand the basic pattern for truncation described in the previous section, you can modify it to come up with any combination of dates. Suppose, for example, that you want to find the last day of the month. One method is to find the first day of the month, add an additional month, and then subtract one day:

```
SELECT DATEADD(day, -1, DATEADD(month, DATEDIFF(month, '19000101',
@InputDate) + 1, '19000101'));
```

An alternative method to find the last day of the month is to add a whole number of months to a reference date that is in itself the last day of a month. For instance, you can use a reference date of **1900-12-31**:

```
SELECT DATEADD(month, DATEDIFF(month, '19001231', @InputDate), '19001231');
```

Note that when using this approach, it is important to choose a month that has 31 days; what this T-SQL does is to find the same day of the month as the reference date, on the month in which the input date lies. But, if the month has less than 31 days, SQL Server will automatically round down to the closest date, which will represent the actual last date of the month in question. Had I used February 28 instead of December 31 for the reference date, the output any time this query was run would be the 28th of the month.

Other more interesting combinations are also possible. For example, a common requirement in many applications is to perform calculations based on time periods such as "every day between last Friday and today." By modifying the truncation pattern a bit, finding "last Friday" is fairly simple—the main trick is to choose an appropriate reference date. In this case, to find the nearest Friday to a supplied input date, the reference date should be *any* Friday. We know that the number of days between any Friday and any other Friday is divisible by 7, and we can use that knowledge to truncate the current date to the nearest Friday.

The following T-SQL finds the number of days between the reference Friday, January 7, 2000, and the input date, February 9, 2009:

```
DECLARE @Friday date = '20000107';
SELECT DATEDIFF(day, @Friday, '20090209');
```

The result is **3321**, which of course is an integer. Taking advantage of SQL Server's integer math properties, dividing the result by 7, and then multiplying it by 7 again will round it down to the nearest number divisible by seven, 3318:

```
SELECT (3321 / 7) * 7;
```

Adding 3318 days to the original reference date of January 7, 2000 results in the desired output, the "last Friday" before February 9, 2009, which was on February 6, 2009:

```
SELECT DATEADD(day, 3318, '20000107')
```

As with the previous example, this can be simplified (and clarified) by combining everything inline:

```
DECLARE @InputDate date = '20090209';
DECLARE @Friday date = '20000107';
SELECT DATEADD(day, ((DATEDIFF(day, @Friday, @InputDate) / 7) * 7), @Friday);
```

A further simplification to the last statement is also possible. Currently, the result of the inner **DATEDIFF** is divided by **7** to calculate a round number of weeks, and then multiplied by **7** again to produce the equivalent number of days to add using the **DATEADD** method. However, it is unnecessary to perform the multiplication to days when you can specify the amount of time to add in weeks, as follows:

```
SELECT DATEADD(week, (DATEDIFF(day, @Friday, @InputDate) / 7), @Friday);
```

Note that, in situations where the input date is a Friday, these examples will return the input date itself. If you really want to return the "last" Friday every time, and never the input date itself—even if it is a Friday—a small modification is required. To accomplish this, you must use two reference dates: one representing any known Friday, and one that is any other day that lies within one week following that reference Friday (I recommend the next day, for simplicity). By calculating the number of days elapsed between this second reference date and the input date, the rounded number of weeks will be one week lower if the input date is a Friday, meaning that the result will always be the previous Friday. The following T-SQL does this for a given input date:

```
DECLARE @InputDate date = '20100423';
DECLARE @Friday date = '20000107';
DECLARE @Saturday date = DATEADD(day, 1, @Friday);
SELECT DATEADD(week, (DATEDIFF(day, @Saturday, @InputDate) / 7), @Friday);
```

By using this pattern and switching the reference date, you can easily find the last of any day of the week given an input date. To find the "next" one of a given day (e.g., "next Friday"), simply add one week to the result of the inner calculation before adding it to the reference date:

```
DECLARE @InputDate datetime = GETDATE();
DECLARE @Friday     datetime = '2000-01-07';
SELECT DATEADD(week, (DATEDIFF(day, @Friday, @InputDate) / 7) +1, @Friday);
```

As a final example of what you can do with date/time calculations, a slightly more complex requirement is necessary. Say that you're visiting the Boston area and want to attend a meeting of the New England SQL Server Users Group. The group meets on the second Thursday of each month. Given an input date, how do you find the date of the next meeting?

To answer this question requires a little bit of thinking about the problem. The earliest date on which the second Thursday can fall occurs when the first day of the month is a Thursday. In such cases, the second Thursday occurs on the eighth day of the month. The latest date on which the second Thursday can fall occurs when the first of the month is a Friday, in which case the second Thursday will be the 14th. So, for any given month, the "last Thursday" (in other words, the most recent Thursday) as of and including the 14th will be the second Thursday of the month. The following T-SQL uses this approach:

```
DECLARE @InputDate date = '20100101';
DECLARE @Thursday date = '20000914';
DECLARE @FourteenthOfMonth date =
    DATEADD(month, DATEDIFF(month, @Thursday, @InputDate), @Thursday);

SELECT DATEADD(week, (DATEDIFF(day, @Thursday, @FourteenthOfMonth) / 7),
@Thursday);
```

Of course, this doesn't find the *next* meeting; it finds the meeting for the month of the input date. To find the next meeting, a **CASE** expression will be necessary, in addition to an observation about second Thursdays: if the second Thursday of a month falls on the eighth, ninth, or tenth, the next month's second Thursday is five weeks away. Otherwise, the next month's second Thursday is four weeks away. To find the day of the month represented by a given date/time instance, use T-SQL's **DATEPART** function, which takes the same date granularity inputs as **DATEADD** and **DATEDIFF**. The following T-SQL combines all of these techniques to find the next date for a New England SQL Server Users Group meeting, given an input date:

```
DECLARE @InputDate date = GETDATE();

DECLARE @Thursday date = '20000914';

DECLARE @FourteenthOfMonth date =
  DATEADD(month, DATEDIFF(month, @Thursday, @InputDate), @Thursday);

DECLARE @SecondThursday date =
  DATEADD(week, (DATEDIFF(day, @Thursday, @FourteenthOfMonth) / 7), @Thursday);
```

```
SELECT
    CASE
        WHEN @InputDate <= @SecondThursday
        THEN @SecondThursday
    ELSE
        DATEADD(
            week,
            CASE
                WHEN DATEPART(day, @SecondThursday) <= 10 THEN 5
                ELSE 4
            END,
            @SecondThursday)
    END;
```

Finding complex dates like the second Thursday of a month is not a very common requirement unless you're writing a scheduling application. More common are requirements along the lines of "find all of today's rows." Combining the range techniques discussed in the previous section with the date/time calculations shown here, it becomes easy to design stored procedures that both efficiently and dynamically query for required time periods.

How Many Candles on the Birthday Cake?

As a final example of date/time calculations in T-SQL, consider a seemingly simple task: finding out how many years old you are as of today. The obvious answer is of course the following:

```
SELECT DATEDIFF(year, @YourBirthday, GETDATE());
```

Unfortunately, this answer—depending on the current day—is wrong. Consider someone born on March 25, 1965. On March 25, 2010, that person's 45th birthday should be celebrated. Yet according to SQL Server, that person was already 45 on March 24, 2010:

```
SELECT DATEDIFF(year, '19650325', '20100324');
```

In fact, according to SQL Server, this person was 45 throughout the whole of 2010, starting on January 1. Happy New Year and happy birthday combined, thanks to the magic of SQL Server? Probably not; the discrepancy is due to the way SQL Server calculates date differences. Only the date/time component being differenced is considered, and any components below are truncated. This feature makes the previous date/time truncation examples work, but makes age calculations fail because when differencing years, days and months are not taken into account.

To get around this problem, a **CASE** expression must be added that subtracts one year if the day and month of the current date is less than the day and month of the input date—in other words, if the person has yet to celebrate their birthday in the current year. The following T-SQL both accomplishes the primary goal, and as an added bonus, also takes leap years into consideration:

```
SELECT
    DATEDIFF (
        YEAR,
        @YourBirthday,
        GETDATE()) -
    CASE
        WHEN 100 * MONTH(GETDATE()) + DAY(GETDATE())
```

```
        < 100 * MONTH(@YourBirthday) + DAY(@YourBirthday) THEN 1
    ELSE 0
  END;
```

Note that this T-SQL uses the **MONTH** and **DAY** functions, which are shorthand for **DATEPART(month, <date>)** and **DATEPART(day, <date>)**, respectively.

Defining Periods Using Calendar Tables

Given the complexity of doing date/time calculations in order to query data efficiently, it makes sense to seek alternative techniques in some cases. For the most part, using the date/time calculation and range-matching techniques discussed in the previous section will yield the best possible performance. However, in some cases ease of user interaction may be more important than performance. It is quite likely that more technical business users will request direct access to query key business databases, but very unlikely that they will be savvy enough with T-SQL to be able to do complex date/time calculations.

In these cases, as well as a few others that will be discussed in this section, it makes sense to predefine the time periods that will get queried. A lookup table can be created that allows users to derive any number of named periods from the current date with ease. These tables, not surprisingly, are referred to as **calendar tables**, and they can be extremely useful.

The basic calendar table has a date column that acts as the primary key and several columns that describe time periods. Each date in the range of dates covered by the calendar will have one row inserted into the table, which can be used to reference all of the associated time periods. A standard example can be created using the following code listing:

```
CREATE TABLE Calendar
(
  DateKey date PRIMARY KEY,
  DayOfWeek tinyint,
  DayName nvarchar(10),
  DayOfMonth tinyint,
  DayOfYear smallint,
  WeekOfYear tinyint,
  MonthNumber tinyint,
  MonthName nvarchar(10),
  Quarter tinyint,
  Year smallint
 );
 GO

SET NOCOUNT ON;

DECLARE @Date date = '19900101';
WHILE @Date < '20250101'
BEGIN
  INSERT INTO Calendar
    SELECT
      @Date AS DateKey,
      DATEPART(dw, @Date) AS DayOfWeek,
      DATENAME(dw, @Date) AS DayName,
      DATEPART(dd, @Date) AS DayOfMonth,
```

```
        DATEPART(dy, @Date) AS DayOfYear,
        DATEPART(ww, @Date) as WeekOfYear,
        DATEPART(mm, @Date) AS MonthNumber,
        DATENAME(mm, @Date) AS MonthName,
        DATEPART(qq, @Date) AS Quarter,
        YEAR(@Date) AS Year;

    SET @Date = DATEADD(d, 1, @Date);
END
GO
```

This table creates one row for every date between January 1, 1990 and January 1, 2025. I recommend going as far back as the data you'll be working with goes, and at least ten years into the future. Although this sounds like it will potentially produce a lot of rows, keep in mind that every ten years worth of data will only require around 3,652 rows. Considering that it's quite common to see database tables containing hundreds of millions of rows, such a small number should be easily manageable.

The columns defined in the **Calendar** table represent the periods of time that users will want to find and work with. Since creating additional columns will not add too much space to the table, it's probably not a bad idea to err on the side of too many rather than too few. You might, for example, want to add columns to record fiscal years, week start and end dates, or holidays. However, keep in mind that additional columns may make the table more confusing for less-technical users.

Once the calendar table has been created, it can be used for many of the same calculations covered in the last section, as well as for many other uses. To start off simply, let's try finding information about "today's row":

```
SELECT *
FROM Calendar AS Today
WHERE Today.DateKey = CAST(GETDATE() AS date);
```

Once you've identified "today," it's simple to find other days. For example, "Last Friday" is the most recent Friday with a **DateKey** value less than today:

```
SELECT TOP(1) *
FROM Calendar LastFriday
WHERE
    LastFriday.DateKey < GETDATE()
    AND LastFriday.DayOfWeek = 6
ORDER BY DateKey DESC;
```

Note that I selected the default setting of Sunday as first day of the week when I created my calendar table, so **DayOfWeek** will be 6 for any Friday. If you select a different first day of the week, you'll have to change the **DayOfWeek** value specified. You could of course filter using the **DayName** column instead so that users will not have to know which number to use; they can query based on the name. The **DayName** column was populated using the **DATENAME** function, which returns a localized character string representing the day name (i.e., "Friday," in English). Keep in mind that running this code on servers with different locale settings may produce different results.

Since the calendar table contains columns that define various periods, such as the current year and the week of the year, it becomes easy to answer questions such as "What happened this week?" To find the first and last days of "this week," the following query can be used:

```
SELECT
    MIN(ThisWeek.DateKey) AS FirstDayOfWeek,
```

```
    MAX(ThisWeek.DateKey) AS LastDayOfWeek
FROM Calendar AS Today
JOIN Calendar AS ThisWeek ON
    ThisWeek.Year = Today.Year
    AND ThisWeek.WeekOfYear = Today.WeekOfYear
WHERE
    Today.DateKey = CAST(GETDATE() AS date);
```

A similar question might deal with adjacent weeks. For instance, you may wish to identify "Friday of last week." The following query is a first attempt at doing so:

```
SELECT FridayLastWeek.*
FROM Calendar AS Today
JOIN Calendar AS FridayLastWeek ON
    Today.Year = FridayLastWeek.Year
    AND Today.WeekOfYear - 1 = FridayLastWeek.WeekOfYear
WHERE
    Today.DateKey = CAST(GETDATE() AS date)
    AND FridayLastWeek.DayName = 'Friday';
```

Unfortunately, this code has an edge problem that will cause it to be somewhat nonfunctional around the first of the year in certain cases. The issue is that the **WeekOfYear** value resets to **1** on the first day of a new year, regardless of what day it falls on. The query also joins on the **Year** column, making the situation doubly complex.

Working around the issue using a **CASE** expression may be possible, but it will be difficult, and the goal of the calendar table is to simplify things. A good alternative solution is to add a **WeekNumber** column that numbers every week consecutively for the entire duration represented by the calendar. The first step in doing this is to alter the table and add the column, as shown by the following T-SQL:

```
ALTER TABLE Calendar
ADD WeekNumber int NULL;
```

Next, a temporary table of all of the week numbers can be created, using the following T-SQL:

```
WITH StartOfWeek (DateKey) AS
(
    SELECT MIN(DateKey)
    FROM Calendar
    UNION
    SELECT DateKey
    FROM Calendar
    WHERE DayOfWeek = 1
),
EndOfWeek (DateKey) AS
(
    SELECT DateKey
    FROM Calendar
    WHERE DayOfWeek = 7
    UNION
    SELECT MAX(DateKey)
    FROM Calendar
)
```

```
SELECT
    StartOfWeek.DateKey AS StartDate,
    (
        SELECT TOP(1)
            EndOfWeek.DateKey
        FROM EndOfWeek
        WHERE EndOfWeek.DateKey >= StartOfWeek.DateKey
        ORDER BY EndOfWeek.DateKey
    ) AS EndDate,
    ROW_NUMBER() OVER (ORDER BY StartOfWeek.DateKey) AS WeekNumber
INTO #WeekNumbers
FROM StartOfWeek;
```

The logic of this T-SQL should be explained a bit. The **StartOfWeek** CTE selects each day from the calendar table where the day of the week is **1**, in addition to the earliest date in the table, in case that day is not the first day of a week. The **EndOfWeek** CTE uses similar logic to find the last day of every week, in addition to the last day represented in the table. The **SELECT** list includes the **DateKey** represented for each row of the **StartOfWeek** CTE, the lowest **DateKey** value from the **EndOfWeek** CTE that's greater than the **StartOfWeek** value (which is the end of the week), and a week number generated using the **ROW_NUMBER** function. The results of the query are inserted into a temporary table called **#WeekNumbers**. Once this T-SQL has been run, the calendar table's new column can be populated (and set to be nonnullable), using the following code:

```
UPDATE Calendar
SET WeekNumber =
    (
    SELECT WN.WeekNumber
    FROM #WeekNumbers AS WN
    WHERE
        Calendar.DateKey BETWEEN WN.StartDate AND WN.EndDate
    );

ALTER TABLE Calendar
ALTER COLUMN WeekNumber int NOT NULL;
```

Now, using the new **WeekNumber** column, finding "Friday of last week" becomes almost trivially simple:

```
SELECT FridayLastWeek.*
FROM Calendar AS Today
JOIN Calendar AS FridayLastWeek ON
    Today.WeekNumber = FridayLastWeek.WeekNumber + 1
WHERE
    Today.DateKey = CAST(GETDATE() AS date)
    AND FridayLastWeek.DayName = 'Friday';
```

Of course, one key problem still remains: finding the date of the next New England SQL Server Users Group meeting, which takes place on the second Thursday of each month. There are a couple of ways that a calendar table can be used to address this dilemma. The first method, of course, is to query the calendar table directly. The following T-SQL is one way of doing so:

```
WITH NextTwoMonths AS
```

```
(
  SELECT
    Year,
    MonthNumber
  FROM Calendar
  WHERE
    DateKey IN (
      CAST(GETDATE() AS date),
      DATEADD(month, 1, CAST(GETDATE() AS date)))
),
NumberedThursdays AS
(
  SELECT
    Thursdays.*,
    ROW_NUMBER() OVER (PARTITION BY Thursdays.MonthNumber ORDER BY DateKey)
      AS ThursdayNumber
    FROM Calendar Thursdays
    JOIN NextTwoMonths ON
      NextTwoMonths.Year = Thursdays.Year
      AND NextTwoMonths.MonthNumber = Thursdays.MonthNumber
    WHERE
      Thursdays.DayName = 'Thursday'
)
SELECT TOP(1)
  NumberedThursdays.*
FROM NumberedThursdays
WHERE
  NumberedThursdays.DateKey >= CAST(GETDATE() AS date)
  AND NumberedThursdays.ThursdayNumber = 2
ORDER BY NumberedThursdays.DateKey;
```

If you find this T-SQL to be just a bit on the confusing side, don't be concerned! Here's how it works: first, the code finds the month and year for the current month and the next month, using the **NextTwoMonths** CTE. Then, in the **NumberedThursdays** CTE, every Thursday for those two months is identified and numbered sequentially. Finally, the lowest Thursday with a number of **2** (meaning that it's a second Thursday) that falls on a day on or after "today" is returned.

Luckily, such complex T-SQL can often be made obsolete using calendar tables. The calendar table demonstrated here already represents a variety of generic named days and time periods. There is, of course, no reason that you can't add your own columns to create named periods specific to your business requirements. Asking for the next second Thursday would have been much easier had there simply been a prepopulated column representing user group meeting days.

A much more common requirement is figuring out which days are business days. This information is essential for determining work schedules, metrics relating to service-level agreements, and other common business needs. Although you could simply count out the weekend days, this would fail to take into account national holidays, state and local holidays that your business might observe, and company retreat days or other days off that might be specific to your firm.

To address all of these issues in one shot, simply add a column to the table called `HolidayDescription`:

```
ALTER TABLE Calendar
ADD HolidayDescription varchar(50) NULL;
```

This column can be populated for any holiday, be it national, local, firm-specific, or a weekend day. If you do not need to record a full description associated with each holiday, then you could instead populate the column with a set of simple flag values representing different types of holidays. This makes it easy to answer questions such as "How many business days do we have this month?" The following T-SQL answers that one:

```
SELECT COUNT(*)
FROM Calendar AS ThisMonth
WHERE
    HolidayDescription IS NULL
    AND EXISTS
    (
        SELECT *
        FROM Calendar AS Today
        WHERE
            Today.DateKey = CAST(GETDATE() as date)
            AND Today.Year = ThisMonth.Year
            AND Today.MonthNumber = ThisMonth.MonthNumber
);
```

This query counts the number of days in the current month that are not flagged as holidays. If you only want to count the working weekdays, you can add an additional condition to the WHERE clause to exclude rows where the DayName is Saturday or Sunday.

If your business is seasonally affected, try adding a column that helps you identify various seasonal time periods, such as "early spring," "midsummer," or "the holiday season" to help with analytical queries based on these time periods. Or you might find that several additional columns are necessary to reflect all of the time periods that are important to your queries.

Using calendar tables can make time period–oriented queries easier to perform, but remember that they require ongoing maintenance. Make sure to document processes for keeping defined time periods up to date, as well as for adding additional days to the calendar to make sure that your data doesn't overrun the scope of the available days. You may want to add an additional year of days on the first of each year in order to maintain a constant ten-year buffer.

Dealing with Time Zones

One of the consequences of moving into a global economy is the complexity that doing business with people in different areas brings to the table. Language barriers aside, one of the most important issues arises from the problems of time variance. Essentially, any system that needs to work with people simultaneously residing in different areas must be able to properly handle the idea that those people do not all have their watches set the same way.

In 1884, 24 standard time zones were defined at a meeting of delegates in Washington, DC, for the International Meridian Conference. Each of these time zones represents a 1-hour offset, which is determined in relation to the Prime Meridian, the time zone of Greenwich, England. This central time zone is referred to either as GMT (Greenwich Mean Time) or UTC (Universel Temps Coordonné, French for "Coordinated Universal Time"). The standard time zones are illustrated in Figure 11-3.

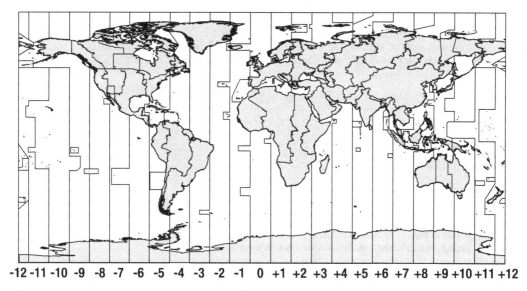

-12 -11 -10 -9 -8 -7 -6 -5 -4 -3 -2 -1 0 +1 +2 +3 +4 +5 +6 +7 +8 +9 +10 +11 +12

Figure 11-3. Standard time zones of the world

The key benefit of defining these standard zones is that, if two people know the offset of the zone in which the other is located, and they are synchronized to the same UTC-specific clock, it is possible to determine each other's time wherever they are on earth.

As I write these words, it's just after 8:15 a.m. in England, but since we're currently observing British Summer Time (BST), this time represents UTC + 1 hour. Many other countries in the Northern hemisphere that observe daylight savings time are also currently 1 hour ahead of their normal time zone. The Eastern United States, for example, is normally UTC – 5, but right now is actually UTC – 4, making it 3:15 a.m.

■ **Note** Different countries switch into and back from daylight savings time at different times: for example, the time difference between the United Kingdom and mainland Chile can be three, four, or five hours, depending on the time of year.

Elsewhere around the world, I can instantly deduce that it is 2:15 p.m. local time in Bangkok, Thailand, which uses an offset of UTC + 7. Unfortunately, not all of the countries in the world use the standard zones. For instance, it is 12:45 p.m. in Mumbai, India right now; India uses a nonstandard offset of UTC + 5.5. Time zones, as it turns out, are really just as much about political boundaries as they are about keeping the right time globally.

There are three central issues to worry about when writing time zone–specific software:

> When a user sees data presented by the application, any dates should be rendered in the user's local time zone (if known), unless otherwise noted, in which case data should generally be rendered in UTC to avoid confusion.

When a user submits new data or updates existing data, thereby altering date/time data in the database, the database should convert the data from the user's time zone to a standard time zone (again, this will generally be UTC). All date/time data in the database should be standardized to a specific zone so that, based on known offsets, it can be easily converted to users' local times. It can also be important to store both the original zone and the local time in the zone in which a given event occurred, for greater control and auditability. There are various ways of modeling such data, as I'll discuss shortly. Given that start and end dates for daylight savings times occasionally change, it can be difficult to derive the original local times from a time stored only in UTC or only with an offset. If you will need to report or query based on local times in which events occurred, consider persisting them as-is in addition to storing the times standardized to UTC.

When a user asks a temporally based question, it's important to decide whether the dates used to ask the question will be used as-is (possibly in the user's local time zone) or converted to the standard time zone first. Consider a user in New York asking the question, "What happened between 2:00 p.m. and 5:00 p.m. today?" If date/time data in the database is all based in the UTC zone, it's unclear whether the user is referring to 2:00 p.m. to 5:00 p.m. EST or UTC—very different questions! The actual requirements here will vary based on business requirements, but it is a good idea to put a note on any screen in which this may be an issue to remind the user of what's going on.

Dealing with these issues is not actually too difficult, but it does require a good amount of discipline and attention to detail, not to mention some data about time zone offsets and daylight savings changes in various zones. It's a good idea to handle as much of the work as possible in the application layer, but some (or sometimes all) of the responsibility will naturally spill into the data layer. So how should we deal with handling multiple time zones within the database? In the following sections I'll discuss two possible models for dealing with this problem.

Storing UTC Time

The basic technique for storing temporal data for global applications is to maintain time zone settings for each user of the system so that when they log in, you can find out what zone you should treat their data as native to. Any time you need to show the user dates and times, convert them to the user's local zone; and any time the user enters dates or times into the application for either searching or as data points, convert them into UTC before they hit the database.

This approach requires some changes to the database code. For example, whenever the **GETDATE** function is used to insert data, you should instead use the **GETUTCDATE** function, which returns the current date/time in Greenwich. However, this rule only applies unconditionally for inserts; if you're converting a database from local time to UTC, a blind find/replace-style conversion from **GETDATE** to **GETUTCDATE** may not yield the expected results. For instance, consider the following stored procedure, which selects "today's" orders from the **AdventureWorks Sales.SalesOrderHeader** table:

```
CREATE PROCEDURE GetTodaysOrders
AS
BEGIN
    SET NOCOUNT ON

    SELECT
        OrderDate,
```

```
        SalesOrderNumber,
        AccountNumber,
        TotalDue
    FROM Sales.SalesOrderHeader
    WHERE
        CAST(OrderDate as date) = CAST(GETDATE() AS date)
END;
```

Assuming that the **Sales.SalesOrderHeader** table contains date/time values defined in UTC, it might seem like changing the **GETDATE** calls in this code to **GETUTCDATE** is a natural follow-up move. However, what if your application is hosted in New York, in which case the majority of your users are used to seeing and dealing with times synchronized to Eastern Standard Time (EST)? In such cases, the definition of "today's orders" becomes ambiguous, depending on whether "today" is measured according to EST or UTC. Although for the most part **CAST(GETDATE() AS date)** will return the same as **CAST (GETUTCDATE() AS date)**, there are 4 hours of each day (or sometimes 5, depending on daylight savings settings) in which the date as measured using UTC will be one day ahead of the date measured according to EST. If this query were to be called after 7:00 or 8:00 p.m. EST (again, depending on the time of year), **GETUTCDATE** will return a date/time that for people in the eastern United States is "tomorrow." The time portion will be truncated, and the query won't return any of "today's" data at all—at least not if you're expecting things to work using EST rules.

To correct these issues, use **GETUTCDATE** to find the current date/time in Greenwich, and convert it to the user's local time. After it is converted to local time, *then* truncate the time portion. Finally, convert the date back to UTC, and use the resultant date/time to search the table of UTC values. Depending on whether or not you've handled it in your application code, a further modification might be required to convert the **OrderDate** column in the **SELECT** list, in order to return the data in the user's local time zone. Whenever your application needs to handle relative dates, such as "today," "tomorrow," or "last week," you should always define these sensitive to the time zone of the user submitting the query, handling conversion into UTC and back again within the query.

Using the datetimeoffset Type

The new **datetimeoffset** datatype is the most fully featured temporal datatype in SQL Server 2008. Not only does it match the resolution and range of the **datetime2** datatype, but it also allows you to specify an offset, representing the difference between the stated time value and UTC. Thus, a single value can contain all the information required to express both a local time and the corresponding UTC time.

At first, this seems like an ideal solution to the problems of working with data across different time zones. Calculations on **datetimeoffset** values take account of both the time component and the offset. Consider the following example:

```
DECLARE @LondonMidday datetimeoffset = '2009-07-15 12:00 +0:00';
DECLARE @MoscowMidday datetimeoffset = '2009-07-15 12:00 +3:00';
SELECT DATEDIFF(hour, @LondonMidday, @MoscowMidday);
```

The time zone for Moscow is 3 hours ahead of London, so the result of this code is **-3**. In other words, midday in Moscow occurred 3 hours before midday in London.

Using **datetimeoffset** makes it easy to compare values held centrally representing times stored in different locales. Consider the following:

```
CREATE TABLE TimeAndPlace (
  Place varchar(32),
```

```
  Time datetimeoffset
);
GO

INSERT INTO TimeAndPlace (Place, Time) VALUES
  ('London', '2009-07-15 08:15:00 +0:00'),
  ('Paris', '2009-07-15 08:30:00 +1:00'),
  ('Zurich', '2009-07-15 09:05:00 +2:00'),
  ('Dubai', '2009-07-15 10:30:00 +3:00');
GO
```

To find out which event took place first, we can use a simple **ORDER BY** statement in a **SELECT** query—the output will order the results taking account of their offset:

```
SELECT
  Place,
  Time
FROM TimeAndPlace
WHERE Time BETWEEN '20090715 07:30' AND '20090715 08:30'
ORDER BY Time ASC;
```

The results are as follows:

Place	Time
Paris	2009-07-15 08:30:00.0000000 +01:00
Dubai	2009-07-15 10:30:00.0000000 +03:00
London	2009-07-15 08:15:00.0000000 +00:00

Note that the rows are filtered and ordered according to the UTC time at which they occurred, not the local time. In UTC terms, the Zurich time corresponds to 7:05 a.m. which lies outside of the range of the query condition and so is not included in the results. Dubai and Paris both correspond to 7:30 a.m., and London to 8:15 a.m.

The **datetimeoffset** type has a number of benefits, as demonstrated here, but it is important to note that it is not "time zone aware"—it simply provides calculations based on an offset from a consistently (UTC) defined time. The application still needs to tell the database the correct offset for the time zone in which the time is defined. Many operating systems allow users to choose the time zone in which to operate from a list of places. For example, my operating system reports my current time zone as "(GMT) Greenwich Mean Time : Dublin, Edinburgh, Lisbon, London." It is not difficult to present the user with such a choice of locations, and to persist the corresponding time zone within the database so that **datetimeoffset** values may be created with the correct offset. Such information can be extracted from a lookup table based on the system registry, and newer operating systems recognize and correctly allow for daylight savings time, adjusting the system clock automatically when required.

For example, in a front-end .NET application, you can use **TimeZoneInfo.Local.Id** to retrieve the ID of the user's local time zone, and then translate this to a **TimeZoneInfo** object using the **TimeZoneInfo.FindSystemTimeZoneById** method. Each **TimeZoneInfo** has an associated offset from UTC that can be accessed via the **BaseUtcOffset** property to get the correct offset for the corresponding **datetimeoffset** instance in the database.

However, even though this might solve the problem of *creating* temporal data in different time zones, problems still occur when performing calculations on that data. For example, suppose that you wanted to know the time in London, 24 hours after a given time, at 1:30 a.m. on the March 27, 2010:

```
DECLARE @LondonTime datetimeoffset = '20100327 01:30:00 +0:00';
SELECT DATEADD(hour, 24, @LondonTime);
```

This code will give the result **2010-03-28 01:30:00.0000000 +00:00**, which is technically correct—it is the time 24 hours later, based on the same offset as the supplied **datetimeoffset** value. However, at 1:00 a.m. on Sunday, March 28, clocks in Britain are put forward 1 hour to 2:00 a.m. to account for the change from GMT to BST. The time in London 24 hours after the supplied input will actually be **2010-03-28 02:30:00.0000000 +01:00**. Although this corresponds to the same UTC time as the result obtained, any application that displayed only the local time to the user would appear incorrect.

What's more, the offset corresponding to a given time zone does not remain static. For example, in December 2007, President Hugo Chavez created a new time zone for Venezuela, putting the whole country back half an hour to make it 4.5 hours behind UTC. Whatever solution you implement to translate from a time zone to an offset needs to account for such changes.

Time zone issues can become quite complex, but they can be solved by carefully evaluating the necessary changes to the code and even more carefully testing once those changes have been implemented. The most important thing to remember is that consistency is key when working with time-standardized data; any hole in the data modification routines that inserts nonstandardized data can cause ambiguity that may be impossible to fix. Once inserted, there is no way to ask the database whether a time was supposed to be in UTC or a local time zone.

Working with Intervals

Very few real-world events happen in a single moment. Time is continuous, and any given state change normally has both a clearly defined start time and end time. For example, you might say, "I drove from Stockbridge to Boston at 10:00." But you really didn't drive only at 10:00, unless you happen to be in possession of some futuristic time/space-folding technology (and that's clearly beyond the scope of this chapter).

When working with databases, we often consider only the start or end time of an event, rather than the full interval. A column called **OrderDate** is an almost ubiquitous feature in databases that handle orders; but this column only stores the date/time that the order ended—when the user submitted the final request. It does not reflect how long the user spent browsing the site, filling the shopping cart, and entering credit card information. Likewise, every time we check our e-mail, we see a **Sent Date** field, which captures the moment that the sender hit the send button, but does not help identify how long that person spent thinking about or typing the e-mail, activities that constitute part of the "sending" process.

The reason we don't often see this extended data is because it's generally unnecessary. For most sites, it really doesn't matter for the purpose of order fulfillment how long the user spent browsing (although that information may be useful to interface designers, or when considering the overall customer experience). And it doesn't really matter, once an e-mail is sent, how much effort went into sending it. The important thing is, it was sent (and later received, another data point that many e-mail clients don't expose).

Despite these examples to the contrary, for many applications, both start and end times are necessary for a complete analysis. Take for instance your employment history. As you move from job to job, you carry intervals during which you had a certain title, were paid a certain amount, or had certain job responsibilities. Failing to include both the start and end dates with this data can create some interesting challenges.

Modeling and Querying Continuous Intervals

If a table uses only a starting time or an ending time (but not both) to represent intervals, all of the rows in that table can be considered to belong to one continuous interval that spans the entire time period represented. Each row in this case would represent a subinterval during which some status change occurred. Let's take a look at some simple examples to clarify this. Start with the following table and rows:

```
CREATE TABLE JobHistory
(
    Company varchar(100),
    Title varchar(100),
    Pay decimal(9, 2),
    StartDate date
);
GO

INSERT INTO JobHistory
(
    Company,
    Title,
    Pay,
    StartDate
) VALUES
('Acme Corp', 'Programmer', 50000.00, '19970626'),
('Software Shop', 'Programmer/Analyst', 62000.00, '20001005'),
('Better Place', 'Junior DBA', 82000.00, '20030108'),
('Enterprise', 'Database Developer', 95000.00, '20071114');
GO
```

Notice that each of the dates uses the **date** type. No one—except the worst micromanager—cares, looking at a job history record, if someone got in to work at 8:00 a.m. or 8:30 a.m. on the first day. What matters is that the date in the table is the start *date*.

The data in the **JobHistory** table is easy enough to transform into a more logical format; to get the full subintervals we can assume that the end date of each job is the start date of the next. The end date of the final job, it can be assumed, is the present date (or, if you prefer, **NULL**). Converting this into a start/end report based on these rules requires T-SQL along the following lines:

```
SELECT
    J1.*,
    COALESCE((
        SELECT MIN(J2.StartDate)
        FROM JobHistory AS J2
        WHERE J2.StartDate > J1.StartDate),
        CAST(GETDATE() AS date)
    ) AS EndDate
FROM JobHistory AS J1;
```

which gives the following results (the final date will vary to show the date on which you run the query):

Company	Title	Pay	StartDate	EndDate
Acme Corp	Programmer	50000.00	1997-06-26	2000-10-05
Software Shop	Programmer/Analyst	62000.00	2000-10-05	2003-01-08
Better Place	Junior DBA	82000.00	2003-01-08	2007-11-14
Enterprise	Database Developer	95000.00	2007-11-14	2009-07-12

The outer query gets the job data and the start times, and the subquery finds the first start date after the current row's start date. If no such start date exists, the current date is used. Of course, an obvious major problem here is lack of support for gaps in the job history. This table may, for instance, hide the fact that the subject was laid off from Software Shop in July 2002. This is why I stressed the continuous nature of data modeled in this way.

Despite the lack of support for gaps, let's try a bit more data and see what happens. As the subject's career progressed, he received various title and pay changes during the periods of employment with these different companies, which are represented in the following additional rows:

```
INSERT INTO JobHistory
(
    Company,
    Title,
    Pay,
    StartDate
) VALUES
('Acme Corp', 'Programmer', 55000.00, '19980901'),
('Acme Corp', 'Programmer 2', 58000.00, '19990901'),
('Acme Corp', 'Programmer 3', 58000.00, '20000901'),
('Software Shop', 'Programmer/Analyst', 62000.00, '20001005'),
('Software Shop', 'Programmer/Analyst', 67000.00, '20020101'),
('Software Shop', 'Programmer', 40000.00, '20020301'),
('Better Place', 'Junior DBA', 84000.00, '20040601'),
('Better Place', 'DBA', 87000.00, '20060601');
```

The data in the **JobHistory** table, shown in full in Table 11-1, follows the subject along a path of relative job growth. A few raises and title adjustments—including one title adjustment with no associated pay raise—and an unfortunate demotion along with a downsized salary, just before getting laid off in 2002 (the gap which, as mentioned, is not able to be represented here). Luckily, after studying hard while laid off, the subject bounced back with a much better salary, and of course a more satisfying career track!

Table 11-1. *The Subject's Full Job History, with Salary and Title Adjustments*

Company	Title	Pay	StartDate
Acme Corp	Programmer	50000.00	1997-06-26
Acme Corp	Programmer	55000.00	1998-09-01
Acme Corp	Programmer 2	58000.00	1999-09-01
Acme Corp	Programmer 3	58000.00	2000-09-01
Software Shop	Programmer/Analyst	62000.00	2000-10-05
Software Shop	Programmer/Analyst	62000.00	2000-10-05
Software Shop	Programmer/Analyst	67000.00	2002-01-01
Software Shop	Programmer	40000.00	2002-03-01
Better Place	Junior DBA	82000.00	2003-01-08
Better Place	Junior DBA	84000.00	2004-06-01
Better Place	DBA	87000.00	2006-06-01
Enterprise	Database Developer	95000.00	2007-11-14

Ignoring the gap, let's see how one might answer a resume-style question using this data. As a modification to the previous query, suppose that we wanted to show the start and end date of tenure with each company, along with the maximum salary earned at the company, and what title was held when the highest salary was being earned.

The first step commonly taken in tackling this kind of challenge is to use a correlated subquery to find the rows that have the maximum value per group. In this case, that means the maximum pay per company:

```
SELECT
    Pay,
    Title
FROM JobHistory AS J2
WHERE
    J2.Pay =
    (
        SELECT MAX(Pay)
        FROM JobHistory AS J3
        WHERE J3.Company = J2.Company
    );
```

One key modification that must be made is to the basic query that finds start and end dates. Due to the fact that there are now multiple rows per job, the **MIN** aggregate will have to be employed to find the real start date, and the end date subquery will have to be modified to look not only at date changes, but also company changes. The following T-SQL finds the correct start and end dates for each company:

```
SELECT
    J1.Company,
    MIN(J1.StartDate) AS StartDate,
    COALESCE((
        SELECT MIN(J2.StartDate)
        FROM JobHistory AS J2
        WHERE
            J2.Company <> J1.Company
            AND J2.StartDate > MIN(J1.StartDate)),
        CAST(GETDATE() AS date)
    ) AS EndDate
FROM JobHistory AS J1
GROUP BY J1.Company
ORDER BY StartDate;
```

A quick note: This query would not work properly if the person had been hired back by the same company after a period of absence during which he was working for another firm. To solve that problem, you might use a query similar to the following, in which a check is done to ensure that the "previous" row (based on **StartDate**) does not have the same company name (meaning that the subject switched firms):

```
SELECT
    J1.Company,
    J1.StartDate AS StartDate,
    COALESCE((
        SELECT MIN(J2.StartDate)
        FROM JobHistory AS J2
        WHERE
            J2.Company <> J1.Company
            AND J2.StartDate > J1.StartDate),
        CAST(GETDATE() AS date)
    ) AS EndDate
FROM JobHistory AS J1
WHERE
    J1.Company <>
    COALESCE((
        SELECT TOP(1)
            J3.Company
        FROM JobHistory J3
        WHERE J3.StartDate < J1.StartDate
        ORDER BY J3.StartDate DESC),
        '')
GROUP BY
    J1.Company,
    J1.StartDate
ORDER BY
    J1.StartDate;
```

This example complicates things a bit too much for the sake of this chapter, but I feel that it is important to point this technique out in case you find it necessary to write these kinds of queries in production applications. This pattern is useful in many scenarios, especially when logging the status of an automated system and trying to determine downtime statistics or other metrics.

Getting back to the primary task at hand, showing the employment history along with peak salaries and job titles, the next step is to merge the query that finds the correct start and end dates with the query that finds the maximum salary and associated title. The simplest way of accomplishing this is with the **CROSS APPLY** operator, which behaves similarly to a correlated subquery but returns a table rather than a scalar value. The following T-SQL shows how to accomplish this:

```
SELECT
    x.Company,
    x.StartDate,
    x.EndDate,
    p.Pay,
    p.Title
FROM
(
    SELECT
        J1.Company,
        MIN(J1.StartDate) AS StartDate,
        COALESCE((
            SELECT MIN(J2.StartDate)
            FROM JobHistory AS J2
            WHERE
                J2.Company <> J1.Company
                AND J2.StartDate > MIN(J1.StartDate)),
            CAST(GETDATE() AS date)
        ) AS EndDate
    FROM JobHistory AS J1
    GROUP BY J1.Company
) x
CROSS APPLY
(
    SELECT
        Pay,
        Title
    FROM JobHistory AS J2
    WHERE
        J2.StartDate >= x.StartDate
        AND J2.StartDate < x.EndDate
        AND J2.Pay =
        (
            SELECT MAX(Pay)
            FROM JobHistory AS J3
            WHERE J3.Company = J2.Company
        )
) p
ORDER BY x.StartDate;
```

This T-SQL correlates the **CROSS APPLY** subquery using the **StartDate** and **EndDate** columns from the outer query in order to find the correct employment intervals that go along with each position. The

StartDate/EndDate pair for each period of employment is a **half-open interval** (or **semiopen**, depending on which mathematics textbook you're referring to); the **StartDate** end of the interval is **closed** (inclusive of the endpoint), and the **EndDate** is **open** (exclusive). This is because the **EndDate** for one interval is actually the **StartDate** for the next interval, and these intervals do not overlap. The results of this query are as follows:

Company	StartDate	EndDate	Pay	Title
Acme Corp	1997-06-26	2000-10-05	58000.00	Programmer 2
Acme Corp	1997-06-26	2000-10-05	58000.00	Programmer 3
Software Shop	2000-10-05	2003-01-08	67000.00	Programmer/Analyst
Better Place	2003-01-08	2007-11-14	87000.00	DBA
Enterprise	2007-11-14	2009-07-12	95000.00	Database Developer

Although the query does work, it has an issue; the **CROSS APPLY** subquery will return more than one row if a title change was made at the maximum pay level, without an associated pay increase (as happens in this data set), thereby producing duplicate rows in the result. The solution is to select the appropriate row by sorting the result by the **Pay** column, in descending order. The modified subquery, which will return only one row per position, is as follows:

```
SELECT TOP(1)
    Pay,
    Title
FROM JobHistory AS J2
WHERE
    J2.StartDate >= x.StartDate
    AND J2.StartDate < x.EndDate
ORDER BY Pay DESC
```

The important things that I hope you can take away from these examples are the patterns used for manipulating the intervals, as well as the fact that modeling intervals in this way may not be sufficient for many cases.

In terms of query style, the main thing to notice is that in order to logically manipulate this data, some form of an "end" for the interval must be synthesized within the query. Any time you're faced with a table that maps changes to an entity over time but uses only a single date/time column to record the temporal component, try to think of how to transform the data so that you can work with the start and end of the interval. This will make querying much more straightforward.

From a modeling perspective, this setup is clearly deficient. I've already mentioned the issue with gaps in the sequence, which are impossible to represent in this single-column table. Another problem is overlapping intervals. What if the subject took on some after-hours contract work during the same time period as one of the jobs? Trying to insert that data into the table would make it look as though the subject had switched companies.

This is not to say that no intervals should be modeled this way. There are many situations in which gaps and overlaps may not make sense, and the extra bytes needed for a second column would be a waste. A prime example is a server uptime monitor. Systems are often used by IT departments that ping each monitored server on a regular basis and record changes to their status. Following is a simplified example table and a few rows of data representing the status of two monitored servers:

```
CREATE TABLE ServerStatus
(
    ServerName varchar(50),
    Status varchar(15),
    StatusTime datetime
);
GO

INSERT INTO ServerStatus
(
    ServerName,
    Status,
    StatusTime
) VALUES
('WebServer', 'Available', '2009-04-20T03:00:00.000'),
('DBServer', 'Available', '2009-04-20T03:00:00.000'),
('DBServer', 'Unavailable', '2009-06-12T14:35:23.100'),
('DBServer', 'Available', '2009-06-12T14:38:52.343'),
('WebServer', 'Unavailable', '2009-06-15T09:16:03.593'),
('WebServer', 'Available', '2009-06-15T09:28:17.006');
GO
```

Applying almost the exact same query as was used for start and end of employment periods, we can find out the intervals during which each server was unavailable:

```
SELECT
    S1.ServerName,
    S1.StatusTime,
    COALESCE((
        SELECT MIN(S2.StatusTime)
        FROM ServerStatus AS S2
        WHERE
            S2.StatusTime > S1.StatusTime),
        GETDATE()
    ) AS EndTime
FROM ServerStatus AS S1
WHERE S1.Status = 'Unavailable';
```

The results of this query are as follows:

ServerName	StatusTime	EndTime
DBServer	2009-06-12 14:35:23.100	2009-06-12 14:38:52.343
WebServer	2009-06-15 09:16:03.593	2009-06-15 09:28:17.007

Some systems will send periodic status updates if the system status does not change. The monitoring system might insert additional "unavailable" rows every 30 seconds or minute until the target system starts responding again. As-is, this query reports each interim status update as a separate interval starting point. To get around this problem, the query could be modified as follows:

```
SELECT
    S1.ServerName,
    MIN(S1.StatusTime) AS StartTime,
    p.EndTime
FROM ServerStatus AS S1
CROSS APPLY
(
    SELECT
        COALESCE((
            SELECT MIN(S2.StatusTime)
            FROM ServerStatus AS S2
            WHERE
                S2.StatusTime > S1.StatusTime
                AND S2.Status = 'Available'
            ),
            GETDATE()
        ) AS EndTime
) p
WHERE S1.Status = 'Unavailable'
GROUP BY
    S1.ServerName,
    p.EndTime;
```

This new version finds the first "available" row that occurs after the current "unavailable" row; that row represents the actual end time for the full interval during which the server was down. The outer query uses the **MIN** aggregate to find the first reported "unavailable" time for each **ServerName**/**EndTime** combination.

Modeling and Querying Independent Intervals

In many cases, it is more appropriate to model intervals as a start time/end time combination rather than using a single column as used in the previous section. With both a start and end time, no subinterval has any direct dependence on any other interval or subinterval. Therefore, both gaps and overlaps can be represented. The remainder of this section details how to work with intervals modeled in that way.

Going back to the employment example, assume that a system is required for a company to track internal employment histories. Following is a sample table, simplified for this example:

```
CREATE TABLE EmploymentHistory
(
    Employee varchar(50) NOT NULL,
    Title varchar(50) NOT NULL,
    StartDate date NOT NULL,
    EndDate date NULL,
    CONSTRAINT CK_Start_End CHECK (StartDate < EndDate)
);
GO
```

The main thing I've left out of this example is proper data integrity. Ignore the obvious need for a table of names and titles to avoid duplication of that data—that would overcomplicate the example. The holes I'm referring to deal with the employment history–specific data that the table is intended for. The primary issue is that although I did include one **CHECK** constraint to make sure that the **EndDate** is after the **StartDate** (we hope that the office isn't so bad that people are quitting on their first day), I failed to include a primary key.

Deciding what constitutes the primary key in this case requires a bit of thought. **Employee** alone is not sufficient, as employees would not be able to get new titles during the course of their employment (or at least it would no longer be a "history" of those changes). The next candidate might be **Employee** and **Title**, but this also has a problem. What if an employee leaves the company for a while, and later comes to his senses and begs to be rehired with the same title? The good thing about the table structure is that such a gap *can* be represented; but constraining on both the **Employee** and **Title** columns would prevent that situation from being allowed.

Adding **StartDate** into the mix seems like it would fix the problem, but in actuality it creates a whole new issue. An employee cannot be in two places (or offices) at the same time, and the combination of the three columns would allow the same employee to start on the same day with two different titles. And although it's common in our industry to wear many different hats, that fact is generally not reflected in our job title.

As it turns out, what we really need to constrain in the primary key is an employee starting on a certain day; uniqueness of the employee's particular title is not important in that regard. The following key can be added:

```
ALTER TABLE EmploymentHistory
ADD PRIMARY KEY (Employee, StartDate);
```

This primary key takes care of an employee being in two places at once on the same day, but how about different days? Even with this constraint in place, the following two rows would be valid:

```
INSERT INTO EmploymentHistory
(
    Employee,
    Title,
    StartDate,
    EndDate
) VALUES
('Jones', 'Developer', '20090101', NULL),
('Jones', 'Senior Developer', '20090601', NULL);
```

According to this data, Jones is *both* Developer and Senior Developer, as of June 1, 2009—quite a bit of stress for one person! The first idea for a solution might be to add a unique constraint on the **Employee** and **EndDate** columns. In SQL Server, unique constraints allow for one **NULL**-valued row—so only one **NULL EndDate** would be allowed per employee. That would fix the problem with these rows, but it would still allow the following rows:

```
INSERT INTO EmploymentHistory
(
    Employee,
    Title,
    StartDate,
    EndDate
) VALUES
```

```
('Jones', 'Developer', '20090201', '20090801'),
('Jones', 'Senior Developer', '20090701', NULL);
```

Now, Jones was both Developer and Senior Developer for a month. Again, this is probably not what was intended.

Fixing this problem will require more than just a combination of primary and unique key constraints, and a bit of background is necessary before I present the solution. Therefore, I will return to this topic in the next section, which covers overlapping intervals.

Before we resolve the problem of overlapping intervals, let's consider the other main benefit of this type of model over the single-date model, which is the support for gaps. Ignore for a moment the lack of proper constraints, and consider the following rows (which would be valid even with the constraints):

```
INSERT INTO EmploymentHistory
(
    Employee,
    Title,
    StartDate,
    EndDate
) VALUES
('Jones', 'Developer', '20070105', '20070901'),
('Jones', 'Senior Developer', '20070901', '20080901'),
('Jones', 'Principal Developer', '20080901', '20081007'),
('Jones', 'Principal Developer', '20090206', NULL);
```

The scenario shown here is an employee named Jones, who started as a developer in January 2007 and was promoted to Senior Developer later in the year. Jones was promoted again to Principal Developer in 2008, but quit a month later. However, a few months after that he decided to rejoin the company and has not yet left or been promoted again.

The two main questions that can be asked when dealing with intervals that represent gaps are "What intervals are covered by the data?" and "What holes are present?" These types of questions are ubiquitous when working with any kind of interval data. Real-world scenarios include such requirements as tracking of service-level agreements for server uptime and managing worker shift schedules—and of course, employment history.

In this case, the questions can be phrased as "During what periods did Jones work for the firm?" and the opposite, "During which periods was Jones *not* working for the firm?" To answer the first question, the first requirement is to find all subinterval start dates—dates that are not connected to a previous end date. The following T-SQL accomplishes that goal:

```
SELECT
    theStart.StartDate
FROM EmploymentHistory theStart
WHERE
    theStart.Employee = 'Jones'
    AND NOT EXISTS
    (
        SELECT *
        FROM EmploymentHistory Previous
        WHERE
            Previous.EndDate = theStart.StartDate
            AND theStart.Employee = Previous.Employee
    );
```

This query finds all rows for Jones (remember, there could be rows for other employees in the table), and then filters them down to rows where there is no end date for a Jones subinterval that matches the start date of the row. The start dates for these rows are the start dates for the continuous intervals covered by Jones's employment.

The next step is to find the ends of the covering intervals. The end rows can be identified similarly to the starting rows; they are rows where the end date has no corresponding start date in any other rows. To match the end rows to the start rows, find the first end row that occurs after a given start row. The following T-SQL finds start dates using the preceding query and end dates using a subquery that employs the algorithm just described:

```
SELECT
    theStart.StartDate,
    (
        SELECT
            MIN(EndDate)
        FROM EmploymentHistory theEnd
        WHERE
            theEnd.EndDate > theStart.StartDate
            AND theEnd.Employee = theStart.Employee
            AND NOT EXISTS
            (
                SELECT *
                FROM EmploymentHistory After
                WHERE
                    After.StartDate = theEnd.EndDate
                    AND After.Employee = theEnd.Employee
            )
    ) AS EndDate
FROM EmploymentHistory theStart
WHERE
    theStart.Employee = 'Jones'
    AND NOT EXISTS
    (
        SELECT *
        FROM EmploymentHistory Previous
        WHERE
            Previous.EndDate = theStart.StartDate
            AND theStart.Employee = Previous.Employee
    );
```

Finding noncovered intervals (i.e., gaps in the employment history) is a bit simpler. First, find the end date of every subinterval using the same syntax used to find end dates in the covered intervals query. Each of these dates marks the start of a noncovered interval. Make sure to filter out rows where the EndDate is NULL—these subintervals have not yet ended, so it does not make sense to include them as holes. In the subquery to find the end of each hole, find the first start date (if one exists) after the beginning of the hole. The following T-SQL demonstrates this approach to find noncovered intervals:

```
SELECT
    theStart.EndDate AS StartDate,
    (
        SELECT MIN(theEnd.StartDate)
        FROM EmploymentHistory theEnd
```

```
        WHERE
            theEnd.StartDate > theStart.EndDate
            AND theEnd.Employee = theStart.Employee
    ) AS EndDate
FROM EmploymentHistory theStart
WHERE
    theStart.Employee = 'Jones'
    AND theStart.EndDate IS NOT NULL
    AND NOT EXISTS
    (
        SELECT *
        FROM EmploymentHistory After
        WHERE After.StartDate = theStart.EndDate
    );
```

Overlapping Intervals

The final benefit (or drawback, depending on what's being modeled) of using both a start and end date for intervals that I'd like to discuss is the ability to work with overlapping intervals. Understanding how to work with overlaps is necessary either for performing overlap-related queries ("How many employees worked for the firm between August 2007 and September 2008?") or for constraining in order to avoid overlaps, as is necessary in the single-employee example started in the previous section.

To begin with, a bit of background on overlaps is necessary. Figure 11-4 shows the types of interval overlaps that are possible. Interval **A** is overlapped by each of the other intervals **B** through **E**, as follows:

- Interval **B** starts within interval **A** and ends after interval **A**.

- Interval **C** is the opposite, starting before interval **A** and ending within.

- Interval **D** both starts and ends within interval **A**.

- Finally, interval **E** both starts before and ends after interval **A**.

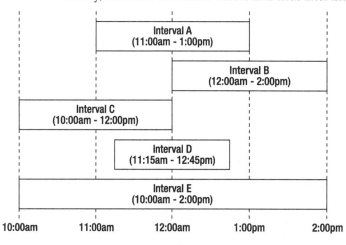

Figure 11-4. The types of overlapping intervals

Assuming that each interval has a **StartTime** property and an **EndTime** property, the relationships between each of the intervals **B** through **E** and interval **A** can be formalized in SQL-like syntax as follows:

```
B.StartDate >= A.StartDate AND B.StartDate < A.EndDate AND B.EndDate > A.EndDate
C.StartDate < A.StartDate AND C.EndDate > A.StartDate AND C.EndDate <= A.EndDate
D.StartDate >= A.StartDate AND D.EndDate <= A.EndDate
E.StartDate < A.StartDate AND E.EndDate > A.EndDate
```

Substituting the name **X** for all intervals **B** through **E**, we can begin to create a generalized algorithm for detecting overlaps. Let us first consider the situations in which an interval **X** does *not* overlap interval **A**. This can happen in two cases: either **X** occurs entirely after interval **A**, or it is entirely before interval **A**—for example:

```
X.StartDate > A.EndDate OR X.EndDate < A.StartDate
```

If the preceding condition is true for cases where **X** does not overlap **A**, then the condition for an overlap must therefore be the complement of this—in other words:

```
X.StartDate < A.EndDate  AND X.EndDate > A.StartDate
```

To rephrase this condition in English, we get "If **X** starts before **A** ends, and **X** ends after **A** starts, then **X** overlaps **A**." This is illustrated in Figure 11-5.

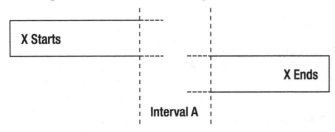

Figure 11-5. If X starts before A ends and X ends after A starts, the two intervals overlap.

Getting back to the **EmploymentHistory** table and its lack of proper constraints, it's clear that the real issue at hand is that it is not constrained to avoid overlap. A single employee cannot have two titles simultaneously, and the only way to ensure that does not happen is to make sure each employee's subintervals are unique.

Unfortunately, this logic cannot be embedded in a constraint, since in order to determine whether a row overlaps another, all of the other rows in the set must be evaluated. The following query finds all overlapping rows for Jones in the **EmploymentHistory** table, using the final overlap expression:

```
SELECT *
FROM EmploymentHistory E1
JOIN EmploymentHistory E2 ON
    E1.Employee = E2.Employee
    AND (
        E1.StartDate < COALESCE(E2.EndDate, '99991231')
        AND COALESCE(E1.EndDate, '99991231') > E2.StartDate)
    AND E1.StartDate <> E2.StartDate
WHERE
    E1.Employee = 'Jones';
```

Note that in order to avoid showing rows overlapping with themselves, the **E1.StartDate <>**
E2.StartDate expression was added. Thanks to the primary key on the **Employee** and **StartDate** columns,
we know that no two rows can share the same **StartDate**, so this does not affect the overlap logic. In
addition, in the case of open-ended (**NULL**) **EndDate** values, the **COALESCE** statement is used to substitute
the maximum possible **date** value. This avoids the possibility of inserting an interval starting in the
future, while a current interval is still active.

This logic must be evaluated every time an insert or update is done on the table, making sure that
none of the rows resulting from the insert or update operation creates any overlaps. Since this logic can't
go into a constraint, there is only one possibility—a trigger. The trigger logic is fairly straightforward;
instead of joining **EmployeeHistory** to itself, the base table will be joined to the **inserted** virtual table. The
following T-SQL shows the trigger:

```
CREATE TRIGGER No_Overlaps
ON EmploymentHistory
FOR UPDATE, INSERT
AS
BEGIN
    IF EXISTS
    (
        SELECT *
        FROM inserted i
        JOIN EmploymentHistory E2 ON
            i.Employee = E2.Employee
            AND (
                i.StartDate < COALESCE(E2.EndDate, '99991231')
                AND COALESCE(i.EndDate, '99991231') > E2.StartDate)
            AND i.StartDate <> E2.StartDate
    )
    BEGIN
        RAISERROR('Overlapping interval inserted!', 16, 1);
        ROLLBACK;
    END
END;
GO
```

The final examples for this section deal with a common scenario in which you might want to
investigate overlapping intervals: when monitoring performance of concurrent processes in a database
scenario.

To start setting up this example, load SQL Server Profiler, start a new trace, and connect to a test
server. Uncheck all of the events except for **SQL:BatchCompleted** and leave the default columns selected.

Begin the trace and then load the RML command prompt. Enter the following query:

```
ostress -Q"SELECT * FROM sys.databases;" -q -n100 -r100
```

The preceding code will perform 100 iterations of a query on 100 threads. The run should take
approximately 1 minute and will produce 10,000 Profiler events—one per invocation of the query. When
the ostress run has finished, return to Profiler and click File ~TRA Save As Trace Table, and save the data
to the database in a new table called **Overlap_Trace**.

Profiler trace tables include two **StartTime** and **EndTime** columns, both of which are populated for
many of the events—including **SQL:BatchCompleted** and **RPC:Completed**. By treating these columns as an
interval and working with some of the following query patterns, you can manipulate the data to do

things such as correlate the number of concurrent queries with performance degradation of the database server.

The first and most basic query is to find out which time intervals represented in the table had the most overlaps. In other words, during the runtime of a certain query, how many other queries were run? To answer this question, the intervals of every query in the table must be compared against the intervals of every other query in the table. The following T-SQL does this using the previously discussed overlap algorithm:

```
SELECT
    O1.StartTime,
    O1.EndTime,
    COUNT(*)
FROM Overlap_Trace O1
JOIN Overlap_Trace O2 ON
    (O1.StartTime < O2.EndTime AND O1.EndTime > O2.StartTime)
    AND O1.SPID <> O2.SPID
GROUP BY
    O1.StartTime,
    O1.EndTime
ORDER BY COUNT(*) DESC;
```

Much like the EmploymentTable example, we need to make sure that no false positives are generated by rows overlapping with themselves. Since a server process can't run two queries simultaneously, the server process identifier (SPID) column works for the purpose in this case.

Running this query on an unindexed table is a painful experience. It is agonizingly slow, and in the sample table on my machine, it required 288,304 logical reads. Creating the following index on the table helped a small amount:

```
CREATE NONCLUSTERED INDEX IX_StartEnd
ON Overlap_Trace (StartTime, EndTime, SPID)
```

However, I noticed that the index was still not being effectively used; examining the query plan revealed an outer table scan with a nested loop for an inner table scan—one table scan for every row of the table. Going back and looking at the original two algorithms before merging them, I noticed that they return exclusive sets of data. The first algorithm returns overlaps of intervals **B** and **D**, whereas the second algorithm returns overlaps of intervals **C** and **E**. I also noticed that each algorithm on its own is more index friendly than the combined version. The solution to the performance issue is to merge the two algorithms, not into a single expression, but rather using **UNION ALL**, as follows:

```
SELECT
    x.StartTime,
    x.EndTime,
    SUM(x.theCount)
FROM
(
SELECT
    O1.StartTime,
    O1.EndTime,
    COUNT(*) AS theCount
FROM Overlap_Trace O1
JOIN Overlap_Trace O2 ON
    (O1.StartTime >= O2.StartTime AND O1.StartTime < O2.EndTime)
```

```
    AND O1.SPID <> O2.SPID
GROUP BY
    O1.StartTime,
    O1.EndTime

UNION ALL

SELECT
    O1.StartTime,
    O1.EndTime,
    COUNT(*) AS theCount
FROM Overlap_Trace O1
JOIN Overlap_Trace O2 ON
    (O1.StartTime < O2.StartTime AND O1.EndTime > O2.StartTime)
    AND O1.SPID <> O2.SPID
GROUP BY
    O1.StartTime,
    O1.EndTime
) x
GROUP BY
    x.StartTime,
    x.EndTime
ORDER BY SUM(x.theCount) DESC
OPTION(HASH GROUP);
```

This query is logically identical to the previous one. It merges the two exclusive sets based on the same intervals and sums their counts, which is the same as taking the full count of the interval in one shot. Note that I was forced to add the **HASH GROUP** option to the end of the query to make the query optimizer make better use of the index. Once that hint was in place, the total number of reads done by the query dropped to 66,780—a significant improvement.

Time Slicing

Another way to slice and dice overlapping intervals is by splitting the data into separate periods and looking at the activity that occurred during each. For instance, to find out how many employees worked for a firm in each month of the year, you could find out which employees' work date intervals overlapped January 1 through January 31, again for February 1 through February 28, and so on.

Although it's easy to answer those kinds of questions for dates by using a calendar table, it's a bit trickier when you need to do it with times. Prepopulating a calendar table with every *time*, in addition to every date, for the next ten or more years would cause a massive increase in the I/O required to read the dates, and would therefore seriously cut down on the table's usefulness. Instead, I recommend dynamically generating time tables as you need them. The following UDF takes an input start and end date and outputs periods for each associated subinterval:

```
CREATE FUNCTION TimeSlice
(
  @StartDate datetime,
  @EndDate datetime
)
RETURNS @t TABLE
```

```
(
  StartDate datetime NOT NULL,
  EndDate datetime NOT NULL,
  PRIMARY KEY (StartDate, EndDate) WITH (IGNORE_DUP_KEY=ON)
)
WITH SCHEMABINDING
AS
BEGIN
  IF (@StartDate > @EndDate)
    RETURN;

  -- Round down start date to the nearest second
  DECLARE @TruncatedStart datetime;
  SET @TruncatedStart =
    DATEADD(second, DATEDIFF(second, '20000101', @StartDate), '20000101');

  -- Round down end date to the nearest second
  DECLARE @TruncatedEnd datetime;
  SET @TruncatedEnd =
    DATEADD(second, DATEDIFF(second, '20000101', @EndDate), '20000101');
  --Insert start and end date/times first
  --Make sure to match the same start/end interval passed in
  INSERT INTO @t (
    StartDate,
    EndDate
  )
  -- Insert the first interval
  SELECT
    @StartDate,
    CASE
      WHEN DATEADD(second, 1, @TruncatedStart) > @EndDate THEN @EndDate
      ELSE DATEADD(second, 1, @TruncatedStart)
    END
  UNION ALL
  -- Insert the last interval
  SELECT
    CASE
      WHEN @TruncatedEnd < @StartDate THEN @StartDate
      ELSE @TruncatedEnd
    END,
    @EndDate;

  SET @TruncatedStart = DATEADD(second, 1, @TruncatedStart);

  --Insert one row for each whole second in the interval
  WHILE (@TruncatedStart < @TruncatedEnd)
  BEGIN
    INSERT INTO @t (
      StartDate,
      EndDate
    )
    VALUES (
```

```
    @TruncatedStart,
    DATEADD(second, 1, @TruncatedStart)
  );

  SET @TruncatedStart = DATEADD(second, 1, @TruncatedStart);
  END;

  RETURN;
END;
```

This function is currently hard-coded to use seconds as the subinterval length, but it can easily be changed to any other time period by modifying the parameters to **DATEDIFF** and **DATEADD**.

As an example of using the function, consider the following call:

```
SELECT *
FROM dbo.TimeSlice('2010-01-02T12:34:45.003', '2010-01-02T12:34:48.100');
```

The output, shown following, contains one row per whole second range in the interval, with the start and endpoints constrained by the interval boundaries.

StartDate	EndDate
2010-01-02 12:34:45.003	2010-01-02 12:34:46.000
2010-01-02 12:34:46.000	2010-01-02 12:34:47.000
2010-01-02 12:34:47.000	2010-01-02 12:34:48.000
2010-01-02 12:34:48.000	2010-01-02 12:34:48.100

To use the **TimeSlice** function to look at the number of overlapping queries over the course of the sample trace, first find the start and endpoints of the trace using the **MIN** and **MAX** aggregates. Then slice the interval into 1-second periods using the function. The following T-SQL shows how to do that:

```
SELECT
    Slices.DisplayDate
FROM
(
    SELECT MIN(StartTime), MAX(EndTime)
    FROM Overlap_Trace
) StartEnd (StartTime, EndTime)
CROSS APPLY
(
    SELECT *
    FROM dbo.TimeSlice(StartEnd.StartTime, StartEnd.EndTime)
) Slices;
```

The output of the `TimeSlice` function can then be used to find the number of overlapping queries that were running during each period, by using the **CROSS APPLY** operator again in conjunction with the interval overlap expression:

```
SELECT
    Slices.DisplayDate,
    OverLaps.thecount
FROM
(
    SELECT MIN(StartTime), MAX(EndTime)
    FROM Overlap_Trace
) StartEnd (StartTime, EndTime)
CROSS APPLY
(
    SELECT *
    FROM dbo.TimeSlice(StartEnd.StartTime, StartEnd.EndTime)
) Slices
CROSS APPLY
(
    SELECT COUNT(*) AS theCount
    FROM Overlap_Trace OT
    WHERE
        Slices.StartDate < OT.EndTime
        AND Slices.EndDate > OT.StartTime
) Overlaps;
```

This data, in conjunction with a performance monitor trace, can be used to correlate spikes in counters at certain times to what was actually happening in the database. This can be especially useful for tracking sudden increases in blocking, which often will not correspond to increased utilization of any system resources, which can make them difficult to identify. By adding additional filters to the preceding query, you can look at concurrent runs of specific queries that are prone to blocking one another in order to find out whether they might be causing performance issues.

Modeling Durations

Durations are very similar to intervals, in that they represent a start time and an end time. In many cases, therefore, it makes sense to model durations as intervals and determine the actual duration for reporting or aggregation purposes by using **DATEDIFF**. However, in some cases, you may wish to store durations using a greater precision than the 100ns resolution offered by SQL Server's **datetime2** type. In addition, it can be difficult to format the duration calculated between two date/time columns for output, sometimes requiring intricate string manipulation.

There are several examples of cases when you might want to model durations rather than intervals. Databases that store information about timed scientific trials, for example, often require microsecond or even nanosecond precision. Another example is data that may not require a date/time component at all. For instance, a table containing times for runners competing in the 300-yard dash may not need a start time. The moment at which the run took place does not matter; the only important fact is how long the runner took to travel the 300 yards.

The most straightforward solution to the issue of inadequate resolution is to store a start date, along with an integer column to represent the actual duration using whatever unit of measurement is required for the accuracy of the application in hand:

```
CREATE TABLE Events
(
    EventId int,
    StartTime datetime2,
    DurationInNanoseconds int
);
```

Using the **Events** table, it is possible to find the approximate end time of an event by using **DATEADD** to add the duration to the start time. SQL Server will round the duration down to the nearest 100ns—the lowest time resolution supported by the **datetime2** type. For the 300-yard dash or other scenarios where starting time does not matter, the **StartTime** column can simply be dropped, and only the duration itself maintained (of course, the results in such cases may not require nanosecond precision as used here).

What this table does not address is the issue of formatting, should you need to output precise data rendered as a human-readable string. Since the lowest granularity supported by the SQL Server types is 100ns, none of the time-formatting methods will help to output a time string representing nanosecond precision. As such, you will have to roll your own code to do so. Once again I should stress that formatting is best done in a client tier. However, if you do need to format data in the database tier (and you have a *very* good reason to do so), the best approach to handle this scenario would be to create a SQLCLR UDF that uses the properties of .NET's **TimeSpan** type to build a string up to and including second precision, and then append the remaining nanosecond portion to the end.

The following UDF can be used to return a duration measured in nanoseconds in the string format **HH:MM:SS.NNNNNN** (where **N** represents nanoseconds):

```
[Microsoft.SqlServer.Server.SqlFunction]
public static SqlString FormatDuration(SqlInt64 TimeInNanoseconds)
{
  // Ticks = Nanoseconds / 10
  long ticks = TimeInNanoseconds.Value / 100;
  // Create the TimeSpan based on the number of ticks
  TimeSpan ts = new TimeSpan(ticks);
  // Format the output to HH:MM:SS:NNNNNN
  return new SqlString(
    ts.Hours.ToString() + ":"
    + ts.Minutes.ToString() + ":"
    + ts.Seconds.ToString()  + "."
    + (TimeInNanoseconds % 1000000000)
  );
}
```

This function could easily be amended to return whatever time format is required for your particular application.

Managing Bitemporal Data

A central truth that all database developers must come to realize is that the quality of data is frequently not as great as it could be (or as we might wish it to be). Sometimes we're forced to work with incomplete or incorrect data, and correct things later as a more complete picture of reality becomes available.

Modifying data in the database is simple enough—a call to a DML statement and the work is done. But in systems that require advanced logging and reproducibility of reports between runs for auditing purposes, a straightforward **UPDATE**, **INSERT**, or **DELETE** may be counterproductive. Performing such data modification can destroy the possibility of re-creating the same output on consecutive runs of the same query.

As an alternative to performing a simple alteration of invalid data, some systems use the idea of **offset transactions**. An offset transaction uses the additive nature of summarization logic to fix the data in place. For example, assume that part of a financial reporting system has a table that describes customer transactions. The following table is a highly simplified representation of what such a table might look like:

```
CREATE TABLE Transactions
(
    TransactionId int,
    Customer varchar(50),
    TransactionDate datetime,
    TransactionType varchar(50),
    TransactionAmount decimal(9,2)
);
GO
```

Let's suppose that on June 12, 2009, customer Smith deposited $500. However, due to a teller's key error that was not caught in time, by the time the reporting data was loaded, the amount that made it into the system was $5,000:

```
INSERT INTO Transactions VALUES
(1001, 'Smith', '2009-06-12', 'DEPOSIT', 5000.00);
```

The next morning, the erroneous data was detected. Updating the transaction row itself would destroy the audit trail, so an offset transaction must be issued. There are a few ways of handling this scenario. The first method is to issue an offset transaction dated the same as the incorrect transaction:

```
INSERT INTO Transactions VALUES
(1001, 'Smith', '2009-06-12', 'OFFSET', -4500.00);
```

Backdating the offset fixes the problem in summary reports that group any dimension (transaction number, customer, date, or transaction type), but fails to keep track of the fact that the error was actually caught on June 13. Properly dating the offset record is imperative for data auditing purposes:

```
INSERT INTO Transactions VALUES
(1001, 'Smith', '2009-06-13', 'OFFSET', -4500.00);
```

Unfortunately, proper dating does not fix all of the issues—and introduces new ones. After properly dating the offset, a query of the data for customer Smith for all business done through June 12 does not include the correction. Only by including data from June 13 would the query return the correct data. And although a correlated query could be written to return the correct summary report for June 12, the data is in a somewhat strange state when querying for ranges after June 12 (e.g., June 13 through 15.) The offset record is orphaned if June 12 is not considered in a given query along with June 13.

To get around these and similar issues, a **bitemporal** model is necessary. In a bitemporal table, each transaction has two dates: the actual date that the transaction took place and a "valid" date, which represents the date that we know the updated data to be correct. The following modified version of the **Transactions** table shows the new column:

```
CREATE TABLE Transactions
(
```

```
    TransactionId int,
    Customer varchar(50),
    TransactionDate datetime,
    TransactionType varchar(50),
    TransactionAmount decimal(9,2),
    ValidDate datetime
);
```

When inserting the data for Smith on June 12, a valid date of June 12 is also applied:

```
INSERT INTO Transactions VALUES
(1001, 'Smith', '2009-06-12', 'DEPOSIT', 5000.00, '2009-06-12');
```

Effectively, this row can be read as "As of June 12, we believe that transaction 1001, dated June 12, was a deposit for $5,000.00." On June 13, when the error is caught, no offset record is inserted. Instead, a corrected deposit record is inserted, with a new valid date:

```
INSERT INTO Transactions VALUES
(1001, 'Smith', '2009-06-12', 'DEPOSIT', 500.00, '2009-06-13');
```

This row indicates that as of June 13, transaction 1001 has been modified. But the important difference is that the transaction still maintains its correct date—so running a report for transactions that occurred on June 13 would not return any rows, since the only rows we are looking at occurred on June 12 (even though one of them was *entered* on June 13). In addition, this model eliminates the need for offset transactions. Rather than use an offset, queries should always find the last update for any given transaction within the valid range.

To understand this a bit more, consider a report run on August 5 that looks at all transactions that occurred on June 12. The person running the report wants the most "correct" version of the data—that is, all available corrections should be applied. This is done by taking the transaction data for each transaction from the row with the maximum valid date:

```
SELECT
    T1.TransactionId,
    T1.Customer,
    T1.TransactionType,
    T1.TransactionAmount
FROM Transactions AS T1
WHERE
    T1.TransactionDate = '2009-06-12'
    AND T1.ValidDate =
    (
        SELECT MAX(ValidDate)
        FROM Transactions AS T2
        WHERE T2.TransactionId = T1.TransactionId
    );
```

By modifying the subquery, it is possible to get "snapshot" reports based on data before updates were applied. For instance, assume that this same report was run on the evening of June 12. The output for Smith would show a deposit of $5,000.00 for transaction 1001. To reproduce that report on August 5 (or any day after June 12), change the **ValidDate** subquery:

```
SELECT
```

```
    T1.TransactionId,
    T1.Customer,
    T1.TransactionType,
    T1.TransactionAmount
FROM Transactions AS T1
WHERE
    T1.TransactionDate = '2009-06-12'
    AND T1.ValidDate =
    (
        SELECT MAX(ValidDate)
        FROM Transactions AS T2
        WHERE
            T2.TransactionId = T1.TransactionId
            AND ValidDate <= '2009-06-12'
    );
```

Note that in this case, the subquery could have been eliminated altogether, and the search argument could have become **AND T1.ValidDate = '2009-06-12'**. However, the subquery is needed any time you're querying a range of dates, so it's a good idea to leave it in place for ease of maintenance of the query.

Using this same pattern, data can also be booked in the future, before it is actually valid. It's common when doing wire transfers, credit card payments, and other kinds of electronic funds transactions to be able to set the posting date on which the business will actually be executed. By working with the valid date, Smith can make a request for an outgoing transfer on June 14, but ask that the transfer actually take place on June 16:

```
INSERT INTO Transactions VALUES
(1002, 'Smith', '2009-06-16', 'TRANSFER', -1000.00, '2009-06-14');
```

Since the transaction date is June 16, a report dealing with transactions that occurred between June 1 and June 15 will not show the transfer. But a business manager can query on June 15 to find out which transactions will hit in the coming days or weeks, and audit when the data entered the system.

Modeling data bitemporally allows for an auditable, accurate representation of historical or future knowledge as data is updated. This can be tremendously useful in many scenarios—especially in the realm of financial reconciliation when you can be forced to deal with backdated contracts that change the terms of previous transactions and business booked in the future to avoid certain types of auditing issues.

■ **Note** When modeling bitemporal data, you may want to investigate the possibility of implementing cutoff date rules, after which changes to transactions cannot be made. For example, the system may have a policy whereby transactions are said to be closed after 90 days. In this case, a simple CHECK constraint would do the trick, to ensure that the ValidDate is within 90 days of the TransactionDate. Another example would be data that has been used to generate an official report, such as for a government agency. In that case, you'd want a rule so that no transaction can be backdated to before the report was run (lest it change the data in the report). In that case, a trigger would be needed in order to verify the date against a table containing the report run history.

Summary

Virtually all data has some form of a temporal component, and every database developer will have to deal with times and dates again and again. Managing temporal data successfully begins with an understanding of the different types of temporal data: instance-based, interval-based, period-based, and bitemporal. By applying knowledge of how SQL Server's native date/time types work, you can intelligently and efficiently do calculations and queries based on temporal data models.

■ ■ ■

CHAPTER 12

Trees, Hierarchies, and Graphs

Although at times it may seem chaotic, the world around us is filled with structure and order. The universe itself is hierarchical in nature, made up of galaxies, stars, and planets. One of the natural hierarchies here on earth is the food chain that exists in the wild; a lion can certainly eat a zebra, but alas, a zebra will probably never dine on lion flesh. And of course, we're all familiar with corporate management hierarchies—which some companies try to kill off in favor of matrixes, which are not hierarchical at all . . . but more on that later!

We strive to describe our existence based on connections between entities—or lack thereof—and that's what trees, hierarchies, and graphs help us do at the mathematical and data levels. The majority of databases are at least mostly hierarchical, with a central table or set of tables at the root, and all other tables branching from there via foreign key references. However, sometimes the database hierarchy needs to be designed at a more granular level, representing the hierarchical relationship between records contained within a single table. For example, you wouldn't design a management database that required one table per employee in order to support the hierarchy. Rather, you'd put all of the employees into a single table and create references between the rows.

This chapter discusses three different approaches for working with these intra-table hierarchies and graphs in SQL Server 2008, as follows:

- Adjacency lists

- Materialized paths

- The `hierarchyid` datatype

Each of these techniques has its own virtues depending on the situation. I will describe each technique individually and compare how it can be used to query and manage your hierarchical data.

Terminology: Everything Is a Graph

Mathematically speaking, trees and hierarchies are both different types of **graphs**. A graph is defined as a set of **nodes** (or **vertices**) connected by **edges**. The edges in a graph can be further classified as **directed** or **undirected**, meaning that they can be traversed in one direction only (directed) or in both directions (undirected). If all of the edges in a graph are directed, the graph itself is said to be directed (sometimes referred to as a **digraph**). Graphs can also have **cycles**, sets of nodes/edges that when traversed in order bring you back to the same initial node. A graph without cycles is called an **acyclic** graph. Figure 12-1 shows some simple examples of the basic types of graphs.

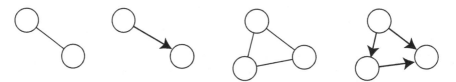

Figure 12-1. Undirected, directed, undirected cyclic, and directed acyclic graphs

The most immediately recognizable example of a graph is a street map. Each intersection can be thought of as a node, and each street an edge. One-way streets are directed edges, and if you drive around the block, you've illustrated a cycle. Therefore, a street system can be said to be a cyclic, directed graph. In the manufacturing world, a common graph structure is a bill of materials, or parts explosion, which describes all of the necessary component parts of a given product. And in software development, we typically work with class and object graphs, which form the relationships between the component parts of an object-oriented system.

A **tree** is defined as an undirected, acyclic graph in which exactly one path exists between any two nodes. Figure 12-2 shows a simple tree.

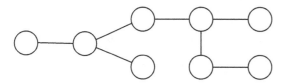

Figure 12-2. Exactly one path exists between any two nodes in a tree.

■ **Note** Borrowing from the same agrarian terminology from which the term *tree* is derived, we can refer to multiple trees as a *forest*.

A **hierarchy** is a special subset of a tree, and it is probably the most common graph structure that developers need to work with. It has all of the qualities of a tree but is also directed and **rooted**. This means that a certain node is designated as the **root**, and all other nodes are said to be **subordinates** (or **descendants**) of that node. In addition, each nonroot node must have exactly one **parent** node—a node that directs into it. Multiple parents are not allowed, nor are multiple root nodes. Hierarchies are extremely common when it comes to describing most business relationships; manager/employee, contractor/subcontractor, and firm/division associations all come to mind. Figure 12-3 shows a hierarchy containing a root node and several levels of subordinates.

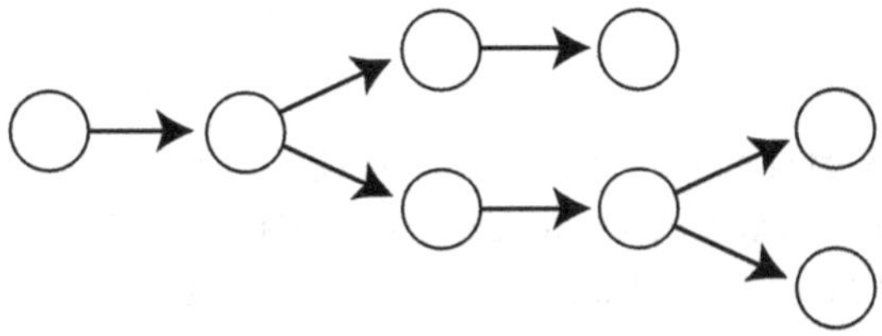

Figure 12-3. A hierarchy must have exactly one root node, and each nonroot node must have exactly one parent.

The parent/child relationships found in hierarchies are often classified more formally using the terms **ancestor** and **descendant**, although this terminology can get a bit awkward in software development settings. Another important term is **siblings**, which describes nodes that share the same parent. Other terms used to describe familial relationships are also routinely applied to trees and hierarchies, but I've personally found that it can get confusing trying to figure out which node is the **cousin** of another, and so have abandoned most of this extended terminology.

The Basics: Adjacency Lists and Graphs

The most common graph data model is called an **adjacency list**. In an adjacency list, the graph is modeled as pairs of nodes, each representing an edge. This is an extremely flexible way of modeling a graph; any kind of graph, hierarchy, or tree can fit into this model. However, it can be problematic from the perspectives of query complexity, performance, and data integrity. In this section, I will show you how to work with adjacency lists and point out some of the issues that you should be wary of when designing solutions around them.

The simplest of graph tables contains only two columns, X and Y:

```
CREATE TABLE Edges
(
    X int NOT NULL,
    Y int NOT NULL,
    PRIMARY KEY (X, Y)
);
GO
```

The combination of columns X and Y constitutes the primary key, and each row in the table represents one edge in the graph. Note that X and Y are assumed to be references to some valid table of nodes. This table only represents the edges that connect the nodes. It can also be used to reference unconnected nodes; a node with a path back to itself but no other paths can be inserted into the table for that purpose.

> ▪ **Note** When modeling unconnected nodes, some data architects prefer to use a nullable Y column rather than having both columns point to the same node. The net effect is the same, but in my opinion the nullable Y column makes some queries a bit messier, as you'll be forced to deal with the possibility of a NULL. The examples in this chapter, therefore, do not follow that convention—but you can use either approach in your production applications.

Constraining the Edges

As-is, the **Edges** table can be used to represent any graph, but semantics are important, and none are implied by the current structure. It's difficult to know whether each edge is directed or undirected. Traversing the graph, one could conceivably go either way, so the following two rows may or may not be logically identical:

```
INSERT INTO Edges VALUES (1, 2);
INSERT INTO Edges VALUES (2, 1);
```

If the edges in this graph are supposed to be directed, there is no problem. If you need both directions for a certain edge, simply insert them both, and don't insert both for directed edges. If, on the other hand, all edges are supposed to be undirected, a constraint is necessary in order to ensure that two logically identical paths cannot be inserted.

The primary key is clearly not sufficient to enforce this constraint, since it treats every combination as unique. The most obvious solution to this problem is to create a trigger that checks the rows when inserts or updates take place. Since the primary key already enforces that duplicate directional paths cannot be inserted, the trigger must only check for the opposite path.

Before creating the trigger, empty the **Edges** table so that it no longer contains the duplicate undirected edges just inserted:

```
TRUNCATE TABLE Edges;
GO
```

Then create the trigger that will check as rows are inserted or updated as follows:

```
CREATE TRIGGER CheckForDuplicates
ON Edges
FOR INSERT, UPDATE
AS
BEGIN
    IF EXISTS
    (
        SELECT *
        FROM Edges e
        WHERE
            EXISTS
            (
```

```
            SELECT *
            FROM inserted i
            WHERE
                i.X = e.Y
                AND i.Y = e.X
        )
    )
    BEGIN
        ROLLBACK;
    END
END;
GO
```

Attempting to reinsert the two rows listed previously will now cause the trigger to end the transaction and issue a rollback of the second row, preventing the duplicate edge from being created.

A slightly cleverer way of constraining the uniqueness of the paths is to make use of an indexed view. You can take advantage of the fact that an indexed view has a unique index, using it as a constraint in cases like this where a trigger seems awkward. In order to create the indexed view, you will need a numbers table (also called a tally table) with a single column, **Number**, which is the primary key. The following code listing creates such a table, populated with every number between **1** and **8000**:

```
SELECT TOP (8000)
    IDENTITY(int, 1, 1) AS Number
INTO Numbers
FROM master..spt_values a
CROSS JOIN master..spt_values b;

ALTER TABLE Numbers
ADD PRIMARY KEY (Number);
GO
```

■ **Note** We won't actually need all 8,000 rows in the Numbers table (in fact, the solution described here requires only two distinct rows), but there are lots of other scenarios where you might need a larger table of numbers, so it doesn't do any harm to prime the table with additional rows now.

The **master..spt_values** table is an arbitrary system table chosen simply because it has enough rows that, when cross-joined with itself, the output will be more than 8,000 rows.

A table of numbers is incredibly useful in many cases in which you might need to do interrow manipulation and look-ahead logic, especially when dealing with strings. However, in this case, its utility is fairly simple: a **CROSS JOIN** to the **Numbers** table, combined with a **WHERE** condition, will result in an output containing two rows for each row in the **Edges** table. A **CASE** expression will then be used to swap the **X** and **Y** column values—reversing the path direction—for one of the rows in each duplicate pair. The following view encapsulates this logic:

```
CREATE VIEW DuplicateEdges
WITH SCHEMABINDING
```

```
AS
    SELECT
        CASE n.Number
            WHEN 1 THEN e.X
            ELSE e.Y
        END X,
        CASE n.Number
            WHEN 1 THEN e.Y
            ELSE e.X
        END Y
    FROM Edges e
    CROSS JOIN Numbers n
    WHERE
        n.Number BETWEEN 1 AND 2;
GO
```

Once the view has been created, it can be indexed in order to constrain against duplicate paths:

```
CREATE UNIQUE CLUSTERED INDEX IX_NoDuplicates
ON DuplicateEdges (X,Y);
GO
```

Since the view logically contains both paths as they were inserted into the table, as well as the reverse paths, the unique index serves to constrain against duplication. Both techniques have similar performance characteristics, but there is admittedly a certain cool factor with the indexed view. It can also double as a quick lookup for finding all paths in a directed notation.

■ **Note** Once you have chosen either the trigger or the indexed view approach to prevent duplicate edges, be sure to delete all rows from the **Edges** table again before executing any of the remaining code listings in this chapter.

Basic Graph Queries: Who Am I Connected To?

Before traversing the graph to answer questions, it's again important to discuss the differences between directed and undirected edges and the way in which they are modeled. Figure 12-4 shows two graphs: I is undirected and J is directed.

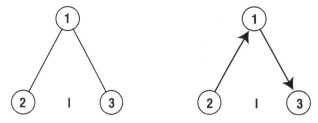

Figure 12-4. Directed and undirected graphs have different connection qualities.

The following node pairs can be used to represent the edges whether or not the **Edges** table is considered to be directed or undirected:

```
INSERT INTO Edges VALUES (2, 1), (1, 3);
GO
```

Now we can answer a simple question: starting at a specific node, what nodes can we traverse to?

In the case of a directed graph, any node **Y** is accessible from another node **X** if an edge exists that starts at **X** and ends at **Y**. This is easy enough to represent as a query (in this case, starting at node **1**):

```
SELECT Y
FROM Edges e
WHERE X = 1;
```

For an undirected graph, things get a bit more complex because any given edge between two nodes can be traversed in either direction. In that case, any node **Y** is accessible from another node **X** if an edge is represented as either starting at **X** and ending at **Y**, or the other way around. We need to consider all edges for which node **Y** is either the start or endpoint, or else the graph has effectively become directed. To find all nodes accessible from node **1** now requires a bit more code:

```
SELECT
    CASE
        WHEN X = 1 THEN Y
        ELSE X
    END
FROM Edges e
WHERE
    X = 1 OR Y = 1;
```

Aside from the increased complexity of this code, there's another much more important issue: performance on larger sets will start to suffer due to the fact that the search argument cannot be satisfied based on an index seek because it relies on two columns with an **OR** condition. The problem can be fixed to some degree by creating multiple indexes (one in which each column is the first key) and using a **UNION ALL** query, as follows:

```
SELECT Y
FROM Edges e
WHERE X = 1

UNION ALL

SELECT X
FROM Edges e
WHERE Y = 1;
```

This code is somewhat unintuitive, and because both indexes must be maintained and the query must do two index operations to be satisfied, performance will still suffer compared with querying the directed graph. For that reason, I recommend generally modeling graphs as directed and dealing with inserting both pairs of edges unless there is a compelling reason not to, such as an extremely large undirected graph where the extra edge combinations would challenge the server's available disk space. The remainder of the examples in this chapter will assume that the graph is directed.

Traversing the Graph

Finding out which nodes a given node is directly connected to is a good start, but in order to answer questions about the structure of the underlying data, the graph must be traversed. For this section, a more rigorous example data set is necessary. Figure 12-5 shows an initial sample graph representing an abbreviated portion of a street map for an unnamed city.

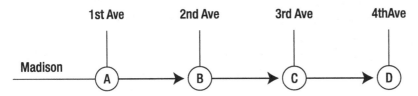

Figure 12-5. An abbreviated street map

A few tables are required to represent this map—to begin with, a table of streets:

```
CREATE TABLE Streets
(
    StreetId int NOT NULL PRIMARY KEY,
    StreetName varchar(75)
);
GO

INSERT INTO Streets VALUES
  (1, '1st Ave'), (2, '2nd Ave'),
  (3, '3rd Ave'), (4, '4th Ave'), (5, 'Madison');
GO
```

Each street is assigned a surrogate key so that it can be referenced easily in other tables.

The next requirement is a table of intersections—the nodes in the graph. This table creates a key for each intersection, which is defined in this set of data as a collection of one or more streets:

```
CREATE TABLE Intersections
(
    IntersectionId int NOT NULL PRIMARY KEY,
    IntersectionName varchar(10)
);
GO

INSERT INTO Intersections VALUES
  (1, 'A'), (2, 'B'), (3, 'C'), (4, 'D');
GO
```

Next is a table called **IntersectionStreets**, which maps streets to their respective intersections. Note that I haven't included any constraints on this table, as they can get quite complex. One constraint that might be ideal would specify that any given combination of streets should not intersect more than once. However, it's difficult to say whether this would apply to all cities, given that many older cities have twisting roads that may intersect with each other at numerous points. Dealing with this issue is left as an exercise for you to try on your own.

```
CREATE TABLE IntersectionStreets
(
    IntersectionId int NOT NULL
        REFERENCES Intersections (IntersectionId),
    StreetId int NOT NULL
        REFERENCES Streets (StreetId),
    PRIMARY KEY (IntersectionId, StreetId)
);
GO

INSERT INTO IntersectionStreets VALUES
    (1, 1), (1, 5), (2, 2), (2, 5), (3, 3), (3, 5), (4, 4), (4, 5);
GO
```

The final table describes the edges of the graph, which in this case are segments of street between each intersection. I've added a couple of constraints that might not be so obvious at first glance:

Rather than using foreign keys to the **Intersections** table, the **StreetSegments** table references the **IntersectionStreets** table for both the starting point and ending point. In both cases, the street is also included in the key. The purpose of this is so that you can't start on one street and magically end up on another street or at an intersection that's not even on the street you started on.

The **CK_Intersections** constraint ensures that the two intersections are actually different—so you can't start at one intersection and end up at the same place after only one move. It's theoretically possible that a circular street could intersect another street at only one point, in which case traveling the entire length of the street could get you back to where you started. However, doing so would clearly not help you traverse through the graph to a destination, which is the situation currently being considered.

Here's the T-SQL to create the street segments that constitute the edges of the graph:

```
CREATE TABLE StreetSegments
(
    IntersectionId_Start int NOT NULL,
    IntersectionId_End int NOT NULL,
    StreetId int NOT NULL,
    CONSTRAINT FK_Start
        FOREIGN KEY (IntersectionId_Start, StreetId)
        REFERENCES IntersectionStreets (IntersectionId, StreetId),
    CONSTRAINT FK_End
        FOREIGN KEY (IntersectionId_End, StreetId)
        REFERENCES IntersectionStreets (IntersectionId, StreetId),
    CONSTRAINT CK_Intersections
        CHECK (IntersectionId_Start <> IntersectionId_End),
    CONSTRAINT PK_StreetSegments
        PRIMARY KEY (IntersectionId_Start, IntersectionId_End)
);
```

```
GO

INSERT INTO StreetSegments VALUES (1, 2, 5), (2, 3, 5), (3, 4, 5);
GO
```

In addition to these tables, a helper function is useful in order to make navigation easier. The `GetIntersectionId` function returns the intersection at which the two input streets intersect. As mentioned before, the schema used in this example assumes that each street intersects only once with any other street, and the `GetIntersectionId` function makes the same assumption. It works by searching for all intersections that the input streets participate in, and then finding the one that had exactly two matches, meaning that both input streets intersect. Following is the T-SQL for the function:

```
CREATE FUNCTION GetIntersectionId
(
    @Street1 varchar(75),
    @Street2 varchar(75)
)
RETURNS int
WITH SCHEMABINDING
AS
BEGIN
    RETURN
    (
        SELECT
            i.IntersectionId
        FROM dbo.IntersectionStreets i
        WHERE
            StreetId IN
            (
                SELECT StreetId
                FROM dbo.Streets
                WHERE StreetName IN (@Street1, @Street2)
            )
        GROUP BY i.IntersectionId
        HAVING COUNT(*) = 2
    )
END;
GO
```

Using the schema and the function, we can start traversing the nodes. The basic technique of traversing the graph is quite simple: find the starting intersection and all nodes that it connects to, and iteratively or recursively move outward, using the previous node's ending point as the starting point for the next. This is easily accomplished using a recursive common table expression (CTE). The following is a simple initial example of a CTE that can be used to traverse the nodes from Madison and 1st Avenue to Madison and 4th Avenue:

```
DECLARE
    @Start int = dbo.GetIntersectionId('Madison', '1st Ave'),
    @End int = dbo.GetIntersectionId('Madison', '4th Ave');

WITH Paths
```

```
AS
(
    SELECT
        @Start AS theStart,
        IntersectionId_End AS theEnd
    FROM dbo.StreetSegments
    WHERE
        IntersectionId_Start = @Start

    UNION ALL

    SELECT
        p.theEnd,
        ss.IntersectionId_End
    FROM Paths p
    JOIN dbo.StreetSegments ss ON ss.IntersectionId_Start = p.theEnd
    WHERE p.theEnd <> @End
)
SELECT *
FROM Paths;
GO
```

The anchor part of the CTE finds all nodes to which the starting intersection is connected—in this case, given the data we've already input, there is only one. The recursive part uses the anchor's output as its input, finding all connected nodes from there, and continuing only if the endpoint of the next intersection is not equal to the end intersection. The output for this query is as follows:

theStart	theEnd
1	2
2	3
3	4

While this output is correct and perfectly descriptive with only one path between the two points, it has some problems. First of all, the ordering of the output of a CTE—just like any other query—is not guaranteed without an **ORDER BY** clause. In this case, the order happens to coincide with the order of the path, but this is a very small data set, and the server on which I ran the query has only one processor. On a bigger set of data and/or with multiple processors, SQL Server could choose to process the data in a different order, thereby destroying the implicit output order.

The second issue is that in this case there is exactly one path between the start and endpoints. What if there were more than one path? Figure 12-6 shows the street map with a new street, a few new intersections, and more street segments added. The following T-SQL can be used to add the new data to the appropriate tables:

```
--New street
INSERT INTO Streets VALUES (6, 'Lexington');
GO
--New intersections
INSERT INTO Intersections VALUES
  (5, 'E'), (6, 'F'), (7, 'G'), (8, 'H');
GO
--New intersection/street mappings
INSERT INTO IntersectionStreets VALUES
  (5, 1), (5, 6), (6, 2), (6, 6), (7, 3), (7, 6), (8, 4), (8, 6);
GO
--North/South segments
INSERT INTO StreetSegments VALUES (2, 6, 2), (4, 8, 4);
GO
--East/West segments
INSERT INTO StreetSegments VALUES (8, 7, 6), (7, 6, 6), (6, 5, 6);
GO
```

Note that although intersections **E** and **G** have been created, their corresponding north/south segments have not yet been inserted. This is on purpose, as I'm going to use those segments to illustrate yet another complication.

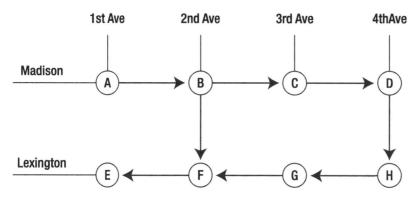

Figure 12-6. A slightly more complete version of the street map

Once the new data is inserted, we can try the same CTE as before, this time traveling from Madison and 1st Avenue to Lexington and 1st Avenue. To change the destination, modify the **DECLARE** statement that assigns the **@Start** and **@End** variables to be as follows:

```
DECLARE
    @Start int = dbo.GetIntersectionId('Madison', '1st Ave'),
    @End int = dbo.GetIntersectionId('Lexington', '1st Ave');
```

Having made these changes, the output of the CTE query is now as follows:

theStart	theEnd
1	2
2	3
2	6
6	5
3	4
4	8
8	7
7	6
6	5

There are now two paths from the starting point to the ending point, but it's impossible to tell what they are; the intersections involved in each path are mixed up in the output.

To solve this problem, the CTE will have to "remember" on each iteration where it's been on previous iterations. Since each iteration of a CTE can only access the data from the previous iteration—and not all data from all previous iterations—each row will have to keep its own records inline. This can be done using a **materialized path** notation, where each previously visited node will be appended to a running list. This will require adding a new column to the CTE as highlighted in bold in the following code listing:

```
DECLARE
  @Start int =  dbo.GetIntersectionId('Madison', '1st Ave'),
  @End int = dbo.GetIntersectionId('Lexington', '1st Ave');

WITH Paths
AS
(
  SELECT
    @Start AS theStart,
    IntersectionId_End AS theEnd,
    CAST('/' +
    CAST(@Start AS varchar(255)) + '/' +
    CAST(IntersectionId_End AS varchar(255)) + '/'
    AS varchar(255) ) AS thePath
  FROM dbo.StreetSegments
  WHERE
    IntersectionId_Start = @Start
  UNION ALL
  SELECT
```

```
            p.theEnd,
            ss.IntersectionId_End,
            CAST(p.ThePath +
             CAST(IntersectionId_End AS varchar(255)) + '/'
             AS varchar(255)
            )
            FROM Paths p
              JOIN dbo.StreetSegments ss ON ss.IntersectionId_Start = p.theEnd
            WHERE p.theEnd <> @End
    )
SELECT *
FROM Paths;
GO
```

This code will start to form a list of visited nodes. If node **A** (**IntersectionId 1**) is specified as the start point, the output for this column for the anchor member will be **/1/2/**, since node **B** (**IntersectionId 2**) is the only node that participates in a street segment starting at node **A**.

As new nodes are visited, their IDs will be appended to the list, producing a "breadcrumb" trail of all visited nodes. Note that the columns in both the anchor and recursive members are **CAST** to make sure their data types are identical. This is required because the **varchar** size changes due to concatenation, and all columns exposed by the anchor and recursive members must have identical types. The output of the CTE after making these modifications is as follows:

theStart	theEnd	thePath
1	2	/1/2/
2	3	/1/2/3/
2	6	/1/2/6/
6	5	/1/2/6/5/
3	4	/1/2/3/4/
4	8	/1/2/3/4/8/
8	7	/1/2/3/4/8/7/
7	6	/1/2/3/4/8/7/6/
6	5	/1/2/3/4/8/7/6/5/

The output now includes the complete paths to the endpoints, but it still includes all subpaths visited along the way. To finish, add the following to the outermost query:

```
WHERE theEnd = @End
```

This will limit the results to only paths that actually end at the specified endpoint—in this case, node **E** (**IntersectionId 5**). After making that addition, only the two paths that actually visit both the start and end nodes are shown.

The CTE still has one major problem as-is. Figure 12-7 shows a completed version of the map, with the final two street segments filled in. The following T-SQL can be used to populate the **StreetSegments** table with the new data:

```
INSERT INTO StreetSegments VALUES (5, 1, 1), (7, 3, 3);
GO
```

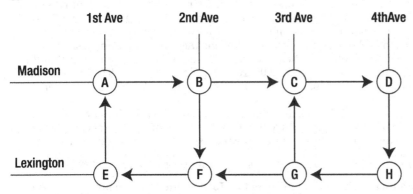

Figure 12-7. A version of the map with all segments filled in

Rerunning the CTE after introducing the new segments results in the following partial output (abbreviated for brevity):

theStart	theEnd	thePath
6	5	/1/2/6/5/
6	5	/1/2/3/4/8/7/6/5/
6	5	/1/2/3/4/8/7/3/4/8/7/6/5/
6	5	/1/2/3/4/8/7/3/4/8/7/3/4/8/7/6/5/
6	5	/1/2/3/4/8/7/3/4/8/7/3/4/8/7/3/4/8/7/6/5/
6	5	/1/2/3/4/8/7/3/4/8/7/3/4/8/7/3/4/8/7/3/4/8/7/6/5/
6	5	/1/2/3/4/8/7/3/4/8/7/3/4/8/7/3/4/8/7/3/4/8/7/3/4/8/7/6/5/
6	5	/1/2/3/4/8/7/3/4/8/7/3/4/8/7/3/4/8/7/3/4/8/7/3/4/8/7/3/4/8/7/6/5/

...

along with the following error:

```
Msg 530, Level 16, State 1, Line 9

The statement terminated.

The maximum recursion 100 has been exhausted before statement completion.
```

The issue is that these new intersections create cycles in the graph. The problem can be seen to start at the fourth line of the output, when the recursion first visits node G (**IntersectionId** 7). From there, one can go one of two ways: west to node F (**IntersectionId** 6) or north to node C (**IntersectionId** 3). Following the first route, the recursion eventually completes. But following the second route, the recursion will keep coming back to node G again and again, following the same two branches. Eventually, the default recursive limit of 100 is reached and execution ends with an error. Note that this default limit can be overridden using the **OPTION (MAXRECURSION N)** query hint, where **N** is the maximum recursive depth you'd like to use. In this case, **100** is a good limit because it quickly tells us that there is a major problem!

Fixing this issue, luckily, is quite simple: check the path to find out whether the next node has already been visited, and if so, do not visit it again. Since the path is a string, this can be accomplished using a **LIKE** predicate by adding the following argument to the recursive member's **WHERE** clause:

```
AND p.thePath NOT LIKE '%/' + CONVERT(varchar, ss.IntersectionId_End) + '/%'
```

This predicate checks to make sure that the ending **IntersectionId**, delimited by **/** on both sides, does not yet appear in the path—in other words, has not yet been visited. This will make it impossible for the recursion to fall into a cycle.

Running the CTE after adding this fix eliminates the cycle issue. The full code for the fixed CTE follows:

```
DECLARE
  @Start int =  dbo.GetIntersectionId('Madison', '1st Ave'),
  @End int = dbo.GetIntersectionId('Lexington', '1st Ave');

WITH Paths
AS
(
  SELECT
  @Start AS theStart,
  IntersectionId_End AS theEnd,
  CAST('/' +
      CAST(@Start AS varchar(255)) + '/' +
      CAST(IntersectionId_End AS varchar(255)) + '/'
      AS varchar(255) ) AS thePath
  FROM dbo.StreetSegments
  WHERE
  IntersectionId_Start = @Start
  UNION ALL
  SELECT
  p.theEnd,
  ss.IntersectionId_End,
  CAST(p.ThePath +
          CAST(IntersectionId_End AS varchar(255)) + '/'
```

```
                AS varchar(255)
        )
    FROM Paths p
    JOIN dbo.StreetSegments ss ON ss.IntersectionId_Start = p.theEnd
    WHERE p.theEnd <> @End
            AND p.thePath NOT LIKE '%/' + CONVERT(varchar, ss.IntersectionId_End) + '/%'
    )
SELECT *
FROM Paths;
GO
```

This concludes this chapter's coverage on general graphs. The remainder of the chapter deals with modeling and querying of hierarchies. Although hierarchies are much more specialized than graphs, they tend to be more typically seen in software projects than general graphs, and developers must consider slightly different issues when modeling them.

Advanced routing

The example shown in this section is highly simplified, and it is designed to teach the basics of querying graphs rather than serve as a complete routing solution. I have had the pleasure of working fairly extensively with a production system designed to traverse actual street routes and will briefly share some of the insights I have gained in case you are interested in these kinds of problems.

The first issue with the solution shown here is that of scalability. A big city has tens of thousands of street segments, and determining a route from one end of the city to another using this method will create a combinatorial explosion of possibilities. In order to reduce the number of combinations, a few things can be done.

First of all, each segment can be weighted, and a score tallied along the way as you recurse over the possible paths. If the score gets too high, you can terminate the recursion. For example, in the system I worked on, weighting was done based on distance traveled. The algorithm used was fairly complex, but essentially, if a destination was 2 miles away and the route went over 3 miles, recursion would be terminated for that branch. This scoring also lets the system determine the shortest possible routes.

Another method used to greatly decrease the number of combinations was an analysis of the input set of streets, and a determination made of major routes between certain locations. For instance, traveling from one end of the city to another is usually most direct on a freeway. If the system determines that a freeway route is appropriate, it breaks the routing problem down into two sections: first, find the shortest route from the starting point to a freeway on-ramp, and then find the shortest route from the endpoint to a freeway exit. Put these routes together, including the freeway travel, and you have an optimized path from the starting point to the ending point. Major routes—like freeways—can be underweighted in order to make them appear higher in the scoring rank.

If you'd like to try working with real street data, you can download US geographical shape files (including streets as well as various natural formations) for free from the US Census Bureau. The data, called TIGER/Line, is available from **www.census.gov/geo/www/tiger/index.html**. Be warned: this data is not easy to work with and requires a lot of cleanup to get it to the point where it can be easily queried.

Adjacency List Hierarchies

As mentioned previously, any kind of graph can be modeled using an adjacency list. This of course includes hierarchies, which are nothing more than rooted, directed, acyclic graphs with exactly one path between any two nodes (irrespective of direction). Adjacency list hierarchies are very easy to model, visualize, and understand, but can be tricky or inefficient to query in some cases since they require iteration or recursion, as I'll discuss shortly.

Traversing an adjacency list hierarchy is virtually identical to traversing an adjacency list graph, but since hierarchies don't have cycles, you don't need to worry about them in your code. This is a nice feature, since it makes your code shorter, easier to understand, and more efficient. However, being able to make the assumption that your data really does follow a hierarchical structure—and not a general graph—takes a bit of work up front. See "Constraining the Hierarchy" later in this section for information on how to make sure that your hierarchies don't end up with cycles, multiple roots, or disconnected subtrees.

The most commonly recognizable example of an adjacency list hierarchy is a self-referential personnel table that models employees and their managers. Since it's such a common and easily understood example, this is the scenario that will be used for this section and the rest of this chapter.

To start, we'll create an simple adjacency list based on three columns of data from the **HumanResources.Employee** table of the **AdventureWorks** database. The columns used will be as follows:

- **EmployeeID** is the primary key for each row of the table. Most of the time, adjacency list hierarchies are modeled in a node-centric rather than edge-centric way; that is, the primary key of the hierarchy is the key for a given node, rather than a key representing an edge. This makes sense because each node in a hierarchy can only have one direct ancestor.

- **ManagerID** is the key for the employee that each row reports to in the same table. If **ManagerID** is **NULL**, that employee is the root node in the tree (i.e., the head of the company). It's common when modeling adjacency list hierarchies to use either **NULL** or an identical key to the row's primary key to represent root nodes.

- Finally, the **Title** column, representing employees' job titles, will be used to make the output easier to read.

You can use the following T-SQL to create a table based on these columns:

```
USE AdventureWorks;
GO

CREATE TABLE Employee_Temp
(
    EmployeeID int NOT NULL
        CONSTRAINT PK_Employee PRIMARY KEY,
    ManagerID int NULL
        CONSTRAINT FK_Manager REFERENCES Employee_Temp (EmployeeID),
    Title nvarchar(100)
);
GO

INSERT INTO Employee_Temp
(
    EmployeeID,
```

```
    ManagerID,
    Title
)
SELECT
    EmployeeID,
    ManagerID,
    Title
FROM HumanResources.Employee;
GO
```

The types of questions generally posed against a hierarchy are somewhat different from the example graph traversal questions examined in the previous section. For adjacency lists as well as the other hierarchical models discussed in this chapter, we'll consider how to answer the following common questions:

- What are the **direct descendants** of a given node? In other words, who are the people who directly report to a given manager?

- What are *all* of the descendants of a given node? Which is to say, how many people all the way down the organizational hierarchy ultimately report up to a given manager? The challenge here is how to sort the output so that it makes sense with regard to the hierarchy.

- What is the path from a given child node back to the root node? In other words, following the management path up instead of down, who reports to whom?

I will also discuss the following data modification challenges:

- Inserting a new node into the hierarchy, as when a new employee is hired

- Relocating a subtree, such as might be necessary if a division gets moved under a new manager

- Deleting a node from the hierarchy, which might, for example, need to happen in an organizational hierarchy due to attrition

Each of the techniques discussed in this chapter have slightly different levels of difficulty with regard to the complexity of solving these problems, and I will make general suggestions on when to use each model.

Finding Direct Descendants

Finding the direct descendants of a given node is quite straightforward in an adjacency list hierarchy; it's the same as finding the available nodes to which you can traverse in a graph. Start by choosing the parent node for your query, and select all nodes for which that node is the parent. To find all employees that report directly to the CEO (**EmployeeID 109**), use the following T-SQL:

```
SELECT *
FROM Employee_Temp
WHERE ManagerID = 109;
```

This query returns the results shown following, showing the six branches of AdventureWorks, represented by its upper management team—exactly the results that we expected.

EmployeeID	ManagerID	Title
6	109	Marketing Manager
12	109	Vice President of Engineering
42	109	Information Services Manager
140	109	Chief Financial Officer
148	109	Vice President of Production
273	109	Vice President of Sales

However, this query has a hidden problem: traversing from node to node in the **Employee_Temp** table means searching based on the **ManagerID** column. Considering that this column is not indexed, it should come as no surprise that the query plan for the preceding query involves a scan, as shown in Figure 12-8.

SELECT
Cost: 0%

Clustered Index Scan (Clustered)
[Employee_Temp].[PK_Employee]
Cost: 100%

Figure 12-8. Querying on the ManagerID causes a table scan.

To eliminate this issue, an index on the **ManagerID** column must be created. However, choosing exactly how best to index a table such as this one can be difficult. In the case of this small example, a clustered index on **ManagerID** would yield the best overall mix of performance for both querying and data updates, by covering all queries that involve traversing the table. However, in an actual production system, there might be a much higher percentage of queries based on the **EmployeeID**—for instance, queries to get a single employee's data—and there would probably be a lot more columns in the table than the three used here for example purposes, meaning that clustered key lookups could be expensive. In such a case, it is important to test carefully which combination of indexes delivers the best balance of query and data modification performance for your particular workload.

In order to show the best possible performance in this case, change the primary key to use a nonclustered index and create a clustered index on **ManagerID**, as shown in the following T-SQL:

```
ALTER TABLE Employee_Temp
DROP CONSTRAINT FK_Manager, PK_Employee;

CREATE CLUSTERED INDEX IX_Manager
ON Employee_Temp (ManagerID);

ALTER TABLE Employee_Temp
ADD CONSTRAINT PK_Employee
PRIMARY KEY NONCLUSTERED (EmployeeID);

GO
```

■ **Caution** Adding a clustered index to the nonkey **ManagerId** column might result in the best performance for queries designed solely to determine those employees that report to a given manager, but it is not necessarily the best design for a general purpose employees table.

Once this change has been made, rerunning the T-SQL to find the CEO's direct reports produces a clustered index seek instead of a scan—a small improvement that will be magnified when performing queries against a table with a greater number of rows.

Traversing down the Hierarchy

Shifting from finding direct descendants of one node to traversing down the entire hierarchy all the way to the leaf nodes is extremely simple, just as in the case of general graphs. A recursive CTE is one tool that can be used for this purpose. The following CTE, modified from the section on graphs, traverses the **Employee_Temp** hierarchy starting from the CEO, returning all employees in the company:

```
WITH n AS
(
    SELECT
        EmployeeID,
        ManagerID,
        Title
    FROM Employee_Temp
    WHERE ManagerID IS NULL

    UNION ALL

    SELECT
        e.EmployeeID,
        e.ManagerID,
        e.Title
    FROM Employee_Temp e
    JOIN n ON n.EmployeeID = e.ManagerID
)
SELECT
    n.EmployeeID,
    n.ManagerID,
    n.Title
FROM n;
GO
```

Note that this CTE returns all columns to be used by the outer query—but this is not the only way to write this query. The query could also be written such that the CTE uses and returns only the **EmployeeID** column, necessitating an additional **JOIN** in the outer query to get the other columns:

```
WITH n AS
(
```

```
SELECT
    EmployeeID
FROM Employee_Temp
WHERE ManagerID IS NULL

UNION ALL

SELECT
    e.EmployeeID
FROM Employee_Temp e
JOIN n ON n.EmployeeID = e.ManagerID
)
SELECT
    e.EmployeeID,
    e.ManagerID,
    e.Title
FROM n
JOIN Employee_Temp e ON e.EmployeeID = n.EmployeeID;
GO
```

I thought that this latter form might result in less I/O activity, but after testing several combinations of indexes against both query forms, using this table as well as tables with many more columns, I decided that there is no straightforward answer. The latter query tends to perform better as the output row size increases, but in the case of the small test table, the former query is much more efficient. Again, this is something you should test against your actual workload before deploying a solution.

Ordering the Output

Regardless of the performance of the two queries listed in the previous section, the fact is that we haven't really done much yet. The output of either of these queries as they currently stand is logically equivalent to the output of **SELECT * FROM Employee_Temp**. In order to add value, the output should be sorted such that it conforms to the hierarchy represented in the table. To do this, we can use the same path technique described in the section "Traversing the Graph," but without the need to be concerned with cycles. By ordering by the path, the output will follow the same nested order as the hierarchy itself. The following T-SQL shows how to accomplish this:

```
WITH n AS
(
    SELECT
        EmployeeID,
        ManagerID,
        Title,
        CONVERT(varchar(900),
            RIGHT(REPLICATE('0', 10) + CONVERT(varchar, EmployeeID), 10) + '/'
        ) AS thePath
    FROM Employee_Temp
    WHERE ManagerID IS NULL

    UNION ALL
```

```
SELECT
    e.EmployeeID,
    e.ManagerID,
    e.Title,
    CONVERT(varchar(900),
        n.thePath +
        RIGHT(REPLICATE('0', 10) + CONVERT(varchar, e.EmployeeID), 10) + '/'
    ) AS thePath
FROM Employee_Temp e
JOIN n ON n.EmployeeID = e.ManagerID
)
SELECT
    n.EmployeeID,
    n.ManagerID,
    n.Title,
    n.thePath
FROM n
ORDER BY n.thePath;
GO
```

Running this query produces the output shown following (truncated for brevity):

EmployeeID	ManagerID	Title	thePath
109	NULL	Chief Executive Officer	0000000109/
6	109	Marketing Manager	0000000109/0000000006/
2	6	Marketing Assistant	0000000109/0000000006/0000000002/
46	6	Marketing Specialist	0000000109/0000000006/0000000046/
106	6	Marketing Specialist	0000000109/0000000006/0000000106/
119	6	Marketing Specialist	0000000109/0000000006/0000000119/
203	6	Marketing Specialist	0000000109/0000000006/0000000203/
269	6	Marketing Assistant	0000000109/0000000006/0000000269/
271	6	Marketing Specialist	0000000109/0000000006/0000000271/
272	6	Marketing Assistant	0000000109/0000000006/0000000272/
12	109	V President Engineering	0000000109/0000000012/
3	12	Engineering Manager	0000000109/0000000012/0000000003/

In order to support proper numerical ordering on the nodes, I've left-padded them with zeros. This ensures that, for instance, the path 1/2/ does not sort higher than the path 1/10/. The numbers are padded to ten digits to support the full range of positive integer values supported by SQL Server's int data type. Note that siblings in this case are ordered based on their EmployeeID. Changing the ordering of siblings—for instance, to alphabetical order based on Title—requires a bit of manipulation to the path. Instead of materializing the EmployeeID, materialize a row number that represents the current ordered sibling. This can be done using SQL Server's **ROW_NUMBER** function, and is sometimes referred to as **enumerating** the path. The following modified version of the CTE enumerates the path:

```
WITH n AS
(
    SELECT
        EmployeeID,
        ManagerID,
        Title,
        CONVERT(varchar(900),
            '0000000001/'
        ) AS thePath
    FROM Employee_Temp
    WHERE ManagerID IS NULL

    UNION ALL

    SELECT
        e.EmployeeID,
        e.ManagerID,
        e.Title,
        CONVERT(varchar(900),
            n.thePath +
            RIGHT(
                REPLICATE('0', 10) +
                    CONVERT(varchar, ROW_NUMBER() OVER (ORDER BY e.Title)),
                10
            ) + '/'
        ) AS thePath
    FROM Employee_Temp e
    JOIN n ON n.EmployeeID = e.ManagerID
)
SELECT
    n.EmployeeID,
    n.ManagerID,
    n.Title,
    n.thePath
FROM n
ORDER BY n.thePath;
GO
```

The enumerated path representing each node is illustrated in the results of the query as follows:

EmployeeID	ManagerID	Title	thePath
109	NULL	Chief Executive Officer	00000001/
140	109	Chief Financial Officer	00000001/00000001/
139	140	Accounts Manager	00000001/00000001/00000001/
216	139	Accountant	00000001/00000001/00000001/00000001/
178	139	Accountant	00000001/00000001/00000001/00000002/
166	139	Accs Payable Specialist	00000001/00000001/00000001/00000003/
201	139	Accs Payable Specialist	00000001/00000001/00000001/00000004/
130	139	Accs Recvble Specialist	00000001/00000001/00000001/00000005/
94	139	Accs Recvble Specialist	00000001/00000001/00000001/00000006/
59	139	Accs Recvble Specialist	00000001/00000001/00000001/00000007/
103	140	Assistant to the CFO	00000001/00000001/00000002/
71	140	Finance Manager	00000001/00000001/00000003/
274	71	Purchasing Manager	00000001/00000001/00000003/00000001/

■ **Tip** Instead of left-padding the node IDs with zeros, you could expose the **thePath** column typed as **varbinary** and convert the IDs to **binary(4)**. This would have the same net effect for the purpose of sorting and at the same time take up less space—so you will see an efficiency benefit, and in addition you'll be able to hold more node IDs in each row's path. The downside is that this makes the IDs more difficult to visualize, so for the purposes of this chapter—where visual cues are important—I use the left-padding method instead.

The downside of including an enumerated path instead of a materialized path is that the enumerated version cannot be easily deconstructed to determine the keys that were followed. For instance, simply looking at the **thePath** column in the results of the first query in this section, we can see that the path to the Engineering Manager (**EmployeeID 3**) starts with **EmployeeID 109** and continues to **EmployeeID 12** before getting to the Engineering Manager. Looking at the same column using the enumerated path, it is not possible to discover the actual IDs that make up a given path without following it back up the hierarchy in the output.

Are CTEs the Best Choice?

While CTEs are possibly the most convenient way to traverse adjacency list hierarchies in SQL Server 2008, they do not necessarily deliver the best possible performance. Iterative methods involving temporary tables or table variables may well outperform recursive CTEs, especially as the hierarchy grows in size.

To highlight the performance difference between CTEs and iterative methods, a larger sample hierarchy is necessary. To begin with, we can add **width** to the **Employee_Temp** hierarchy. This means that the hierarchy will maintain the same depth, but each level will have more siblings. To accomplish this, for each row below a given subtree, both the employee IDs and manager IDs can be incremented by the same known amount, thereby producing a duplicate subtree in place. The following T-SQL accomplishes this, running in a loop five times and doubling the width of the hierarchy on each iteration:

```
DECLARE @CEO int;
SELECT
    @CEO = EmployeeID
FROM Employee_Temp
WHERE ManagerID IS NULL;

DECLARE @width int = 1;

WHILE @width <= 16
BEGIN
    INSERT INTO Employee_Temp
    (
        EmployeeID,
        ManagerID,
        Title
    )
    SELECT
        e.EmployeeID + (1000 * @width),
        CASE e.ManagerID
            WHEN @CEO THEN e.ManagerID
            ELSE e.ManagerID + (1000 * @width)
        END,
        e.Title
    FROM Employee_Temp e
    WHERE
        e.ManagerID IS NOT NULL;

    SET @width = @width * 2;
END;
GO
```

There are two key factors you should pay attention to in this example. First is the **@width** variable, which is doubled on each iteration in order to avoid key collisions as the keys are incremented. Second, look at the **CASE** expression in the **SELECT** list, which increments all IDs except that of the CEO. This ensures that the duplicate subtrees will be appended to the tree as a whole, by virtue of the roots of those subtrees being subordinates of the CEO's node, rather than the node at the top of each subtree becoming an additional root node.

Once this code has been run, the **Employee_Temp** hierarchy will have 9,249 nodes, instead of the 290 that we started with. However, the hierarchy still has only five levels. To increase the **depth**, a slightly different algorithm is required. To add levels, find all managers except the CEO, and insert new duplicate nodes, incrementing their employee IDs similar to before. Next, update the preexisting managers in the table to report to the new managers. The following T-SQL does this in a loop four times, producing a hierarchy with a depth of 50 levels and 31,329 nodes:

```
DECLARE @CEO int;
SELECT
    @CEO = EmployeeID
FROM Employee_Temp
WHERE ManagerID IS NULL;

DECLARE @depth int = 32;

WHILE @depth <= 256
BEGIN
    DECLARE @OldManagers table
    (
        EmployeeID int
    );

    --Insert intermediate managers
    --Find all managers except the CEO, and increment their EmployeeID by 1000
    INSERT INTO Employee_Temp
    (
        EmployeeID,
        ManagerID,
        Title
    )
    OUTPUT inserted.EmployeeID - (1000 * @depth) INTO @OldManagers
    SELECT
        e.EmployeeID + (1000 * @depth) as newemp,
        e.ManagerID,
        'Intermediate Manager'
    FROM Employee_Temp e
    WHERE
        e.EmployeeID <> @CEO
        AND EXISTS
        (
            SELECT *
            FROM Employee_Temp e1
            WHERE e1.ManagerID = e.EmployeeID
        );

    --Update existing managers to report to intermediates
    UPDATE Employee_Temp
    SET ManagerID = EmployeeID + (1000 * @depth)
    WHERE
        EmployeeID IN
        (
```

```
            SELECT EmployeeID
            FROM @OldManagers
        );

    SET @depth = @depth * 2;
END;
GO
```

Be careful when adding additional depth to an experimental hierarchy. I've found that depth has a much greater performance impact than width, and extremely deep hierarchies are not especially common—for instance, even the largest companies do not normally have more than 20 or 30 levels of management.

To iteratively traverse the hierarchy using a table variable, think about what recursion does: at each level, the employees for the previous level's managers are found, and then that level becomes the current level. Applying this logic iteratively requires the following table variable:

```
DECLARE @n table
(
    EmployeeID int,
    ManagerID int,
    Title nvarchar(100),
    Depth int,
    thePath varchar(900),
    PRIMARY KEY (Depth, EmployeeID)
);
```

The **Depth** column maintains the level for nodes as they are inserted. The table is clustered on the combination of **Depth** and **EmployeeID**; at each level, the depth will be queried first, and we know that **EmployeeID** will be unique so we can exploit it as a method of ensuring that the key itself is unique.

To start things off, prime the table variable with the node you wish to use as the root for traversal. In this case, the CEO's node will be used, and the path is started with **1/**, as I'll be implementing the enumerated path output shown in the previous example:

```
DECLARE @depth int = 1;

INSERT INTO @n
SELECT
    EmployeeID,
    ManagerID,
    Title,
    @depth,
    '0000000001/'
FROM Employee_Temp
WHERE ManagerID IS NULL;
```

After the first row is in place, the logic is identical to the recursive logic used in the CTE. For each level of depth, find the subordinates. The only difference is that this is done using a **WHILE** loop instead of a recursive CTE:

```
WHILE 1=1
BEGIN
```

```
INSERT INTO @n
SELECT
    e.EmployeeID,
    e.ManagerID,
    e.Title,
    @depth + 1,
    n.thePath +
        RIGHT(
                REPLICATE('0', 10) +
                    CONVERT(varchar, ROW_NUMBER() OVER
                        (PARTITION BY e.ManagerID ORDER BY e.Title)),
                10
            ) + '/'
FROM Employee_Temp e
JOIN @n n on n.EmployeeID = e.ManagerID
WHERE n.Depth = @depth;

IF @@ROWCOUNT = 0
    BREAK;

SET @depth = @depth + 1;
END
```

Finally, the output can be queried from the table variable. Like before, an **ORDER BY** clause is necessary:

```
SELECT
    EmployeeID,
    ManagerID,
    Title,
    thePath
FROM @n
ORDER BY
    thePath;
```

This method uses over 50 percent more code than the CTE, is quite a bit less intuitive, and has many more potential areas in which you might introduce logic bugs. However, its performance is quite a bit better than the CTE. The enumerated path CTE performs 347,282 reads and runs in 27.6 seconds on my laptop against the enhanced **Employee_Temp** table. The iterative method, on the other hand, requires only 173,536 reads and runs in 13.2 seconds.

Despite the clear performance improvement in this case, I do not recommend this method for the majority of situations. I feel that the maintainability issues overshadow the performance benefits in all but the most extreme cases (such as that demonstrated here). For that reason, the remaining examples in this chapter will use CTEs. However, you should be able to convert any of the examples so that they use iterative logic. Should you decide to use this technique on a project, you might find it beneficial to encapsulate the code in a multistatement table-valued UDF to allow greater potential for reuse.

> ■ **Note** If you're following along with the examples in this chapter and you increased the number of rows in the `Employee_Temp` table, you should drop and re-create it before continuing with the rest of the chapter.

Traversing up the Hierarchy

For an adjacency list, traversing "up" the hierarchy—in other words, finding any given node's ancestry path back to the root node—is essentially the same as traversing down the hierarchy in reverse. Instead of using **ManagerID** as a key at each level of recursion, use **EmployeeID**. The following CTE shows how to get the path from the Research and Development Manager, **EmployeeID 217**, to the CEO:

```
WITH n AS
(
  SELECT
    ManagerID,
    CONVERT(varchar(900),
      RIGHT(
        REPLICATE('0', 10) +
        CONVERT(varchar, EmployeeID) + '/', 10)
      ) AS thePath
  FROM Employee_Temp
  WHERE EmployeeID = 217

  UNION ALL

  SELECT
    e.ManagerID,
    CONVERT(varchar(900),
      n.thePath +
      RIGHT(
        REPLICATE('0', 10) +
        CONVERT(varchar, e.EmployeeID),
        10) + '/'
      ) AS thePath
  FROM Employee_Temp e
  JOIN n ON n.ManagerID = e.EmployeeID
)
SELECT *
FROM n
WHERE ManagerID IS NULL;
```

This query returns the path from the selected node to the CEO as a materialized path of employee IDs. However, you might instead want to get the results back as a table of employee IDs. In order to do that, change the outer query to the following:

```
SELECT
  COALESCE(ManagerID, 217) AS EmployeeID
FROM n
ORDER BY
```

```
CASE
  WHEN ManagerID IS NULL THEN 0
  ELSE 1
END,
thePath;
```

In this case, the **COALESCE** function used in the **SELECT** list replaces the CEO's **ManagerID**—which is **NULL**—with the target **EmployeeID**. The **CASE** expression in the **ORDER BY** clause forces the **NULL** row to sort at the top so that the target **EmployeeID** is returned first. All other sorting is based on the materialized path, which naturally returns the CEO's row last.

Inserting New Nodes and Relocating Subtrees

In an adjacency list hierarchy, inserting new nodes is generally quite straightforward. Inserting a leaf node (i.e., a node with no subordinates) requires simply inserting a new node into the table. To insert a nonleaf node, you must also update any direct subordinates of the node you're inserting under, so that they point to their new manager. This is effectively the same as inserting a new node and then relocating the old node's subtree under the new node, which is why I've merged these two topics into one section.

As an example, suppose that AdventureWorks has decided to hire a new CTO, to whom the current Vice President of Engineering (**EmployeeID 12**) will be reporting. To reflect these changes in the **Employee_Temp** table, first insert the new CTO node, and then update the VP's node to report to the new CTO:

```
INSERT INTO Employee_Temp
(
    EmployeeID,
    ManagerID,
    Title
)
VALUES
(
    999,
    109,
    'CTO'
);
GO

UPDATE Employee_Temp
SET ManagerID = 999
WHERE EmployeeID = 12;
GO
```

That's it! This same logic can be applied for any subtree relocation—one of the advantages of adjacency lists over the other hierarchical techniques discussed in this chapter is the ease with which data modifications like this can be handled.

Deleting Existing Nodes

Removing nodes in an adjacency list is only slightly trickier than inserting a new nonleaf node. This time, the first step is to relocate any subordinates that report to the node to be deleted—the key is that *subordinates* is plural this time, as there may be more than one. Once those subtrees are relocated to their new manager, the leaf node can simply be removed.

Suppose that on her first day at the office, the new CTO won the lottery and decided that she would rather race her yacht than continue to work at AdventureWorks. Removing her from the organizational hierarchy requires relocating her reports back to the CEO, and then deleting her node, which will then be a leaf. Due to the self-referencing foreign key on the table, nonleaf nodes cannot be deleted—this is another nice fringe benefit of adjacency lists.

The following T-SQL can be used to relocate subordinates of the CTO to her immediate manager, and then remove the CTO's node:

```
UPDATE Employee_Temp
SET ManagerID =
    (
        SELECT ManagerID
        FROM Employee_Temp
        WHERE EmployeeID = 999
    )
WHERE ManagerID = 999;

DELETE FROM Employee_Temp
WHERE EmployeeID = 999;
```

This code works by finding the manager for the node to be removed, and updating all of the node's direct subordinates to point to that manager (in other words, the "grandfather" node for each of the subordinates becomes their "father" node). Once the update is complete, the node is a leaf, and so can be removed.

Constraining the Hierarchy

Each of the hierarchical traversal examples shown in this chapter makes a very important assumption about the data: it is taken for granted that there are no cycles or other data issues that would breach the rules of a valid hierarchy. The main benefit of this assumption is that the resultant code can be made a lot simpler; the problem is that the simpler code is prone to various problems should bad data creep in—and as most readers are no doubt aware, bad data can and *will* creep in if given the opportunity.

Simple code is a good thing, so instead of making the code more complex, we have a choice: either cross our fingers for luck and hope that the system never has occasion to melt down at runtime, or better, actually constrain the data to ensure that it remains valid. From a defensive point of view, I highly recommend the second approach.

There are two possible issues that can make life difficult for hierarchical queries: forests and cycles. **Forests** occur when there are multiple root nodes in the hierarchy. And although they may make sense for some types of data, for organizational charts they do not. **Cycles** occur when, somewhere downstream from a given node, that node is suddenly referenced again. For example, if George manages Ed, Ed manages Steve, and Steve manages George, a cycle has been formed—this is not only unrealistic, but also cause for a runtime exception due to an endless loop!

The `Employee_Temp` table we've been working with already has a couple of constraints that help guard against certain issues: a primary key and a self-referencing foreign key. The primary key, which is on the **EmployeeID** column, guards against most cycles by making it impossible for a given employee to have more than one manager. And the self-referencing foreign key guards against most forest issues because every node must be connected to another node that already exists—unless it's a root node.

The first thing that must be constrained against is multiple root nodes. One method that might come to mind to handle this is using a trigger, but I find it slightly more interesting to employ an indexed view:

```
CREATE VIEW OnlyOneRoot
WITH SCHEMABINDING
AS
  SELECT
    ManagerID
  FROM dbo.Employee_Temp
  WHERE
    ManagerID IS NULL;
GO

CREATE UNIQUE CLUSTERED INDEX IX_OnlyOneRoot
ON OnlyOneRoot (ManagerID);
GO
```

The view returns all rows in the table with a **NULL** manager ID, and the index, because it is **UNIQUE**, only allows one such row to be inserted.

While this approach works well to prevent multiple root nodes from being created, it does not enforce the hierarchical condition that there should always be *exactly one* root node. For example, it doesn't stop someone from assigning a manager to the root node (the unique constraint can only enforce rows that exist, and by updating the table, the **NULL** manager ID would no longer exist at all). To solve this problem, a trigger can be used to make sure that there is always at least one **NULL** manager ID in the table:

```
CREATE TRIGGER tg_AtLeastOneRoot
ON Employee_Temp
FOR UPDATE
AS
BEGIN
  SET NOCOUNT ON;

  IF NOT EXISTS
  (
    SELECT *
    FROM Employee_Temp
    WHERE ManagerID IS NULL
  )
  BEGIN
    RAISERROR('A root node is required', 16, 1);
    ROLLBACK;
  END
END;
GO
```

To eliminate the possibility of cycles, we need to think about what kinds of cycles can exist in the table. To begin with, the simplest cycle—and one that's not constrained against by either the primary key or the foreign key—is an employee managing herself. This is easily solved with a check constraint:

```
ALTER TABLE Employee_Temp
ADD CONSTRAINT ck_ManagerIsNotEmployee
    CHECK (EmployeeID <> ManagerID);
GO
```

This constraint does nothing for deeper cycles, where an employee manages himself one or more levels below. For instance, if George manages Ed and Ed manages Steve, someone could issue an update to the table so that Ed manages George. This would create a deeper cycle that the constraint would not be able to catch. In order to solve this problem, a trigger can be employed. The trigger should start with the updated row, traversing up the tree toward the root node. Should it encounter the same employee a second time before hitting the root, it is apparent that there is a cycle. Following is the code for such a trigger:

```
CREATE TRIGGER tg_NoCycles
ON Employee_Temp
FOR UPDATE
AS
BEGIN
  SET NOCOUNT ON;

  --Only check if the ManagerID column was updated
  IF NOT UPDATE(ManagerID)
    RETURN;

  --Avoid cycles
  DECLARE @CycleExists bit = 0;

  --Traverse up the hierarchy toward the leaf node
  WITH e AS
  (
    SELECT EmployeeID, ManagerID
    FROM inserted

    UNION ALL

    SELECT e.EmployeeID, et.ManagerID
    FROM Employee_Temp et
    JOIN e ON e.ManagerID = et.EmployeeID
    WHERE
      et.ManagerID IS NOT NULL
      AND e.ManagerID <> e.EmployeeID
  )
  SELECT @CycleExists = 1
  FROM e
  WHERE e.ManagerID = e.EmployeeID;

  IF @CycleExists = 1
```

```
    BEGIN
        RAISERROR('The update introduced a cycle', 16, 1);
        ROLLBACK;
    END
END
GO
```

This type of cycle can only be caused by either updates or multirow inserts, and in virtually all of the hierarchies I've seen in production environments, there were no multirow inserts. Therefore, this trigger is set to only fire on updates. Remember to change the trigger definition if you need to work with multirow inserts in your environment.

■ **Caution** Excessive or inappropriate use of triggers can degrade query performance. While the solution proposed in this section solves the problem of cycles using triggers in the database, you might want to consider enforcing this kind of business logic in an application layer instead, if it makes more sense to do so.

Persisted Materialized Paths

The adjacency list model, while both a de facto standard for modeling hierarchies and extremely easy to work with from a data manipulation point of view, suffers from inefficiencies due to the fact that the hierarchy must be traversed using either recursion or iteration. In this section we'll look at an alternative technique that avoids this problem: **persisted materialized paths**. While this technique can act as a stand-alone replacement for adjacency lists, I recommend using it in conjunction with existing adjacency list hierarchies. In the following sections, I will show you how to maintain both hierarchy types alongside each other in the Employee_Temp table, using a series of triggers.

In the previous section's examples, a materialized path was used to provide an ordered representation of the hierarchy for output purposes. This same path can be persisted in the table to allow you to answer all of the same hierarchical questions as with an adjacency list, but without the necessity for recursion or iteration.

To add and populate a materialized path column to the Employee_Temp table, first add a new column of type **varchar(900)** and then update the table using a recursive CTE used to get the path for each node:

```
ALTER TABLE Employee_Temp
ADD thePath varchar(900);
GO

WITH n AS
(
    SELECT
        EmployeeID,
        CONVERT(varchar(900),
            '/' + CONVERT(varchar, EmployeeID) + '/'
            ) AS thePath
    FROM Employee_Temp
    WHERE ManagerID IS NULL
```

```
    UNION ALL

    SELECT
      e.EmployeeID,
      CONVERT(varchar(900),
        n.thePath +
        CONVERT(varchar, e.EmployeeID) + '/'
      ) AS thePath
    FROM Employee_Temp e
    JOIN n ON n.EmployeeID = e.ManagerID
)
UPDATE Employee_Temp
  SET Employee_Temp.thePath = n.thePath
  FROM Employee_Temp
  JOIN n ON n.EmployeeID = Employee_Temp.EmployeeID;
GO
```

varchar(900) is important in this case because the materialized path will be used as an index key in order to allow it to be efficiently used to traverse the hierarchy. Index keys in SQL Server are limited to 900 bytes. This is also a bit of a limitation for persisted materialized paths; a path to navigate an especially deep hierarchy will not be indexable and therefore will not be usable for this technique.

As with a pure adjacency list hierarchy, the best indexing scheme for a persisted materialized path should be determined through careful testing of your particular workload. That said, I can all but guarantee that a clustered index will never be the right choice. Since the paths can grow quite large, and every nonclustered index inherits the clustered index's keys, clustering on the path will grow the page sizes of every index created on the table. The path doesn't bring any value in its nonindexed form, so I don't recommend trying that technique. Instead, create a nonclustered covering index, and use the INCLUDE clause to bring along any columns that are commonly used in conjunction with hierarchical searches of the data. In the case of the Employee_Temp table, the index will include the Title and EmployeeID columns so that the same output shown before can be most efficiently produced via the materialized path (the table is clustered on ManagerID, so that does not have to be explicitly included):

```
CREATE NONCLUSTERED INDEX IX_Employee_Temp_Path
ON Employee_Temp (thePath)
INCLUDE (EmployeeID, Title);
```

Finding Subordinates

Since the materialized path is a string, we can take advantage of SQL Server's LIKE predicate to traverse down the hierarchy. The path for every given node N that is a subordinate of some node M starts with node M's path. Looking back at the results of the enumerated path contained in the last section, notice that since all nodes are descendants of EmployeeID 109 (the CEO), every path starts with the string 109/. Likewise, moving down the hierarchy, every subordinate node inherits its parent's path and adds its own ID to the end.

Therefore, searching for all subordinates of a given employee is as simple as using the LIKE predicate and adding the wildcard character, %. The following query finds all subordinates of the Vice President of Engineering (EmployeeID 12), using the materialized path:

```
DECLARE @Path varchar(900);
SELECT @Path = thePath
```

```
FROM Employee_Temp
WHERE EmployeeID = 12;

SELECT *
FROM Employee_Temp
WHERE
    thePath LIKE @Path + '%'
ORDER BY thePath;
```

Performance of this query compared to the CTE solution, even against the small table, is fairly impressive. To find all subordinates of the Vice President using the CTE, the query engine must perform 187 logical reads. To do the same thing using the materialized path requires only 6.

Finding only the direct reports for a given node is just a bit trickier. This time, a naked wildcard does not do the trick, as it will return the input node, its children, and children of its children. To eliminate the input node, we can change the predicate to **thePath LIKE @Path + '%/'**. This will return **false** for the input node, since the additional oblique stroke is not present in its path. However, this still includes all children nodes, as each has a path suffixed by a stroke. To eliminate children of children, the following **NOT LIKE** predicate must be added: **AND thePath NOT LIKE @Path + '%/%/'**. Essentially, this predicate says that the target path can only have one more stroke than the input path—and therefore, that path is one level of depth below. The following T-SQL finds the direct reports for the Vice President of Engineering:

```
DECLARE @Path varchar(900);
SELECT @Path = thePath
FROM Employee_Temp
WHERE EmployeeID = 12;

SELECT *
FROM Employee_Temp
WHERE
    thePath LIKE @Path + '%/'
    AND thePath NOT LIKE @Path + '%/%/';
```

Navigating up the Hierarchy

One of the limitations of persisted materialized paths is that there is no especially efficient way to use them to navigate up the hierarchy in order to produce the "how do we get to the CEO from the current node" report. However, the materialized path itself already contains all of the information necessary—it's just that the data needs to be manipulated a bit to get it into a usable format.

The path for each employee is a stroke-delimited ordered list of the nodes that lead from the root node to the given employee. In order to generate a table from the list, it must be split up based on its delimiters. This can be done by recursively using the **SUBSTRING** function. By putting this logic in a recursive CTE, we can take the substring of each node in the path on each iteration. Simultaneously, we can remember the order of the nodes in the list so that the output can be ordered properly. The following CTE finds the path to the CEO starting at the Research and Development Manager:

```
WITH n AS
(
  SELECT
    CONVERT(int,
```

```
      SUBSTRING(thePath, 2, CHARINDEX('/', thePath, 2) -2)) AS EmployeeID,
    SUBSTRING(thePath, CHARINDEX('/', thePath, 2), LEN(thePath)) AS thePath,
    1 AS theLevel
  FROM Employee_Temp
  WHERE EmployeeID = 217

  UNION ALL

  SELECT
    CONVERT(int,
      SUBSTRING(thePath, 2, CHARINDEX('/', thePath, 2) -2)),
    SUBSTRING(thePath, CHARINDEX('/', thePath, 2), LEN(thePath)),
    theLevel + 1
  FROM n
  WHERE thePath LIKE '/%/'
)
SELECT *
FROM n
ORDER BY theLevel;
```

The output of this query is as follows:

EmployeeID	thePath	theLevel
109	/12/3/158/217/	1
12	/3/158/217/	2
3	/158/217/	3
158	/217/	4
217		5

Aside from the expression used to pull out the current first node, another expression I used in both the anchor and recursive members cuts the first node out of the path, so that the path progressively shrinks as the CTE recurses at each level. This time, the cut starts just after the first delimiter—and takes the entire remainder of the path.

Although the **EmployeeID** column is probably the only one necessary in the output, I've left the other columns in so that you can see how the path is affected by the CTE's logic at each level.

Inserting Nodes

Whenever a new leaf node is added to the hierarchy, its parent's path must be determined, and the new node appended to the path. This logic can be encapsulated in a trigger such that whenever new nodes are inserted into the adjacency list, their paths will automatically be updated. The following trigger handles this logic:

```
CREATE TRIGGER tg_Insert
ON Employee_Temp
FOR INSERT
AS
BEGIN
  SET NOCOUNT ON;

  IF @@ROWCOUNT > 1
    BEGIN
      RAISERROR('Only one node can be inserted at a time', 16, 1);
      ROLLBACK;
    END

  UPDATE e
    SET e.thePath =
      Managers.thePath +
      RIGHT(
        REPLICATE('0', 10) + CONVERT(varchar, i.EmployeeID),
        10) + '/'
    FROM Employee_Temp e
    JOIN inserted i ON i.EmployeeID = e.EmployeeID
    JOIN Employee_Temp Managers ON Managers.EmployeeID = e.ManagerID;
END;
GO
```

The logic of this trigger is relatively simple: find the updated row in the **Employee_Temp** table by joining on the **EmployeeID** columns of both it and the inserted virtual table, and then join back to **Employee_Temp** to get the manager's path. Finally, concatenate the employee's ID onto the end of the path.

The most important thing to mention about this trigger is its limitation when it comes to multirow inserts. Due to the fact that SQL Server does not have any guarantees when it comes to update order, it is possible to create invalid paths by inserting two nodes at the same time. For instance, try disabling the row count check and inserting a subordinate first, followed by a manager, in the same statement:

```
INSERT INTO Employee_Temp
(
    EmployeeID,
    ManagerID,
    Title
)
VALUES
(1000, 999, 'Subordinate'),
(999, 109, 'Manager');
```

Since the order in which the **UPDATE** processes rows is not guaranteed, the result of this operation is nondeterministic. The subordinate may therefore end up with a **NULL** path, since at the moment its row is updated the manager's path has not yet have been processed. It may be possible to solve this problem by traversing any hierarchy present in the **inserted** table using a cursor, but I decided not to attempt this as I have never seen a situation in a real-world project in which this limitation would be a barrier.

Relocating Subtrees

Data modification is the real downside of the persisted materialized paths technique. Any time you affect a node's path, you must cascade the new path to all of its subordinates. This can mean that some updates are extremely expensive—should one of the vice presidents replace the CEO, every node in the hierarchy must be updated! Luckily, the average cost is not huge; the following T-SQL finds the **span of control** or average number of subordinates—four, as it turns out—for all nodes in the **Employee_Temp** hierarchy:

```
SELECT AVG(NumberOfSubordinates)
FROM
(
  SELECT COUNT(*) AS NumberOfSubordinates
  FROM Employee_Temp e
  JOIN Employee_Temp e2 ON e2.thePath LIKE e.thePath + '%'
  GROUP BY e.EmployeeID
) x;
```

Relocating a materialized path's subtree involves finding the new manager's path and replacing it in the updated node as well as all of its child nodes. This becomes clearer through example, so consider what would happen if the Engineering Manager (**EmployeeID 3**) gets a promotion and now reports directly to the CEO. Her path will change to the CEO's path with her employee ID concatenated to the end: **0000000109/0000000003/**. This operation will also invalidate the paths of the Design Engineer and the Senior Tool Designer, both of whose paths depend on that of the Engineering Manager. So the same operation—replacement of the beginning of the path—has to happen for all three nodes. It also has to happen for any of their subordinates, all the way down the tree, since every subordinate inherits its manager's path.

Once again, a trigger can be employed to automatically perform this update when a subtree is located based on the adjacency list. The following trigger handles the logic:

```
CREATE TRIGGER tg_Update
ON Employee_Temp
FOR UPDATE
AS
BEGIN
  DECLARE @n int = @@ROWCOUNT;

  IF UPDATE(thePath)
    BEGIN
      RAISERROR('Direct updates to the path are not allowed', 16, 1);
      ROLLBACK;
    END

  IF UPDATE(ManagerID)
    BEGIN
      IF @n > 1
        BEGIN
          RAISERROR('Only update one node''s manager at a time', 16, 1);
          ROLLBACK;
        END
```

```
    --Update all nodes using the new manager's path
    UPDATE e
    SET e.thePath =
      REPLACE(e.thePath, i.thePath,
        Managers.thePath +
        RIGHT(
          REPLICATE('0', 10) + CONVERT(varchar, i.EmployeeID),
          10
        ) + '/'
      )
    FROM Employee_Temp e
      JOIN inserted i ON e.thePath LIKE i.thePath + '%'
      JOIN Employee_Temp Managers ON Managers.EmployeeID = i.ManagerID
  END
END
GO
```

There are a few things to discuss in this trigger. Starting at the top, the trigger first obtains the number of rows affected by the update operation. Just like when dealing with inserting new nodes, relocation of subtrees must be serialized to one node at a time in order to avoid logical ambiguities. However, an error is not thrown right away in this case; it is possible that someone might be updating a different column in the table, such as changing all of the "Production Technicians" to "Production Specialists." As long as the update is not to the hierarchy, multirow updates are certainly allowed.

The first error check done is for direct updates to the path—this is not allowed, since it's the job of the trigger. Next, the trigger checks to see whether the **ManagerID** column is being updated. If not, it has nothing to do. If so, it then throws an error if multiple rows have been affected. Finally, if there are no issues, the paths of the affected node and all subordinates are updated based on the new manager's path. The logic used is to find the previous path of the updated node—using the **inserted** virtual table, which will still have that original path because direct updates to the path are not allowed—and replace it in all nodes with the new path.

As before, this trigger could probably be made to handle multirow updates by using a cursor, but I do not feel that the effort required to implement such a solution would be worthwhile.

■ **Note** If you're using the **tg_AtLeastOneRoot** trigger in conjunction with the **tg_Update** trigger, you'll have a problem if you need to swap the root node, because to satisfy the **tg_AtLeastOneRoot** trigger's logic, the update must end with a root note in place, and this will require a multirow update. Luckily, that's not generally something that has to happen very often, but if you do need to do it, remember to disable one of the triggers before making the change, and reenable it immediately afterward to make sure that other callers don't introduce data inconsistencies in the interim.

Deleting Nodes

Thanks to the fact that the adjacency list is being used in conjunction with the materialized path, deleting nodes requires no additional logic. Due to the self-referential constraint on the adjacency list, only leaf nodes can be deleted. Leaf nodes have no subordinates and therefore there is nothing to cascade—the row will be deleted, and no further logic is necessary. This is one of the main benefits of keeping both hierarchical models in the same table—each inherits the other's constraints, helping to ensure greater data integrity.

Constraining the Hierarchy

All of the logic mentioned in the previous "Constraining the Hierarchy" section (which dealt with adjacency lists) still applies to materialized paths. However, with a materialized path, it's much easier to detect cycles, so there is no need to use the **tg_NoCycles** trigger. Instead, a simple check constraint should be used that makes sure the given employee only appears once, at the end of the path:

```
ALTER TABLE Employee_Temp
ADD CONSTRAINT ck_NoCycles
  CHECK
  (
    thePath NOT LIKE
    '%' +
    RIGHT(REPLICATE('0', 10) + CONVERT(varchar, EmployeeID), 10) +
    '/%' +
    RIGHT(REPLICATE('0', 10) + CONVERT(varchar, EmployeeID), 10) +
    '/'
    );
GO
```

■ **Note** There is a subtle difference between the logic expressed here and the logic used to prevent endless loops in the section "Traversing the Graph." In that section, the nodes in the path were not left-padded with zeros, so the first node had to be delimited in order to make sure to detect a cycle involving it. This was done to prevent a false alarm in case of a path like **123/456/3**. In this case, the left-padding means that there is no way to misinterpret a section of one ID as another, so we do not have to modify the basic path logic already established.

The hierarchyid Datatype

In the preceding section, I discussed one of the limitations of the materialized path approach—namely, that the string encoding makes it difficult to work with deep hierarchies. Fortunately, in SQL Server 2008, the **hierarchyid** datatype was introduced, which essentially stores hierarchical data using materialized paths that are serialized into a CLR datatype. While this doesn't provide much additional functionality on top of what was possible using the materialized path approach described previously, it does make querying hierarchical data much easier, as I will demonstrate in this section.

The **hierarchyid** datatype comes with a set of defined methods for working with hierarchical data, and the first method of interest to us is the **Parse()** method, which instantiates a new item of **hierarchyid** data based on a supplied string representation of a materialized path. Fortunately for us, the string format expected by the **Parse()** method is exactly the same as we used in the **thePath** column created in the previous section—using an oblique stroke between each node in the path.

The following code listing creates and populates a column of **hierarchyid** values representing rows in the **Employee_Temp** table based on the existing materialized path.

```
ALTER TABLE Employee_Temp
ADD hierarchy hierarchyid;

UPDATE Employee_Temp
 SET hierarchy = hierarchyid::Parse (thePath);
```

Finding Subordinates

Having populated the **hierarchyid** column, let's put it to the test by performing the same set of common queries as we did for the other methods. The first requirement is to identify all those rows that are subordinates of a particular manager. To do this, we can use the **IsDescendantOf()** method, as shown in the following query:

```
SELECT * FROM Employee_Temp
WHERE hierarchy.IsDescendantOf('/109/6/') = 1;
```

The preceding query returns all those rows that are subordinates of the Marketing Manager (whose **hierarchy** path is **/109/6/**), as follows:

2	6	Marketing Assistant	/109/6/2/	0xE02EE568
6	109	Marketing Manager	/109/6/	0xE02EE5
46	6	Marketing Specialist	/109/6/46/	0xE02EE5CBD0
106	6	Marketing Specialist	/109/6/106/	0xE02EE5E02D40
119	6	Marketing Specialist	/109/6/119/	0xE02EE5E047C0
203	6	Marketing Specialist	/109/6/203/	0xE02EE5E0EDC0
269	6	Marketing Assistant	/109/6/269/	0xE02EE5E26EC0
271	6	Marketing Specialist	/109/6/271/	0xE02EE5E26FC0
272	6	Marketing Assistant	/109/6/272/	0xE02EE5E28440

There are a couple of important points to note about the result obtained from the preceding query:

- Notice that the value supplied to the IsDescendantOf() method, like all string representations of hierarchyid data, both begins and ends with an oblique stroke. This style of syntax is probably familiar to all developers who have previously used XQuery functionality in SQL Server or elsewhere.

- The hierarchyid values are returned in the result set in their native binary format. To get the string representation of a hierarchyid value, you must call the ToString() method.

- Note that even though we were attempting to identify subordinates of the Marketing Manager, the Marketing Manager himself is returned in the results. This is an interesting quirk of the hierarchyid type in that, for any given node x, x.IsDescendantOf(x) = 1. This is by design, and is useful in some circumstances, but may not seem that intuitive.

- The IsDescendantOf() method returns true for all descendants of the given node, not just direct children, but grandchildren, great-grandchildren, and so on.

To restrict the results to only return *direct* descendants of a node (and also to exclude the node itself from the results), we can take advantage of the **GetLevel()** method, which returns an integer representing the "level" of a node in the hierarchy. The root node is level 0, and at each level of the hierarchy underneath the root node this value increases by one. Therefore, the direct subordinates of a given node will always be one level greater than their parent. The following code listing demonstrates how to constrain the results to only include direct subordinates of the Marketing Manager:

```
DECLARE @Parent hierarchyid = hierarchyid::Parse('/109/6/');
SELECT * FROM Employee_Temp
WHERE hierarchy.IsDescendantOf(@Parent) = 1
AND hierarchy.GetLevel() = @Parent.GetLevel() + 1;
```

This is a very flexible structure that can be used to specify exactly how many levels of descendants to traverse under a given node—for example, to return children and grandchildren, you can include all those nodes where the difference between the two levels is less than or equal to 2.

Navigating up the Hierarchy

Since the **hierarchyid** datatype is essentially just a materialized path serialized as a CLR datatype, each individual **hierarchyid** value already contains the full path back to the root node. In order to display this path in a readable format, we simply need to call the **ToString()** method. For example, consider the path from the CEO to the Production Technician, **EmployeeID 100**:

```
SELECT
 EmployeeID,
 ManagerID,
 Title,
 hierarchy.ToString() AS hierarchyPath
FROM Employee_Temp
WHERE EmployeeID = 100;
```

The results of this query are as follows:

EmployeeID	ManagerID	Title	hierarchyPath
100	143	Production Technician - WC20	/109/148/21/143/100/

Notice how the path obtained from the **hierarchyid ToString()** method is exactly the same as the path we created in the **thePath** column earlier. Fortunately though, navigating up through this hierarchy doesn't involve any of the string manipulation we had to perform previously—instead we can use the **GetAncestor()** method, which provides similar functionality to **IsDescendant()** but from the opposite point of view. Rather than returning a Boolean response indicating whether a given node is descended from another node, the **GetAncestor()** method is invoked on a child element and used to return a **hierarchyid** node representing an ancestor of that child. The **GetAncestor()** method can not only return the direct parent of a node—it accepts an argument to determine how many levels of hierarchy should lie between the given node and the ancestor.

To demonstrate, the following code listing uses that **GetAncestor()** method with the argument **1** to determine the immediate parent of each node in the **hierarchy** column. This value is then used to return only those nodes that report directly to the Marketing Manager, **EmployeeID 6**:

```
DECLARE @Parent hierarchyid;
SELECT @Parent = hierarchy
FROM Employee_Temp
WHERE EmployeeID = 6;

SELECT * FROM Employee_Temp
WHERE hierarchy.GetAncestor(1) = @Parent;
```

Inserting Nodes

In order to insert a new node, we need to calculate the appropriate **hierarchyid** value representing the path to that node. This can be done using the **GetDescendant()** method on the node that is to become the parent of the newly inserted node. **GetDescendant()** accepts two arguments that determine the lower and upper values of the range in which the allocated **hierarchyid** node will lie. To demonstrate this method, suppose that the Shipping and Receiving Supervisor, **EmployeeID 85**, needs to hire an office administrator. By providing **null** values for both arguments, the following code uses the **GetDescendant()** method to allocate an arbitrary **hierarchyid** value for the new employee:

```
DECLARE @Parent hierarchyid;
SELECT @Parent = hierarchy
FROM Employee_Temp
WHERE EmployeeID = 85;

SELECT @Parent.GetDescendant(null, null).ToString();
```

The result, **/109/148/21/85/1/**, is guaranteed to be a new node that is a direct descendant of the supplied parent node, but the actual identity of the new node may vary. In some situations, this may cause problems. For example, consider instead what would happen if the Production Supervisor, **EmployeeID 16**, were to hire a new member of staff. To assign a hierarchy node for the new employee using the preceding pattern, we might initially try something like this:

```
DECLARE @Parent hierarchyid;
SELECT @Parent = hierarchy
FROM Employee_Temp
WHERE EmployeeID = 16;

SELECT @Parent.GetDescendant(null, null).ToString();
```

The result returned, **/109/148/21/16/1/**, is a valid node that reports to the Production Supervisor, but the problem is that this node *already exists* in the hierarchy. It is assigned to **EmployeeID 1**, who is a technician reporting to this production supervisor. In order to avoid such cases, we can supply a parameter value to the **GetDescendant()** method representing the minimum value that the newly created child node must be greater than. To do this, we will find out the maximum currently assigned child node for the chosen parent, as follows:

```
DECLARE @Parent hierarchyid;
SELECT @Parent = hierarchy
FROM Employee_Temp
WHERE EmployeeID = 16;

DECLARE @MaxChild hierarchyid;
SELECT @MaxChild = MAX(hierarchy)
FROM Employee_Temp
WHERE hierarchy.IsDescendantOf(@Parent) = 1;

SELECT @Parent.GetDescendant(@MaxChild, null).ToString();
```

The result, **/109/148/21/16/248/**, is now guaranteed to be a unique node in the hierarchy. The second parameter that can be supplied to **GetDescendant()** represents the maximum node value that the newly created node must lie before. In this case, I've left it **null** as I don't want to enforce a maximum.

Of course, in the current model, the value of each node in the materialized path is based on the **EmployeeID** of the associated employee. So long as the **EmployeeID** field remains unique, you could continue to model all individual node values based on that and not have to worry about the possibility of creating duplicate **hierarchyid** values. However, there are many other scenarios in which such an identity value is not available, in which case, the **GetDescendantOf()** method becomes a very useful way to allocate values for new child nodes. If you wanted to retain both the adjacency list modeled on **EmployeeID** and the **hierarchyid** model within the **Employee_Temp** table, you would of course need to modify the **tg_Insert** trigger created previously to automatically update the **hierarchy** column based on the **EmployeeID** of the inserted row.

Relocating Subtrees

To relocate a **hierarchyid** node, we use the **GetReparentedValue()** method. Note that this method doesn't actually alter a **hierarchyid** value—rather, it returns a node representing the new path to a node if it were to be reparented to the supplied new parent node. To move the node, you must then update the **hierarchyid** value to be equal to this result.

To demonstrate this in action, consider what would happen if we were to remove one of the production supervisors, **EmployeeID 64**, from the hierarchy, and relocate all of their direct employees to report to one of the alternative supervisors, **EmployeeID 74**.

To start with, we need to identify the nodes that represent both the old parent that nodes are moving from, and the new parent to which they will be reporting, as follows:

```
DECLARE @FromParent hierarchyid;
SELECT @FromParent = hierarchy
FROM Employee_Temp
WHERE EmployeeID = 64;
```

```
DECLARE @ToParent hierarchyid;
SELECT @ToParent = hierarchy
FROM Employee_Temp
WHERE EmployeeID = 74;
```

Having identified the two parents between which nodes are to be moved, we can then update all those descendants of the old parent using the **GetReparentedValue()** method as follows:

```
UPDATE Employee_Temp
SET hierarchy = hierarchy.GetReparentedValue(@FromParent, @ToParent)
WHERE
hierarchy.IsDescendantOf(@FromParent) = 1
AND EmployeeID <> 64;
```

This query uses the **IsDescendantOf()** method to identify all those rows that report to the old parent, **EmployeeID 64**, and updates them to report to the new parent. The final condition is required to prevent the original parent node being moved (remember that, based on the **IsDescendantOf()** method, a node is a descendant of itself).

As with row inserts, if you wanted to maintain this solution in a production environment alongside the adjacency list, you would need to modify the **tg_Update** procedure to update the **hierarchy** column when nodes were moved.

Deleting Nodes

Hierarchies modeled using the **hierarchyid** datatype do not enforce any kind of inherent referential integrity. As such, any node may be removed from the hierarchy, potentially leading to orphan nodes if the node removed is a nonleaf node. Fortunately, as with the string materialized path described previously, in this example we are using the **hierarchyid** datatype in conjunction with the constraints provided by the existing adjacency list on the **Employee_Temp** table. These constraints mean that only leaf nodes can be deleted, which reduces the chances of orphans or multiple root nodes being introduced into the structure of the hierarchy.

Constraining the Hierarchy

Since the **hierarchyid** datatype is essentially just a wrapper around a materialized path construct, the same rules apply for how to constrain the hierarchy in order to prevent cycles or forests. A further consideration is how best to index columns of **hierarchyid** data. Placing a unique index on the **hierarchy** column can prevent duplicate entries, as well as improve query performance against the hierarchy, but you should devote a little time to consider how hierarchies are ordered in a single index.

By default, SQL Server 2008 indexes **hierarchyid** values in a **depth-first** order. That is, the nodes that are listed down a particular path through the tree are listed next to each other. This sort of indexing is efficient for fulfilling queries that involve traversing up (or down) several levels of subtrees, such as "Find the managers two levels immediately above this employee." The following code listing creates a depth-first index on the **hierarchy** column:

```
CREATE UNIQUE INDEX idxHierarchyDepth
ON Employee_Temp(hierarchy) ;
GO
```

It is also possible to index **hierarchyid** data in **breadth-first** order, in which case all the siblings who are immediate children of a particular parent node are listed next to each other in the index. This kind of index is best suited for queries such as "Find all the employees who report directly to this manager." Of course, you don't need to choose exclusively between these two types of index—you can create both. To create a breadth-first index, we will make use of the **GetLevel()** method once more to populate a persisted column representing the level of each node. By including this column in the index, we will ensure that nodes at the same level of the hierarchy are indexed next to each other, as expected in the breadth-first index:

```
ALTER TABLE Employee_Temp
ADD hierarchyLevel AS hierarchy.GetLevel();
GO

CREATE UNIQUE INDEX idxHierarchyBreadth
ON Employee_Temp(hierarchyLevel, hierarchy);
GO
```

Summary

Graphs and hierarchies are extremely common throughout our world, and it is often necessary to represent them in databases. By utilizing adjacency lists, you can describe virtually any graph's form, and recursive CTEs allow you to navigate graphs with relative ease. Hierarchies—special types of graphs—can also be modeled using adjacency lists, but other techniques can be employed to make querying them much more efficient, without the need for recursion or iteration.

There are a lot of ways to solve hierarchical problems, but in the end it comes down to the best choice for the given scenario you're faced with. As always, the most important thing you can do as a developer is to carefully consider your options, and test whenever possible to find the optimal solution.

Index

■ **E**